SERMONS FROM DUKE CHAPEL

WILLIAM H. WILLIMON, EDITOR

Sermons from Duke Chapel

VOICES FROM "A GREAT TOWERING CHURCH"

Duke University Press   Durham and London

2005

2nd printing, 2005

© 2005 Duke University Press

All rights reserved

Designed by C. H. Westmoreland

Typeset in Fournier by Tseng Information Systems, Inc.

Library of Congress Cataloging-in-Publication Data appear
on the last printed page of this book.

Thanks to Dr. William E. King, former archivist at Duke University, who helped to secure sermons, and to Seth Dowland, George Linney, and David Wilmington for their help in transcribing the sermons for publication in this book.

Contents

SERMONS FROM DUKE CHAPEL

A Terrible, Wonderful Place to Preach

For the past twenty years I have had the task of preaching the gospel from a pulpit that offers the preacher quite a challenge. As one of our guest preachers commented, after the service at which he had preached, "Duke Chapel is one of the most difficult places in the world to preach."

Perhaps he overstated the challenge, but I knew what he meant. At the beginning of a sermon the preacher looks into a dark, cavernous gothic expanse. Because of the lighting, or lack of it, the preacher can see no farther than the first five or six rows of pews. Preaching is not only an acoustical but also a visual phenomenon, and Duke Chapel is a place where it is difficult for a preacher to see or be seen while speaking.

One Sunday, after I had preached as well as I knew how, a woman grasped my hand as I stood at the door and said, "Would you please tell the lady who preached this morning that I thought she had a thoughtful sermon?"

I prayed that she had been seated in the last row.

As for the acoustics, the natural but unnerving reverberation of the Chapel's limestone walls and floors was, during the installation of the Chapel's third organ in the 1970s, "enhanced." An already unmanageable acoustical environment was exacerbated, for the sake of the music. The reverberation level increased more than three seconds. A speaker hears the sound of his or her voice coming back a few seconds after the words are spoken; the congregation must sort through a cacophony to get the point that is being made. Sounds bounce off the walls and ricochet back and forth. A baby's competing squeal is amplified. A dropped hymnal becomes a thunderous peal.

After a high-volume sermon by a distinguished African American Pentecostal, both preacher and congregation emerged from the experience shaken by auditory overload. And after one of my sermons, when my tendency to drop the endings of my sentences had proved lethal to the reception of my message, one grande dame of the congregation told me, "I could tell from your gesticulation that you were agitated about some matter of importance but, unable to make out a word of your sermon, I had no clue about the object of your disease."

Duke Chapel is a tough place in which to preach.

But any church, limestone walls or wood, small steeple or tall, in Durham or Durban, offers a challenge for the articulation of the Christian message. In

1928, about the time that James B. Duke was forming his dream of a university built around "a great towering church," a young pastor in Switzerland, Karl Barth, was beginning what was to become a revolution in Christian theology. Barth encapsulated the challenge that preachers faced: "As ministers we ought to speak of God. We are human, however, and so cannot speak of God. We ought therefore to recognize both our obligation and our inability and by that very recognition to give God the glory. This is our perplexity." (*The Word of God and the Word of Man*, trans. Douglas Horton, 186.) Barth points to a perplexity inherent in any attempt to put God into human speech. If God is the God whom Christians claim God to be, then there will be an unavoidable dissonance, a disconnect between almost anything we say about God and the reality of God.

Yet it is the Christian claim not that God is omnipotent, omniscient, and omnipresent but that God speaks, that God speaks to us. It is the nature of the Trinity to be communicative, to establish, through speech, communion, and community. All Christian preaching rests upon a conviction of God's discourse. The same God who, by speech, brought a world into being (Genesis 1) continues to create, to bring something out of nothing, to order chaos, to shed light, and to raise the dead through the power of the word. It is the nature of the God of Israel and the church to be loquacious. All Christian homiletics has its right and its origin in the statement of faith, "And God said . . ."

Paul believed that "faith comes through hearing" (Romans 10:17). The Christian faith is a peculiarly acoustical affair, a uniquely auditory phenomenon. Each Christmas Eve, about midnight, when in the Service of Lessons and Carols I rise before the packed congregation and read those sonorous phrases from the first chapter of John's gospel, congregation and preacher are reminded of how very much is at stake in the church's speaking of the gospel. "In the beginning was the Word, and the Word was with God, and the Word was God. . . . And the Word became flesh and lived among us, and we have seen his glory. . . ."

When James B. Duke directed that this new university in the South would be known by its "great towering church," he seems not to have had any particular program or mission in mind for this neo-gothic building other than some sort of vaguely "spiritual influence" on the youth who studied at the university. The Chapel was a lovely place for periodic university convocations, for monthly moral exhortations from President William Preston Few, and for quiet meditation. Speaking at the 1931 baccalaureate, President Few saw the Chapel, then being built nearby the auditorium where he spoke, as a sort of sermon to the university, a bulwark of a civilization's "great and enduring values," an architectural embodiment of Duke's motto, *Eruditio et Religio*:

> The architectural harmony and strength . . . suggest unity and fullness of life. Here stand side by side science and religion — science . . . given to the full, untrammeled pursuit of the truth and religion with its burning passion for righteousness in the world. The Chapel, hard by the library and laboratories and cooperating with the University in its every effort to promote truth and serve humanity, will dominate this place . . . symbolical of the truth that the spiritual is the central and dominant thing in life . . . Can this ideal be realized in our world and can religion and education engage successfully in a great formative, common undertaking to make this a better world . . . ? Duke University . . . and its Gothic architecture . . . will proclaim the beautiful hope that righteousness and truth, gentleness and strength, goodness and beauty can live together . . . can build a world that will sustain a civilization with great and enduring qualities.

Larger than even Few's vision, from the very first Duke Chapel became a center of vibrant articulation of the Christian faith. When the Chapel was dedicated on a hot June afternoon in 1935, President B. R. Lacy of Union Seminary in Richmond, Virginia, enthusiastically portrayed the Chapel as a sermon in itself: "The Chapel says to the world that here God has the preeminence and that all life should be lived under His shadow, within the sound of His voice, and under the influence of His beauty and holiness."

Shortly thereafter, a group began gathering at the Chapel on Sunday mornings for worship, calling themselves the "Duke University Church (Interdenominational)." A "Preacher to the University" was secured, a professor from the Divinity School, and a tradition began. In the early days, most of the guest preachers came from the ranks of the university faculty. But before long, services were attracting large numbers of worshippers, the great choral tradition began with the formation of the Chapel Choir, and the Chapel ministers were seeking the great voices of mid-twentieth-century American Protestantism as guests in their pulpit. James T. Cleland, a transplanted Scot and a popular preacher on the collegiate circuit, served as the Chapel's beloved and longest-tenured Dean of the Chapel. Cleland developed the tradition of linking Duke Chapel to the teaching of homiletics in the Duke Divinity School, a linkage that continues in the work of the present Dean.

3

Over the years, the chaplains and university ministers who have led Duke Chapel have invited the best preachers in America to the Chapel pulpit, and over the years the very best have come, have preached their best sermons; nearly all of their sermons have been carefully preserved in the Duke University Archives. This collection, spanning seventy-five years, represents a remarkable display of homiletical art, a testimony to the extraordinary intellectual vitality of this particular medium of communication, and a sweeping panorama of American preaching from one century to the next.

The sermons in this seventy-fifth-anniversary collection have been selected on the basis of their meeting most of these editorial criteria: *The sermon is interesting; the preacher is a noteworthy practitioner of a particular type of preaching in a particular period of homiletical history; the sermon, even today, is memorable and exhibits why millions of Americans, and many more millions elsewhere, still listen to sermons with attention and care.*

Without much fear of contradiction, I think that the reader of these sermons will find among those selected the greatest preachers, at least the greatest in American Protestantism, over the past seventy-five years. The toughest task was not selecting a preacher, but selecting only one sermon from a preacher, for some of these preachers have preached many great sermons here. Over half of these sermons had to be transcribed from audiotapes because our collection of printed sermons is uneven. Though transcription was a large undertaking, sermons that are transcribed from tapes probably give readers a better indication of how the sermon sounded in its original presentation than could be had in the edited and printed version left by the preacher.

The first woman to preach in Duke Chapel was Dr. Georgia Harkness, renowned Methodist theologian, in 1939. Sadly, neither tape nor transcript remains of that groundbreaking sermon. We lack many sermons from the first decade of Duke Chapel Sunday worship; our earliest predecessors probably had little appreciation for how prominent and vital would be the tradition they were initiating. After Georgia Harkness, the Chapel has been host to just about every prominent woman preacher in American Protestantism. I counted about a dozen Catholics and four rabbis who had preached at Duke Chapel over the years. The representation of African American preachers is commendable.

During the months that I spent in the Duke University Archives selecting the sermons for this collection, I was reminded of how many great sermons have been preached in this place and also somewhat surprised by how many not-so-great sermons have been heard here. Many of the early sermons sound somewhat pompous and pedantic to my contemporary ears, suggesting not only that the preachers are using a style that is long passé but also that they are intimidated or at least overly deferential to both the building and the academic setting. Those early sermons that begin with, "In this great center of learning and erudition, I would invite you to ponder the following . . ." rarely rise above the status of an ill-timed lecture.

Before beginning this project, I had assumed that preaching was in decline from its former eloquence and brilliance. But now (and this may again be a sign of my contemporary prejudices) I think that many contemporary preachers are more biblical, more engaging, and more theologically faithful than some of our predecessors. There is a confidence bordering on smugness in many of the early preachers, as if they speak in the sure conviction that they are addressing "our" world, a world in which Protestant Christianity reigns supreme. By the late 1960s, one senses that Chapel preachers felt that they must contend for a hearing, that they must exercise some degree of artful persuasion. Perhaps some of these contemporary interpreters of the faith are a bit too troubled by the prejudices and limits of a contemporary academic congregation and are apt to be just a bit too sly, giving away a bit too much of the faith to modern sensibilities. Still, it is probably a good thing for preachers not to assume too great a level of interest among their listeners.

Another observation: sermons through the 1950s are full of annotations and references to contemporary social scientists and works of drama and fiction. These preachers seem awfully concerned to demonstrate to the congregation that they are well read and fully conversant in the best products of contemporary high culture. By the 1970s, Chapel preachers appear to have lost interest in reading anything but the Bible. There are few references to extra-biblical material and many sermons that are mostly a walk through the various movements of a biblical text. This move away from the preacher as presumed cultural critic to the preacher as biblical expositor may be attributed to interesting advances in biblical studies and theology in the later part of the twentieth century and to the explosion of Lectionary-based biblical study aids for the preacher. There may also be a sense among preachers that Christianity's "cultured despisers," as Schleiermacher would have labeled many in the Chapel's Sunday congregation, ought not be flattered by a preacher's references to their passing cultural icons.

The turn toward the Bible and the retelling and paraphrasing of biblical texts in the sermon may also be part of the preacher's recognition that increasingly the congregation is becoming biblically illiterate. Subtle references to a biblical text, vague allusions to an episode in the life of Jesus, are no longer sufficient for a congregation that has not been nurtured in scripture. Therefore the text must be told, retold, reiterated, walked through, and explicated in full detail.

I hope that readers of these sermons might find them to be a challenge to my opening assertion of the grave difficulties of preaching in a place like Duke Chapel. Although this building — inspired by the High Middle Ages, when preaching was not highly regarded in the church's liturgical life, a building that is more kind to the sound of the organ than to the preacher's voice, a place where seeing and hearing (stock in trade of oral communication) are difficult — makes preaching a challenge, by the grace of God something significant is said and heard here. It is probably a good thing for preachers to feel that they must really work to get a good hearing.

When I came to Duke Chapel in 1984, after four years in an inner-city parish, a friend told me, "You may find that chapel pulpit difficult. You have been able to get away with saying some wild things because you are such a conscientious pastor. You visit your parishioners, give them close pastoral care. Therefore they let you say almost anything in Sunday sermons. At Duke Chapel you won't have any of that pastoral work to prop you up. All you will have is your preaching. It may be tough."

There was truth in some of what my friend said. It was as if at Duke Chapel I was part of a controlled experiment in the power of preaching. Here, with many of the typical parochial props removed — the personal relationships with listeners, the full range of pastoral care, the halo effect that surrounds "our" pastor — it was as if we had created a liturgical setting in which preaching was the sole means of contact between pastor and people. How much weight could preaching bear? How much could be heard when most of my Sunday listeners knew me no further than the sound of my voice?

In twenty years here, I have come to an even more extravagant view of the preaching office. I am routinely amazed at what people hear. I am astounded by the students who make major moves in their lives, major steps toward the faith on the basis of nothing more than what they heard in a sermon. Thus I have learned that Duke Chapel is a wonderful place to preach because it is proof of how much people continue to value preaching as well as a validation of how much spiritual weight a twenty-minute sermon is able to bear.

The contemporary university, with its competing truth claims, its mix of voices, its limited modes of thinking, its innate prejudice against many of the claims of the Christian faith, is not always congenial for the proclamation of the Christian message. Dr. Few's originating faith, which proclaimed Duke Chapel to be an enduring testimony to the fact that "the spiritual is the central and dominant thing in life," and that here religion and education would "engage successfully in a great formative, common undertaking to make this a better world," has proved to be problematic in the Chapel's intervening years. Though the Chapel's current Sunday congregation is the largest of any at a university chapel in America, only a minority of the Duke community is present on Sunday at eleven. More people hear a Chapel sermon on the web than listen to the sermon at the Chapel. Most Duke faculty and administrators see the Chapel and its programs to be on the periphery of university life, just one option among others for students on a weekend, rather than the dominant and organizing focal point of the university. The self-confident, mainline Protestant hegemony that one summer's day saw its dominance over American life confirmed in the erection of Duke Chapel is now being sidelined in the new American religious pluralism. The central, dominating building on Duke's campus is as much the new parking deck as Mr. Duke's "great towering church."

Yet Christian communicators have always shown great resourcefulness in their ability to speak their truth to various competitors and counterclaimants to faith. The contemporary university and those inculcated into its peculiar forms of thinking can be a challenge for Christian preachers, but the preachers in this volume demonstrate that it is not an insurmountable one. The hundreds who gather in this Chapel on a Sunday, or the thousands who download sermons from the Chapel website, are evidence that Christian preaching can hold its own against any other competing testimony within the university. At Duke Chapel, a crowd still gathers on Sunday expecting to hear a good sermon, confirming the continuing vitality of the seventy-five-year-old tradition that is celebrated in this book.

As Barth went on to say in his lecture on the difficulties of Christian preaching, a sermon is ultimately to be judged not on the basis of its ability to evoke listeners' interest, its preacher's rhetorical expertise, or its poetic shape, but by the truth. Our best listeners come to church, said Barth, not simply asking, "Is this relevant and useful information?" but rather, "Is this true?" Is this a truthful account of what is really going on in the world? Is it a living representation of the One who is called not only Jesus but also "the way, the truth, and the life" (John 14:6)?

As long as the university is dedicated to the pursuit and the enjoyment of truth, then these sermons indicate that a place like Duke Chapel is a wonderful location to hear a good sermon. I hope that you will agree after reading these sermons from seventy-five years of preaching at Duke Chapel.

WILLIAM H. WILLIMON

Twenty-third Sunday after Pentecost

November 16, 2003

Duke Chapel

Duke University

Durham, North Carolina

On a hot summer evening in 1935, Duke University Chapel was dedicated in a grand service. Dean Lynn Harold Hough of Drew University delivered the dedicatory sermon. His sermon typifies the spirit of the age. With America, particularly this part of America, still in the throes of the Great Depression, standing on the threshold of another great war, with Duke Chapel as a stunning symbol of ecclesiastical and academic aspirations at this newly wrought university, an eloquent word was needed and Hough rose to the occasion. His sermon represented the earliest attempt to reflect upon the significance of a modern university campus with a late gothic cathedral at its center, the first indication of what Duke Chapel was to become.

The Cathedral and the Campus

Dedicatory Sermon — Eight-thirty in the evening
June 2, 1935

LYNN HAROLD HOUGH

The theme to which I wish to invite your attention tonight is "the Cathedral and the Campus," and the text is in the Book of Proverbs, the ninth chapter and the first verse, "Wisdom hath builded her house."

Does the campus of a modern university have a place for a cathedral? It depends of course upon what you mean by a cathedral. If you mean the central church of a diocese, with the throne of the bishop, then of course you cannot associate a campus and a cathedral. But the great *Oxford Dictionary*, which has made slaves of us all, throws, I think, a little extra light on this word *cathedral*. It quotes an English writer of 1643 who says: "Let England then keep the honor to be the cathedral of other nations." And this sentence is quoted in connection with a definition of the word "cathedral" as signifying "a chief center of authority and learning." In this sense surely there is a place for a cathedral upon a campus — "a center of authority and learning." In any event it is in this sense that I shall speak tonight about the cathedral on the campus.

There is something very extraordinary about stone, about buildings. Indeed there is something very extraordinary about everything. Get a few sounds together, as Browning has said, and you will have not another sound, but a star. Get a few bits of material together and you have something of such rare and exquisite beauty, of such gracious and glowing loveliness, that it seems that it can scarcely be associated with the materials which together have somehow wrought this strange magic of beauty, this gracious loveliness, this summoning grandeur so solidly buttressed in material things.

Now what is the cathedral on the campus? It is to be seen as a kind of glorified, solid monument of that authority and learning for which the university stands. It is the material symbol of the ideal elements which give unity to life. Personally I should want the cathedral on the campus somehow to reach out arms wide enough, if I may put it so, to give every human being who comes within its walls a home for his highest ideals. However hard we may be, however cynical, however bitter our experiences may have been, however proud we may be in our belief that we have tossed away those ideals we once possessed, there is in us some exquisite glorious thing, which cannot quite be destroyed by cynicism or covered up with mud, and when that thing speaks in our hearts, we know that just that ideal is what gives significance to life. I know how we sin against this inner ideal; I know how we toss it aside; I know how we say it is quite impractical. And yet around some strange, quiet corner of experience life does manage to give its final testimony. And so whatever our religion, or lack of religion, we confront a blazing ideal whose authenticity we cannot honestly deny. And in the name of just this ideal the cathedral is constantly speaking with a kind of imperial power.

I should like the cathedral on the campus to utter a note which would give to every person who comes into it the feeling that his own — her own — rarest mood and the cathedral belong together. Mrs. Edith Wharton describes one of her heroines very briefly by saying that she carried about constantly a face which expressed her rarest mood. The thought of having a countenance which perpetually expresses one's rarest mood is arresting enough. Most people know the discomfort of faces which suggest anything but their rarest mood. Did you ever think what it means to have on the campus a building which captures the rarest, the most radiant mood of the university and gives it permanent expression in stone? Did you ever think what it means to have a building which is all the while telling you of the poetry of the dreamers who hoped great things for the university — the ideals of those who were not caught in the clutches of a mechanistic interpretation of life, but believed in truth and goodness and beauty as the goal of the human adventure?

Surely you need to keep in your heart the perpetual challenge of the university's rarest mood. If you recall the history of the greatest universities in the world you will see this matter in clear perspective. The ancient city of learning which is Oxford University has had a checkered history. Since the twelfth-century gathering of students it has known golden centuries and centuries which were not golden. But the golden times have defined the university. Cambridge University has not always been dominated by Platonists, but the Cambridge Platonists give the true note of the university. In all the vicissitudes of human understanding it is good to have on the campus a building which says: *"This sort of rare and radiant beauty was in the minds and was splendid in the thought of those who made this university."* What those founders really wanted was to be contributing to that subtle something, which is not in the body, which is not hard and sordid and selfish, but which reaches out friendly arms to all the world, and which comes to the world with eyes on fire with golden expectation, with a heart warm with belief in the great things you may do with life.

Indeed, unless this is true, why have a university? Unless there are ideals which give unity to life, why have such a place as this? Whatever a man's views of thousands of disputed things this should be the first great experience in the university's cathedral. A man should be brought out of his ordinary hard complacency and as he feels the exquisite meanings of life, which are expressed in the great building, he should hear a voice which is saying: "What you have for a moment in your own heart now I am keeping here for you all of the time."

I have a photograph or two in my home—I will not say of very beautiful people—but each photograph captures a kind of splendor of something more than physical, something lofty which is possessed by these friends of mine. Once in a while I take out these photographs. And as I look at them I recall the things these great and good friends are expecting of me. That is what this building is saying. Choir, transept, nave—all are saying to every student, "Duke University expects you to build your life into forms of nobility and beauty. Do not dare to base your thought of life on a lower standard. Do not dare to conceive of your life on a lower level." And all that this glorious building is saying really has to do with that invisible cathedral which the human spirit builds and of which the cathedral stone is a symbol.

In the next place, the cathedral on the campus ought to be the expression of real values, a material symbol of the values which give significance to human experience. As a matter of fact knowledge is a terrible thing. Intellectual power is a terrible thing. For knowledge may be made the instrument of evil purposes, and intellectual power may give strength to dark and sordid enterprises. Socrates, you will remember, had two pupils, Plato and Alcibiades, almost equal in intellectual power. Sometimes I think that Alcibiades was diabolically clever. You may have heard the story of the day when as a young man Alcibiades was talking with Pericles, then the most powerful man in Athens. The younger man with expansive assurance was telling the older how Athens ought to be governed. For a while Pericles listened with a twinkle in his eye. Then, becoming rather tired of the self-confidence of Alcibiades, he said with obvious irony: "When I was your age, Alcibiades, I used to talk just as you are talking now." Without a moment's hesitation Alcibiades replied, "Oh, Pericles, how I should like to have known you when you were at your best!" Whatever a clever mind could do for a man was done for Alcibiades. Plato took the training of Socrates and gave a soul to Athens. Alcibiades, the product of the same training, betrayed Athens and for all his intelligence proved a knave and a fool. Knowledge may be misused. Knowledge may become the very instrument for wounding civilization, for stabbing friendship, for assassinating virtue, for breaking down every noble and splendid thing in the world. So this is the problem of the university — the saving of knowledge from prostitution to evil purposes. It is a good old word, that word "salvation," and knowledge needs salvation badly enough. How is knowledge to be saved? We must have on every campus a building reminding us of those values, loyalty to which will bind all knowledge to noble purposes in life, and will make us safe in the possession of those vast powers of control over nature which modern discoveries have brought within our reach. Values! Values! There is not a kidnapping which tears our heart, there is not the explosion of a machine gun on our pagan city streets, which does not represent the tragedy of technical knowledge unrelated to permanent values. And the university which knows only the realm of knowledge and does not know the realm of values is doomed. There must be one spot where the mighty miracle is wrought by which knowledge is turned to a sense of values, and values direct us in our use of knowledge — the values which give significance to life. This the cathedral on the campus is all the while doing. It reminds us by every subtle quality of its pointed arches; it reminds us by every support of its buttresses, it reminds us through the sense of distance and of height, of those intangible realms of value without which civilization is but a name.

The cathedral on the campus is an expression of the principle that it is the very nature of the material to wear the livery of the spiritual. As you sit in a university chapel like this one you feel the marvelous fashion in which the material may take on an almost incredibly spiritual grandeur and a grace and loveliness of rare and exquisite beauty. The principle involved is of the most far-reaching character. We are not to think of the material as belonging to a world which is antagonistic to the spiritual. We are to think of the material as in its very nature to be used by the spiritual for its own high purposes. At this point we have often gone wrong in our interpretation of life and of religion. Perhaps the Puritan tradition has had its effect here — but however that may be, somehow the fear of the beautiful, as if beauty were necessarily corrupting; somehow a fear of life in the world, as if it could not be bent to high purposes; somehow a suicidal asceticism has come like a strange poison through some of the noblest things of religion.

The material should express the spiritual. Life is not to be torn apart at this point. You are not to hate the body; you are to shoot it through with the glory of the moral and the spiritual. Everything indeed which has to do with this world is an object for the mastery of spiritual power. Of course that is what this chapel is saying every moment. You come here all alone, you sit in the nave, you look at the great heights, and somehow through the material this miracle has been wrought, and the inexpressible beauty of the spiritual life glows in your mind, becomes incandescent in your imagination, and exquisite in your thought. And this is a symbol of the fashion in which all physical experience is to come at last to spiritual meaning. How many people could have been saved from heartbreak if they had understood that.

Whenever a boy or girl takes the wrong track, that boy or that girl has most tragically lost the key to the golden chest in which the real meaning of physical experiences is to be found. The physical life is a sacrament and it is not meant to lose its connection with spiritual meanings.

In my twenty-five years in the pastorate I used to have occasion to go into homes where a tiny child had just arrived. Sometimes, knowing the parents, I would wonder a little about it all. Then I would go into the house and the baby would be introduced to me. I would look into the mother's face and I would see a transformation. How did it happen? God has a way of whispering into the hearts of the most careless girls marvelous secrets when they become mothers. You cannot go through life's characteristic experiences without feeling around many a corner that you have looked into the eyes of God. The very genius of the material is to be linked with the spiritual, to be the vehicle of the spiritual.

This is what Jesus meant when He took the bread and said, "This is my body." In one tremendous act He claimed the material as the symbol of the spiritual. If we had understood that, many things in our lives would have been different. Even our social and industrial and political life would have possessed a new spiritual quality. I never go into a great cathedral — like the Minster of York, or one of those old European cathedrals echoing with the sobs of wounded hearts in many a century, shining with the bright hopes of eager young people who lived hundreds of years ago — but I remember that it is the very genius of the material to express the spiritual.

The cathedral on the campus is to be the symbol in stone of that harmony without which life becomes "a tale told by an idiot signifying nothing." Francis Bacon spoke of the one good custom which might corrupt the world, and John Galsworthy has reminded us that small and mutually exclusive loyalties may have devastating effects. Life must be organized into the sort of harmony where individual loyalties find their place in larger loyalties and these in still larger loyalties, until all our knowledge and all our purposes unite in a noble completeness. We can turn our backs upon the thought of harmony if we will. And if we repudiate it, life will break us. We will be putting a poison into our life which, by and by, will do its desperate work.

And so we need to be reminded all the while of that dream of harmony in whose presence we are a little abashed, and in speaking of which we become oddly self-conscious. We need to be reminded of the bright crimson of the new day, of the iridescent sunset, of the strange beauty of the moonlit ocean, of the beautiful things we have seen in human faces, of the sudden revelations we have seen in wistful eyes. We need to be reminded of that harmony without which we cannot really live. Of course, it is rather like bringing coals to Newcastle to say this in the South. For this is the part of North America where there has been a fuller and firmer sense that life itself should be made a beautiful art than anywhere else in this republic. And if I may say so there are some of us in other parts of the country who are counting on you. We think of southerners as those who make living an art. We are not quite comfortable with those from the South who come north and seem to be completely absorbed in learning our commercial cunning. It is your service to the republic to keep alive something very precious and beautiful which was at the very heart of the life of the Old South. And we must all learn that what Beethoven did in his great compositions we have to do with life itself. The thing for which we really live is the achievement of harmony. So there is a noble fitness about the cathedral on the campus. It is like a stately presence which, seeing the wistful longing for harmony in our eyes, speaks to us words of high encouragement, as it says, "Do not give up that dream."

The cathedral on the campus is the perpetual witness to the imperial place of religion in human life. I know that there are a good many people who will say that the economic motive is the dominant motive in human action. That, if you will allow me to say so, is sheer nonsense. Why do you want to succeed in the world? There is somebody somewhere you want to please. There is somebody somewhere you want to make happy. After all, let us be fair. There is not so much hard, grim avarice in the world as we might think. The very ambition for wealth arises from love for something, somebody, and we want the power of wealth to use that power for what we love. Sir Henry Jones tells in his autobiography of how as a little lad in Wales he lived in a house so tiny and with brothers and sisters so many that they could never get all together for a meal. He tells how he was walking in the hills of Wales one night with one of his boyhood companions. There in the moonlight, looking each other in the eye, they promised each other that they would meet at one of the great universities of the world. Something in that flash from eye to eye was inexplicable. They had begun to feel and to see the invisible. You cannot compress that scene into any set of material relationships. You cannot explain life in economic terms. And all the vast meanings of life which cannot be expressed in merely material or economic terms move on until they come to full fervor in religion. Here is something which transcends all facts and thoughts and actions, something in which they find their meaning and their right to be, which gives a soul to human experiences, which tells us that we must indeed live as if seeing the invisible. This has come to living form in the greatest of the existing religions. It touches the deepest depths of the life of mankind. The cathedral on the campus speaks in its name. It is the worthy expression of the imperial nature of religion.

The cathedral on the campus embodies in stone the very genius of the Christian religion. Transept, nave, and choir—always the representation in stone of the Cross; and a thousand things it would require hours to tell, in which Christianity is caught here and there and everywhere in the mighty building; all these express the very quality of Christianity frozen, if we may paraphrase Goethe, into a perpetual music in stone. The Christian interpretation of hope and fear, joy and sorrow, the battle with evil, the tragedy of defeat and the glory of victory, all live in a thousand features in the great buildings which have come out of the history of which they have been a part. If a young man is inclined to think of Christianity as a thing of a day, the slightest acquaintance with a great cathedral will confront him with the marvel of a tale splendid with twenty centuries of achievement, drenched, it is true, by twenty centuries of agony and evil, but glorious with moral and spiritual victory, with the sunlight always falling upon it.

What is there to keep us from barbarity in a civilized world? There is the greatness, the splendor, the intellectual and spiritual achievement coming to fulfillment in twenty centuries of Christian history. Sometimes one has a feeling of sharp shock in one of the older cathedrals of Europe, as he thinks how age after age men have here remembered the moral passion of the Hebrew prophets, the glory of the life of Jesus, that haunting passion which we cannot forget, which changes us even when we turn back to it. People did not learn how to build cathedrals until Christianity had come into the world. And if there ever comes a day when Christianity has waned in power, men will come into buildings like this and say: "What majesty of thought lived in the mind of man before it was flung out in this magnificent nave." And they will go back and listen again to the words of Jesus, and they will go back to the long centuries of Christian history, and the old faith will once more command their minds and dominate their conscience and bend their will to its purpose.

The cathedral on the campus is a summons to men to find the synthesis of all experiences in Jesus Christ. This very type of architecture is the crystallization in permanent form of a devotion which century after century has offered unquestioning loyalty to Jesus Christ. Arch and buttress, window and spacious overarching roof, every feature of the vast building tells the story of an integration which has been made possible in stone because of a mighty loyalty to the central figure in history.

The cathedral on the campus is a perpetual call to worship. Students entering its portals for a few quiet moments between classes find themselves in an atmosphere where worship becomes almost inevitable. The invisible in some strange and beautiful fashion has indeed become visible, the impalpable has been brought within reach, and as perhaps the great organ expresses the beauty already in stone, in a perfect beauty of sound, all of experience seems moving toward one central act of devotion.

The cathedral on the campus is a summons to Christian action.

> Our God is still the Lord of might,
> In deeds, in deeds He takes delight.

That which rises in the human spirit in the hour of profound devotion is to come forth in radiant and effective action for the glory of God and for the good of men.

> Beat down yon Beetling mountain
> And raise yon jutting cape.
> A world is on the anvil,
> Now smite it into shape.
> Whence comes that iron music
> Whose sound is heard afar?
> The hammers of the world-smiths
> Are beating out a star.

The cathedral on the campus is the symbol of an eternal hope. The other day I heard an address by a Christian leader of great eminence. I walked away from the building with a man whose name you would recognize. "It was a notable address, was it not?" I said to my friend. "Yes," he replied, "it was a great speech." He was silent a moment. Then he added: "I am over eighty years of age. He told me nothing about what I can hope for when I make my great adventure." One of the great French proverbs tells us that to understand earth you must have known heaven. All that we have said and all the reality which lies back of what we have said comes to one consummation in a hope in the presence of which time is an impertinence and for whose fulfillment eternity is inevitable. Of the cathedral too it may be said, "God hath put eternity in its heart."

The cathedral on the campus is most of all to be more of a voice. It has many voices—music of much loveliness, architecture of beauty beyond words. But the voice of the preacher will come with peculiar power. From the pulpit of the cathedral is to sound forth that message in which the glory of the Timeless breaks into time, and the passing days carry the splendor of the life of God in the soul of man. There is a sense in which the university chapel comes to its supreme moment as the home of a voice which is at once the voice of a man, and by some strange and beautiful divine grace the voice of God.

"Wisdom hath builded her house." It is a great thing when God puts it into the heart of a human being to do what has been done in the building of this chapel. By and by not only here, but about the United States and out over the world the influences of this chapel will be felt. It is a living symbol of the imperishable riches of the Gospel of Jesus Christ. It will have a share in producing that consummation when love not hate, truth not falsehood, faith and not fear, justice and not injustice shall rule in the hearts and lives of men. In the meantime, it will give gracious inspiration to spiritual pilgrims, and it will speak its deepest word to those who have been captured by the incredible love of Jesus Christ.

Paul Tillich, who served for many years on the faculty of Union Theological Seminary in New York City, was one of the twentieth century's greatest theologians. Tillich took existentialism, the reigning philosophy of the postwar years, and used it as a medium for translating the Christian faith into a language which Tillich judged to be more accessible for educated, enlightened, modern people than traditional Christian thought. In this sermon, preached at the height of his popularity as a theologian, Tillich meditates on the concept of strength in our lives, correlating a passage from Paul's letters into a message of encouragement for a contemporary congregation.

Be Strong

March 13, 1955

PAUL TILLICH

I Corinthians 16:13–14 The text for our sermon is taken from First Corinthians 16:13–14: Be watchful, stand firm in your faith, be courageous, be strong. Let all that you do be done in love. Out of this well-known passage, I choose two words, on which I want you to center your attention in this hour—the words "Be strong!"

How can I attain strength? This is the question asked in all ages of man's life and in all periods of human history. It is a question asked with passion and despair in our time and asked most impatiently by those who are no more children and not yet adults.

In our text Paul uses several times the imperative. *Be* strong, he asks the Corinthians. We easily slip over it. But it should arrest our attention as fully, perhaps even more than the other words in our text. For the demanding verb "be" contains in its two letters the whole riddle of the relation of man to God.

Paul asks of the Christians in Corinth not something which is strange to them. He asks them to be what they are—Christians. All the imperatives he uses are descriptions of something that is, before they become demands for something that ought to be. Be what you are, that is the only thing one can ask of any being. One cannot ask of a being to be something it is not according to its true nature. But *this* one can and must ask. One has a feeling as if life in all its forms desires to be asked, to receive demands. But no life can receive demands for something which it is not. It wants to be asked to become what it is and nothing else. This seems surprising, but a little thought shows us that it is true.

Nobody questions that one cannot ask fruits from thorns, or grain from weed, or water from a dry fountain, or love from a cold heart, or courage from a cowardly mind, or strength from a weak life. If we ask such things from beings who do not have them we are foolish, and either they will laugh at us or they will move against us as unfair and hostile toward them. We can ask of anything or anyone only to bring forth what he has, to become what he can become. Out of what is given to us, we can act. Receiving in all life precedes acting.

Be strong, says Paul; he says it to those who have received strength as he himself has received strength in his weakness, when the power of a new reality grasped him on his road to Damascus. Now some of us will ask: What about us who feel that we have nothing received, that we don't have faith and courage and strength and love? We are wanting in all those, so the commanding "be" of Paul is not said to us. Or if somebody says it to us, must we not remain unconcerned or become hostile to him who says it? We are not strong, so nobody can ask us to be strong! We are weak, shall we remain weak? Shall we fall into resignation, and become cynical about such demands, and say, "They may be for others, they are not for us"? I hear many people, more than we believe, saying this. I hear whole classes of young people speak like that. I hear many individuals in the older generations repeat it.

And I don't find any consolation in the Bible. There is the parable of the different soils on which the seed of the divine message falls and of which only *one* soil brings fruit. There is the word of the many who are called and the *few* who are elected; there is the terrifying, realistic statement of Jesus that those to whom much is given will receive more, and that *from* those to whom little is given, even this will be taken away. There is the contrast between those who are *born* out of light and have become its children and those who are *born* out of darkness and have become *its* children. There is the parable of men as clay which cannot revolt against God the potter, whatever the potter does to the clay. *We* would like to revolt when we hear this, and many Christians revolt and have revolted. I have heard many of them whenever they read or heard these words. They close their ears against such hard words because they cannot stand them. We would like to revolt when we hear them also. But if we look around us into the life of men we are forced to say they are true. The Bible at least sees reality as it is, even if the preaching of the Bible does not. We would like to say in good democratic phrasing: "Everyone gets a chance by God to reach fulfillment, but not everybody uses it. Some do, some don't. Both have their ultimate destiny in their own hands." We would like that it were so. But we cannot escape the truth that it is *not* so. The chances are *not* even. There is only a limited number of human beings to whom one can say "Be strong," because they have received strength. And the others, to whom many of us may belong? The only thing, the only honest thing I could say to them is: Accept that you are weak, don't pretend that you are strong. And if you dare to be what you are, this will be your strength, the only one you can have now. Accept that you are weak; that is what we should say to those who *are* weak. Accept that you are a coward; that is what we should say to those who are cowardly. Accept that you are uncertain about your faith: that is what we should say to those who are not firm in it. And to those who don't love, we should say, accept it that you are not able to love.

This sounds strange! But everyone who knows the human soul, above all who knows his own soul, will understand what is meant. He will understand that for the weak ones the first thing is to acknowledge and to accept their weakness. He who does this will cease to deceive himself by saying: I have at least something of what the apostle demands. He can demand it from them, for partly at least I have it. There are perhaps people who could rightly speak this to themselves, but *they* just would not do it. Yet there are others for whom it is self-deception if they judge themselves in this way. And to them we must say: Accept that you are weak for you are weak; be honest toward yourselves.

Let me say a word to those who are responsible for others, as parents, teachers, ministers, counselors, friends: Don't say the demanding "be" to anybody without fear and great hesitation. If you use it, even if you use it toward yourselves, you touch at the mystery of a person's destiny in the perspective of the eternal. You touch at the mystery of your own eternal destiny.

And now let us hear what Paul says to those whom he considers to be strong and whom, therefore, he can ask to be strong. The first thing he says is that they shall be watchful. He knows there is a non-Christian in every Christian; there is a weak one in every strong one. There is cowardice in every courage and unbelief in every faith and much hidden hostility in every love. Watchfulness means that the Christian never can rest on his being a Christian, that the strong one never can rely on his strength. He must rely on something else. Paul calls it faith. He asks the Corinthians to stand on a firm ground, on a ground which cannot be shaken when all other foundations have shaken — the ultimate, the divine ground. To stand on this ground means to stand in the faith.

Paul, of course, thinks of the faith in the form in which he has brought it to the Corinthians. But in this faith, the faith itself is present, namely the standing on the ultimate ground below any shaking and changing ground. To break the way to this ultimate ground is the meaning of the Christ. Stand firm in your faith means, don't give up that faith which alone can make you ultimately strong by giving you the ultimate ground on which to stand. And everybody needs a ground to stand on. Standing firm in one's faith does not mean to adhere to a set of beliefs; it does not request us to suppress doubts about Christian or other doctrines; but it points to something which lies beyond doubt in that depth in which man's being and all beings is rooted. To be aware of this ultimate ground, whatever its name, is to live in it, and out of it is ultimate strength. Be strong and stand in faith is one and the same demand. But now, remembering what we first said about the limits of every imperative, some may reply: "We do not stand in any faith. Doubt or unbelief is our destiny but not faith. We know, they continue, that you are right, that there is no strength where there is no faith. But we have no faith, and there is some strength in us, it is — we can call it so — the strength of honesty, the unwillingness to subject ourselves to faith which is not ours, be it for conventional reasons, be it for obedience to our parents, be it because of our own longing for strength, be it under the impression of emotion-arousing evangelists as with so many of our contemporaries. Our strength," they say, "is to resist all this and to reject strength coming out of the sacrifice of our intellectual integrity." Some of the best in our time would speak like this. To them I answer: Your honesty proves your faith and, therefore, your honesty is your strength! You may not believe in anything which can be stated in doctrines. But you stand on the ultimate ground, you stand firm in your faith as long as you stand in honesty and take your doubt and your unbelief seriously without restriction. Become aware of the faith which you *have*, and perhaps you will find words for it, perhaps not. Perhaps you will find even Christian words for it, perhaps not. But with or without words, be strong; for you *are* strong. You are strong in the seriousness of your honesty.

There is another enemy of strength even more powerful than the lack of faith. It is the disunity within ourselves and the lack of courage coming out of it, the weakness which prevents us to say "yes" to ourselves. For the affirmation of oneself demands the greatest courage. He who is united with himself is invincibly strong. But who is? We all are dominated by forces which conquer parts of our being and split our personality. We lack the strength which is given with a united, centered personality. We are disrupted by compulsions, formerly called demonic powers. And who could tell a split personality: Be strong! To which side of the personality can such a command be addressed? But something else can happen to such a personality and perhaps it has happened to some of us. Healing power, coming through men, but ultimately coming from the ground on which we stand, can enter the personality and can unite it with itself so that an act of courage can become possible. I speak of the courage which takes upon itself the anxiety of our split personality. This courage is the innermost center of faith. It dares to affirm ourselves in spite of the deep anxiety about ourselves. Out of this courage the greatest strength emerges. It is the strength which overcomes the powers splitting our soul and our world. Be courageous! Say "Yes," Yes to yourselves, Yes to your God in spite of the anxiety of the No which is always working within you.

And now Paul adds something to what he asks of the strong personality, something which seems to be almost the opposite of it. He says: "Let all that you do be done in love!" The strength of the personality whom Paul has in mind is based on something beyond courage and faith. It is not the strength of the hero. It is the strength of him who surrenders the praise which he would have received as a hero, as a strong personality, to the humility of love. We know strong personalities, perhaps in our family, in our friendship, in public life whom we admire, but of whom we feel that something is wanting. And this something is love.

One can be strong by subjecting oneself to a strong discipline, and by suppressing much in oneself and becoming powerful in relation to others. It is often this type of man which is called a strong personality. And, certainly, strength without the ability to direct oneself is impossible. But those who have this ability, and I admire the strong personalities, should ask themselves whether something is wanting. They should ask themselves whether their strength is not without love. Perhaps in order to confirm themselves to say yes to themselves, they force upon others the same restrictions of life they have imposed on themselves. Their domineering strength creates opposition or submissiveness, and in any case, weakness in others. There is a profound ambiguity about the strong Christian personality. Christianity could not live, society could not go on without them. But many Christians, many persons who perhaps could have become strong themselves, are destroyed or reduced to mental weakness and often illness by them. Be watchful when you are considered or consider yourselves strong. Be watchful and don't demand of those around you to be what you are and what they are not. You will destroy them by your strength.

Without love the strong one becomes a law for the weak one. And the law makes those who are weak even weaker. It drives them into despair or rebellion or indifference. Strength without love destroys first the others, then itself. Love is not something which may or may not be added to strength, but it is an element of strength. One cannot be strong without love. For love is not an irrelevant emotion, but it is the blood of life, it is the power of reunion of the separated. Strength without love leads to separation, to judgment, to control of the weak. Love reunites what is separated, it accepts what is judged, it participates in what is weak as God participates in our weakness and gives us strength by His participation. Amen.

H. Shelton Smith was a distinguished historian of American Christianity at Duke and director of graduate studies in religion when he preached this courageous sermon. One of Smith's most renowned books was his In His Image but . . . Racism in Southern Religion, 1780–1910, *a devastating look at the southern church's support of slavery in antebellum times and racial segregation in the present. One hears echoes of his academic work in this sermon, delivered while the South awaited moral awakening in the civil rights movement. A university chapel ought to be at the forefront of the church's moral deliberation. This sermon shows such a moment at Duke Chapel.*

Moral Crisis in a Troubled South

April 29, 1956

H. SHELTON SMITH

Acts 9:1–20   At no time in the present century has the South been so deeply troubled in soul as it is today. This anxiety is, of course, partly the result of pressures arising out of a far-reaching decision of the Supreme Court. But its root goes deeper. Unless I am seriously mistaken, it stems from a growing conviction that our legally imposed color bar is in basic conflict with both the democratic ethic and the Christian faith. This conflict is involving us of the South in a deepening moral crisis which I feel constrained to discuss with you today.

In meditating upon our present crisis, my thought has turned often to that dramatic story which was read to you this morning (Acts 9:1–20). In passionate loyalty to his ancestral tradition, Saul of Tarsus earnestly tried to wipe out the early Christians. Where persuasion would not work he did not hesitate to persecute, to imprison, even to murder. Yet at the very height of his frenzied zeal, while hurrying to Damascus, a light from heaven brighter than the sun flashed through his conscience, and a voice said to him, "Saul, Saul, why do you persecute me?" "Who are you?" stammered Saul. "I am Jesus, whom you are persecuting," replied the heavenly visitor. "It hurts you to kick against the goads."

Note one thing: the more fiercely Saul persecuted the early Christians, the more brightly the moral flame burned within his conscience, until at last the scales fell from his blinded eyes and he was transformed into an advocate of that which he had formerly opposed.

Are not we of the South experiencing an inner moral conflict which broadly parallels that of Saul of Tarsus? Is not the light from above disturbing our consciences? Will the heavenly flame eventually burn through our clouded visions and transform our racial perspectives?

My considered answer, based finally upon faith in the sovereignty of God, is a strong yes. Our moral road to Damascus may be long and tortuous, but we are on our way. When I say we are on our way, I mean simply that thousands of white southerners, including especially youth, can no longer morally justify the principle of racial segregation. To be sure they are still a minority group, yet their numbers are steadily growing. They do not, like some noisy demagogues, shout their views from the housetops, but their convictions lie deep nevertheless.

One fact is worth emphasizing at the outset. This new spiritual outlook did not start on May 17, 1954, when the Supreme Court first ruled against the Plessy doctrine of separate but equal. In fact, ever since the First World War, the South has been the scene of the prophetic labors of such men as the late Will Alexander and Howard Odum, to whom the color bar was anathema. Through the actions of interracial councils and commissions, through research and publications, they sowed the seeds of a greater South. While they labored patiently within a biracial framework, they foresaw the day when it would be abandoned.

Four years before the Supreme Court handed down its historic decision, the Presbyterian Synod of Alabama declared, "Segregation is living on borrowed time." Both the federal Constitution and the Christian conscience, the Synod added, have written doom upon the brow of legalized segregation. Southern groups in all the other major denominations were expressing similar convictions. Meanwhile church-related colleges, graduate and professional schools of state universities, and theological seminaries were opening their doors to all qualified students.

Hence, when the Supreme Court finally struck down the Plessy doctrine, the leaders of most of the religious bodies in the South were already prepared to sanction its ruling. Episcopalians, in their Southeastern Provincial Conference, called the decision "just and right." A Texas Methodist Conference declared it to be "but the legal assertion of the position of the Christian Church." The General Assembly of Southern Presbyterians commended the Court's ruling and called upon all church members to support it. The Southern Baptist Convention acknowledged the decision to be "in harmony with the constitutional guarantee of equal freedom to all citizens, and with the Christian principles of equal justice and love for all men." Catholic and Jewish agencies in the South were equally affirmative in their actions. These church groups, be it noted, were not so-called outside meddlers, but native southerners.

For a brief interval after the Supreme Court rendered its verdict it looked as though a good many cities and communities in the South would take steps to keep faith with the Court. Indeed, local school boards in some of the more progressive cities began taking actions toward compliance.

But alas, this affirmative spirit soon encountered a different temper. Tough-willed resistance movements began emerging, springing up first of all in the lower South, led by ardent segregationists whose more extreme members openly defied the Supreme Court. They insisted on the freedom of their respective states to do as they pleased, but yet they did not tolerate that same freedom within their own borders. Rigid conformity was demanded, even at the price of coercion if necessary.

This spirit of resistance later spread to the upper South as well. Although revealing itself in sweeter words, the overall effect was the same. Almost everywhere the prevailing mood has been to prevent any local community from cracking the wall of segregation. This holds not only for public schools, but largely also for many other public facilities such as city halls and recreational centers. Even where the color bar has been outlawed, as in public education, the Negro is exhorted to volunteer to remain segregated. This frozen temper says, "Don't give an inch, or you will have to give a mile."

Grave dangers lie ahead of a South in this inflexible mood. First of all, we are in danger of jeopardizing our public schools. The movement to assign to local communities the final decision on questions of vital school policy, hitherto reserved to state boards of education, can easily scuttle the hard-won standards which have been a half-century in building. This backward-looking trend threatens the South with all the evils of the old district school system. The outcome could be not a statewide system, but a patchwork of uneven policies, standards, and programs, Add to this the legal option of any local community to abolish its public schools altogether, and the prospect becomes alarming. Some may call this power to close a local school "a safety valve," but it seems far more like a time bomb. If we in the South ever become so unbalanced as to wipe out our public schools, we will sentence our children to the tyranny of ignorance and poverty.

A second danger is that the South will cut itself off from the main currents of the nation — industrial, political, cultural. Our twentieth-century form of secession could be secession not from the political household of the Union, as in 1860, but from the mainstream of democratic civilization. It is as true of a region as it is of an individual that if it tries to live unto itself, it will shrivel up and die of stagnation.

This decaying process would be hastened by the migration of our abler youth to freer sections of the nation, as in the wake of the Civil War. Meanwhile, the present flow into our region of industrialists, scientists, skilled technicians, and vocational specialists would slow down to a trickle. This two-way loss of creative leadership would leave the South to the inevitable ravages of political demagogues, cultural drones, and moral bigots.

Yet another danger is that we will so bungle our interracial relations as to cripple America's moral leadership in the larger world community. Remember, two out of every three people in the world are colored, and our behavior is an open book to them. The shameful Lucy spectacle and the barbaric Emmett Till murder were unfolded daily to the Chinese, the Africans, the Indonesians, and other colored peoples who are coming to power in the greatest revolution of modern history. They measure our morality and our goodwill not by our words, but by our deeds. When the Voice of America proclaims to them the virtue of our Declaration of Independence and our Bill of Rights, they read our professed ideals through the lenses of our daily actions.

When the Supreme Court first ruled against segregated public schools, totalitarian governments interpreted it as a fraud palmed upon the world, and they predicted that in any case the South would not abide by it. Shall we in the South fulfill their cynical prophecies? If we do, my brethren, we will give aid and comfort to the mortal enemies of democracy.

But that which should give us the deepest concern of all is the tragic fact that we dare to risk all these dangers because of a fundamentally anti-Christian assumption about a group of our fellow men. After taking a wide-ranging poll of southern sentiment, Howard Odum declared that the heart of our credo can be summed up in these words: "The Negro is a Negro, and nothing more." In other words, the Negro is humanly inferior to the white man. In the final analysis, our dual racial structure in the South rests upon that belief.

Let us then face squarely our southern credo in the light of the Christian revelation which came to Saul as he paced the road to Damascus. Without question, he did more than any other follower of Jesus to emancipate the early church from the bonds of Judaism and transform it into a fellowship of all races. For this very reason his fellow Jews conspired to kill him.

Nevertheless, he "was not disobedient to the heavenly vision." When Peter later wavered in his supraracial views, Paul boldly rebuked him. "Is God the God of the Jews only?" Paul asked the Christians at Rome. "Is he not the God of Gentiles also? Yes, of Gentiles also, *since God is one*" (Romans 3:29–30).

Note well his decisive words, "since God is one." Paul here laid the very cornerstone of Christian community. It is faith, not race, which determines the range of our Christian fellowship. Where there is true faith in one God there is no color bar. "There is neither Jew nor Greek, . . . neither slave nor free; . . . for you are all one in Christ Jesus" (Galatians 3:28).

Is it not clear, then, why we white churchmen are conscience-stricken? We do not presume to be better than our worthy forefathers, yet we do believe, as most of them apparently did not, that a racially segregated church is a tragic denial of that community which is inherent in One Lord, One Faith, One Baptism. Since God is one, we are members one of another — equally subject to God's judgment and mercy; equally accountable to Him; equally valuable in His sight. Hence, to discriminate against a single one of His children on the ground of race is to impugn the moral character of God. Human equality is the gift of God; therefore, human equality is an unalienable spiritual attribute of every child of God.

When we consider the Supreme Court's decision from this Christian perspective, we are bound to admit that it is morally right. If therefore this ruling is being bitterly assailed in the South, it is due in no small measure to the moral infirmity of our Christianity. Many of the most rabid enemies of the Court's ruling are members of our Protestant churches. Let us ministers in particular take this fact seriously to heart, pondering our faith and our stewardship. Had we been fully surrendered to the will of God, it is hard to believe that so many lay pillars in our churches would now be party to an un-Christian movement to obstruct the course of human justice.

How long will be our journey to Damascus? It will be as long as we persist in our un-Christian belief that our colored brother is only a Negro, and nothing more. A fundamental change of heart may require a very long journey, a journey of trial and tribulation. Nevertheless, since the moral flame from heaven is already penetrating our consciences, the Eternal Light will eventually burn away the scales which obscure a larger vision of the Kingdom of God.

Symbolic of that new day is a generally unknown act which was performed by the South's greatest Civil War hero. Within a year after the Confederate surrender at Appomattox, an unwanted Negro entered one of Richmond's fashionable churches while Holy Communion was being served, made his way down the aisle, and knelt at the Communion Altar. The congregation sat aghast, and emotions quickened. Sensing the situation, a distinguished layman arose in his pew, stepped forward to the altar, and knelt beside his colored brother. Captured by his spirit, the congregation followed his magnanimous example.

That layman was Robert E. Lee. On that Sunday morning he won the greatest battle of his career. For "greater is he that mastereth his spirit than he that taketh a city." By the grace of God, Robert E. Lee lighted a spiritual torch that will never go out until we of the South, black and white, are transformed into a fellowship as broad and as enduring as the love of Christ.

Eugene Carson Blake, a Presbyterian, was a great ecumenical leader, presi-
dent of the World Council of Churches in the postwar years. In this sermon Blake
meditates on the prophetic poetry of Isaiah, helping his congregation to see the
contemporary significance of these ancient words.

Even the Desert Shall Bloom

April 7, 1957

EUGENE CARSON BLAKE

Isaiah 55:1 My text is Isaiah 55:1 — "Ho! Everyone that thirsteth, come ye
to the waters. And he that hath no money, come ye, buy and eat. Yea, come,
buy wine and milk, without money and without price."

Poetry is often hard to interpret. This 55th chapter of Isaiah is acknowledged to be great and beautiful poetry. Anyone with literary sensibility is
moved by the beauty of its images, the grandeur of its language. But most of
us — even those who like poetry — would probably be put to it, familiar as it
is, to interpret the full sense of the chapter. What does it all mean anyway?
What was the situation that called this writing forth? What did it signify
to the people to whom it was originally addressed? What does it mean, if
anything, to us gathered here this morning?

Poetry is different from prose. We know that. But the exact difference is
sometimes hard to analyze or to express. I remember studying for a whole
term in a college English course on this very subject. Even when we were
finished and I passed the course, none of us were quite sure that we knew
what exactly made a poem a poem, much less what made a good poem a
good poem. But there is one thing that remains with me still from that course
in poetics after all of these years. It is that poetry is pictures, images, con-
creteness. Prose may contain pictures, too, but prose is often abstract.

During World War II, at the darkest hour of Britain's trial, when it looked
as if the mighty power of the Nazi army and air force was just waiting until
it could come and take over Britain, Winston Churchill made a speech. Part
of what he said to the beleaguered British people was this: "We shall go on
to the end. We shall fight in France. We shall fight on the seas and oceans. We
shall fight with growing confidence and growing strength in the air. We shall
defend our island, whatever the cost may be. We shall fight on the beaches.

We shall fight on the landing grounds. We shall fight in the field and in the straits. We shall fight in the hills. We shall never surrender."

Churchill was speaking pure poetry. Put in prose, all that the prime minister said was that wherever the Germans attack us, we will fight them, and we won't give up. Clear enough, too. But no pictures—no images, no flashes in your mind, no warming in your heart. To understand poetry, the first requirement is to see the picture. Seeing the pictures, if we can, if we will, in quite prosaic fashion, we must understand what those pictures mean.

> Ho! Everyone that thirsteth, come ye to the waters. And he that hath no money, come ye, buy and eat. Yea, come, buy wine and milk, without money and without price.

Let's look at the picture behind that text. It's a picture of a dry land, where water is scarce. And where, because of the scarcity, food and drink of all kinds were becoming more and more expensive each year, and more and more out of the reach of ordinary people. For a thousand years and more, this land of Mesopotamia had been the center, the cradle of culture and civilization. Even before history began to be written, there were traditions that this fertile land lying between the Tigris and the Euphrates had been inhabited by peoples extinct long before men had begun to write. Even the Garden of Eden had been placed in Mesopotamia by the ancient stories that had been told and retold. The cities of the plain had been sought for prizes by barbarian empire after barbarian empire, which had risen and fallen through the centuries of recorded history. Synachre, Assurnasirpal—they had conquered them. Rameses of Egypt had tried and failed. Even now, Cyrus the Persian was on the march toward these great cities of the plain.

During all that time of history, Mesopotamia had been watered well by its two great rivers, flowing from their sources far to the north in the snow-capped mountains of Iran. But of late, in the last century or two, water had begun to be a problem. Too many of the hills had been deforested. The flood-waters each spring carried more and more of the precious topsoil into the sea. Dry seasons came with increasing frequency. Hot winds would blow away in fine dust more and more of the precious, life-giving soil. It came to be, finally, that in normal seasons, the rains became a mixed blessing. They ran off so fast over that sun-baked soil. The soil itself was almost as hard as the clay bricks, from which they had built their palaces and houses. The sun-baked soil soaked in but little of the needed water.

Man had been ingenious. Canals and irrigation ditches crisscrossed the whole land. Still, year after year, water became scarcer. And because of it, food became more expensive — not merely in money prices (for that can be adjusted), but food became more expensive in the labor required to produce and to transport it. Thus, by the time our prophet poet wrote, even the fairly thoughtless ordinary people had become aware of the fact that water was the most precious of all commodities — that a gentle rain was the gift of life itself.

What we were watching was the caving in of a great civilization, due to lack of water. Babylon was doomed, although it had not died yet. At this time, the prophet was speaking his message to his fellow captives from Israel, who had been transported there to Babylon a generation or two before. Nor was it long after, as history is measured, that Babylon and the whole region between the rivers was no longer a center of culture at all, but had turned into a sun-baked, sleepy outpost of civilization, which it remained until oil was found. A few scattered remnants of people eked out a living in poverty, where once great cities had stood proudly, with their fabled hanging gardens and the great marketplaces teeming with life and with beauty.

This is the background of the prophet's poem. In it he pictured an open marketplace. Hawkers and farmers are calling out their various wares to the crowds: the produce, which is for sale. But prices are high — terribly high! So high that business is slack because people don't have money even to buy the basic necessities. Suddenly, above the other voices of the marketplace sounds out a new cry: "Ho! Everyone that thirsteth, come ye to the waters." Water was being sold now; it was so expensive, so scarce. "Ho! Everyone that thirsteth, come ye to the waters. And he that hath no money, come ye, buy and eat. Yea, come, buy wine and milk, without money and without price."

You can picture for yourself the surprise, the incredulity, the wonder of those poor and discouraged people. What kind of bad joke is this? Free wine, free milk — can't be true. As the prophet spoke his poem to the people gathered near him at day's end, he caught their attention with his startling picture of free food, water, wine, and milk.

But of course, he made it clear at once that the picture was not a literal one. He had no more water than they. He was as poor. They understood that he was teaching them in poetry about their God, about the God of Israel, whom they had almost forgotten, so long had they been exiled from their land, and so hard were the economic realities of life as it pressed in upon them.

Always in hard times, men and women seem to think a little more about religion. Not that hard times make people religious, but hard times make people think more about religion. When the materials of life become harder and harder to get, there is naturally more interest in possible spiritual goods.

Men ask, "After all, what does life mean? Is it worth it? What must I do to be saved? How can I find God?"

Those who become really interested in religion tend to think of spiritual goods as hard to get—that they, too, must be struggled for as other goods. That faith and hope and peace and power require the same type of competitive effort that water and food and milk require. What the prophet was saying to them in his poem, what this preacher was saying to this people, this thirsty and hungry people—thirsty as much for God as they were for water; hungry for God almost as much as they were for bread and milk—to these thirsty and hungry people the prophet was saying, "God's not hard to find. He's not far off. He's not the end or the goal of a long and difficult search. Your God is near, as near as the marketplace. His word of hope and comfort and power are free—no price at all! All you must do is listen. Heed what he says to you. Hear, hear, and your soul shall live."

God as this prophet pictured him is continually offering us the greatest bargains imaginable in the very things we most want and need: peace in a troubled world, forgiveness to men who are accustomed to being bargained for the final penny of their indebtedness. This word, freely coming from God, will produce fruit in your life, just as rain will make flowers blossom when it gently falls on fertile soil.

> Seek ye the Lord while he may be found. Call ye upon him while he is near. Let the wicked forsake his way and the unrighteous man his thoughts, and let him return unto the Lord, and he will have mercy upon him, and to our God, for he will abundantly pardon. For as the rain cometh down and the snow from heaven, and returneth not thither, but watereth the earth, and maketh it bring forth and bud, that it may give seed to the sower and bread to the eater. So shall my word be that goeth forth out of my mouth. It shall not return unto me void, but it shall accomplish that which I please, and it shall prosper in the thing whereto I send it.

One very simple idea is essential to that word of hope to people of long ago. God, a God of mercy, generous at heart, rich with grace—God was seeking them. He had gifts, and they were free. Reach forth your hands, receive them. And rich would be first the blossoming and then the fruitage in barren lives.

Religion is not, essentially, the struggle we so often make it. Faith is the end of struggle. God is good. He is gracious. He cannot be won by our effort, nor bought with our money. God is a God of grace whose gifts are yours for the asking.

Let me pause a moment here to note the result of this prophet's preaching. For the result was almost unbelievable. Those people heard! They heeded. And what's more, they repented and turned to God. They soon returned, many of them, to their own land. Based upon their new insight and understanding of what faith could be, they built a new culture and a new civilization in the Holy Land, a culture and a civilization good enough for Jesus Christ to grace by His birth and by His life.

If any religious message could so create a new blossoming in the desert of this world, we may well ask what this ancient poem means to us this morning. With minor and unimportant variations, our need, our human need, is about the same as was theirs so long ago. That God is seeking us out in His grace, always before we think to seek for Him. That faith is, after all, not won by our human struggle, but rather by our acceptance of God's end of false and worthless struggling. That God is willing to make a covenant with you and me, a bargain so generous on His part, that skeptically, we're sure it's too good to be true.

"Wherefore do you spend money for that which is not bread? And your labor for that which satisfieth not?" You want life. You want joy. You want to find it. All of us are on this quest: true happiness. Then turn to God. Receive His gifts. His word, planted in your heart, will blossom even in a barren desert's soil. This is the gospel, the good news of God. When we Christian preachers try to make you see it, we have the more specifically Christian poem, full of beauty and of power, to save even more than did the ancient prophet. The late Cannon Streeter once put it this way: "There is an ancient story. Is it a parable, or something more?" (He might have asked, Is it a poem?) "There is an ancient story, which has a strangely moving power. First of all, the scene is set in heaven, before all worlds. It changes for a while to Earth under Pontius Pilate. Then we're back in heaven until the final end of things."

Very God of Very God, for us men and our salvation, so the story runs, so the poem has it. Very God of Very God, for us men and our salvation, came down from heaven, was incarnate of the virgin, and was made man. Crucified also for us, He rose again, ascended into heaven, sitteth on the right hand of the father, and shall come again with glory to judge both quick and dead.

This is the story-poem that is told and retold at all Christian churches in every way we speak. The coming of God to His people in Jesus Christ. But we must remember that it is a poem, a mighty work of God to move us. We must see its imagery with the Spirit's eyes until it finds its place in our barren lives. Part of the wonder of it is that when we find this Christian faith, when we really hear this word to us from God, we find that we have not found an

34

escape. We are not turning our backs upon the hard and harsh realities of daily life—the marketplaces and the high prices and the too little water for irrigation and lack of rainfall for the fields or any of the other, more modern economic problems. No, we find that the end of the story, as the prophet pictures it and as it is truly, is not some bodiless, spiritual existence that Christ and His gospel bring to men.

Rather, we find ourselves committed to a rescued, redeemed earth as well. "The mountains and the hills will break forth before you in singing, and all the trees of the fields shall clap their hands!" That's poetry, all right—the image of a fertile, peaceful earth. The prophet continues, "Instead of the thorn shall come up the fir tree. And instead of the brier shall come up the myrtle tree." That's the climactic end of the poem, a very accurate description, by the way, of what must grow upon the hills—fir trees instead of cacti—if the earth is to produce abundance, and if there is to be peace and prosperity among men.

There are two kinds of people to whom I speak this morning. Those of you, first, who find religion an effort, hard, like all the rest of life, a struggle, an unequal competition, a strain. To you, once more, comes the gospel promise. God is near. His gifts are free. Receive them now. And to those of you who hardly know you want God at all, so busy you have been in searching for bread which doesn't satisfy and the other things and the other trinkets with which men try to fill their days and satisfy restless hearts, you, too, are athirst for God, though you know it not. To you, too, comes the invitation, framed in the ancient prophet's words: "Ho! Everyone that thirsteth, come ye to the waters. He that hath no money, come ye, buy and eat. Yea, come and buy wine and milk, without money and without price."

Let us pray.

O thou gracious heavenly Father, God of the past and of this hour, Father of our Lord Jesus Christ, who has called us to be thy sons, we pray thee that hearing thy word of truth, we may respond to it in our hearts and with our lives, that receiving thy good gifts we may learn to share them with all thy children everywhere. And the peace of God which passeth all understanding keep your hearts and minds in the knowledge and love of God, and of His Son, Jesus Christ our Lord. May the blessing of God Almighty, the Father, Son, and Holy Ghost, rest upon you and remain with you always.

Waldo Beach served for many years as a professor of ethics at the Divinity School. With his teacher, Richard Niebuhr, Beach was the coauthor of a widely used text of Christian ethics. In this Palm Sunday sermon, Beach challenges the university's reigning notion of success, comparing it with the story of Jesus. Beach's sermon is a word of critique, from inside the university establishment, to an increasingly affluent congregation in the late 1950s.

Education for Failure

Palm Sunday
April 14, 1957

WALDO BEACH

One of our favorite American words is the word "success." Like a great blinking neon light, the word success presides over our culture, our business, our politics, our churches, our clubs, our entertainment, even our campus. What we are here for is to succeed. There is no clear consensus as to exactly what the word means, but it is usually taken to mean the delight in winning the prize on the TV show, arrival at the top of the ladder, being over someone not as fortunate or as hard-working. It means a sales record for cars or for class enrollment that beats everybody else. It means getting to wherever you set out for. It means hitting the jackpot. It means winning the championship, copping the Oscar.

University culture mirrors this American ideal very faithfully. A phrase common among educators and college catalogues is "education for success — training for successful living." Our community life here is set up as a kind of rehearsal in the small of the great American success story. Everyone aims to be the successful student, the leader, the president of this or that, tapped for Omicron Delta Kappa, elected to Phi Beta Kappa. His quality points shine in his crown at graduation, promising him success in the next chapter of his life. Fraternities are commended because they provide connections that will help one get established in the business jungle after college — or at least that is what is said during rush. The *Chanticleer* is a kind of bible of campus success, full of kings and queens and heroes. The reason it is so thick every year is that it must do honor to all the leaders, all the students most likely to succeed. And in such a place as this, we have too many chiefs and not enough Indians.

No one dares stop in the great rat race to suggest that the American ideal of success may be a mirage. Or, if he does suggest it, he is written off as dour or cynical. The American dogma is that every story must have a happy ending. Everybody is destined for success if only they take advantage of the opportunity and mail in the entry blank. Everybody has to be a winner; it's just a law of the universe. This is dramatized daily in the arrangements made in the TV giveaway quiz shows, which are Roman circuses, for even the loser to be the winner. "I'm so sorry," says the emcee, "that you can't name five generals in World War II. Do take this small check for $500 just for *trying* so hard." And then there is great applause. Everybody will come to some pot of gold at the end of the rainbow. This is the gospel of Hollywood and TV and pocket-sized magazines and cereal boxes.

Much of the psychological quackery that passes for religion helps to sustain and to perpetuate this American dream of success. Vital, successful living is guaranteed if you practice these scientific ten steps. It's so simple, you can't lose. It is rare that anyone challenges this abracadabra. But the fatal weakness in the whole scheme is suggested by an exchange of letters in the newspaper some time back. Somebody wrote a testimonial describing glowingly how a certain athlete of indifferent ability, by virtue of practicing the ten steps to success, had won the 440 race handily in the next meet. Then somebody else wrote in: "Alright, but what if the ten steps to success had been practiced by all the runners in the meet?" That question punctures neatly the whole inflated, fantastic ideal of success.

Everybody can't be a winner. There have to be also-rans. Everybody can't be an "A." There have to be B's, and C's, and D's, and F's. This is life's built-in grade curve. There is a great peril in the whole idea of education for success, and especially the way success is understood on campus, as meaning coming in first, winning out.

I suspect that we are vaguely aware of the falsity of success once in a while. We talk about "senior jitters," as common an ailment as spring fever this time of year, or falling in love. Senior jitters arise from the awareness that sneaks up on us some April morning (with two months of college to go) that along the line somewhere, somebody fooled us. Quality points and prizes and comps and crowns look a little small, a little dingy. Even the Big Man on Campus, who has worked for four years to get himself on top, may find himself disillusioned to discover that the elevation is slight.

Woe to the student who takes campus success as his goal in life, as the be-all and end-all of his days. There is nothing more pathetic than the May Queen who never quite got over it. And there is a distinct shock in store for the young alumna who comes back for a visit and finds the women's student government operating remarkably well without her services. The common trouble with the successful student who has had no sense of the falsity of the mirage of the BMOC is that like all big wheels, his center is a long way from the ground.

To educate for success is to arrive at a fall, sooner or later. To assume that life is a movement toward a happy ending is to set us up as easy victims for disillusionment and despair. We need also to educate for failure, for tragedy, for the perversities of human nature, the letdowns of human existence, for the gremlins who inhabit our universe as surely as fairy godmothers. To educate for failure means the equipment of mind and heart to meet the tragic element, which is built into the structure of human life. It means preparation for being up against it. It's curious that in that phrase "being up against it," "it" always refers to something tragic.

Tragedy comes in many forms. It may mean a sudden catastrophic blow. Sudden death smashes in our house of serenity, leaves us numb and powerless—unless we have acquired some resources of spirit and mind to draw on. Everyone encounters some smashing tragedy of this sort, or at least has a brush with it along the way. Yet our education is so carefully oblivious to this radical evil in life, so preoccupied with successful and happy living, the specter of death and tragedy is avoided until unavoidable. We practically have a phobia about it, like William Randolph Hearst, who refused to have anyone mention the word "death" in his presence. The catastrophic, devastating emergency just doesn't fit our scheme. So we are not unlike third-grade schoolchildren in a civil defense air raid test. They must be considerably mystified about human destiny when they crawl down under their desks during the air raid, and then crawl out to resume reading *Cinderella* where they left off before the siren sounded.

Though there are the sharp and sudden tragedies, the usual types of failure are of another sort. These are the small and seeping failures of daily living, the gradual dying of hopes and dreams, the gray disenchantment of the years, the slow attrition of time's blows, the unspectacular failures of talent and intelligence into a dull mediocrity, the settling down of bright courage into a tired, middle-aged cynicism. Countering at every point in life the hope for a better day tomorrow, the hope for an achievement surpassing the old and winning out, is the opposite, limiting factor, which turns back the hope, which makes living a slow form of dying.

Arthur Miller's *Death of a Salesman* was a play that struck home sharply to its audiences because it epitomized the failure of the American success story. Willy Loman is a pathetic, bewildered product of education for success, and he had no resources with which to meet failure. Willy's sons, whom he tried to indoctrinate with the formula for success, are disillusioned when Willy proves much less than a hero and a paragon of virtue. The play puts well one of life's continual processes of disillusionment: when we realize that our parents, beneath their elaborate disguises, are not heroes and saints, but about average, about C-minus people. Or when our children fail to realize our hopes for them, and they turn out to be about average, too.

Is this a fitting word to speak to undergraduates for a mother-daughter weekend in the springtime of the year? Life looks like an upward road full of bright promise. Time enough later, you say, for the troubles. For now we live by hope that stands a shining ray far down the future's broadening way. But what of the fact that the future is a narrowing way?

If there be a running down of life as much as a running up, should not education equip us somewhere, if it claims to see life steadily and wholly, to reckon with this tragic element, this dark tone? Somehow to be mindful of the transience, the passing away of all hopes, all persons. Somehow to remember the biblical note, "As for man, his days are as grass. As a flower of the field, so he flourisheth. When the wind passeth over it and it is gone, and the place thereof shall know it no more."

There are many kinds of responses of faith to the failures of life, either its stark tragedies or its small letdowns, in which men repeat ancient answers. One, I suppose, would be a kind of Epicureanism, which simply refused to face the tragic. Continue to have fun; life is a comedy and a farce, a continual cabin party to be played for the kicks. But sooner or later, the morning after comes, and the funnyman has nothing to say.

Or the response of faith to failure may be a kind of grim Stoicism, which sees the whole show as tragic, concocted by a perverse demon as a cruel joke. We are here to sweat it out and to brave it through, like, perhaps, Housman's lad. The troubles of our proud and angry dust are from eternity and shall not fail. Bear them we can, and if we can, we must. Shoulder the sky, my lad, and drink your ale.

The Christian faith offers a profoundly different answer to the problems of failure. For Christianity, the drama of human existences is neither a farce nor a grim tragedy, but a drama for the education of the soul, wherein it can learn—by way of failure or success—the true purpose of life and the true understanding of what we are here for. The point of relevance of the Christian faith to this issue is that it provides an answer beyond success or failure. According to the Gospels, according to Christian theology—where the sign of the faith is the cross—life is not a success story, everybody a winner. At this point, Christianity becomes the criticism of the American fable. It educates us to see how misleading the American ideal is at its heart.

But more importantly, the Christian faith enables us to redefine the content of success and failure. If the last question asked by American culture is, "Were you successful? Did you win?" the last question asked by Christianity is, "Were you faithful?" It is integrity, not success, which is the Christian mark of worth. Though it may take some long time to find this out—and perhaps a long way around—it is the Christian answer that goes beyond success or failure.

To be a little more specific, what most of you confront after college is far from glamorous, romantic, successful—far from being queen. Rather, it is life in the ranks, life in the level of gray Monday morning doings. There are the drudgeries of the menial and the humdrum, miles from shoe-and-slipper weekend. There are miles of typewriter ribbon to bang. On the average, there are 39,000 dishes to wash—per housewife, per year.

There is considerable contrast between white duchy and dirty diapers, and by this fact there is not much success, by *Chanticleer* standards. But education informed by the Christian faith can equip the student ahead of time to realize that the meaning of life does not consist in success but in faithfulness, in trust, in love, in patience, in long suffering, in the daily meeting of human need, in thankless devotion. We are here not to succeed, but to love—whether our love has a happy ending or a sad one. Its worth stands in failure as much as in success.

In this sense, Christian faith is disenchantment with the success fable, but it is re-enchantment with authentic success. Christianity never should be construed to offer the cash prize, the straight "A," the presidency. What it does offer is the reward of serenity and confidence, which is nonchalant about success and which is serene within failure. It is education in equanimity for life or death. This is what St. Paul means when he says, "Whether we live or whether we die, we are the Lord's." Unless a Duke student gets some inkling of this ideal, he is headed for sure despair and frustration. But if he has learned to see beyond the mirage of success to the truth of the cross, he will even now be putting on something of the armor of God.

In a curious way, the Palm Sunday story can be seen as appropriate to this Christian truth. It is usually taken, in a Hollywood sense, as being a success story. The triumphal entry into Jerusalem, the shouts of the crowd, what a happy day when the Messiah arrives. But this is entirely the wrong way to take it. It just wrenches it out of its context in Holy Week. It is rather a day of tragic irony, where success and failure are all mixed up. The crowd missed the point of the story in the entry. They took Christ for what he was not. They missed the symbolism of his riding on a colt, the symbol of the suffering servant. They took him for a military hero who would bring them political success through some magical trick. In the grand manner of a Cecil B. DeMille, Christ alone understands the irony. He knows the thinness of their loyalty. He knows their disillusionment. He can see the shadow of the cross prefigured over the palms of the Jerusalem road. Amid all the parading and rejoicing, he weeps. Jerusalem does not know the time of its visitation.

Palm Sunday is not a success story; it is a story of failure by the standards of the world. But it is a story of integrity and faithfulness, even unto the cross of Good Friday, where man's faithfulness within failure is transmuted into victory.

Let us pray.

Almighty God, who has granted to us the perilous gift of freedom, and thus set our way amid hard choices of good and evil, grant us by thy grace the wisdom to discern the eternal from the temporal, the treasures of heaven from the treasures of earth, that in seeking first thy kingdom and thy righteousness, we may learn and possess the peace, which the world can neither give nor take away. Now unto him who is able to keep you from falling and to present you faultless before the presence of his glory, with exceeding joy to the only wise God, our Savior, be glory and majesty, dominion and power, both now and evermore. Amen.

Bishop Gerald Kennedy was a great leader in the Methodist Church, pastor of First United Methodist, Pasadena, California, and a popular preacher. With elegantly illustrated sermons, a colloquial preaching style, and an optimistic, liberal theology, Kennedy set the tone for preaching in his denomination for more than a decade. Though he begins his sermon by saying that "the spoken word is hardly necessary for the worship of God" in "one of the most beautiful churches in the world," still Kennedy manages a most hopeful, encouraging word.

June 2, 1957

GERALD KENNEDY

Romans 12:2 After one has come in to what is certainly one of the most beautiful churches in the world and listened to this great music, it takes a good deal of courage to stand up and to try to preach. One has the feeling that the spoken word is hardly necessary for the worship of God. You'll understand therefore why I count it such a very high honor to be in this pulpit this day and to speak on this occasion.

There has come down to us from 1650 a list of the names of the jurymen of Sussex County, England. They were all Puritans, apparently, and they all had names expressing their faith. One man's name was "Fight the Good Fight of Faith White." Another one was called "Peace of Mind Knight." (That sounds modern.) One man was called "Kill Sin Pimble." And there was another name, "Renewed Wiseberry."

The English essayist E. B. Lucas says that if he could choose a name that was descriptive of his life, he would prefer to be called "Renewed." He says that is what everybody is looking for: renewal, to start over again freshly, not weary, not cynical, not disillusioned. And I suppose he is right. There is in every man's life an almost inescapable nostalgia for good old days. When we get old, we want to begin again; we think of the days of our youth as the great days of our lives — fresh beginnings, great hopes.

Renewal: as I have been thinking about that during these past days, there came to my mind that great verse read this morning from Romans, where St. Paul is saying to those early Christians, "Be not conformed to this world, but be ye transformed by the renewal of your mind." He seems to be saying that one of the gifts of the gospel is the gift of renewal. This sense of fresh beginnings and of a new start and of a fresh dream — I want to talk about that for a little bit this morning.

I read some time ago that a professor from the Middle West had remarked that if you do not want your children to overhear what you are saying, act as if you are talking to them. So this morning I'm reversing that a little. I'm talking primarily to what I think is going to happen a few years from now in hopes that maybe the graduating class may overhear something I say.

The first thing I want to say this morning is rather pessimistic, yet I feel sure it's true. So far as a vast majority of people are concerned, life is a gradual running down. That's inevitable, of course, physically speaking. There comes a time when suddenly we realize that we are run down considerably, physically speaking, and that life, in a sense, is a process of gradually dying.

That comes as a very hard blow to us, a very great shock. That first time when we have to admit to ourselves that we get more weary than we used to become, that the print is a little smaller, and the blocks are a lot longer. That would not be so bad in some countries, I think, where they honor age. There are some cultures where the elderly man is a man respected. And a man can know that as he grew older, at least he would obtain something that made up for this loss of physical vigor. But not in America. We do not, for the most part, honor age. This is a young country. We worship youth; we worship action. So a man has to act young, even if it kills him. And sometimes it does.

This thing does not always come as it does to an athlete: the realization to a baseball player, for example, that he is an old man at thirty-eight. Or a boxer who is probably toward the end when he is thirty-two. It sometimes comes very gradually to us. But it comes in a way that brings about what some psychologists call the "dangerous age," when a man or woman in desperation to recapture youth does something silly, like trying to find a new wife or a new husband. It's a bad time, and we all have to get ready for it, because it's coming.

The son of Robert Benchley said that his father always thought he should exercise and stay in good condition, but he hardly ever did. He said that his father bought a rowing machine, brought it home, put it under the bed, and never used it once. He paid enough rent on a sun lamp to buy it several times over and never turned it on. He called the couch that he had in his study his track. And he would announce blithely that he was going to take a couple of turns around the track, by which he meant that he was going to take a nap. After he became a spectator sportsman, he always insisted that the toughest sport was jai alai because the steps at the hippodrome were the longest he had to climb. And he speaks for most of us, because we come to that time ultimately when, suddenly, we know that we have run down.

In a more serious way, we run down mentally. I do not know whether the faculty would agree with me on this or not, but about the saddest thing I see is the average college graduate ten years after he has graduated. He is run down. He is an individual who has given up all intellectual interests, for the most part. No more does he think; no more does he study. He has been too busy becoming a success. And so, perhaps, he may now and again glance through his trade journal or professional magazine. He may take a hasty look at *Life* (at the barbershop, usually). He may read an article or two from the *Reader's Digest*. But it has been a long time since he really wrestled with an idea: the social conditions of his time and the political situation in his country, the international problems—all these things pass him by. He is no longer interested. He has run down mentally. This is something that can happen so easily and we know it not. It comes up on us, and we don't know exactly what has happened, but here it is, it has happened. And it is a desperate thing.

I speak to you this morning of that possibility, almost probability (if you're not careful), that you become a part of the majority of people for whom life is just running down.

The late Stephen Vincent Benét (one of America's great poets, I think) wrote some lines a good many years ago—just four of them—which he called, interestingly, "35." I happened to find them when I was just about that age, and they struck me hard. This is what he wrote:

> The sun was hot, the sky was bright
> And all July was overhead.
> I heard the locusts first that night,
> Six weeks till frost, they said.

He was speaking of that moment when suddenly we know, like all our fathers, we will grow old. And one day we will die—that moment when this becomes real. And it can become a very destructive, tragic moment in our lives.

The second thing I want to say this morning is that in our generation we assume there is some physical answer to this problem, that if we are running down, we can find some physical things that will wind us up again, so to speak. If you will read the magazines, you will see that we assume there is a physical answer to every problem that is facing you. The young lady having trouble with her romance only has to change her toothpaste, or maybe she needs a new shampoo. The young man who is not getting along very well in business is wearing the wrong kind of shirt. He needs the kind that the fellow wears with the patch over his eye, or something like that. There is a physical answer to the thing. If you are not succeeding, all you have to do is discover what it is. Somewhere, you can find it—something that will solve the whole business: romance, success, friendship, family life. It's amazing how the whole pressure upon us is to make us believe that somewhere there is a product that will take care of this whole business.

Some years ago, the novelist Ernest Hemingway had a crackup in a plane and narrowly escaped death. He was in Africa. I remember seeing a picture of him shortly after that accident; I'm sure some of you saw it. He stands just at the edge of the jungle. He hasn't shaved for a long time. In one hand he has a bunch of bananas, in the other a bottle of gin. As one of my friends says, rather cynically, "By looking at Hemingway, you can't tell whether he is emerging from the jungle or going back into it." But here it is: jungle philosophy. All you need, on the one hand, enough to eat, and on the other hand, enough to drink, and all is well. There is a physical answer to the problem that you face.

There is even a physical answer, we believe, if we go stale, if life suddenly caves in on us. You need to travel! Buy yourself a ticket on a plane or a ship and go to some other country. Discover a new environment. Put yourself from here over there and you will feel good again. Life will have meaning for you again. Well, I wish it were true. (There are so many Americans traveling today; I wish it were true.)

I think it is a good thing that we travel a great deal. I'm glad Americans are traveling. Many who can't afford it are traveling—they can pay later. But it is a good thing that we are seeing other cultures and other nations, because then we understand our own better. We understand our place in the world, and I hope we have a growing appreciation of our oneness as a world. It's good.

But it won't solve many problems for you. The fellow that's a bore in Des Moines will be one in Honolulu, almost certainly. The man who finds it difficult to discover meaning in his life in Durham probably won't find it in Hong Kong either. There are any number of these Americans traveling who do only one thing: criticize everything they see in terms of what they had back home. And they come back just as they left: still unhappy, still bored, still lacking any real purpose or meaning in their lives. There is an old Spanish proverb that sums it up. It says, "He who would bring home with him the wealth of the Indies must take the wealth of the Indies with him." What a man is here, he will be there. You can never leave yourself behind. This doesn't solve it. It is a wonderful thing to travel, but don't think it is going to change your life very much.

I don't know whether many of you have been in one of those old country stores or not. Some of the older people in this congregation, I'm sure, have

been. When I was bishop of the Portland area, I had Alaska under my juris-
diction. And many a time in those frontier Alaska communities, I went in to
an old-fashioned country store. Everything that community had to have had
to be in that store—there was only one. And you ought to see them, piled
up this way and that. I don't know how anyone could ever find anything. I
remember a sign I saw. It said, "We have it if you can find it."

That's our belief today: We have it if you can find it. We have an answer
if you can discover it. If it isn't this product, it will be this one. Search for
it. Well, I don't believe it.

The third thing I want to say is, all healing, all renewal has to come from
inside. It has to be something from within. They don't have it. And you can't
find it. It has to come from inside.

Not that many years ago, when I graduated from college, I was talking
with a man who had been a friend of our family's for a long time. He knew
that it was a sacrifice for me to go to college; in fact, he had discouraged me
from doing so. It had been a hard grind for me. Then I saw him and he said,
"Well, do you think it was worth it?" I said, "Yes." He asked, "What did you
get out of it?" And I spoke off the top of my head: "I got an attitude." He
thought that was a rather flippant answer; maybe he thought it was stupid.
Yet as I have lived a number of years and thought back on that moment, I
would still say the same thing. I got an attitude—a critical attitude, a horror
at becoming a victim of high-powered propaganda, a belief in and love of
the truth, a desire (if possible) to understand the truth and to find it, and a
willingness to weigh without first accepting—a critical attitude. I believe
that was the thing I got from college that I value the most. Most of the information I received I have forgotten or lost. I have discovered where it
could be found (where my secretary can find it for me!). But the main thing
that came from that experience (and it was a great experience, a changing
experience) was an attitude of the critical mind—something inside.

The psychiatrists, the psychologists, all those who deal with the mind, do
not always agree on the right explanation of why we do what we do, but
there is one thing on which they all agree: that a man's healing has to come
from inside. We are discovering in these days that a man's physical strength
correlates with his inner strength and his physical health with his mental
health. We are discovering in this day that if inside of us we have something
that is the center of resentment and hatred and fear, until that's removed,
there is nothing that can heal us—not from the outside. It has to be an inner
healing, if we are to be healed at all.

Jesus said something one time that we have rather ignored. We do not
preach on it very much. We do not discuss it. It's a radical statement. He said,

"Blessed are you when you are persecuted for righteousness' sake." What does that mean? He was saying, blessed are you; fortunate are you; lucky are you; happy are you when you are persecuted, because it means you have a conviction. Because at the end of the day, despite all of the unpopularity that has surrounded you, you can live with yourself and say, "I stood by what I believed." Happy are you—this is where it comes from, he's saying. This is health. This is success: inside, nowhere else.

Have you read that little classic, *The Lonely Crowd*, where Riesman speaks about the outer-directed and the inner-directed people? The poor man who was merely the victim of the most pressure? Who goes wherever the pressure pushes him? The outer-directed who is no longer actually a person but simply the result of whatever other people want him to be? Contrast that over against that inner-directed individual who has certain great convictions from within on which he stands. That's the thing I'm speaking of. This promises strength to men.

John Wesley, who was the spiritual father of the Methodist Church, lived to be an old man of eighty-eight. He started with poor health as a child, did enough work to kill one hundred men, rode up and down England in all kinds of weather, preached any number of times a day, and seemed to thrive on it. He died at eighty-eight. Toward the end of his life, somebody asked what the secret of his health was. He said, "The main thing was that I got up at four every morning, and I preached at five. It's the best exercise in the world." I take his word for it. I haven't tried it! But I think what he was saying was this: when a man has a sense of a high purpose in life—when he is doing something he knows is worth doing—somehow it even affects his physical strength. He doesn't get tired. He has great resources, great reservoirs of power. The man whose life is meaningless never finds renewal and power from within.

There is a very cynical book in the Old Testament called Ecclesiastes. It's always been a favorite of mine. This man who has looked around and who has studied some of the clichés that they were speaking in his generation turns his back to them. He says in one place, "The race is not always to the swift, nor the battle to the strong."

I have lived long enough to understand something of the meaning of that. I have seen the young man who has everything in his favor, who ought to run swiftly to the top, falter some way. That young man who you were not very impressed with, perhaps, proves to have inside himself tremendous swiftness and speed that carry him on and on to the heights.

I have watched those battles where you said at the beginning, this cause can't win—look what's against it. All the newspapers, all the powerful people in the community on the other side, what chance does it have? Till you discover that a few people dedicated to a high purpose win, because inside they had power that no one saw and no one understood.

I'm saying this morning that renewal comes from inside, not outside. Power is from within and not from without. Have you read that famous biography of Johnson by Boswell? I expect most of you have. You may recall that little incident where Boswell is reporting to Johnson about a condemned criminal. He said this man had lived a very evil life. And now, just in the last days before his execution he had suddenly turned to religion and studied it with great intentness. Johnson said, "Sir, when a man is going to be hanged in a fortnight it wonderfully concentrates his mind."

The truth is, when we come up against any great crisis in our lives, suddenly we know that all we have is our mind. All we are is what we are inside. All we have to stand upon is the quality of our characters and the faith by which we live. You're not going to be renewed by buying that product. You're not going to change your life by some physical answer. You're going to find it inside, or as Paul put it, "by the renewal of your mind."

The last thing I want to say this morning is that this, in my judgment, is one of the greatest gifts of religion. It is a special gift that God gives us through Christ: the renewal of our minds. He does it by giving us hope. This may not have happened to you yet—and I hope it never does—but it has happened to some of us. We come to the realization that we have done something that is utterly unforgivable. We did not think it could ever happen to us, but it did. And in that desperate moment, what we need above anything else is hope that somehow, once more, we can believe in ourselves. I believe that one of the great things Christ does for men is to perform this miracle of restoring faith in ourselves when we have done something that is utterly unforgivable, and we know it. Yet we hope again, and we try again.

You may not have had this experience—and I hope you never shall—but you might. Some of us have. When a friend that we trusted and would have bet our lives on sold us out. There are some here this morning who can think back with me on such an occasion when the heavens caved in, and you said, "I can never believe in anyone again." But He came and performed that miracle on us. Again we began to understand there were things in this man's life that we never knew, and there are people who are trustworthy. We began to believe in people again. He brought us the renewal of our hope.

It may be that we shall have that experience of taking the wrong turn or coming one day to the dead end, when all life seems to be is a tale told by an idiot—sound and fury signifying nothing. Then, instead of sitting down and feeling sorry for ourselves, He may give us grace to believe we were at fault, not life. Somewhere back there we have to return and to take the other track. This is what's wrong with the generation of novelists of our time. They have been writing their stories about men who have ignored every moral law of life, every decent convention. Then when life caves in on them, they cry out as if life had let them down—not once facing up to the truth that maybe, they let life down. They were wrong, and not life.

He comes to us when we have taken that wrong turn in order to make us hope again that life is right. Life is full of meaning and excitement and adventure and dignity. We have to find the way again, and our hope is renewed.

One of my very close friends on the Council of Bishops is Bishop Frank Smith of Houston. He is retiring in 1960. They say that he can take a young man who has to go out to the most difficult and discouraging job in the conference, put his hand on that boy's shoulder and talk to him for a little while, and the boy straightens his back and goes out as if he was facing the greatest opportunity there is, and does a wonderful job. So one of Bishop Smith's friends has suggested they make him chaplain of Huntsville Prison after he retires. That's where they execute bad Texans. This friend says that Bishop Smith can put his hand on the shoulder of a man going to the electric chair and make him think he is facing the greatest opportunity he has ever faced, so that he would be willing to pull the switch himself, probably.

This gift of encouragement, this gift of a new hope, this gift that goes beyond the present difficulty—what a gift that is in men! To bring encouragement to another. But of course, above all that we can do, it is His gift through Christ, to make us hope again, to teach us that we live by faith. No man can live for ten minutes on the basis of what he can prove. We choose this faith that has within it the promise of God. And we test it as Paul tells us to do, this will of God for us. As we live by this faith and find that every day is a new life, that there is no boredom connected with this, we can hardly wait for the next year to see what life has to give us. Never forget this. When Robert Browning wrote those oft-quoted lines, "Grow old along with me / The best is yet to be," he was a Christian. He was speaking as a Christian. It made no sense to the pagan, and it never will.

I look around about me at some people whose life has grown weary, and I wonder about them. What's happened to them? Bernard Berenson, one of the great art critics of our time and one of the great art philosophers, said recently, because he is an old man now and yet has so much work in front of him, that he is afraid he will die before he finishes it. He said he would like to stand on the street corner like a beggar with his cap in his hand and beg for some extra hours from the passers-by who are wasting them.

I speak to you this morning of the kind of life—the life of hope, the life of faith, the life of love — that is a constant life of renewal, so that every day man begins anew with expectation and hope for the future. The renewal of your mind.

I close with this. One of the outstanding priests in the Church of England is a man called Father Dowling, who spent a good many years in Portsmouth. His parish was down in the slum section. He was the poor man's priest. He had a great sense of mission to this parish, to improve the living conditions in that section of the city. He discovered, for example, that the sewer system of the city of Portsmouth had not extended itself into this section of Portsmouth. There were no drains there. It upset him so much that he began to organize opposition among these formerly acquiescent and humble people. They began to put pressure on the mayor, for a change. The mayor, who was a good politician, did not want things stirred up. He thought everything was all right as it was. So he went to the bishop and asked, "Can't you quiet this priest?"

The bishop called Father Dowling in to talk to him and said in a nice way that this was out of his bailiwick. He told Dowling, "You're doing things the priest has no business doing. Yours is a spiritual task. You are supposed to teach these people religion and theology and faith. You're supposed to tell them what they ought to believe. You have no business interfering in this." Father Dowling, who was notoriously slow in speech and fumbled his words, suddenly burst out and said, "My Lord! The reason I am making a fuss about the drains is that I believe in the Incarnation. I believe in the dignity of life. I believe that God came into life in a real way. I believe in every man who has to live. My task, therefore, is to make life better for every man."

I submit to you this: no man that believes in the Incarnation will ever discover that life is dull. He will discover that faith being central in his life is a renewing thing, every day of his life. "Be not conformed to this world, but be ye transformed by the renewal of your minds."

Let us stand together for the benediction.

Now, O Lord, we commend unto thee in a special way these young men and young women who graduate from this great university. We ask thy blessing upon them. We pray especially that this experience that has been theirs shall be to them through all the years of their lives like a well of water springing up to give them the water where that they drink, they shall not thirst again. May the grace of the Lord Jesus Christ, the love of God, and the fellowship of the Holy Spirit rest and abide with you, now and evermore.

James T. Cleland came to Duke Chapel from Amherst College in 1945, having come from his native Glasgow to New York in the 1920s to study at Union Theological Seminary. For nearly thirty years, the voice of this playful Scot was the voice of Duke Chapel. He was the first Dean of the Chapel, one of only two in the Chapel's history. He was also a professor of preaching at the Divinity School and even coach of Duke's soccer team. One of his most popular courses at the Divinity School was his "Preaching from Non-Biblical Sources," in which Cleland mined contemporary fiction, music, and drama as sources for sermons. This sermon, in which Cleland related Arthur Miller's most famous play to the situation of Americans in the 1950s, is typical of Cleland's way with contemporary drama. The sermon also demonstrates his preference for ordered (note the subheadings), carefully crafted sermonic form. What made such a sermon live, and endeared him to the hearts of the congregation, was Jim Cleland's sprightly delivery and wit.

Postmortem on a Salesman

February 1, 1959

JAMES T. CLELAND

Matthew 6:19–34 On this particular Sunday in the academic year—between exams and the new semester—when some of our classmates are academically dead, let us look together at a very famous play which begins in anxiety and ends in suicide. It is Arthur Miller's *Death of a Salesman*, winner of the Pulitzer Prize and the Critics Circle Award, published in a special readers' edition by Bantam Books. It may say something to us, because—as one critic has pointed out—"the blood of Willy Loman"—the central character, who takes his own life—"flows in all of us." The academic deaths of our roommates, of ourselves, were not due to murder deliberately and premeditatedly planned by the faculty. They were not caused by manslaughter, which is killing without malice aforethought. They were not even the result of justifiable homicide, though some faculty members might rightly plead such a defense. They were suicide: academic death at one's own hand. Some of you may have heard how Dr. Manchester, when he was dean of freshmen, used to utter this factual prophecy at the first meeting of each new class of Trinity freshmen: "Look to your right and look to your left. If the two boys sitting on each side of you are here in four years, you won't be. If you are here, one of them won't be." One third of each new class in Trinity dies academically each college generation, so far as Duke is concerned, and the usual verdict is "suicide." Let us look at the death of Arthur Miller's salesman, to find if it says anything by way of explanation, or warning, or prevention.

Death of a Salesman is a tragedy, in that it involves the ruin of the leading character. It is realistic in that it holds the mirror up to nature. Perhaps in that fact lies its popular appeal. You recall how the play opens. The salesman crosses the entire stage in full view of the audience, carrying his sample cases which weigh his shoulders down. He seems tired. "As he comes to a halt at the door to the kitchen and takes out his key, it is clear that he has just barely made it home" (5). The main characters are the salesman, Willy Loman, and his distraught, devoted wife, Linda, and their two sons, who live in a state of constant conflict with their father. They are drawn to him and repelled by him almost at the same moment. Here is a man who dreamed of worldly success for himself and his sons and achieved a most ordinary failure, which addled his thinking, frenzied his emotions, and drove him to a blissful suicide, which was meant to be an act of atonement and turns out to be a flat flop. He dies. There is no doubt of that. The drama ends in a cemetery at his graveside. Here are the last words of the play as sobbed by his widow: "Forgive me, dear. I can't cry. I don't know what it is, but I can't cry. I don't understand it. Why did you ever do that? Help me, Willy, I can't cry. It seems to me that you're just on another trip. I keep expecting you. Willy, dear, I can't cry. Why did you do it? I search and search and I search, and I can't understand it, Willy. I made the last payment on the house today. Today, dear. And there'll be nobody home. We're free and clear. We're free. We're free . . . We're free . . ." (151).

The final act of suicide is, in one way, a very lovely gesture. Realizing that despite the continual wordy brawls, the family was one in which love was latent, Willy Loman took his own life so that the insurance money might give the others, particularly his elder son, the capital to make good. But we would be wrong if we accepted this as the motivation without a more careful examination: because Willy Loman had tried to commit suicide before, before he realized that his family could be a community in goodwill. He kept a rubber pipe in the cellar ready to attach to "a new little nipple on the gas pipe" (61).

Let us examine this character, not in a physical autopsy, but in a spiritual postmortem.

We must look, then, at the salesman as he is depicted throughout the entire play. Are there spiritual symptoms which suggest that suicide may be his answer to life's problems? There are repeated suggestions.

In the first place, he was a man of disparate moods. No one can foretell with accuracy how he will react in a situation. His wife never knows, when he enters the house, whether "he may turn upon her in anger, or may pull her to his breast with a love so desperate as to stun her" (6). The comment continues: "She is always preparing for a crisis" (6). On the one hand he is, vocally, full of self-confidence. His son truthfully affirms: "Pop! I'm a dime a dozen, and so are you!" The answer, given in an uncontrolled outburst, is: "I am not a dime a dozen! I am Willy Loman and you are Biff Loman!" (143). Yet on the other hand, he admits that he is not impressive: "I'm fat. I'm very — foolish to look at . . . they do laugh at me. I know that" (35). One can even find both moods in a single utterance: "Oh, I'll knock 'em dead next week. I'll go to Hartford. I'm well liked in Hartford. You know, the trouble is, Linda, people don't seem to take to me" (34). How does a man live sanely within such conflicting moods? There is no singleness to his life.

In the second place, he relives the past, a victim of hallucination. People and situations from his early life, right back to his childhood, are re-enacted for us, not as flashbacks but as the very present experiences of a disordered nervous system — a kind of sober delirium tremens. There are the joyous moments of his sons' youth as they polish the Chevrolet and carry in the wash for their mother. There are the puzzled moments when his successful pioneer brother returns from Alaska with true tales of fabulous riches. Memory haunts and taunts and plagues Willy Loman. He is chock-full of wishful thinking, of what-might-have-been. The return to what-is offers a devastating adjustment. This is a sick man whom we are watching, a sick man with enough physical power left to murder — others or himself.

In the third place, when memory fails to please, there is always a refuge in daydreams. And how he dreams! But notice the content of the dreams: the cult of personality, contacts, and the salesman's golden tongue. Here is his own confession of faith: "It's who you know and the smile on your face! It's contacts . . . contacts! . . . and that's the wonder, the wonder of this country, that a man can end with diamonds here on the basis of being liked!" (91). "It's not what you say, it's how you say it — because personality always wins the day" (67). His younger son spots his father's delusion: "Dad is never so happy as when he's looking forward to something" (118). That may be salutary in your twenties, but at sixty, in connection with your job, it is soul-shattering. But Willy dreams of success as a salesman; even his funeral will be a success: "That funeral will be massive! They'll come from Maine, Massachusetts, Vermont, New Hampshire! All the old-timers with the strange license plates . . . I am known! Rhode Island, New York, New Jersey—I am known!" (137). Yet they do not come. His widow asks, at the graveside: "But where are all the people he knew?" (149).

Moodiness, hallucinations, daydreams—anyone could foresee trouble, dire trouble, ahead.

Now, let us go behind the symptoms to the cause. Perhaps no one word can embrace all the facets of the suicide urge. Maybe a phrase may cover the cause: the lonely insecurity of frustration. All he did, all he loved, all he might have been, all was vain and ineffectual. Life, in every relation, was a confusing, perplexing, disjointed concatenation of pieces in a jigsaw puzzle which produced no single picture. Therefore he drew within himself, but even there found no united self to give him security, protection from his disintegrating fears. His love for his wife was haunted by his unfaithfulness to her in a Boston hotel room. His affection for his boys was thwarted by their latent contempt for him as a failure. His hard work in his job became more and more a hated chore and less and less a satisfying joy. Routine was his only authority; and habit is a poor master, though a fine servant. So he crept within himself at the deepest level of life, while barging into the existence of others in ordinary daily contacts. His wife said of him: "He's only a little boat looking for a harbor" (78). His elder son said: "He had the wrong dreams. All, all wrong . . . He never knew who he was" (150). He said of himself: "I still feel—kind of temporary about myself" (53).

There is no meaning to his life. His worldliness let him down, and there was no net to catch him. The stage setting of his small frame house, dwarfed by Brooklyn tenements, is symbolic of a little man crushed by a world in which he thought he had to live and which he could not comprehend. The lonely insecurity of frustration is hardly a foundation for richness of living.

Remedy

There can be no regeneration in this life for Willy Loman. He is dead, in a suicidal car smash, which he hoped—probably in vain—that the insurance company would consider an accident. But what about the other Willy Lomans still living around us, even at Duke, especially at mid-years? There are three complementary parts of the remedy for his sickness.

First a man should know who and what he is. Willy Loman was not really a salesman with a city home for a base and miles of roads as the web of his livelihood. There are numerous statements throughout the play revealing that he was a carpenter who ought to be living in the country with a small garden to potter in at the end of a day's work. Listen. His son Biff is speaking: "There were a lot of nice days. When he'd come home from a trip; or on Sundays, making the stoop; finishing the cellar; putting on the new porch; when he built the extra bathroom; and put up the garage. You know something, Charley, there's more of him in that front stoop than in all the sales he ever made" (150). Here is Willy himself speaking to his wife: "You wait, kid, before it's all over we're gonna get a little place out in the country, and I'll raise some vegetables, a couple of chickens . . . And they'll get married, and come for a weekend. I'd build a little guest house. 'Cause I got so many fine tools, all I'd need would be a little lumber and some peace of mind" (74).

What was he doing just before he drove off on his last journey? Planting carrots, beets, and lettuce in a plot of ground about the size of a tablecloth, where the sun seldom shone because the garden was at the foot of an artificial canyon hewn by apartment skyscrapers. If this kind of man is to be cured, if any man is to be cured, he had better first know who he is, and what he is cut out to do.

Second, a man should find a community to which he can give himself and from which he can draw strength when he needs it. Willy Loman thought that his firm was such a community, and he was devastated when he discovered that it was not. Listen to him pleading for another chance to make good in the company where he had worked for a generation. The new owner is mercilessly objective about worn-out salesmen. Willy blurts out: "I'm talking about your father! There were promises made across this desk! You mustn't tell me you've got people to see — I put thirty-four years into this firm, Howard, and now I can't pay my insurance! You can't eat the orange and throw the peel away — a man is not a piece of fruit!" (85).

There is no community here. Well, he might have found it in his home. There was some understanding, even appreciation, in the individual members. But they could never all be understanding or appreciative at the same time. Willy says of his wife — and he means it: "You're my foundation and my support, Linda" (13). She affirms of him: "He's the dearest man in the world to me, and I won't have anyone making him feel unwanted and low and blue" (57). The elder son remarks to the prostitute he is with, as his father leaves them: "You've just seen a prince walk by. A fine, troubled prince. A hardworking, unappreciated prince . . . A good companion. Always for his boys" (122–23). Yes, there is individual appreciation of one another. But because there is no commonality in their mutual concern, there is no community in fact. Yet man is made to live in community. The Willy Lomans of this world must find fellowship if they are to re-find themselves.

But there is a third part of the cure, and it is ultimately a matter of theology. A man requires a center of loyalty outside of himself, greater than himself, more lasting than himself which both commands and sustains him. The arresting fact about this play is that God is totally absent. He is not damned, or pooh-poohed. He is just ignored, conspicuously disregarded. He does not amount to anything, or count for anything in the life of any character. They are all practical atheists, and John Buchan, Lord Tweedsmuir, has defined an atheist as one who has no invisible means of support. Conrad Hilton, of hotel fame, is in some ways a successful Willy Loman. Hilton, too, worked hard and daydreamed, but his mother, a devout Roman Catholic, added one more ingredient: prayer (*Be My Guest*, 16–17). It is not my desire to make a success story out of religion; there is a cross in Christianity and much suffering in Judaism. But Christianity and Judaism survive not only because young men work and old men dream dreams but because both add prayer. God was, and is, the invisible means of support. The Willy Lomans need to be aware that life does take on meaning when they know themselves, first as creatures of God, and then as sons of a heavenly Father. That is what gives lasting dignity to a person's life. That is what our Lord was getting at when He suggested we lay up treasure in heaven rather than on earth (Matthew 6:19–20), and that we seek the Kingdom first (6:33) and the things of earth will not only fall into their proper place but will provide us with the necessities of daily living (6:25–30). The fundamental answer is theological. That Willy Loman never knew.

But what method of treatment can be used to implement this theoretical remedy? Like the theory, it too will fall into three parts. In order to help folk suffering from the lonely insecurity of frustration, we must first help them to discover who and what they are. That may call for the assistance of the wise counselor, perhaps even of the psychiatrist. They can bring a man face to face with the inevitable facts, the facts a man has avoided by moodiness, hallucination, and daydreaming. I am grateful for my colleagues in counseling and in medicine.

But once the Willy Lomans know these facts, they are going to need the support of a community, especially a community which has experienced and understood and been redeemed from the fears the would-be suicides would abolish through death. We know the successful work of Alcoholics Anonymous. Have we ever thought of what the Gideons, the Christian Commercial Travelers' Association of America, do for salesmen? You know funny stories about the Gideons. So do I, some of which should not be told from the pulpit. But this is the kind of group which might have saved Willy Loman if he had lived on as a salesman. This is the kind of work fraternities and sororities might do on this campus, if they would take their responsibilities seriously. Willy's wife saw his need, though she didn't know how to handle it alone, and sought the woeful help of her sons: "I don't say he's a great man. Willy Loman never made a lot of money. His name was never in the paper. He's not the finest character that ever lived. But he's a human being, and a terrible thing is happening to him. So attention must be paid. He's not to be allowed to fall into his grave like an old dog. Attention, attention must be finally paid to such a person" (58).

Attention must be paid to such a person. That is a job for a community of folk who know and understand love.

The third step is for the Church. Here is the organized society which believes in the invisible means of support. Here Willy Loman can be cleansed of the ghastly guilt of his marital infidelity. "Neither do I condemn thee. Go and sin no more," were Jesus' words to the woman taken in adultery (John 8:11). In corporate worship a person can present his life to God, in the company of like-minded folk, for examination, for correction, for blessing. The president of a fine small New England college told me that he made his decision to accept the presidency at the Sunday morning service in his home church. Here we see — or should see — life *sub quadam specie aeternitatis*, that is, under the eye of God. And the pieces begin to fall into place. We begin to know what comes first, and what follows a long way after, if at all.

This is all going to take time, and patience, and group effort. There will be moments of encouragement and hours of disappointment. Willy Loman was sick for years; his convalescence would have required months. But it could have been done. It can still be done for his spiritual younger brothers and sisters.

Conclusion

Yes, *Death of a Salesman* is quite a play. It ran a long time on Broadway, perhaps because "the blood of Willy Loman flows in all of us." Do you know any Willy Lomans on this campus, or any of his sisters on East? Are you he? Then we stand ready to help them and you, if we can but make contact with you, before it is too late. As a Christian university, our job is the care and cure of souls, and you would be surprised at the willingness to help if you have never tapped this resource for yourself or others — denominational chaplains, deans of men and women, doctors, psychiatrists. Suicide, academic or otherwise, is not our desire for you at Duke. We are bold enough to say —

however feeble we are to implement—our Lord's words, about seeking to save those who are lost.

Almighty God,
Whose will it is that none of these little ones should perish;
Grant unto us goodwill and wisdom and learning and skill
To be agents of Thy salvation,
That men and women may be brought to the knowledge of Thy saving
    health and live lives worthy of Thy Son, Jesus Christ, our Lord.
Amen.

Though one of the early preachers to the university was a Quaker, few Quakers have preached in Duke Chapel. D. Elton Trueblood, then professor of philosophy at Earlham College, in Richmond, Indiana, was a notable exception. Trueblood preached this sermon in 1960, in which he linked courage with caring, noting that Christian caring is a dangerous, insecure activity.

The Courage to Care

February 14, 1960

D. ELTON TRUEBLOOD

I Corinthians 13 In a poll that was taken partly with the help of the Department of the Interior, a poll that was a spot check, it was found that 96 percent of the people in this country over the age of thirteen claim to have some religious affiliation. This does not mean that the affiliation is deep, or important, or genuine; it does mean that we are ashamed not to claim it, and this is very nearly universal. The attendance at public worship in our country is tremendous; even today, with this storm across the country, there are undoubtedly millions in places of worship at this very hour. Many churches now have to have three services on Sunday morning in order to take care of the people, because attendance at public worship is today popular, conventional, expected, part of the pattern of our current American life. And yet the shocking fact is that often the worst cases of prejudice come in the very areas where the attendance is the greatest.

The Chicago Police Department's dishonesty has taken place in an area of Chicago where the people are very religious, where there are many churches, and where there is a great deal of attendance at public worship. This is the thing to shock anybody: to recognize that the high points of our popular religion have coincided exactly with a moral sickness of which the TV scandals of last fall are only one symptom among many. You can have religion, and yet not have by any means what is enough.

And so this famous and glorious passage of scripture says, "Though I have faith so as to remove mountains, and yet do not have 'something else,' I am worth precisely nothing." Now this is where the Christian religion has something tremendously relevant to say to our modern world, as we open this seventh decade of the twentieth century of storm and stress. The greatest word of Christianity is a Greek word which is so important, so significant, that it takes an entire chapter of the New Testament to try to define it: the chapter that I read in your hearing a few moments ago. Now this word is *agape*. It is very hard to translate. But this is what Christianity has to say to the world: you can have all these other things—big colleges and universities, technology, factories, armies, money, religious attendance, membership, faith, all these things. But if you do not have the one thing needful, which is *agape*, you never have enough. The others are not sufficient for the good life of man.

Now, how do you translate this word? Maybe it was a mistake ever to try to translate it. We could have kept it in the Greek, and we would now be reasonably familiar with it, but we did not elect to do this, for some reason. When the great scholars of 1612, under King James, got together, they decided to translate this key word of Christianity as "charity." They were influenced here by Latin equivalents. But nearly every one of us today recognizes that this will not do. The word "charity" has been somewhat debased in our world, as many words are; and in our modern language it means practically the same as philanthropy, or "do-goodism," and certainly will not suffice. Very likely, there is hardly a person in the room who would choose this as the translation of our greatest word. Dr. Phillips, in what I read to you, follows the revised versions and uses the word "love," which is undoubtedly better for us than charity. And yet it has a great deal against it because for so many people it means nothing but a passing emotion, and is not for many of our ears sufficiently deep.

What then can we substitute for this greatest word? And here comes a suggestion that really arises out of contemporary existentialism; namely, that the one word that could mean this, that does mean this, and that has not been debased, is the word "caring," and the basic word "care." And then you can read, "Though I speak with the tongues of men and of angels, and do not care, I am as a sounding brass or a tinkling cymbal. And though I understand all prophecies, but do not care, I am nothing. Caring never ends . . . caring is never glad when others go wrong; caring is never possessive . . . And now there abide three great, enduring values, faith, hope, and caring, and the greatest of these is caring."

There is hardly any word that could be more appropriate to an academic congregation. For one of the major dangers in our academic life is that we lack the courage to care. We have pose; we have a cult of detachment. This is the reason that the word "cool" is, in spite of its vulgarity, still a word of approbation even in many academic circles. It means you stand off, never enter into a mood, observe, analyze, judge as from a superior eminence, but don't get drawn in. Therefore, the maxim is, don't stick your neck out; don't go out on a limb. Remain indifferent to all causes. And in scores of our colleges and universities this is supposed to be the smart and the advanced thing. There is no doubt that this is safe. You see, what people are so afraid of is being ridiculous. If you care greatly for a movement, if you care greatly for a person, you run the risk of being ridiculous. You can be shown wrong, perhaps. You throw yourself into a movement, and then what? The movement fails. You look silly, don't you? I'll tell you how to avoid that: never give yourself to anything unapologetically, or thoroughly; and then nobody can ever say, "I told you so." But it is also true that at the same time you will never find out anything important.

What about people? Do you want to play it absolutely safe? Never get married. Don't fall in love. You know, some marriages fail. Sometimes the person turns out not to be the person you thought. You stand before an altar like this, and you say, "I, John, take thee, Mary, for better, for worse, for richer, for poorer, in sickness and in health, so long as we both shall live." It's a tremendous gamble. It has no "if-clause." It is unconditional, it is commitment, it is not a contract. It is not cool detachment. It is the complete involvement of two people in each other's lives and destinies and fortunes and sins and virtues and characters. It's risky, but potentially glorious. But if you want to avoid all risk, or avoid anybody's being able to say "I told you so," stay away from it. The same comes in having a child. How do you know the child will love you? Will be worth it? You don't know. Some aren't. And sometimes the worst hatred arises between child and parent, and parent and child. It's pathetic, it's tragic, it occurs. You can avoid it: never have a child. But if you never have, you may miss some of the greatest joys of all this world.

You see, it takes courage to care; for caring is dangerous. It is the opposite of security. But all the greatest things in the world come by involvement. How do you really know another person? By standing off and looking at him, critically, objectively, detachedly? You won't know very much about him that way. You may know how big his body is, you may know a little about his mind, but you won't know very much else. You never really know another person unless somehow you become involved with that person, you care about that person and have a sense of concern; you see that other person's life as from the inside, to look at the world through his eyes. We sometimes say that love is blind, meaning that it hides from us the defects of the beloved; and there's a little truth in this—not very much. The far greater and the neglected truth is that love is the organ of knowledge, that it is only by caring greatly for another person that you begin to know who that other person is. Have you never noticed in the New Testament that it was only when the apostles had already come to love Christ that they knew who He was? The Pharisees did not know; the Herodians did not know; the popular observers did not know. The ones who knew were the ones who cared. Caring is the greatest thing in the world. It is the heart of the faith that has brought us into this company this morning. Not one of us follows it completely; but to know that it is the greatest thing in the world: this is to know something very important. For then at least we know when we go wrong.

Let us pray.

O Lord, wilt thou bring in to our hearts a divine disturbance. Wilt thou make us see ourselves as we are, in all our failure and in all our potential glory. Help us to see every man and woman whom we meet as through the eyes of Jesus Christ our Lord.

And now unto God's eternal keeping we commit you: in your going out and in your coming in, in your labor and your leisure, in your laughter and your tears, from this day and forevermore.

A university chapel has a number of occasions that one finds on no other church's liturgical calendar. Duke Chapel celebrates Opening Sunday (when the school year begins), the Last Sunday of the School Year (when the school year ends), and Founders' Sunday (when the university pauses to remember its founders). With president and trustees in attendance, this Sunday gives the community an opportunity to reflect on its mission and, at least at Duke, its unique identity as a university with Christian roots. In this Founders' Sunday sermon from 1961, Robert E. Cushman, longtime dean of the Divinity School, engages in such reflection, noting his own difficulty in finding a suitable scriptural text for what he feels led to say to the university. One wonders if by the end of this sermon Cushman's listeners were confused as to whether they had heard a sermon or a lecture; they surely knew that they had been in the presence of a great mind who loved the university well. Cushman was a leader of the Methodist Church, Wesleyan theologian, expert on Plato's philosophy, and erudite interpreter of the faith.

The Idea of a University

January 29, 1961

ROBERT E. CUSHMAN

Proverbs 8:1—Doth not wisdom cry, and understanding put forth her voice?

Now and then it has been said of a sermon that its alleged scriptural foundation was rather more a pretext than a text. That there be no dissembling, I warn that such may be the case this morning. For I have in mind to say something about the idea of a university, and I trust wisdom will cry, and understanding put forth her voice. But we may as well be frank; the Scripture nowhere has any explicit word about the university. It speaks much of wisdom, truth, and knowledge, of faith, hope, and love, but neither school nor academy is anywhere noted as the special place of insemination or dissemination. To be sure, the synagogue was a school of sorts and the early church a focus of instruction. But the Scripture neither knows nor heralds the academy, and thus, so far as Scripture is concerned, we will have to shift for ourselves.

Suppose on some mid-year examination—happily behind us—you had been asked to state the aims of the university and enlarge upon its nature and function, how would you have fared? Perhaps your ingenuity would not have been so taxed as your surprise that the question should be asked at all — so customary is it for us to take for granted the institutions we are involved in, without scrutiny of their purposes. Well, then, how would it go with the faculty, if positions were reversed, and you the students had asked us what is the enterprise called the university: what does its name imply, what is its reason for being, and how does your particular subject matter inhere in its total economy of disciplines, and with what justification?

Frankly, I do not know whether the ingenuity of students or of faculty would be the more severely strained. I suspect that the position of either would be about equally discomfiting with that of the rank and file of civil servants pressed to define the aim of politics and the purpose of government, or as uneasy as churchmen required to define the Church, its reason for being, and their place in it. The fact is, nothing is commoner than for all of us to participate in institutions without defined or acknowledged consensus about their intrinsic meaning or essential purpose.

In point of fact, within limited periods, institutions seem inclusive and hospitable of differing aims and varying purposes, and some of the aims and purposes are mutually compatible. Some are incompatible, but there is no evident difficulty, no overt crisis, until some aims become imperious enough to be at strife with others, or until the prevailing aims are contested by new and emergent ones that seek to supplant the old. Then there will be signs of ferment and inner turmoil, indicating that the institution is in transition. If it is a university, consideration might properly be given to the nature of the emergent forces, the consequent and likely shape of the future, and, above all, to the question what is, not just the *existing*, but the *essential* idea of a university. This also, then, would be part of long-range planning; and if this is not done first, then planning is either piling on more of the same or it is subterfuge.

Let us have a look, then, at some ideas of a university with a view to sorting them out. Webster's definition has remained unchanged for decades, indicating no very lively reflection about it or re-examination: "It is an institution organized for teaching and study in the higher branches of learning and empowered to confer degrees in special departments as in theology, law, medicine, and the arts." It is plain to see that Webster's definition is only a rough description and pretends nothing concerning the essential nature of what it describes.

The historian Mosheim helps us a little in suggesting that the School of Paris, founded in the twelfth century, first properly earned the name "university" because it was first to embrace *all* the arts and sciences. This implies that the word "university," deriving from the Latin *universitas*, refers to a whole, the whole universe of studies. Cicero used the word *universitas* to signify "the world." In a sense, then, the university would be a kind of microcosm, or miniature world within the world and in which, in some measure, the actual world is represented in knowledge—a microcosm within the macrocosm. And that perhaps is the denotation actually attached to the word "university" in the later Middle Ages. To the university, therefore, students would resort who desired something like a synoptic view of reality as it was apprehended.

This may have been the idea of the university in the thirteenth century, perhaps even in the seventeenth, but by the nineteenth century this conception was disavowed. In the twentieth it was all but eclipsed. Endless specialization in the natural and social sciences foreclosed upon a synoptic view of reality, so that in our own time, no less an Oxonian than William Temple could declare that a university "is a place where a multitude of studies are conducted, with no relationship between them except those of simultaneity and juxtaposition"; and Arnold Nash, of nearby Chapel Hill, has adequately demonstrated that "in theory the (modern) liberal university rejects the attempt to teach a unified conception of the world" (*The University and the Modern World*, 259).

Thus, the older conception of the university as the unified world of knowledge within the larger world—the microcosm within the macrocosm—is gone, succeeded by a shapeless galaxy of truths, spawned by the several sciences, in general disarray and devoid of inclusive pattern or comprehensive rationale. No longer a cosmos, the university became a storehouse of *truths* with no sure grasp on *Truth*: "Doth not wisdom cry, and understanding put forth her voice!"

So a new conception of the university came of age, reached maturity, and some think is in its dotage. It based itself upon the announced program of seventeenth-century "natural philosophy," which accorded to the experimental method the privileged, if not the exclusive, prerogative of determining truth and falsity in human judgments. Nothing was true that was not verified by the method, and nothing that the method verified was other than a particular truth. The whole of Truth fractured like Humpty-Dumpty, and couldn't be put together again. Men had to content themselves to await the results of the next experiment from the laboratory or the anticipated findings of the political or sociological statistician. Endlessly multiplying data burst the walls of libraries as monographs added more and more to the mounting lore of less and less.

In principle, the university came to disavow responsibility for the Truth men live by — moral or aesthetic or religious — and, with professional solemnity, blandly accepted a kind of cultural schizophrenia; that is, a fixed gulf between the truths of the sciences and the Truth men live by, if they live at all. If any were to attain the latter, it must needs be outside the university. Indeed the situation is known to have gone so far as that what is recognized in the outside world as crime and immorality has been, in the university, innocuously styled incompetence. "Doth not wisdom cry, and understanding put forth her voice!"

As the matter stands, there is little doubt that this second ideal of the university I have mentioned — the one which enshrines the all-sufficiency of scientific methodology, with its endless proliferation of truths — has had its special part to play in the present "failure of nerve" of liberal democracy. To be sure, some of its devotees have contrived to content themselves with some departmental findings and inductible dogmas — envisioning reality through their particular crack. But for the most of us, the situation entails an incomprehensible pluralism of truths, without Truth, that has eroded inherited structures of value and meaning until the intelligible fabric of life dissolves in meaninglessness, or the threat of it.

Meanwhile wisdom cries out for unity, the *One* that gives form and structure to the *many*, and halts, as Plato saw and said, "The dreadful slithering of thought into the infinite abyss." Without unity there is no difference, and without difference — that is, intelligible structure — there is no presiding Truth to be found in the many. There is only the *Nihil*, the Nothing, and the will of man, invoked by no commanding vision, is mired in the impotence of indecision. Thus, it is an unaccountable anachronism to find this idea of a university resurgent at Duke or elsewhere in this day of the world's life when the existence of western Hellenic-Christian culture is militantly challenged by a unified world view that however benighted, bids well to capture with its partial meaningfulness the disinherited of the earth.

A third idea of the university, closely allied with the second, derives from the dictum of Francis Bacon: "Knowledge is power." It is justified by its utility. The "true and lawful goal of the sciences," declared Bacon, "is that human life should be endowed with new discoveries and powers." In this way, man could "become a God to man" and "the kingdom of man founded on the sciences" might easily rival and probably outstrip the kingdom of God in significance, certainly in utility (cf. *Novum Organum*, 99, 113).

There is no doubt that over the years Bacon has had a hearing in the university. The ascendancy of technology and the decline of the humanities, the denaturing of philosophy, and the eclipse of theology are witnesses to that. Moreover, it was through the universities that "the Bomb" was devised as the dreadful and consummate achievement of Bacon's program. The "kingdom of man founded upon the sciences" was apparently also to be destroyed by them. Now, man could become a god to man, at least for his annihilation. No prophecy of good was ever so well fulfilled in its reverse as Bacon's. Nemesis and frustration, thy name is man! President Kennedy's inaugural address of January 20th posed the issue simply: it is destruction or peace, "before the dark powers of destruction unleashed by science engulf all humanity in planned or accidental self-destruction." Do you know what dropped out of the skies near Goldsboro this week? Almost surely enough atomic power to have pulverized eastern North Carolina, if it had gone off! This is the kind of providence that is going on over our heads.

From what resources, then, of science and technology shall peace come? This has been the frantic question of the Association of Atomic Scientists who have rehearsed the peril for fifteen years without hitting upon an answer. Plainly, the powers unleashed by science are either diabolical or beneficent depending upon the *men* who use them. But what is man, and what are the springs of his motivation, and how may these be altered for the good? Whence comes the will to righteousness, and what are the sources of goodness? And the university that has downgraded the humanities, pigeonholed philosophy, banished religion, and sniped at theology has no answer. "Doth not wisdom cry, and understanding put forth her voice!"

But there is another, a fourth idea of the university, which gives full place to the "humanities." It had classical statement in the work of John Henry Newman, that brilliant and controversial British churchman of the nineteenth century. Said Newman a hundred years ago, the university "is a place of teaching universal knowledge." This implies that its object is, on the one hand, intellectual, not moral; and on the other, that it is "the diffusion and extension of knowledge rather than advancement." Newman could not accept the university as a place of research. He was perplexed to know how, if its purpose was discovery, it should bother with students. And it may be conceded that this has been to many university researchers an insistent dilemma as well as a present nuisance.

But what is central in Newman's theory is his cogent plea for knowledge as its own sufficient reward, and intellectual value as its own chief end. Such is the constitution of the human mind, thinks Newman, that "knowledge is capable of being its own end" (*The Idea of a University*, 92). He approves of Cicero's view that "as soon as we escape the pressure of necessary cares, forthwith we desire to see, to hear, to learn." So it seems to Newman that the end of university education "is a comprehensive view of truth in all its branches, of the relations of science to science, of their mutual bearings and their respective values" (91). This is a liberal education. It engenders the philosophic temper, a "habit of mind," or serene composure, "which lasts through life, of which the attributes," he says, "are freedom, equitableness, calmness, moderation, and wisdom" (90).

Newman's idyllic picture answers authentically, not alone to the fancy, but to the aspiration of the true academician. The figure of the sage, perhaps of Socrates himself, presides over the composition; and in the background, nineteenth-century English gentlemen stroll past, soberly debonair, from the cricket field to four o'clock tea. Perhaps it is a romantic nineteenth-century version of Plato's Academy or Aristotle's Lyceum. At least for Newman, the university retains its role as seat of universal learning — the learned cosmos within the larger cosmos. And there is the advantage that in this view of the university, the intelligible world has a chance to remain standing.

But what is this intellectualistic purism by which Newman is content to divide *knowledge* from *virtue* and finds within the former the self-sufficient domain of university endeavor? When we ask this question, we should recall that this is also our own purism. We have been tricked by this idyll of Newman and others into believing that Socrates' moderation was without commitment, that wisdom was without moral earnestness, and that knowledge was without passion. By this nineteenth-century idyll we have been encouraged to forget that Plato linked knowledge with *eros*, wisdom with devotion to justice, and that he made all truths answerable to the true Good. Patron of the intellect alone, the academician can hardly credit the fact that Plato explicitly said in the *Laws* that "ignorance is no great evil but much more to be feared is a knowledge of many things without knowledge and reverence for the Good."

No, with all his admirable exaltation of intellectual values, Newman fosters the fundamental error of the liberal democratic university — its divorce of knowledge from virtue and its irresponsibility toward the moral good and the spiritual structures of social existence. Small wonder that the university earns the reputation of irrelevancy among embattled men in the workaday world, as an "ivory tower" of secure asylum from the agonizing demands of day-by-day decision!

But Newman's idea of a university did contain a corrective ingredient. He knew that his university might breed gentlemen, but gentlemen nevertheless haughty toward the prophets and contemptuous of the saints. So he was disposed to concede that "knowledge is one thing, virtue is another; good sense is not conscience, refinement is not humility. Liberal education makes not the Christian, but the gentleman. It is well to be a gentleman, it is well to have a cultivated intellect, a delicate taste . . . but still they are no guar-

68

antee for sanctity or even for conscientiousness; they may attach to the man of the world, to the profligate, to the heartless." And then Newman adds: "Quarry the granite rock with razors, or moor the vessel with a thread of silk; then you may hope with such keen and delicate instruments as human knowledge and human reason to contend with those giants, the passion and the pride of men" (106–7).

In these words Newman concedes the bankruptcy of his own idea of a university in so far as its purpose is to exalt alone the intellectual value in abstraction from the moral and religious. Its *paideia*, its way of education, is helpless to deal remediably with the existing distortions of the human spirit. It yields hardly more than the idealized sage, in a glass case, who never existed. By his own admission, Newman teaches that the university that takes no responsibility for the moral implications of knowledge is sterile so far as its contribution to the actual world of decision is concerned. Therefore, Newman explicitly looked to the Church to supply to the university what he called its "integrity."

We have glanced at the four historically controlling ideas of a university. Each has its values. Each exists by way of half-truth. Each, save the first, has its vicious defects. "Doth not wisdom cry, and understanding put forth her voice?" Wisdom does cry; it cries out that despite the university's vaunted openness to truth, it is no more really open to criticism nor capable of self-criticism than the Church or a political party. Its priests are as bound by the shackles of their own unexamined presuppositions and the inherited dogmas of the schools as are the devotees of other ways of life and other endeavors, with the added disadvantage that they are especially prone to the occupational disease of intellectual pride.

But wisdom cries out something else, and understanding puts forth her voice to admonish us in our day: Wisdom and understanding declare that the knowledge which preserves man's existence does not derive exclusively from the scientific method, that utility is a false criterion of truth, that intellectual refinement is not necessarily trustworthy. Wisdom and understanding plainly declare that unless, in the idea of a university, reverence is joined with knowledge, the university is not only irrelevant to the actual human situation but, quite possibly, a downright peril to the future.

Therefore, as you leave this Chapel today, mark well the two figures sculptured in stone on either side of the entrance to the nave. They embody the educational vision of the founders of this university. They are there permanently enshrined in stone, but let it not be only in stone! They are reverence, *religio*, on the one hand, and learning, *eruditio*, on the other. Tennyson put it rightly:

Let knowledge grow from more to more,
But more of reverence in us dwell,
Till mind and heart, according well,
Shall make one music, as before—but vaster!

I believe that inseparably and together, these two do constitute a new idea of a university suited for our day and for which wisdom cries and understanding puts forth her voice. Amen.

Martin Niemöller was a courageous German pastor who was imprisoned in Dachau by the Nazis. After surviving that ordeal, Niemöller became a world-renowned preacher in the postwar years. He preached this sermon while visiting Duke Chapel as president of the World Council of Churches. In this sermon he movingly speaks of his own experience in a concentration camp and how that taught him something about the God whose "strength is made perfect in weakness."

Human Weakness and Divine Strength

February 24, 1963

MARTIN NIEMÖLLER

II Corinthians 12:9

Grace be unto you and peace from God our Father and from the Lord Jesus Christ! Amen.

"And he said unto me, my grace is sufficient for thee, for my strength is made perfect in weakness. Most gladly therefore will I rather glory in my infirmities, that the power of Christ may rest upon me."

Certainly, this word of St. Paul—we know it and we may have heard it many times—is a very queer and most surprising statement. If it really stands as valid and true, we feel that those people who say that the days of Christianity are passing by quickly or may have gone already might be right, that we in our generation have entered the post-Christian era, since our everyday thinking and living has become incompatible with this kind of attitude and claim. Ours is an era marked by the tremendous progress and success of science and knowledge, of ability and efficiency, human possibilities seem to us as being unlimited and boundless—we are very near to conquering and to governing the universe. So our conception of nature and our relationship to nature has changed basically; we do no longer feel that there may be regions which will remain out of our reach and dominion. Human power really is something in which we may trust, and our task of today and tomorrow is only to adapt our faculties in the right and best way to the chances we have.

Strength, power, might—human strength, human power, human might —they are the things that matter, and to get rid of all complexes of inferiority is an aim worth striving for. The ideal surely is not to be weak, but to be strong; human existence is getting so complicated that only an austere and disciplined vigor will cope with it.

To depend on any help and assistance from outside, to trust in somebody except yourself, is suspect of being a trait of weakness and a lack of self-confidence. At least, this opinion and conviction is in keeping with the general spirit of our present age. Therefore, the religious element in human nature is losing ground and the consciousness of dependence, the very basis of religion, is dwindling away. Today's atheism therefore is in no way surprising, but just a logical by-product of modern evolution. We do feel able to explain everything—if not yet at present and today, then certainly tomorrow or in the near future. And we trust that we shall deal with all newly accomplished insight successfully, when we consult only, and rely upon, our own reason and judgment.

Evolution means progress; this we do take for granted, and this is why we are facing the present decline of religion among civilized nations, and especially the regress of Christianity in our formerly "Christian" world.

Today this retrogression is quite obvious and notorious; but it has developed already for a considerable time, through decades and maybe even for more than two centuries. It began when people began to omit or to pass over those parts of the Christian gospel and message, which no longer were in accordance with their general feeling and with their understanding of human nature and human life. When they began to become aware of their great talents and when they began to achieve unprecedented progress in science and technology, they wanted—whether consciously or not—to forget everything which might reduce or even destroy their optimistic self-confidence. There was no room anymore for the message of sin and of redemption, for the praise of service and of weakness and the like; but still they clung to everything in the teachings of Jesus which seemed to call for a heroic and idealistic and active life. They clung to the Christian religion because they were convinced that it had furthered and in the end accomplished the abolition of slavery as well as the equal status of women, and that thereby it had proved a genuine factor of human progress. It really was, it really has been!

But with this curtailment and alteration of the gospel message, through which the continuation of Christianity became possible in those days and for a considerable time, the gospel lost its life-center. Its master and Lord was no longer needed, His place at the bottom and in the midst of the Christian message was filled with His teachings; they were regarded as the main truth, based upon themselves, no longer connected with, and dependent on, the Master's person. And so the faith in Jesus the Christ was replaced by the belief in His doctrine, His precepts, His rules; the personal relationship was abandoned in exchange for a system of moral commandments.

So then, in some parts of the world Christianity has become something very different from what the New Testament understands by Christian faith. There Christian faith means that Christians are the Lord's disciples and followers, subject to His authority and attached to him, knowing His spirit and willing to obey His directives, responsible to our living Lord, who — according to His promise — is present as our counselor and guide; and we may ask Him — no, we must — what He wants us to do: "Lord, what wilt thou have me to do?"

But when we deal only with His teaching, with His rules and precepts, we may derive from His commandments a number of principles which we take into consideration ourselves. Principles are subject to our own judgment, and we select from them by making our own choice, putting aside what is not convenient to us, and, by doing this, we maintain our own and decisive authority. There are many Christians who call such a selection of principles their "faith"; they do believe in them as far as they agree; but there are some among them which they think to be too difficult and too exaggerated and which therefore they do not acknowledge, e.g., "love your enemies, bless them that curse you, do good to them that hate you, and pray for them which despitefully use you and persecute you!" This simply does not belong to their Christian faith, and there are quite a number of directives among the words of Jesus which meet with similar doubts and objections. And — to be sure — none of these Christians, who believe in principles of their own decisive selection, has ever agreed, or will ever agree, with St. Paul's confession: "Most gladly will I rather glory in my infirmities, that the power of Christ may rest upon me!"

This whole kind of Christian religion, which is based on a collection of principles, wants strength and power and might, wants something with which to live, with which to work, with which to succeed. And those who adhere to this type of Christianity cannot and will not take the risk of "infirmities." What they have in mind is rather how to avoid all sorts of weakness and all possibilities of defeat; they believe in progress, at least they want to, and they long for accomplishing their justification on their own account. Everything else would violate and hurt their pride, their claim to mastery and sovereign independence. Here it becomes clear and evident that this

Christianity is absolutely indifferent to God and also to Jesus, the Christ, and utterly revolts against the gospel. For the gospel announces the Kingdom of God, and it is announced as being at hand in the reign of Jesus, the human being, in whom God Himself meets with us, His human children, in order to gain us over and to bring us home again.

The power of this Lord, what is it? Nothing, it seems! At least, the power of His opponents proves to be stronger than all He can do; and so He finishes His commission in suffering and death, in total defeat.

And yet, all inimical power of human pride and self-concern, of hatred and vindictiveness cannot overcome Him, cannot make Him use the same means of power and violence, not even in self-defense, cannot seduce Him to the spirit and attitude of retaliation. And so He becomes and remains more than a conqueror, for in dying He prays forgiveness for His murderers, His hangman, His guardsmen, His persecutors, His traitor, His enemies, His faithless friends, and in praying He dies for them all and for all of us: more than a conqueror, a Saviour, the Saviour.

In the last year of my imprisonment in one of Hitler's ill-famed concentration camps, at Dachau, a gallows was transplanted, transferred from the general camp into the courtyard of the "bunker," the prison inside the camp. And the upper part of this gallows looked into my solitary-confinement cell, through the window bars. How often has this gallows induced me to pray for my comrades who were hanged on it, and how often every day I had to control myself, when the idea arose: If these people will pull me out of my place here to that gallows, I shall shout at them, "You criminals, you murderers, wait and see — there is a God in heaven and he will show you!" And then the torturing question: What would have happened if Jesus, when they nailed him to his gallows, to the Cross, had spoken like this and had cursed his enemies? Nothing would have happened, only there would be no gospel, no Christian Church, for there would be no message of great joy; for then he would have prayed against his enemies, not for them, and would have died against them and not for them. Thank God! He prayed, he died a different way, "Father, forgive them, for they know not what they do!"

And there it was, that He said unto me: "My strength is made perfect in weakness, and therefore my grace is sufficient for thee." This then is the crucial, the decisive question: Do we, do I, really know that He prayed for me, that He died for me there on Calvary, on his Cross?

No, Christian principles will not do. Paul, the apostle, is right when he renounces every idea of being anything for himself. All that matters is He, Jesus, and all that really counts is His power of sacrificial love, by which He makes me His brother and thereby His father's child and my fellow's brother at the same time. But I need Him, not just His words and directives; but Himself, His person and His love. I need Him. Most gladly therefore will I rather "glory in my infirmities," that the power of Christ may rest upon me! And that I may confess: "I live, yet not I, but Christ liveth in me!" Amen.

Bill Coffin's ministry at Yale epitomized the heady, conflicted, prominent days of campus ministry in the 1960s. Antiwar activist, gadfly to the academic establishment, motivator of protesting students, Coffin was everything that many campus ministers of the sixties aspired to be. In this sermon he takes off from a story of Jesus into a mocking attack upon intellectual immobility in the face of the great crises of our time.

Burdened with Erudition and Paralyzed with Indecison: A Sermon on Learned Paralytics

March 12, 1967

WILLIAM SLOANE COFFIN JR.

Hosea 11:1–9 and Mark 2:1–12 "And when Jesus returned to Capernaum after some days it was reported that He was at home and many were gathered together so that there was no longer room for them, not even about the door. He was preaching the Word to them. They came to Him bringing a paralytic carried by four men and when they could not get near Him because of the crowd they removed the roof above Him and when they had made an opening they let down the pallet on which the paralytic lay. When Jesus saw their faith, He said to the paralytic, 'My son, your sins are forgiven.' Some of the scribes were sitting there questioning in their hearts. Why does this man speak thus? It is blasphemy; who can forgive sins but God alone? And immediately Jesus receiving in His spirit that they thus questioned within themselves said to them, 'Why do you question thus in your hearts? Which is easier to say: your sins are forgiven or rise and walk? I say to you that you may know that the son of man has authority on earth to forgive sins.' He said to the paralytic, 'I say to you, rise, take up your pallet and go home.' And he arose and immediately took his pallet and went out before them all. So that they were all amazed and glorified God saying they never saw anything like this." May God bless unto us this the reading of His Holy Word.

Earlier this week unseasonable warmth melted most of Connecticut's remaining snow. But thanks to a truly genuine drainage system on what we call the Old Campus at Yale none of the snow was lost. It simply rearranged itself in an unending series of puddles. While most of these were muddy, some few were clear. By that afternoon it was possible for me to rediscover the childhood joy of puddle gazing. We wonder in youth how so vast an expanse of earth and sky can be contained in such a small body of water. No less wondrous is how so much of the story of earth and heaven can be captured in small biblical narratives.

We just read the story of Jesus and the paralytic; how Jesus the great disseminator of life healed the man whose life had become one long suicide. Here we see the eternal disseminator of God's freedom confronting the eternal paralysis of the human will. Once again we are prompted to reflect on that phrase on which we cannot reflect too much: to serve God is the highest freedom. It is man's natural, proper role to rebel against God and I think that we can safely surmise that in all human history God never met an opponent more redoubtable than Jesus Himself. With typical power and imagination, *The Last Temptation of Christ* portrayed the young Jesus racked with conflicting desires but with none more passionate than the desire to escape the burden of divinity. Sensing the nature of the struggle and all excited by it, his rabbi approaches Jesus' mother: "Hail Mary, God is all powerful, His designs are inscrutable. Your son might be a prophet!" But Mary, whose eyes by now are drained dry with the agony of watching her son struggle, cries out, "Have pity on him! Prophet? No, no! And if God has written so let Him rub it out. I want my son like everyone else. Nothing more. Nothing less." Rabbi leans heavily on his crosier and gets up. "Mary," he says severely, "if God listened to mothers, we would all rot away in the bog of security and easy living." Then he goes to her son and says in all tenderness, "Jesus, Jesus, my child, how long are you going to resist Him?" Then the entire cottage shakes with a savage shout, "Until I die! The soil of Israel is in labor, unable to give birth and screaming."

But out of the struggle of man with God, the Messiah comes. Man's anxiety becomes God's love in person honored. Jesus abandoned the struggle of man with God to take up the struggle of God with man, abandoned all self-protection for utter vulnerability. What I am trying to say is that a submission which comes too quickly is simply a façade for repressed rebellion. Jesus' struggle was long, and hard, and ends in voluntary, total self-surrender. And that is why His authority is peculiar. A writer in a recent essay points out sympathetically: "The truth has not only a persuasive but a coercive nature; with the result, the truth teller tends toward tyranny. Not so much because of a character weakness, as because they are under restraints and strong compulsions." This is something for good Christians to remember, for when piety becomes fanaticism, then faith becomes arrogance, and goodness inevitably becomes cruelty. But Jesus is no fanatic, no tyrant. While He confronts people with His and their beliefs, never does He try to do their believing for them. And I suppose what I am really trying to say is that a truly strong man is always tender.

So it must have been this combination of strength and tenderness that drew the crowds of Capernaum to the home of Peter and Andrew, and prompted the four friends to bring to Jesus the man who had become such a burden to them and to himself. I think that we must assume that the man was crippled not by any lesion of a nerve, a trauma of the cerebral cortex, but by a total paralysis of the will. His was that paralyzing cry for the soul that one sees in mental hospitals, more properly called in Russia hospitals "for the soul-sick" because the mental derangement is an effect and not a cause. In short, as we can see in mental hospitals, this man was quite literally scared stiff! Now as such he lies there, on his pallet as a symbol of us all, partially paralyzed as we all are, but whose hand here is free, free to be extended to anyone, whose eyes are free to see the truth as it is because all our eyes are in part paralyzed by these status symbols of ours; whose feet are free, free to walk in any walk of life. No, in all honesty we are not born into freedom. We are born into lack of freedom and the church is right, only with baptism does freedom begin to enter in. Only with God behind us does freedom lie before us. So we must take our stand with baptism against birth, witness to our given freedom against our inherited lack of freedom. This becomes strikingly clear when we realize that the question of freedom is not the question from what, but the question toward what. He is truly free who is unhindered for what he counts to good. Freedom of choice, to be or not to be; that is the form of freedom, but to be able to choose to be, that is the meaning of freedom.

Modern technology, for instance, cannot free us to serve what we count to be good. In a strange way modern civilization, far from solving our difficulties, seems rather to externalize them. We are better cared for, but we have more cares. Physical support of modern society is more than offset by the psychological pressures. Which is why Berdyaev correctly prophesied that when bread has been assured, then God becomes a hard and inescapable reality instead of an escape from harsh reality. Modern education, too, cannot free us for what we count to be the good. For often does not education drive a wedge between thought and action instead of enabling action of a higher kind? Modern education, designed as it so often is to help people meet outer demands at the expense of their capacity to set inner goals, is turning out people who are burdened with erudition and paralyzed with indecision. The academic community is often as not a crowd of learned paralytics. But let us recognize that this is always bound to be the case, for anguish is born of fear and fear is born of knowledge and hence history of paralysis begins at the foot of the tree of knowledge.

How unfree are we? It becomes clearer yet when we realize that this whole nation of the most advanced technology, and in many ways the most advanced educational system in the world, is today paralyzed in a kind of lock-step to a world ideological view already doomed beyond reprieve to belong to a bygone age. Again and again Europeans are shocked at our paralysis of thought and action. I shall never forget how shocked I was when two East European Marxists stopped by not long ago, and their question was, "How do you do it, how do you do it?" And knowing that they were just back from the Midwest, I assumed and thought they were talking about our great agricultural achievements, because as you know the Soviets are still planting that miracle grain, planted in the Ukraine and it comes up in Canada! But not at all. What they had in mind, they quickly made clear, was something quite different. We have, they said, watched CBS, NBC, ABC; what's the difference? Your radio programs are equally as uniform (they were nice enough to say not uniformly bad). With the exception of certain editorials in the *St. Louis Dispatch* and *New York Times* and *Louisville Courier*, all your editorial policy across the country seems to be very much the same. How do you do it? How do you achieve such effective thought control without resorting to terror? What an irony, that soon communists will be coming to the leading democracy of the world in order to study effective methods of thought control. Perhaps this nation has its symbols in our story. Perhaps this nation is symbolized by Capernaum, whose inhabitants apparently were worse off than the cripple because their pride's swollen face had so closed up their eyes that they were unable to perceive their own paralysis. So we read the prophecy, "And you Capernaum, will you be exalted in heaven?" No. You will be brought down to Hades the way that great powerful Roman is pictured in Michelangelo's *Last Judgment* being brought down to Hades, one hand over his eye and a look of dire understanding on his face. He understood, but too late. The prophecy was singularly fulfilled, for one of the most difficult tasks in sacred typography is to discover the site of Capernaum.

But let us get back to the paralytic. The problem we are dealing with is deeply personal and deeply religious. And the prayers we heard earlier, which I think were said for most of us certainly, intimated love (if we are talking about God's love it is not blind but visionary). And as an x-ray pierces the body to perceive the disease, so Jesus' love pierced the heart of this man and perceived that his will was paralyzed by guilt. The guilt of all who dare to fail to be themselves. But Jesus is not judging, as no doubt the moralistic Scribes expected Him to do, for that would have been to humiliate him at the level of his deepest failure. God is not trying to turn us all into miserable little heaps of humanity. Nor did Jesus punish him because punishing by assuaging guilt makes the old way of life bearable anew. Rather, He simply said to him, and His words combine a kind of somber explicitness with a kind of vibrant warmth, "My son, your sins are forgiven." Then the miracle takes place. The man believes Him, believes that there is more mercy in Christ than sin in him. And he is free, free at last from the powers of death militant; and one of the most joyful hieroglyphics in the early Christian art is a picture of a man bouncing along the road with a terribly light bed on his back.

And now the final, crucial word. We are more like the others in Capernaum of whom we were speaking and therefore roles have been tragically reversed. In the story it is the cripple who is in agony, not Christ. But when we meet Christ it is not in the house of Peter and Andrew but at Calvary, and the pain that is ours because we cannot love is totally overshadowed by the pain of Him who can but love. What is so killing to Jesus is not the nails and the spears, but having so much love to give and so few to receive it. "O Jerusalem, Jerusalem, how often would I, and you would not?" It is man's natural role to rebel, to argue with God, to shake angry fists at God. And let's be honest in this Lenten season, take your rebellion to the foot of the Cross, look up, see what's going on and hear that great cry from the heart still calling out, "Father, forgive them," and go ahead and argue. What have you got to say? What is there for any of us to say, except perhaps, "O Lamb of God that taketh away the sins of the world, have mercy upon us."

Let us pray: Almighty God, unto Whom all hearts are open, all desires known, and from Whom no secrets are hid, cleanse the thoughts of our hearts by the inspiration of Thy Holy Spirit, that we may perfectly love Thee and worthily magnify Thy Holy Name, through Jesus Christ our Lord. Amen.

Jürgen Moltmann came to the attention of the North American theological com-
munity through his "Theology of Hope." His fame was spreading when he
preached this Communion sermon in Duke Chapel in the late 1960s. Moltmann's
sermon concerns a predominate theme of that era: the healing of human divisions
through devotion to the expansive love of God in Christ.

Communion Meditation

October 1, 1967

JÜRGEN MOLTMANN

"For as many of you as were baptized into Christ have put on Christ. There is neither Jew nor Greek. There is neither slave nor free. There is neither male nor female. For you are all one in Christ Jesus and if you are Christ's then you are Abraham's offspring, heirs according to promise." And may God bless unto us the reading of his Holy Word.

This communion meditation is based upon the verses from Galatians which we have just heard. *Who am I really?* This is a crucial question we all have to answer in our lifetime. When we are young, we compete in games to find out how strong we are physically. Later, we take a job to prove to ourselves and others what we can accomplish with our total being. And when we have exhausted ourselves in the demands and responsibilities of our everyday concerns, we often cry out, "I have lost myself. I want to find myself again. I don't know at all who I really am." And so the question of our self-identity keeps hounding us to the grave. Man is hidden to himself. All his life, he is in search of his true being.

Dostoevsky wrote, "The ant knows the formula of her ant-hood. The bee knows the formula of her beehive. They do not know their formula in a human way, but in their own way. And I don't need to know more. Only man does not know his formula. Thus man is always man on the go. You risk an adventure and a hope. He can gain everything, but he can also lose everything. He can find heaven and he can find hell as well."

In his preaching, St. Paul opens up two ways of life for us, that of a slave and that of a son. What does he want to say? A man can try to find his terrified identity by enormous works? Who he really is, then, depends on what other people see him doing. Here he places himself under the law. Every day he hears the command of his conscience, "You must accomplish something big today. You have to be somebody. You have to prove to yourself and to others that you are a good guy or a charming woman. You have to do better than others." And this voice evokes ambition in a man and his anxiety eggs him on. He looks for approval in the eyes of his fellow men and seeks self-respect from their compliments. On the other hand, however, he is also constantly to humiliate others in order to exalt himself. I am not like this tax collector, said the Pharisee. I am not like this Jew or that Negro or like the communist, some say today. But this way of life is life under the law. If we live this way we are slaves, slaves of our own anxiety. Seeking approval through works is a characteristic of slaves. A slave has to make something out of himself because he is nothing in himself.

St. Paul points to another way of life by proclaiming that Christ to us. Don't look upon yourself. Don't become dependent in your work, whether in pride over the good ones or despair over the bad ones. Look upon Christ, who gave Himself up to death for you. In Him you will find yourself — whoever you are — deeply loved forever. In Christ we recognize the love of the Father and whenever we experience this love we become free. The frantic struggle for approval stops. The anxiety of coming up on the short end of life disappears. We can accept ourselves as we are because of being accepted by God in His love. We can have confidence as a son who trusts his father. We are at home everywhere and can breathe freely, because we are surrounded by His love from all sides. No one can earn this, for no one becomes a son by doing good works, but only by the love of his parents. Ye all are sons of God by faith in Christ Jesus, St. Paul tells the Galatians. I don't think they were better people than we are. They were probably just as hopeful and just as disappointed, just as proud and just as sad as we are. And nevertheless, they and we are sons of God by faith in Christ because they and we find in Christ the costly love of God to His mankind. And in this love, we are changed from proud and unfortunate slaves to children of His joy — to sons to whom belongs the world, to heirs of the coming kingdom in which all things will be new.

Every fish needs water in which to swim. Every bird needs air for flying; and we human beings need love to live in freedom. The boundless love of God is like the utmost fear in which we grow up to a truly free and human life. We find ourselves where we find this very love of God. Let us say, therefore, seeking approval in words is a sign of slaves, but the freedom found in faith expresses the true dignity of the children of God.

And there is another negative characteristic of man involved in St. Paul's reflections that needs to be mentioned. Whenever men come together they easily draw apart from each other at once as if separation were a rule of their nature. The Israelites considered themselves separate from the gentiles by divine election. The Greeks claimed to be better than the barbarians because of their education. Today, some Christians take non-Christians to be worse people. We separate ourselves from other people by pride in the superiority of our origin or education, wealth, class, race, and countless other ways which we invent day by day. We are naturally inclined to congregate with people whom we consider equals. Birds of a feather flock together. And one crow doesn't pick out the eye of another. These proverbs go back to the Greeks, who thought that only brotherly love, *philia*, can bring together free citizens in society. Their political society consisted of an assembly of the priests and the lords—an assembly rigidly excluding slaves. We all know that this attitude of exclusiveness is a basic motive for hate, for wars, and even revolutions. The scheme of hate is rooted deeply in the souls of servile men. It is the result of tainting all of human reality in black-and-white terms. People divide each other up into neat categories, friends and foes, equals and unequals. Usually they need an enemy who creates in them anxiety and fear, precisely in order that they may solidify their own group and their own nation. Communists do in fact need an enemy who is guilty of all evil. And many in the western world, no less, seem to need the bad communist to serve as a focal point of anxiety. Because man is not free to discover the guilt that is his own. He urgently needs a whipping boy or a scapegoat whom he can accuse in order to excuse himself. Why do people act this way privately as well as in public life? I think because they are slaves of their own anxiety and are not free. God's love liberates us from this anxiety. We simply lose fear whenever we experience everlasting love. And because God's love creates peace on Earth, we can see in the Christ of God—who died not for His friends but for the enemies of God—what this love means. It is not brotherly love, *philia*, as the Greeks said, but love of enemy, *agape*, as the New Testament says. Jesus associated not with the equal, but with the one who was different, the unequal, the ostracized, the despised, the humiliated one. To the amazement of the Pharisees, Jesus associates with prostitutes and tax collectors, social outcasts and political nobodies. In His love, equal doesn't associate with equal. God justifies the godless and accepts sinners and always loves them. This love is not like a playboy love which is attracted by outward glamour and what appears lovable; it is a love which seeks the lost and creates new life where otherwise hate kills everything.

Through Christ we learn of this new creative love because we experience it only in Him. If we are recreated to a new life by this love, we are enabled to love our enemies. I think this is the creative reality of the Christian community. Here our boundaries are infiltrated and the walls of separation men themselves erect from mutual isolation are raised. Here is neither Jew nor Greek, neither bond nor free, neither male nor female, and, let us say, neither friend nor foe, for all are one in Christ Jesus. All are alike as sinners, and yet all are equally loved by God. We can become a Christ to the other for we have put on Christ, as St. Paul says. That we can become a brother and a helper and in this way a redeemer to the other.

A wave of freedom went through the ancient world when people left behind their presuppositions and their nations, classes, and races to find a new humanity in the worldwide community of the church. They were called the new people of God and the third species. A movement of peace went through the medieval world when people left behind them their everlasting struggle for blood revenge and came to the Lord's Supper for reconciliation. It is especially at similar frontiers that we have to seek the creative reality of the church today, where enemies make friends. Their contempt is replaced by appreciation. Their hate changes into kindness. There is the true Christian community. Christ is not against the communists—he died for them. Christ is not against our private, our public enemies—he died for them. If we understand that and follow him in the ministry of reconciliation, then the Christian community is what it has to be—the advance guard of the coming new world of God where mankind shall live in peace.

Well, it is true that what we are able to realize in this life are fragments beginning only with very small steps, but it belongs to the vision of the Christian hope to see the fragments of the coming whole: in the ambiguous beginning, the unequivocal perfection, and in the earthen vessel, the beauty of the coming kingdom of God. What we are able to realize as kindness and peace in our Christian community is always very human and puny and often altogether much too human. But at the same time, this reality is a sacrament of the great hope for the future of mankind.

Today is Worldwide Communion Sunday. Throughout the world people are celebrating the Supper of our Lord. Everywhere, people are becoming free sons of God out of proud or desperate faith. Greek and barbarian, bond and free, male and female, Germans and Poles, black and white are entering the brotherhood of Christ, leaving behind what separates them and makes them enemies. Now they are becoming a unity in the midst of all disunity. They are celebrating the festival of freedom that crosses all boundaries. They hope in peace on Earth because they believed in the reconciliation of the world through the life of Christ. This is presented as a great offer to each of us. God offers us His open hand to recreate us from slaves to sons. From all

84

continents and nations, brothers stretch out their hands to find the brother in us. Do not let these hands remain empty. Seize these hands and hold firm. It is the offer of true life in the midst of death. And herein we can experience what we really are. We are the sons of God by faith. We are all one in Christ Jesus and we shall live in the peace of God. Amen.

For four decades Thomas A. Langford was a strong spokesperson for and an un-
deniable embodiment of the Christian faith at Duke. In his person he combined
Duke's motto, eruditio et religio. *He was a fine scholar of both philosophical*
theology and Wesleyan theology. He was a renowned academic administrator,
serving as chair of Duke's department of religion, dean of the Divinity School,
and provost of the university. Yet he was also a United Methodist preacher. In
this sermon, preached during the university's homecoming weekend, Langford
combines insights from literature, scripture, and even a song by the Beatles with
his personal wisdom to craft a beautiful sermon that elevates the notion of home-
coming to an encounter with the gospel.

Homecoming

Homecoming and Dad's Day
October 22, 1967

THOMAS A. LANGFORD

Psalm 127 I want to begin with a passage from a novel which captures both
the mood of this time of year as well as the reality of change in which we are
involved. I am reading from Thomas Wolfe's novel *Of Time and the River*:

> October had come again, and that year it was sharp and soon: Frost was
> early, burning the thick green on the mountainsides to massed brilliant hues
> of blazing colors, painting the air with sharpness, sorrow and delight . . . It
> was October, and that year, after years of absence and wandering, he had
> come home again.
>
> October is the richest of seasons: the fields are cut, the granaries are full,
> the bins are loaded to the brim with fatness, and from the cider-press the
> rich brown oozings of the York Imperials run . . . The corn is shocked . . .
> The barn is sweet with hay and leather, wood and apples . . . The sweat,
> the labor and the plow are over . . . Meanwhile the leaves are turning. . .
>
> Summer is dead and gone, the earth is waiting, suspense and ecstasy are
> gnawing at the hearts of men, the brooding prescience of frost is there . . .
> And the great winds howl and swoop across the land: They make a dis-
> tant roaring in great trees, and boys in bed will stir in ecstasy, thinking of
> demons and vast swoopings through the earth . . .
>
> And often the night there is only the living silence . . . and the moon,

the low and heavy moon of autumn, now barred behind the leafless poles of pines . . .

Then a chime of frost-cold bells may peal out on the brooding air, and people lying in their beds will listen. They will not speak or stir, silence will gnaw the darkness like a rat, but they will whisper in their hearts: "Summer has come and gone, has come and gone. And now — ? "

But they will say no more, they will have no more to say: They will wait listening, silent and brooding as the frost, to time, strange ticking time, dark time that haunts us with the briefness of our days. They will think of men long dead, of men now buried in the earth, of frost and silence long ago, . . . and they will think of things they have no words to utter.

And in the night, in the dark, . . . what will they say?

October. This time of fulfillment and foreboding; a time which ends a time and a time which begins a time. Culminating the past, it portends a future. October, October is here in Durham and at Duke: everything, perhaps too much, is gathered together all at once. Dad's Day, football, parties, decorations, and dates. A time of fulfillment and a time of foreboding; the meeting of the past with the present. Parents and old graduates are among us: gaping at our dress and language, shocked by our activities and iconoclasm, peering gingerly into the coffeehouse, questioning their investment of money in education, and resenting the smiles of indulgence by the youths they pass. They realize how quickly things have changed, and for a moment they are aware of their middleageness.

And those of you who are students. You have gone your own ways this weekend: delighting in your ability to shock or to cushion the shock which your parents have received from visiting you. Entertaining alumni with those "irrepressible smiles and happy thoughts," exhibiting your ability to get through school without working. You have been busy, staying on the run and it has been fun, hectic fun, but fun. But now as the weekend comes to an end there may also be those moments of wonder and self-questioning. With a hard-to-describe taste in your mouth, you might return to your dorm or walk the campus tonight being aware of . . . October, of the transition of life.

October. This richest of seasons. The time of the fruition of friendship. There are moments in life which seem to make it all very worthwhile. Would you believe it, one student actually confessed to me this week that he was looking forward to seeing his father come down, and I smilingly asked why. He replied, "Because I always enjoy him." The couples on campus, some with a deep sense of the meaning and meaningfulness of relationship. A time of harvest. A time when one begins to reap the many things he has sown and some are good. This is the richest time of year. But this time, which is a fulfillment, can also produce foreboding and some of you, when the pre-science of frost surrounds you, will lie in your beds tonight and tomorrow night thinking of demons and vast swoopings through the earth. And in the night silences you will listen and brood, and perhaps like Thomas Wolfe, you will think of men long dead, of men now buried in the earth, of cold silences long ago, of the movement of things and of some thought which you have no words to utter.

As you scan with a sensitive eye, you will wonder about love and hate—yourself and your parents, yourself and that girl, that boy, yourself . . . perhaps just yourself. You will also wonder about the difference between the moon's pale glow across the chapel steeple and across a rice paddy in Vietnam; you will wonder about wealth and poverty—the chill of the wind as it blows across the preserved grass of Duke campus and as it flows through the unprotected homes in Edgemont. You will wonder about riots and race, frustrated ambitions and fractured lives and . . . October. The changing of life, the nakedness of the earth, youth and old age, life and death.

And in the midst of it all you will remember that this weekend was Homecoming, that time which tends to tie the past to the present. Homecoming. But what is home and how do we get there? How difficult it is to be at home, even at home. G. K. Chesterton perhaps spoke for many when he mentioned "Men who are homesick in their homes" (in "The House of Christmas"). Gaps grow between generations, splitting crevasses separate person from person, an abyss seems to stand between God and men.

This weekend I had the opportunity to speak with several parents on campus, and again the haunting side of Homecoming came through as one father commented, "I think I have never known my son." One does not have to speak to parents to know this; one can also speak to students and sit as I did for a couple of hours one afternoon hearing a story of a life which was torn because her life and others are torn, because of agony, despair, solitude, and loneliness.

Perhaps the Beatles wake us to reality, for we feel a sensation of recognition when they sing:

> She's Leaving Home
> Wednesday morning at five o' clock as the day begins
> Silently closing her bedroom door
> Leaving the note that she hoped would say more
> She goes down stairs to the kitchen clutching her handkerchief

Quietly turning the backdoor key
Stepping outside she is free.
She's leaving home
She's leaving home after living alone
For so many years, Bye, bye.
(from "Sgt. Pepper's Lonely Hearts Club Band")

Some leave home and others come home. But even some of the home-comings are destitute of meaning. Harold Pinter, in his current Broadway play *The Homecoming*, has depicted the emptiness, the sham, and the mockery of at least one effort to return home.

Some are coming home just as others are leaving. And in the strange passage of bodies in time so few people seem to meet. Perhaps now that it is October, we can once again hear the goblin footfall crossing the earth—and perhaps a shudder runs down our spines. Homecoming, home leaving, homesick, and sick of home, pretense, love, joy, fear of the past, fear of the future; all of these are within us, all of these things are us. And as we come back home to this moment of richness and of foreboding, we are reminded of those relationships which have been meaningful and full and we are reminded of those relationships attempted which have failed. We want and we do not want to come, yet we are here. Hoping that life is also made up of meetings which lead to joy and the richness of the season may portend the richness of our own lives.

As Thomas Wolfe reflected on the difficulties of returning, he offers what amounts to a prayer. Continuing, then, from where I was reading before, we hear him say:

> Come to us, Father, in the watches of the night. Come to us as you always came, bringing to us the invincible sustenance of your strength, the limitless treasure of your bounty, the tremendous structure of your life that will shape all lost and broken things on earth again into a golden pattern of exultancy and joy.
>
> Come to us, Father, while the winds howl in the darkness, for October has come again bringing with it huge prophecies of death and life and the great cargo of the men who will return. For we are ruined, lost and broken if you do not come. And our lives, like rotten chips, are whirled about us onward in the darkness to the sea. (*Of Time and the River*).

"Come to us, Father." Is it possible for us still to speak these words? Can we still call upon a father? Is this a name for God? Homecoming. Can we still hope for home, and where is it, if we hope for it? Perhaps home is not a place at all but rather a Presence. Home is not only where we come from or where we are going, it's the present and a Presence. We are at home when we are in fellowship. We are home when we are with Another who makes everyplace and everytime our place and our time.

In Samuel Beckett's *End-Game*, there is a sad conversation between two men, Hamm and Clov, who are talking about living with one another; Hamm is making an offer to Clov to stay with him and says:

> HAMM: I'll give you one biscuit a day, One and a half, Why do you
> stay with me?
> CLOV: Why do you keep me?
> HAMM: There's no one else.
> CLOV: There's nowhere else.

This is tragic, but the other side of tragedy is the possibility of joy and to us who feel, at least at some moments, that there is no one else and no place else there comes a word which we need to hear. In the midst of our struggle to find our way in the constant change of life, in the midst of our efforts to find others, in our search for love, in our coming and in our going there is one word which perhaps we can still speak. Perhaps we can still say, "Father."

With a kind of haunting anxiety Thomas Wolfe said, "If you do not come, Father, our lives are like rotten chips whirled about us." But this anxiety we do not need to share. For before we can speak or call, God has already spoken. God has already come. He has not waited for us. Into a frost-laden world he came, and silhouetted among the trees of our October bareness there stands a cross, and riveted upon that cross is an exposed man who feels the vast swoopings through the earth, the chill winds of human antagonism and the senseless inability to love and to share life. He is in the midst of change and with us. We are no longer alone, no longer in our solitary confinement, because the cross has been buried in our earth and that exposed man has lived in the midst of our exposed situation. He has broken into time's claim upon us and calls us into relationship with Him.

"Come to us, Father?" God has not awaited our call. He has already come! Not to destroy October, not to deny the reality of its change, but He has come to stand in its midst, to embrace its transition. God has come and His presence is the promise of our place, and coming home, we can once again say to Him, "Father," and He receives us.

In the name of the Father, the Son, and the Holy Spirit. Amen.

Albert C. Outler, longtime professor of theology at Perkins School of Theology, Southern Methodist University, began his academic career at Duke, as he notes in the beginning of this sermon. He was one of the century's finest interpreters of the theology of John Wesley and was a great intellectual leader among Methodists. In this Founders' Sunday sermon, while he refers briefly to scripture, Outler mainly uses the lessons of history as his source—his personal history at Duke and the rather short history of Duke—for his reflection upon our duties as contemporary beneficiaries of the vision and sacrifice of those who have preceded us.

And So What Have You Done for Me Lately?

A Founders' Day Sermon
December 10, 1967

ALBERT C. OUTLER

Matthew 7:7–28 There was no resisting Chaplain Wilkinson's invitation to return to Duke for this Founders' Day celebration, not merely because of the great honor of such an assignment, but much more because of the vivid, warm memories I have of the best seven years of my life invested in this place, away back when. I first came to Duke in '38, the year of the Centennial, and I still remember being bemused by the paradox of a school so obviously new having a hundred years of history behind it. I have a host of other memories, too—of President Few (so gentle and modest that it was never clear just how he brought it all off!), of Shelton Smith and Harvie Branscomb (who continued my theological education after the Yale faculty had cried quits!), of an unbeaten, untied football season, of the mustering service in this chapel on the day after Pearl Harbor, twenty-six years ago. I have, however, come to the age when reminiscing gets out of hand all too easily and I must forgo its selfish pleasures. It is enough if you can realize that all those cherished experiences help me to feel very much at home on this campus, a living relic of a part of that past we are gathered to commemorate.

Over the years, whenever I have thought of the men and women who are enrolled as the "Founders" of this university, there are two Scripture passages that come readily to mind, and say essentially the same thing. One is Jesus' parable about the so-called talents (in Matthew 25:14–30)—about two men who made the most of what they were given and one who goofed off and then excused himself with a brave show of self-righteousness. The other passage is Luke 12:48—this one not a parable but an aphorism: "To whom much is given, from him much shall be required."

Here is an obviously square, uptight moral maxim: God's rightful expectation of us that we put our human freedom to constructive use. Moreover, this maxim comes from the mouth of Jesus; He evidently took it seriously. The notion that a man's life may be measured by his response to his opportunities sounds dreadfully moralistic, but who will deny that Jesus understood it as integral to a fully human style of life? And who will further deny that it was one of the ordering principles of those forebears whom we rejoice to honor here today?

And yet it strikes a discord in our modern ears—and this is itself a clue to the climate of our age. These are the days of the NOW generation (there is a soft drink that makes a pitch about its "NOW taste" and a new university that advertises itself as "the NOW university"). The past goes unremembered and the future is dreaded. Change is the only constant in the relentless flux of continuing social revolution. Mutations come so fast we cannot assimilate them and so slowly that the discontented go unsatisfied. Ours is an epoch that mingles idealism and outrage, when disintegrating value systems pose dangers as dire as the specter of disintegrating atoms.

All this has been given trenchant commentary by Eric Hoffer, our wonderful modern Montaigne. It is his thesis, in *The Temper of Our Times*, that "the presence of a global population of juveniles" (his irreverent term for *young folks*) "spells trouble for everybody. No country is a good country for its juveniles, . . . even in normal times every society is in the grip of a crisis when a new generation passes from boyhood to manhood" (93). But ours are not normal times. Our "social chemistry has gone awry; no matter what ingredients are placed in the retort, the end-product is more often than not an explosive . . . The chief trait which characterizes the temper of our time is impatience. Tomorrow has become a dirty word. The future is now, and hope has turned into desire. The adolescent cannot see why he should wait to become a man before he has a say in the ordering of domestic and foreign affairs." He is "panting to . . . act as a pathfinder in the van of mankind . . . Rudeness has become a substitute for power, for faith and for achievement" (99–100).

One of the obvious side effects of such a mood is that in it, the past is readily dismissed, by common consent, as more of an incubus than a blessing. "The Past is Prologue"—so runs the motto on the portal of our National Archives (with a nod to Shakespeare's *Tempest*)—but most of my young friends feel strongly that *their* prologue was a flawed affair, which they would rather shed than celebrate. God knows, they say, the world we had foisted on us is in a pluperfect mess (or stronger words to the same effect). It is so grimly unsatisfactory that many are trying to opt out of it. Others turn to destructive protest, fiercely self-righteous. There are those who really do believe that they can "grasp the sorry scheme of things entire, shatter it to bits and then remold it—nearer to their hearts' desire." And so they turn away from their past in conscientious ingratitude. They know that they are heirs of a legacy once called great but they scorn to be beholden to it. They are like the wheeler-dealer in the old wheeze, who came to foreclose on an old family friend. The victim's plea for mercy was a recital of what he had done for his tormentor in times past: given him his first job, introduced him to his wife, bailed him out of bankruptcy, etc., etc. At the end, the entrepreneur brushed it all aside with a scornful question: "And so, what have you done for me *lately?*"

What, then, can Founders' Day mean in such a climate, when it is also true what our Founders did for us is so plainly insufficient that we have to keep on building and rebuilding and developing and planning—when, for example, the financial goal of your Fifth Decade Program is nearly thrice the sum of your original endowment? What word is there from this particular past that remains worth hearing in the present, and for the future? This much at least, in the spirit of our parable: that *we* are as responsible for making the utmost of *our* unmerited gifts as *they* did with *theirs.* This may sound trite but to accept and affirm it is the purest honor in our power to offer to their memory today.

I am as willing as Antony was to bury the past and not to praise it—but not without a word of witness about its achievements and their present import. As a member emeritus of more successive "NOW generations" than I care to remember, I claim the right to call attention to those convictions and passions that fueled and guided our forefathers—not merely in their praise, but in solemn testimony that *their* best convictions and passions are still urgently relevant for *us,* here and now. The Founders that I knew, or knew about, didn't spend a great deal of time looking back either—only enough to gain and keep perspective—but what they would ask of us is that we review the past for its insights, that we plot the future with hopeful plans for real action.

In such a testimony, my first point is that history has a striking way of confounding contemporary judgments as to who the real swingers and the real squares are. Frederick Morton has spoken recently of the current *nouveau avant,* the frenzied and failing struggle of "moderns" to keep pace with modernity, to stay "in," to make the changing scene. Naturally enough, it's more than flesh and blood can manage—hence the desperate recourse to drugs and herd behavior in lieu of self-reliance. And then there was the pathetic story in the *Times* two weeks ago of how ex-professor Timothy Leary has now become the ex-guru of the League for Spiritual Discovery. I've no quarrel with the league's message that "you are free to do your own thing," but it is always fair to ask if a given "thing" is a *real doing* or a disastrous self-deception. And it comes to mind that the now bedraggled motto "Tune in, turn on, drop out" is a fairly close paraphrase of the alibi of the unprofitable servant in our parable: "I took your money, wrapped it in a sock and left it be while I went about my tripping — see, here it is!"

For all their faults and shortcomings, our Founders saw life with clearer eyes than this. They were, for the most part, compulsive types who were enchanted by goals and dreams that seemed unreal to most of their contemporaries. They sometimes drove themselves and others to tasks that we might wish had been conceived in other terms. They were nonconformists but in a different style than nowadays — when nonconformity has to run in packs and wear uniforms in order to sustain itself.

It is not that they were heroes or saints — or that they ever saw the fullness of their dreams come true. The men who led the way from the Union Institute to Trinity College to Duke University were constantly engaged in an unequal struggle between need and resources, with inadequate support, in a climate where the correlation of *eruditio et religio* was suspect by the pious — as indeed it still is, though now for quite opposite reasons, by the non-pious! When I came to Duke in '38, it could still be said that the buildings were more imposing than the academic community that dwelt therein. And yet it was that first century, and most especially its last two decades, that created the exciting and demanding future that lies before *you* now. You are heirs not only of a tradition of great philanthropy but of a lifestyle, a gospel of opportunity and duty that is still more relevant and valid than most of its alternatives.

Its gist was this: that the enduring significance of a man's life lies in what he does with his abundance, whatever that is. It is, I take it, a truism that human culture in all its higher reaches is the product of the use or abuse of surplus accumulations of various sorts in a given population — food, wealth, invention, creative intelligence, etc. When human energy is absorbed in the prime necessities of self-maintenance, only a meager margin is left for being really and fully human. On the other hand, when there is ample food and shelter and fun and games, but no passion to surpass, society stagnates and calcifies. It is with *surpluses* and the concern for their *creative* use that the agony of culture begins — and it *is* an agony for, with the same sort of surplus, the "haves" can oppress the "have-nots" and the wise and good can create those values that mark off civilization from savagery. What a man does with what he does not really need for mere survival defines his true humanity and writes his real epitaph.

In amassing and managing one of the great American fortunes, the Dukes and their associates were conspicuous for both their energy and enterprise and yet also for their human concern and their *effective* generosity. There are not many comparable cases to match the results they achieved, relative to their means and potential, in American education and in their contributions to church and society. They were children of their age and their clay feet were badly exposed. But they were creative men: visionaries, architects, builders. They were disciplined men, desiring to be judged by results and not merely good intentions. They were men of character and code — self-accepted, self-administered, self-assessed. Their kind has been shrewdly analyzed by Leon Harris in his superb recent biography of a kindred soul in this same tribe — Godfrey Lowell Cabot: "He [Godfrey Cabot] was a hero in the Greek sense, but in the only sense in which we have heroes left: a man who performs over and above his duty by normal standards, who marches to his own drums and is willing to take risks in doing so; who is dedicated, in the literal sense of self-placement without stint; not driven to a position but self-given and whose life is ordered by such presently unfashionable words as *duty*, *probity*, *integrity*, and *character*" (xiii–xiv).

But surplus money, even in quantity and without strings, cannot build a university without yet another surplus fruitfully managed: *leisure time*. Too many of us have forgotten, or never knew, that the Greek original for our word scholar, *scholē*, means "leisure time" or, by extension, "a man with time to think and the disposition to do so." Your predecessors here — faculty and students — had far less leisure than they needed, or than would now be thought minimal for academic excellence. My first teaching load was twice what would be normal now. Moreover, our amassed capital from the leisure of other men — which, being interpreted, is the *library*! — was still comparatively meager, even in my time. The status of eggheads in the environing society of this region was only barely respectable — and their influence in practical affairs was negligible. And yet it was *these* men and women who rooted the scholarly tradition here, who cultivated the arts and sciences of critical inquiry and taught others to do so, who blazed a trail that has not yet been followed to its end.

And so the story goes — of men who wrought well with *their* abundances, and who have earned the right to ask us how well we are doing, or propose to do, with *ours*. It is just here that our salute to the Founders becomes an arresting challenge to our own self-examination and self-dedication. For there never was a generation so immersed in abundance as our own. There is, indeed, a sort of surfeit of it—as the flower children are trying to tell us in their garish ways. And as all the prophets prophesy, there will be more leisure and more gadgets and more affluence. There will be more people with more time and at least the technical means to manage larger surpluses more creatively than ever before since Eden.

And yet we already know, and the knowledge strikes panic in our hearts, that our equivalents of the achievements and contributions of our forebears will demand of us a discipline and dedication—of heart and mind and will—that we are loath to impose upon ourselves and that cannot be imposed on us by others. It is *closed* to us to replicate the feats and the failures of the Founders. It is, however, *open* to us to receive from them our heritage, gratefully to renew its imperatives of noblesse oblige in our own time and circumstances, to stretch out our vision of NOW to include our duty to the future, to make the most of change and not merely to endure its happenings. There is the challenge of poverty in an affluent society; there is the challenge of human equality and harmony in a morbidly race-conscious society; there is the challenge of license and violence in a free and ordered society. There is the anguished hope of peace in a war-torn world, haunted by the terrors of incineration and irradiation. But most of all, there is the challenge of being truly human ourselves—of finding the wisdom and the will to distinguish license from liberty, outrage from moral indignation, tantrums from significant witness and real results.

It will not do to plead the enormity of the issues and tasks before us. By any fair comparison, our forebears underwent as much as ever we must face. And if they bequeathed us a world in agony, let us beware lest we insure that the agony will never end—or else end in some final flash of meaningless destruction. They were men who hated to lose on their investments. *We* are their *chief* investments and they would happily forgo all our eulogies of them in exchange for evidence that we had caught something of their spirit and faith.

And thus we come at last to the heart of the matter. The vision of the good society is fatally blurred by men who suppose that it is no more than a human task, a human achievement. "The secular city" is finally unfit for human habitation without the reconciling forces of love and hope and faith. The parable of the talents makes sense only in the context of the Kingdom of God, the righteous rule of God in the hearts and lives of men. Humanity will never experience the fruition of its hopes and expectations apart from the acknowledged Lordship of Jesus Christ, the man who makes our manhood actual and real, through God's sovereign love incarnate in him.

It was no mere whim of Mr. Duke's that placed this chapel in the center of the campus, and it has been no accident that its influence in this community, both symbolic and actual, has made an enormous difference in the life of this university and the region — which can be measured merely by imagining how it would be here now if there had never been such a symbol of *religio* here to match the omnipresent tokens of *eruditio*.

Founders' Day is a day for remembrance, for reverence, for gratitude, for renewed perspective. It is also a day of resolution and dedication — "it is rather for us, the living . . ." and all that! This, then, is no mere ritual episode, no merely routine ceremonial. For, on our response to what is here remembered and portended, hangs the verity of our faith and the sincerity of our confessions that (as we shall hear again, in a moment in the Hallelujah Chorus) the Lord God omnipotent *does*, indeed, reign and *shall* reign, forever and forever.

Let us pray.

Almighty God, who has given us a goodly heritage beyond our deserving and has set us to tasks and goals beyond our powers of full achievement, forgive us our failures of nerve, hope, and vision, strengthen our hearts and wills to make the utmost of our futures — in faith and love — and so enable us honestly to honor the memory and the purposes of those we gratefully name as our Founders in this place. Let our heritage from the past inspire us, let the good in the present give us courage, let the challenge of the future beckon us, through the grace and love and leading of Jesus Christ our Lord and Savior. Amen.

How many sermons, once planned, are tossed away before Sunday due to the exigencies of that moment in time? Probably some of the best sermons are those that were preached on short notice, when the preacher took his or her cues not only from the scriptural text but also from the contemporary context. Thor Hall was a professor of preaching and theology at Duke when he preached this powerful, straightforward sermon in the aftermath of "another shocking week in the history of our time and this country." Hall, who was noted for his commitment to a solid theological basis of the sermon, forsakes the sermon that he had planned to preach in the Chapel and uses this occasion for an eloquent plea for nonviolence in a terribly violent land.

Thou Shalt Not Kill

June 9, 1968

THOR HALL

Matthew 5:17–24 This has been another shocking week in the history of our time and of this country. Within a period of two months two of the finest young men of this nation have been shot to death by assailants and opponents. Once more, the whole nation has been called to observe a day of mourning and a period of penitence. And we all do, on one level or another. Most of us are stunned still. We do not know what to say that makes sense in this situation. Some of us don't even know what to think — and even if we do, thoughts do not seem to make much difference anymore. We need to know, perhaps more desperately than anything else, what to do, or more basic yet what to be.

You will understand that the subject announced in the bulletin is not the subject for this sermon. It is not at all relevant today.

I had planned to preach on "Shaping Up the Church for Tomorrow." That would, I thought, have been a way to look at the many church assemblies held during this past week — Methodist, Baptist, Presbyterian — and compare their feeble attempts at affirming the church's commitment to the principle of unity, in the church, in society, and in the world, with the clear needs of the times on the one hand, and with the strong imperatives of the Christian gospel on the other. I thought I could say something significant about the future.

But in the meantime the present forced itself into focus, refusing to allow the leisure of long-term reflection and projection. Honestly, I am so shaken, saddened, and torn apart by the cumulative effect of the events of these last ten weeks that I am afraid I shall not be able to present a calm, seasoned, and polished sermon. But I do have something to say, something that forces itself on me. It is not my word, the kind of word I like to speak. I find it hard to give it voice, because it cuts like a two-edged sword, judging me as it does all of us.

It crystallizes itself into one short, terse phrase, a commandment we have all learned to be part of God's will for us, a truth we thought was obvious in the law of life itself. It says simply: "Thou shalt not kill."

There has been a great deal of talk in recent years about love of neighbor, civil rights, and personal freedom. As a matter of fact, most high ideals of thought and conduct have plenty of spokesmen today. Reference to Christian principles of love and justice, unity and equality, abound in the language of our time. General concepts of human liberties, racial integration, respect for law, equal opportunity, and open housing all have eloquent proponents. And that is good. In fact, it is very good.

But behind the glamour of the high idealism of our time there is an awesome sickness eating away at the very vitals of our life. Occasionally, it signals its presence in clear and unmistakable symptoms, as in the assassination of Martin Luther King, as in the killing of Robert F. Kennedy. But it is there, working its way to the very marrow of our existence, all along. It is a basic disrespect for life that issues in a propensity for killing, expressing itself all the way from the field of international military conflict to the nation's highways, to the streets of our cities, to the backyard games of neighborhood kids.

The weekly progress of the war in Vietnam is summarized in the chilling statistics of U.S. and enemy dead.

Motion pictures like *Bonnie and Clyde* are hailed and awarded for the realism and flair with which they describe the dynamics of killing and being killed.

In the daily drama of social or personal tension we are seldom thought to feel very strongly about things unless we are willing to give or take life to advance our cause.

Threats are spoken in the language of killing. Commitments are proclaimed with the voice of violence. Entertainment thrives on playmaking with murder. Even our jokes are penetrated with the disdain for life.

This last Thursday, of all times, on the cash register of a drive-in restaurant, there was a postcard saying: "We shoot every third salesman we see. The second one just left." Oh well, it's all so innocent and harmless, isn't it?

No it isn't, not any more. Not after the last two months.

For we are doing something to ourselves and to our culture which undercuts the value of all our idealism. We are fostering the hypocrisy which says that if all our principles are high our practice is irrelevant. We nurture the deceit that if we know the good it doesn't matter if we do evil. We feed the falsehood that those who have heard the gospel of a great society can forget the law of all previous covenants.

This is dreadfully wrong! It is wrong on whatever level of discourse we might operate.

It is true, of course, that violence is as American as apple pie. The country was settled as a result of threats against the lives of people in the old world. Its frontiers were pushed to the full expanse of this continent by means of the musket, the Colt, and the Remington. It gained its freedom by way of war. It guarded its unity by armed conflict. And in our time it polices the world by means of lethal power.

All that is history. It may explain who we are and how we got here. But it doesn't make it right to think that the power of law lies in the weapon that enforces it, or that one's right to property gives one the right to kill. And it doesn't point a way to a better and more civilized future.

A generation or more ago, Albert Schweitzer was struggling to coin a phrase that would serve to express the essence of a deeper and stronger ethic than that built on Nietzsche's "will to power." He had been searching for it for years. Then one day, on a trip upriver from Lambarene, it struck him like a flash: Reverence for life! That's what he was after!

In that phrase, Schweitzer expressed what to him was the fundamental fact of human awareness, namely "I am life that wants to live, in the midst of other life that wants to live." Says Schweitzer: "A thinking man feels compelled to approach all life with the same reverence he has for his own. Thus, all life becomes part of his own experience. From such a point of view, 'good' means to maintain life, to further life, to bring developing life to its highest value. 'Evil' means to destroy life, to hurt, life, to keep life from developing. This, then, is the rational, universal, and basic principle of ethics" ("Albert Schweitzer Speaks Out," *World Book Yearbook 1964*, 142).

If Schweitzer is right and reverence for life is the most foundational principle of human ethics, then our generation is judged to the core as immoral, sick, unthinking, and evil. Our disrespect for life and our propensity to killing make a mockery out of everything else, however lofty, that we profess to stand for.

Now, in case someone among us should still think that the fundamental law of God regarding the sanctity of life can be disregarded and set aside, in deference to the historical truths of our traditions or the high ideas we have for the future or in view of needs and expediencies of the present, let me remind you of a point or two in the Scripture reading of the morning.

It was from the Sermon on the Mount. Jesus was about to launch his re-interpretation of the old law, setting over against what had been taught in the past what was now to be the new shape of truth in the future.

Before he did that, however, he was eager to point out that he had not come to do away with the Law of Moses or the teachings of the prophets, but to give them real meaning: " 'Remember this,' he said, . . . 'whoever breaks even the smallest of the commandments, and teaches others to do the same, will be least in the Kingdom of heaven' " (Matthew 5:18–19).

That, I think, is a significant word for us today. We have been stressing that Christianity is summed up in the double commandment, "You shall love the Lord your God with all your heart, with all your mind, with all your soul, and with all your strength" and "You shall love your neighbor as yourself," but we have neglected to emphasize the actual content of the law of God to which this formula is the summary. And that law has within it the clear commandment "Thou shalt not kill." And it has others: "Thou shalt not commit adultery," "Thou shalt not steal," "Thou shalt not bear false witness against thy neighbor," and so on. Those who obey these, says Jesus, will be "great" in the Kingdom of heaven.

What Jesus seems to be saying is this: You have advanced toward the fulfillment of the commandment to love only in so far as you obey the fundamental commandments of God regarding life.

That, I think, is an important corrective for us.

But there is something more involved in our Scripture reading.

When Jesus went on to draw up his own teaching of the law, and by the way his first point had to do with the commandment against murder, he did something which forever after puts the actual deed of killing within its proper context. He said: "You have heard that men were told in the past, 'Do not murder; anyone who commits murder will be brought before the judge.' But now I tell you: whoever is angry with his brother will be brought before the judge; whoever calls his brother 'You good-for-nothing!' will be brought before the Council; and whoever calls his brother a worthless fool will be in danger of going to the fire of hell" (Matthew 5:21–22).

The point could not have been made more clearly. Most of us have tended to take the commandment "Thou shalt not kill" on face value, and we say, "Right. I am clear on that score. I have not murdered anyone. Hold that commandment up before those who do such things." But Jesus leaves us no such opening. Killing, to him, is a function of anger. Anger is the result of disrespect for another's life. And disrespect of another's life is the expression of selfishness and pride.

What Jesus makes so crystal clear is this: the commandment "Thou shalt now kill" does not only include the few among us who actually execute an act of murder. It includes us all. It reaches into the secret caverns of our minds, and aims its light at every dark dimension of our relationships, and it says, "You shall have reverence for life."

Numerous commentators and political leaders have reflected in recent weeks on the corporate guilt of the entire American community, in creating an atmosphere of hate and violence that gives nurture to sick and twisted individuals in the actual performance of shooting or burning or robbing or raping. Others react to a wholesale condemnation of our society on the basis of the dastardly acts of certain individuals or small groups of people.

We shall never resolve such controversies.

The president of the United States, expressing what appears to be a growing consensus in the country, has asked for stronger measures for controlling the flow of weapons and checking the spread of violence in the streets. Others feel that unless the hearts of men are changed and the conditions breeding hopelessness, rage, and riots are alleviated, increased government control and stronger police forces will not only be ineffective, they will even create greater explosions of violence.

I see no solution to that controversy either.

Even with the shock of these last few weeks and the self-scrutiny that has been initiated among us, every instinct tells me that we have not seen the end to violence. The world is not finished with killing. For the basis of our life together is still the "will to power," rather than "reverence for life." Even in such moments when that reverence occurs among us, it is still partial and selective — not reverence for life but for a certain kind of life, our kind.

I do not know what hope we can have for a new order in the world. The war in Vietnam is probably not the last war we shall know. And Robert Kennedy is not likely to be the last political martyr. It is an old truth that those who live by the sword will die by the sword. Equally hallowed by history is the fact that every Jerusalem kills its prophets and refuses the servant who will gather it into one.

But perhaps a bare minimum of hope can be placed with those among us who find ourselves moved to renounce power and pride, and to cleanse ourselves of anger and disrespect, and who grope for an elementary basis of a new order in our life, in reverence for life, in pursuit of a "good" which simply means, in Schweitzer's terms, "to maintain life, to further life, to bring developing life to its highest value." That movement must surely have been inspired by the Lord of life himself.

And that is perhaps all we can say today. Perhaps it is also enough to say, for those who believe.

As Robert Kennedy once said: "Some men see things as they are, and say, 'Why?' I dream things that never were and say, 'Why not?' "

Let us pray: Almighty God, Lord of life, whom to know is life eternal: breathe Thy life into our being, that we shall live, let live, and revere life in truth and word and deed. Through Christ, Thy son, we pray. Amen.

Browne Barr, then the minister of First Congregational Church, Berkeley, California, had a front-row seat for the campus turmoil of the late 1960s. Before coming to Berkeley, where he preached for seventeen years, he had been a professor of preaching at Yale. Among his homiletical gifts was an ability to lay the Christian faith alongside contemporary dilemmas. In this sermon Barr moves from the disciples asleep during Jesus' Passion to insights about our own tendency to sleep through life.

Now I Lay Me Down to Sleep

October 26, 1969

BROWNE BARR

Psalm 139 This text confronts us with a common human everyday crisis. It is a crisis which every one of us faces day in and day out. Perhaps it will sound inappropriate to speak of it in the same breath with Christ's agony, for it is the common crisis of *sleep*.

Of course, the center of this drama, the profoundly religious event, is the struggle of Jesus in the anguish of the decision to die. But the nature of that event and its significance may be opened up for us who are no spiritual giants if we move the focus of our attention from Jesus to the ordinary men in the shadows who were asked to stay wide awake but who fell asleep—not once but *three* times.

Twentieth-century Christians may take some comfort in supposing that had we been there we would not have slept. Sleep comes hard for many of us, especially serious-minded religious people. We are so *anxious* about the struggle in the world's Gethsemanes, Vietnam, Edgemont, and your Allen Building that we lie restlessly awake night after night. We would not have slept then, Lord—surely! Yet without the renewal which regular and natural sleep brings, how are we to face the issues of the day at all! To fall asleep is an act of profound trust. It is a gift of faith. It is a religious experience in which the whole self is surrendered, given over. It may well be argued that all the paraphernalia which we have devised and accumulated to help us sleep—Nembutal, warm milk, lightweight electrical blankets which do not bind the toes, clock radios which soothe us with music till dawn and turn off when their mothering is done—perhaps all our helps to sleep, if they become necessary accessories in daily life, are symbols of the poverty of our faith.

Now if you are troubled by insomnia, you may feel that this sermon is a direct personal attack. I cannot claim that it is not addressed to you, but it is not an attack. It is more a confession or consultation. Your hostility may be reduced to the point of staying awake *now* to listen further if you know that one night this week as I lay wide awake at 4:10 a.m., I asked myself: Now what in heaven's name is keeping me awake? O yes, it is that sermon for the Duke Chapel — that sermon about sleep.

This Gethsemane text suggests two sources of sleepiness. We will look at them in turn. The first is this: *We are half awake when we sleep because we are half asleep when we are awake.* We cannot sleep in bed at night in proper season because we sleep at our desk or in our pew out of season.

You will note that Jesus did not commend the disciples for sleeping. Quite to the contrary. He rebuked them because it was not the time or place for sleeping. He asked them to watch with him, to be alert, to be helpful. When he found them sleeping, he said, "Could you not watch one hour?" Could you not stay awake and attend fully to the business at hand? It was the proper time for wakefulness, not for sleep. Could you not pay attention for twenty minutes? Our sleeping problems begin, you see, not in the night but in the day, not when we go to bed, but when we get up; it begins when we go through the waking, vital, producing, living hours half asleep. The problem some of us will face of wakefulness tonight when we go to bed begins in the fact that we are half asleep now. So Erich Fromm suggests that "the paradoxical situation with a vast number of people today is that they are half asleep when awake, and half awake when asleep" (*The Art of Loving*, 128).

The remedy lies, he claims, in developing the art of living in what he calls "concentrated" fashion, to be concentrated in "everything" one does, in listening to music, in reading a book, in talking to a person, in seeing a view. The activity at this very moment must be the only one that matters, to which one is fully given. We know that when we are concentrating very hard, maneuvering through high-speed freeway traffic or trying to figure out directions for putting up a can opener, we do not get drowsy or fall asleep. That happens when we are not giving the matter at hand our full attention, are not fully awake, fully concentrating, fully alive.

In what circumstances then are we best enabled to concentrate? That comes, does it not, when we are engaged in something about which we have intense concern, commitment, interest — enjoyment in the most profound sense. How readily we find wakefulness, energy, for the activities we relish.

Dorothy Sayers was probably speaking for herself when in one of her mystery stories Harriet Vane says of writing prose, "When you get the thing dead right, and know it's dead right, there's no excitement like it. It's marvelous. It makes you feel like God on the Seventh Day" (*Gaudy Night*, 180). And we might add that the rest God found on the Seventh Day was the beautiful response to six days of concentrated activity, the scriptural symbol of the gift prepared for those who have been fully awake while it is day.

It is in large measure a sleeping-tablet generation which is under fire by wide-awake youth today. If you want to eradicate the drug cult don't begin with the kids and their marijuana, begin with their parents' bedside tables, handbags, and medicine closets or begin with the generation which has often made vocational and even avocational decisions on the basis of what will bring status or money rather than on the basis of what is eternally important or truly enjoyable. Even the service professions—especially medicine and the law (but not excepting the ministry and education or even the thirty-four San Francisco Bay Area dentists telephoned one Sunday at off hours before one could be found who was willing to see an afflicted visitor)—these professions have largely succumbed to this distortion of wakefulness; comfort, convenience, status, income, rank, power become the pursued goals. John W. Gardner reminds us, "How many times have we seen middle-aged people caught in a pattern of activities they don't care about at all—playing bridge with people they don't really like, going to cocktail parties that bore them, doing things because 'it's the thing to do.' Such people would be refreshed and renewed," he writes, "if they could wipe the slate clean and do *one little thing* that they really cared about deeply, one little thing that they could do with burning conviction" (*Renewal*, 17). The sickest insomnia-ridden corners of every campus from faculty houses to classrooms are occupied by anxious people doing things because it's the thing to do rather than because it's their "thing."

So as we search for the first clue to sleeplessness, we find it, oddly enough, in the disciples' sleepiness, in their absence of intense concentrated activity when it was much needed. Such concentrated giving of self, such involvement in the wonderful and worrisome world of the waking hours is the source of the true *tiredness which is the prelude to natural sleep*.

As we stir ourselves a bit and try to be concentrated awhile longer on the text at hand, our eyes still settle on those sleeping disciples. And there, still with the sleepers, is revealed a *second source of sleeplessness*: it is symbolized in their huddling, in their staying together, in their leaning on one another. They were destined to fitful guilty slumber because instead of detaching themselves from one another and really coming to grips with their own fear and anxiety, they settled for the limited comfort and support of one another's company. It was similar to that time they were out on the lake in the storm, all huddled together in their togetherness, group therapy in a sinking ship, and there was little hope for them until one of them forsook that comfort of community and launched out by himself, alone, toward the Lord. So here again Jesus suggests that hard requirement. He draws apart even from his friends and enters that aloneness where a man must come to grips with himself and what he really believes to be. The terror of wakefulness at night is the existential fright which comes when all the supports and disguises to self are gone: conversation is stopped, distracting food and drink are put away, the mystery story or the TV is closed — and the self and its ultimate values slowly approach the most reluctant self and call it out from hiding — self meeting self. Jasper's "limit situation" — the sinner's bench, the anxious seat — the creative crisis of personal knowledge and awareness of finiteness.

But we sleepless ones beat a fast retreat, back to the comfort of other people — actually or by proxy through the printed page or the flickering tube. Please talk to me until I fall asleep; or I'll read for a while to put myself to sleep or look at the late, late show, and then we sleep all the night long with the light on — unhappy symbol of our fear and our flight. "Not even the darkness shall cover us." So the facing of self is avoided and we become skillful fugitives from self. And fugitives we may well remain all our days if when detached from others and thus all alone we hold on to the edge of our composure by counting sheep. The promise of faith is quite otherwise that alone we will find we are not alone and discover far more than sheep to count:

> How precious also are thy thoughts unto me, O God!
> How great is the sum of them.
> If I should count them, they are more in number than the sand:
> When I awake, I am still with thee.
> *Sleep is an act of trust; it is a gift of faith.*

During student days many of us had a favorite professor. He was a true and consistent religious liberal, a man of courage and integrity and of deep social conviction. His name and energy were linked to important causes of the day. One time he cited as an example of spiritual immaturity a prayer many of us knew, "Now I lay me down to sleep, I pray the Lord my soul to keep." From that day on I rejected that prayer along with the other childish things which an adolescent learns must be put away when one becomes a man.

Recently I have been thinking about it again. What was it that this man found so distasteful? Surely the opening lines are appropriate for the mature man, the man of that natural tiredness which follows upon concentrated wakefulness: "Now I lay me down to sleep, I pray the Lord my soul to keep." If one believes in prayer at all, that line should not cause any trouble. I suspect, however, that it was the next two lines on which he gagged: "If I should die before I wake, I pray the Lord my soul to take."

Such dark and gloomy thoughts had no place in the nurseries of sunny optimism presided over by the religious liberals of the 1930s, where that insipid euphemism for death, "passed away," wormed its inauthentic witness into the Christian vocabulary. Certainly a child should be protected from thoughts of death and how could even an adult ever sleep if his last thought at night was of his own mortality, of the possibility that he might never rise again from that bed? How morbid can you be! So just about the time our professor and friend told us that it was dreadful to teach a little child to pray, "If I should die before I wake," just about that same time Camus was writing, "There is but one *freedom*, to put oneself right with death" (*Notebooks 1942–51*, trans. Justin O'Brien).

To come to grips with the fact of one's own death is to concentrate fully on existence, it is to be wide awake ultimately. It is also to be *separated*, detached from everyone. There we must at last go alone. But the Gethsemane scene endures because He, for love's sake, chose to die as the pioneer of the race, breaking the grip of darkness with His grace and truth. As sleep is the restorer of strength, so is death the agency and liberator of life. And the anxiety of the night, of our limit-situation, is eased and sleep is welcomed, the sleep of one night or the last sleep of all the nights. Thus it is that a child's prayer confidently embraces the darkness of Gethsemane because its foothold is in Resurrection's dawn:

> Now I lay me down to sleep
> I pray the Lord my soul to keep.
> If I should die before I wake,
> I pray the Lord my soul to take.

A Sunday congregation could have no better guide through a Christian classic like the story of the Prodigal Son than Eduard Schweizer, distinguished professor of New Testament at the University of Zurich. In this sermon Schweizer walks through this familiar story and finds unfamiliar treasure. Identifying us with the older brother who was "so very right," the preacher then turns the tables upon us and we experience anew not only a great story of Jesus but also the grace of God in Christ.

God's Helplessness—Our Help

April 12, 1970

EDUARD SCHWEIZER

Luke 15:25–32 "Lo, these many years I have served you, and I have never disobeyed your command; yet, you never gave me a kid . . . But when this son of yours came, who had devoured your living with harlots, you killed for him the fatted calf." Right he is, totally and absolutely right. We may count whatever way we want to, he is right. Twelve hours of labor every day, 300 times a year, are 3,600 as a minimum; and it might be some five years, since that day when the younger brother left the house of the father to throw away all his father's money for drinks and women—which makes about 20,000 hours of hard work. And on the other side of this account there is not even an occasional kid, let alone the festivities with calf steaks and old wine. Right he is, this elder one, perfectly right. As right as we are.

I know of a university hospital in which desperate students destroyed the whole card index of all the patients so that it became extremely difficult to treat these patients until all the cards had been renewed in a long and difficult process. It is clear that the doctors there became more than angry. Or there is a husband who insults his wife like a madman, because she is again expecting a child from him. And all the world just sees that effective and successful husband, and nobody knows about that quiet and inconspicuous wife. Is she not right, right without any doubt, when she complains of her husband and thinks that nobody could live with such a man? Or there is that youngster who had to start his military service early in the morning in one of our mountain towns. The evening before, his parents phone him and are told that he would come on his very old and rather decrepit motor bike. About midnight, he is tired of riding his bike, goes to a hotel, and thinks that he might go by rail early in the morning. His father, more than anxious, starts at 2 a.m., drives over two or three mountain passes in search of his son, and comes back next morning very much alarmed — to hear that his son had arrived by train an hour ago. But everybody admires the charm of that modern, racy young man, and nobody cares for the father when he flares up. At least, his son could have phoned, although it was, of course, nonsense from the beginning to try that night ride over Swiss mountain passes.

All of us, we are so totally right. As right as the elder brother here in our parable. There are younger brothers and husbands and sons and students with whom it is simply impossible to live. And so often, they are the ones that are admired by everybody, and nobody asks about those who have to put up with them day by day. And this is not only true in our individual lives, where it might still be more or less harmless. It is also true in the world of politics, and it seems to become more and more true. There are younger nations and races that are threatening our peace and our comfort, and so many things that they do are not commendable.

Where in this world of turmoil and injustice is God? Where is this God of whom the Christians say that he loves his world? There are patients and wives and fathers suffering because of the nonsense of some of the "younger brothers." And there are nations dying in blood because of rebelling younger nations. And sometimes they are really innocent. Where is God, this loving God?

"His father came out and entreated him." Here he is, this father. He is with his elder son in his outrage and accusations. He is with him, as he was, in his heart, day by day with his younger son when that one went to seek, entertaining prostitutes and feeding swine. No, the father is not in the banqueting hall in all luxury and comfort; the father is where his lost and outraged sons are. What does Jesus say? Did we hear correctly? He says that God is not in a golden heaven, in which all the problems are solved, far away from the turmoil and all the misery and wretchedness of the world. He says that God is there, where a man doubts and rebels against him and his fellow men.

What should move us most in this short story is the helplessness of this father. No, he is not simply the almighty. He is staying outside the gate, and he has nothing but his word, by which he tries to invite his son. Certainly, he could call two of his servants and command them to drag his son into the banqueting hall. But what would he gain? The heart of his son would not be there. Love and joy cannot be forced upon anybody. And because the father desires nothing but the love and the joy of his son, he can stake nothing but his word. And into this word he puts all his love, his courting, his being ready to do whatever he could do. But this is not all that is left for him. Also with the younger son, he did not call the police in order to get him home. Also with him, he has had nothing but his burning love which was waiting for him. He has had no means to force him to accept it. This is God's helplessness and powerlessness. Because God desires our heart, its love and its joy, He has to stay outside of the gate, far from the banqueting hall of heaven, and has to wait. He has no means to drag us home by force. He has but His word into which he puts all His love.

But His word? This Word became flesh to call us back to God's festival meal. And just then, its total helplessness became obvious. They cried, "Where is God?" and looked up to the sky and thought of some golden heaven and a throne with God upon it. They supposed that He should sit there and play policeman and step in with brutal force, when so many outrageous things happen on earth with husbands that oppress their wives, and children that drive their parents to despair, and directors that exploit their employees, and . . . and . . . and . . . But the word of God had long ago become flesh and was, in its total helplessness, hanging just above them on a cross and did not descend in a miraculous way, but did nothing but invite, even in its silence, and call and tell about the burning love of the father. This is the powerlessness of God, who is not content with less than our heart. One may call, invite, and even entice to love, but one can never force it on anybody. To be sure, we may tell John: "Listen, my boy, if you behave as you did last time and refuse the welcome kiss to aunty, you will learn it the hard way," and John will probably behave and dutifully kiss his aunt. Love, however, will not be in the kiss. This is God's helplessness, that He has decided to create a world, in order to share His bliss and joy with creatures that would love Him from their hearts, because it is only in the freedom of our hearts that we are able to love and to praise and to find real joy.

And yet, this seemingly so helpless Word of God, even nailed on a cross and, as everybody thought, reduced to a deadly and definite silence, is still speaking and goes on speaking. It is something like the balance in a clock, which keeps the world on its move. As it had spoken in the prophets, it speaks in Jesus, for centuries and centuries. It reaches us today, all of us, who might be so dreadfully right in our complaints. It says: "Son, you are always with me, and all that is mine is yours." Indeed, we may not have realized it, but this is what God means. He has given us his creation to use it. We are free to use it or to misuse it. This is our freedom with all its dangers and all its almost inconceivable hope. And God tells us: "You should make merry and be glad." This is what God invites us to, this God who is helplessly nailed to a cross and yet is still inviting us to the banquet.

To make merry and be glad, do we ask, with such a husband and such children and such oppressors and such a world of suffering and terror? But God's decisive question is still waiting for us: Do we want to be with Him or not? The elder brother is standing a few inches from the father and yet, he is miles away from him in his heart. It is the elder one, the one who is so totally right, as right as we may be. And with all this rightness he is so far from the father. It is just his counting and arguing which separates him from the father. As long as he sees his 20,000 hours of hard work, he cannot see the love and the joy, he cannot enjoy the steaks or the wine, he cannot understand that there are men of weaker character or with the blood of an adventurer, perhaps born this way, perhaps consciously or unconsciously brought up in this way by an older generation; in short, he cannot understand that there is a question which is even more important than that about the hours of his hard work, namely that about his openness to love.

The parable ends with this elder son. Jesus leaves us alone with him. This means that he leaves us with that question which threatens us at the end of His story. It is the question whether we are really with the father. We might be as close to Him as the elder son, perhaps just a few steps from the altar of our church, and yet miles from His heart. There might be others, seemingly far away, perhaps in a banqueting hall or a pub at the time of the church service, and yet close to His heart. It is the question whether we are able to let ourselves be loved and to learn to become happy from all our heart, because we are learning to love. This will be impossible as long as we are still standing on our rights, whether in our Christian righteousness or in our atheism. The people who stood under the cross, have, perhaps, been more right than we. Doubtless there were Jews who did not care for the laws of God and who behaved in a shocking way. And there were pious ones, who donated 10 percent of their incomes to God every week, like, for instance, the Pharisees. But just by being so right, they could no longer understand Jesus who ate and drank with tax collectors and sinners. And in their total righteousness, they crucified him.

But where a heart opens itself for this invitation of the Word of God, things begin to happen. I remember a young couple sitting in my study. We just started talking about the marriage ceremony and I quoted the beginning of our liturgy: "You, John Miller, desire Mary Smith as your wife and . . ." At that moment I was interrupted by the young man who said: "But this is just what I do not desire, I just have to marry her, because she is expecting a baby from me." This was the beginning of a very long talk together, in which I realized how much his wife had understood of the invitation of God to love of which we have spoken. I saw her for years in a very difficult matrimony, in which she certainly would have been right a hundred times over against her husband, but remained quiet and loving and bearing husband and children. And I remember the notice in the newspapers about the president of Zambia, Africa, a devoted Christian, who sent all his ministers into the small villages, which are still living in the stone age, for living there and experiencing every day what life means for most of the citizens of his country, instead of living in the capital, which is almost like any North American or European city. Thus, the helpless, powerless God wanders through the world and becomes a power which makes families and nations new and good.

Might it not be the meaning of all life on earth, even of all suffering in it, that we might learn to love? To love God, out of a free heart, and by learning this, to learn also to love our younger or elder brothers who might not be so perfect as we are ourselves, perhaps even by far not? Might it not be the meaning of all life, even of all suffering, that in it, we might learn to accept this invitation of the father and to find in it the real, eternal happiness?

Father, you have talked to us, and we have tried to listen to you. We have felt a bit of your burning love. And yet, we are still uncertain whether we have heard adequately. We know ourselves. We like so much to be right, and we dislike so much to be helpless and powerless. And tomorrow, there will be all those who make our lives so difficult. We do not know whether we shall be able to remain close to you in your helplessness and love, close to the cross to which we nailed your incarnate love, lest we should listen to it. Therefore we pray. Sometimes, there is so much storm and turmoil in us, and sometimes, we are too much at rest, so that nothing can move us. Whatever it may be, we pray: come out of the banqueting hall to join us, and let your word become the unrest of our life, until we learn to accept your invitation and to let your love overcome us. Here we are sitting in your presence with all the ups and downs of our hearts and with all the misery of the world. We have nothing but you. Therefore, we are waiting for you. Break into our coming week and into our whole world with all its problems and sufferings, and let your love become contagious so that it affects us and through us, the world.

There was a sort of tough, Yankee straightforwardness in the preaching of Ed-mund Steimle. He was a Lutheran in theology and in style, firm believer in the finitude of humanity and in the triumphant grace of God. While a professor of preaching at Union Theological Seminary in New York City, Steimle came down to Duke to preach this Lenten sermon in which he tells those in the congregation who doubt and question that they may be in a better position to profit from the season of Lent than those of us who manage to be unperturbed by the silence and absence of the God of the hidden face.

Address Not Known

March 7, 1971

EDMUND A. STEIMLE

Psalm 13 and Matthew 25: 1–13   In W. H. Auden's "Victor, A Ballad," Victor is betrayed by his wife. So . . .

> Victor walked out into the High Street
> He walked to the edge of the town;
> He came to the allotments and the rubbish heap
> And his tears came tumbling down.
> Victor looked up at the sunset
> As he stood there all alone;
> Cried: "Are you in Heaven, Father?"
> But the sky said "Address not known."

I suspect this experience is not an unfamiliar one to any one of us here. It may be brought on with a personal crisis, as with Victor, or perhaps by a kind of endless national crisis when the statements of our policy in Vietnam seem to yield no end to the frustration and the agony of war; or maybe simply as a result of the wearing down by the years when all this talk of a good and loving father in heaven seems absurd, when there seems to be no "ground of existence anywhere" so far as we can see . . . when life seems quite literally to be no more than a "tale told by an idiot." And to our attempts to "find" God somewhere, to listen to his voice, to get some assurance that there really is a "Father" up in the sky somewhere or in the depths of our being, or at work in the world as the saying goes these days, the answer is the same: "Address not known."

Some, of course, will say that we are simply growing up—outgrowing the superstition of years past—and that all talk of "God" is foolish talk. Some theologians have talked of God being "dead." Some scientists throw up their hands at any kind of God-talk; he's obviously not to be found in measurable, verifiable terms anywhere. We now are living in a secular world and have to get along by ourselves as men, without this God-crutch, this pie-in-the-sky-bye-and-bye, this residue of another day when men filled the vast gaps in their knowledge of themselves, of nature, of history with talk about God.

But what is so often forgotten in all this is that way back, up in that never-never land of the Bible—when it seems that God was apparently so obviously present, forever coming to men in dreams and visions, His voice so clear and unmistakable in the mouths of patriarchs and prophets and, of course, in the man, Jesus—what is so often forgotten in all this is that the overriding and normal experience of God in those days was not of God present, but of God absent! The Psalms, for example, those soaring outpourings of faith are full of it: "Will the Lord spurn forever and never again be favorable? Has His steadfast love forever ceased? Are His promises at an end for all time? How long, O Lord? How long wilt Thou hide [Thy] face from me?" Over and over again, the theme is God not momentarily absent, like the sun disappearing for a moment behind a cloud, but a *prolonged* absence. To be sure, there were visions and voices and men who spoke of God as the living God; but these were the *occasional*, the momentary experiences. The ordinary day-by-day, year-by-year experiences were of God absent: "How long, O Lord, wilt Thou forget me, forever?"

Not only in the Old Testament, that record of centuries, is God occasionally experienced as present but normally absent; in the New Testament, too, the same experience is reflected. And surprisingly enough, we find it in that familiar parable of the wise and foolish bridesmaids, read just a few moments ago, which on the surface seems to point to the necessity of being forever on the *qui vive* because God might arrive at any moment and we might not be ready. It seems to be a story about God's coming. And the last line, "Watch therefore for you know neither the day nor the hour," simply misses the point! Scholars agree that this line was added by some ancient editor to the original story. And this line throws us off the track. All the bridesmaids fell asleep, the wise as well as the foolish. And there apparently was nothing wrong in that. It was a long wait. And *that* is precisely the point. It *was* a long wait. The bridegroom was delayed. And the foolish bridesmaids were unprepared for *that*—for the delay, for the absence. It was originally a word to the hyped-up followers of Jesus, and to a hyped-up early church, to cool it! Be ready for God's absence. It may be a long time before you will have unmistakable assurance that God is present. The wise bridesmaids were ready for the bridegroom when he arrived, precisely because they had taken along extra oil for their lamps in the event of a long wait.

So how then do we wait in the face of the delay, in the face of God's absence or His silence? Well, if we fail to take into account the necessity of waiting, of long waiting, chances are we'll start looking around for God, for the assurance of His presence, in the wrong places.

The late Samuel Miller quotes a delightful story of a former Munich comedian, Karl Valentin: "The curtain goes up and reveals darkness; and in this darkness is a solitary circle of light thrown by a street lamp. Valentin, with his long-drawn and deeply worried face, walks round and round this circle of light, desperately looking for something. 'What have you lost?' a policeman asks who has entered the scene. 'The key to my house.' Upon which the policeman joins him in his search; they find nothing; and after a while he inquires: 'Are you sure you lost it here?' 'No,' says Valentin, and pointing to a dark corner of the stage: 'Over there.' 'Then why on earth are you looking for it here?' 'There is no light over there,' says Valentin" (Samuel H. Miller, *The Dilemma of Modern Belief*, 58–59).

So, maybe—just maybe—we look for God in the wrong places, not in the dark places where we might have lost sight of Him, but in the "light." Chances are we'll look for God's presence in the Bible, in the creeds, in the liturgy, in worship, in the places where obviously there seems to be some "light"—in religion. But maybe He's to be found not in "religion" at all, but in the dark places: in the gaunt body of a mutilated child in Laos, or in a broken-down tenement in Harlem, in the grief of a widow of some Viet Cong, or in the deaths of American men daily in Vietnam, or maybe in the beard and long hair of a student rebel. As Samuel Miller says, "We never see Him directly; He is always mediated by the very things that seem to deny Him."

And of course that's why so many in the New Testament missed Him entirely and finally decided to rid the world of this obvious impostor. Imagine! God—born of peasant stock, walking around incognito as Mary's son! Spending his time with call girls and racketeers. That was obviously too dark a spot to look for a lost God. If He was around at all, He'd be in the Temple or in the synagogue or with the learned and pious pillars of the church—in the brightly religious spots on the landscape, not hiding off in the shadows. And maybe that's why He often seems to be "absent" or "silent" for us too.

Or it may be that we spend our time waiting by asking the wrong questions. And the most familiar and often agonizing question while we wait is "Why?" Why, if there is a good and loving God, the misery in ghettos and cancer wards? Why the overwhelming misery of hungry people in the third world? Why the recurring agony of war? Why the persistent and pernicious evil in the world—and in you and me? Why are we forever messing up our lives with too much alcohol, too much sex, too much drugs, or with too much fear—of others, of ourselves, of the future, of change? Why God, the persistent absence? It all comes to a burning point in that cry on the cross: Why, God, why have you forsaken me—why are You silent?

But God dispenses no information. No daily press release to let us in on what is going on at the heavenly White House. No voices in the ear, no visions. Even on the cross, no answer—no "angels came and ministered unto Him as in the wilderness." As someone has written, "The Cross was God's greatest silence . . . Then the demons were unleashed and the most dreadful passions since the fall of Adam were given free rein. And God had nothing to say. There was simply the cry of the Dying asking of the silence, why? . . . God was silent even when dumb nature began to speak in eloquent gesture and the sun withdrew its light. The stars cried out, and God was silent" (Helmut Thielicke, *The Silence of God*, 14).

Apparently God gives out no information when we demand to know why. And yet in answer to other questions, that dark spot in history, that unlikeliest of unlikely places for God to be hiding—that dying man—has told us worlds about the mystery of God.

But there's another reason why God seems to be absent, why He doesn't seem to be around, and it may be the deepest reason of them all, because in the depths of our beings we really couldn't stand it if He were. You know— to be known, all through, not only in the depths but in the trivial and superficial—to have the evasions and hypocrisies in every last one of us, laid bare for Him and for all the world to see.

I'm sure there's a god we wouldn't mind having around, the god who is our best instincts writ large, a kind of magnified Me in my best moments. But that isn't the God Jesus is talking about certainly. This is the God who slams the door in the face of those not prepared to wait, with the terrible words "I do not know you." It's the God who demands everything as well as gives everything; the kind of God who demands the crucifixion of His only obedient One. Job had his moments when he hated this God, the God who will never leave us alone. After all, who wants a companion like that, from whom we can never be separated, who haunts us from morning till night and on through the long night He watches, like the hound of heaven that He is? Who in the fury of His love terrifies as well as heals? Small wonder we find *that* God absent, for many's the time we *want* Him absent.

But supposing, now, we do desire this "presence," this healing fire, then how shall we prepare ourselves for the delay, for the times of His absence? Well, first of all we have to disabuse ourselves of any notions that the experience of the absence is unusual; rid ourselves of all those sentimental notions of wanting to get back to a time when God was apparently present and His presence was as plain as the nose on your face. "If only I could have been with Him then!"

As someone once said, "It's very hard to make out what God is doing, anywhere, at any time. Where would you have liked to live, and when, just to be sure?" (Paul Scherer, *The Word God Sent*, 168.) In Pilate's shoes, for example? With Jesus in the wilderness? With Paul in prison, in shipwreck, stoned and beaten with lashes? With Peter in the courtyard taunted by a girl? Or with Luther splitting the church into bits? My God, we can't even stand a little tension and disagreement in a typical church—It's not Christian! There was no time when God's presence was as plain as the nose on your face. He delays. He refuses to answer the question, Why? And when you come right down to it isn't this what faith is all about? And our freedom as His creatures? If He were forever whispering in our ear, tapping us on the shoulder, tripping us up just to let us know He's around, He wouldn't be the Father of Abraham, Isaac, and Jacob—the Father of our Lord Jesus Christ.

So there will be the willingness not to "have" Him—in our ears or vest pockets, or in Bible creed or liturgy, or in some specific social action—or to long nostalgically for a never-never time when others "had" Him in a way we don't. God has never been had. There have been only three times when men and women very much like ourselves struggled with His absence as well as with His presence, and the record of that struggle you will find in Bible, creed, and liturgy. An evidence of that struggle occasionally crops up, as in the march on Selma or in a quarter of a million marching on Washington for peace.

But beyond that, it may be that God speaks to us most clearly and is closest to us simply in the awareness of His absence. Paul Scherer finds the answer to Paul's prayer about the thorn in his flesh to which God was silent at first. Do you remember how he prayed to God three times that it be removed and all he got was silence for an answer until the words came, "My grace is sufficient for you"? (*The Word God Sent*, 249–50). It is suggested that the answer came in silence rather than in some mysterious voice in his ear. For isn't it so? The only possible time we can know His "grace" is "sufficient" is precisely when He's not at our beck and call.

Of course, that is not all that we have to say. To be sure, we ought to be on the *qui vive* lest God's presence, like any thief in the night, catch us unawares. But we will miss any coming, any visitation, any assurance of presence, if we are not first prepared for the delay, for His absence, for silence. The foolish ones in the parable were ready for a "coming," for a "presence," but not for a delay and for those foolish ones there was no coming at all, no visitation. The door was shut. "I do not know you."

I suppose it all adds up to whether in the face of the question "Are you in heaven, Father?" we can take the reply "Address not known" and hang in there and wait. And maybe that is what this season of Lent is all about. At any rate, if you who are here this morning are here because you are more disturbed by a delay, by absence, by silence, then you are in better shape religiously than those who are not. At least, so this parable reads.

Let us pray: O God, our Father, keep us faithful precisely when we most need to be kept faithful, when your face is veiled, when there is no voice, when your presence is most deeply felt in absence. Through Christ our Lord. Amen.

When Howard C. Wilkinson, chaplain at Duke and director of religious ac-
tivities during the tumultuous 1960s and early 1970s, enlisted a student, C. G.
Newsome, football player and graduating senior, for a "dialogue sermon," did
he know that they would give us a lasting example of experimental preaching?
It was a time when old forms of communication and piety were under attack.
Hence, some preachers like Wilkinson attempted new approaches to the sermon.
An older, established preacher in planned "dialogue" with a younger person was
a favorite medium. "What Is Religion All about, Anyway?," the youthful inter-
locutor asks. Thus begins a sermon on a traditional theme that was delivered in
a most nontraditional manner.

What Is Religion All about, Anyway?

A Dialogue Sermon

Opening Sunday
September 5, 1971

CLARENCE G. NEWSOME AND HOWARD C. WILKINSON

James 1:27, Joshua 4:15–24, and Matthew 11:2–5

WILKINSON: You good people are about to hear a dialogue sermon, in case
you are wondering what two of us are doing standing up here in front, at
the moment the program calls for a sermon.

NEWSOME: Some of you probably wondered, when you saw the two of us
come out, whether that meant the sermon was going to be twice as long
as usual, but we assure you that won't be the case.

W: Actually, though, C.G., ALL sermons are dialogue sermons, and the chief
difference between this one and the others is that in this dialogue BOTH
sides of the dialogue will be heard.

N: What do you mean by that, Chaplain?

W: I mean that almost always, when one person gets up to preach a sermon
by himself there is a silent partner who is "dialoguing" with him, and that
silent partner is the man in the pew. The preacher opens his mouth and
says, "All of you folks out there in the congregation are sinners." The man
in the pew doesn't open his mouth but he's silently thinking, "How about
the man in the pulpit? Is he a sinner, too?"

N: That's probably true, and I think it also is true that even though you and I are going to be standing up here engaging in a dialogue between ourselves, the freshmen sitting there in the pews are going to be second-guessing *both* of us.

W: Right you are! And speaking of the freshmen, that's how we got ourselves into this topic we're examining today. Earlier in the summer I sent out a letter to all the incoming freshmen, asking them to return a card to me, on which they were to indicate their religious preference — or lack of it — and then I passed along this information to the various denominational chaplains. Well, at the bottom of the cards was room for a question or a comment. Quite a few wrote questions which added up to the big question which we're facing in this dialogue: "What is religion all about, anyway?"

N: Chaplain, you frighten me when you say that. Do you mean to imply that you and I have the responsibility, in this sermon, to answer that big question?

W: Now look who's scaring whom! When you phrased it the way you did you put a panic into me! So to comfort both of us, and to avoid misleading our friends in the congregation, let's agree that we're going to "chicken out" on any pretense to give a full and sufficient answer to the question of what religion is all about, and simply attempt to explore the question, perhaps hitting at some directions in which all of us can move as we find our own answers.

N: Yes, I think that's a more realistic posture to take. However, I do think it is possible for us, even in a twenty-five-minute sermon, to identify some of the false notions with which some people have regarded this question.

W: What do you mean, C.G.?

N: I mean that a great many intelligent people seem to have some pretty unintelligent ideas of what religion is all about, and even if we can't say today all of the things religion means, we can begin by bulldozing some of the false notions.

W: Like what, for instance?

N: Like the idea that religion is getting God to see to it that we beat Florida in football this Saturday; or that we pray to God to help us napalm the women and children in Vietnam; or the idea that God wants black folks to be subservient to the whites; or the idea that religion consists entirely of just going to church; or the thought that a person is religious in proportion to how many verses of the Bible he has memorized; or the belief that a person is religious if he claims to believe everything in the Apostle's Creed and he's NOT religious if he questions any part of it; or—

w: Hey, wait a minute! You're going too fast for me! Before you add anything else to your catalogue of what you call unintelligent ideas, how about my asking you a question about each one of those you've mentioned?

n: OK.

w: Let's start with the first one, the one about getting God on our side in Saturday's game at Tampa. Are you implying that religion has nothing to do with winning football games?

n: Before I tackle that question, let me make it perfectly clear that I am a football player, that I very much prefer winning over losing, and that when I'm in a game I do everything I know to do that will help my team to win. Have I made that much clear?

w: You have!—both by your rhetoric just now and by your performance on the field! But what were you going to add to that?

n: I was going to add that God is intelligent enough to know that the members of the Florida team have a keen desire to win also, and God loves them as much as He loves me. Therefore I'm not going to kid myself into thinking that I can coax God into giving us an unfair advantage over Florida next Saturday, and by the same token I'm not afraid that some prayerful player on their team is going to trick God into giving them an unfair advantage over us.

w: I'm glad to hear you put the matter in those terms, but you still haven't fully answered my question about whether religion has NOTHING to do with winning football games.

n: OK—Well, the only other thing I'll say about that is, in my opinion if a person is truly religious it tends to make him do a better job of every worthwhile thing he sets himself to do. It makes him more unselfish, more inwardly disciplined, more responsible in his attitude toward his fellow man, and things like that. So in that sense religion makes a player a BETTER player than he might otherwise be.

w: All right, then: let me ask what you mean about bulldozing the idea that religion is a way to get God to help us napalm the poor people of Vietnam?

n: The unfortunate conclusion we come to from reading history books is that ever since the time of Christ, so-called Christian nations have tried to claim Christ's blessings on their wars against other nations, and again and again we have seen two nominally Christian nations fighting each other, both praying to the same God to help them slaughter each other! How stupid do we think God is?

w: I say "Amen" to that! I'm not even going to ask you a question about the third false notion you listed. That was the one which held sway too long in America, to the effect that religion endorsed the practice of black people always being the servants of white people, whether under a system of political slavery or under a system of economic slavery. I recall the short poem by Countee Cullen, "Epitaph: A Lady I Know":

She thinks that even up in heaven
Her class lies late and snores,
While poor black cherubs rise at seven
To do celestial chores.

Any such concept as this should be labeled for what it is: pure blasphemy!

I do want to raise a question about your comments on church attendance and memorizing portions of the Bible. Am I right in guessing that these activities are important so long as we don't treat them as the MAJOR thrust of religion?

N: I could perhaps agree with that way of stating it, except that I think we ought to point out that some pastors, some parents, and some church officers have emphasized church attendance to such an extent and in such a way that without actually saying so, they have created the impression that church attendance is what religion consists of.

W: OK, I get your point, C.G., and I assume you feel approximately the same way about memorizing portions of Scripture and about reciting the Apostle's Creed. Several years ago I heard Dr. Carl Michaelson give a modern parable about the Bible, while preaching a sermon in this Chapel. He said, "Let's imagine that a group of Duke students want to go to Raleigh. They ask about the way to get there and are told to go west of the campus, get on the 15-501 bypass, and then follow the signs. A fellow student decides later that he wants to join the group in Raleigh, so he jumps in his car, goes to the 15-501 bypass, follows the signs, and is speeding on his way to Raleigh when, on the east end of Durham, he spots the car of his friends parked at the side of the highway and sees the friends seated on the ground in a circle. So he stops his car, walks back to the group and asks what they are doing. They point to a highway sign in the middle of their circle, and the sign reads, 'To Raleigh,' and it has an arrow pointing toward Raleigh. The student who arrived late is mystified and asks what that has to do with their sitting on the ground. They answer that they wanted to go to Raleigh and that the sign says 'To Raleigh,' so they have reached their destination." Dr. Michaelson said that the logic of that hypothetical group is no worse than the logic of those who make the Bible the center of their religion, rather than God Himself.

N: Chaplain, we've been identifying a few of the false notions of what religion is all about. Perhaps we should now suggest some directions in which a person could move to find an affirmative answer to the question.

W: C.G., there is a verse in the Bible which gives a brief and succinct answer to that question, and it suggests that the answer to a sacred question is to be found in the secular order. What is religion all about? James 1:27 answers this way: "Pure religion and undefiled before God and the Father is to look after orphans and widows in their distress, and to keep himself uncontaminated by the world." So when we ask a sacred question, "What is pure religion?," we receive a secular answer, "Get involved in caring for the needy!"

N: That seems to be the clear implication of this verse in the Epistle of James, but is that verse typical of the Bible in general, or is it an exception?

W: From my own studies of the Bible, and from reading the reliable studies of others more competent in textual matters than I am, I have come to the conclusion that the thrust of the Judeo-Christian Scriptures as a whole is definitely in this direction.

One of the finest examples of it is the passage in Joshua (4:15–24) which Lucy Austin read a little while ago. Let me briefly summarize the story. The ancient Israelites were in slavery to the Egyptians. They cried out to their masters for liberty and were denied. They cried out to Jehovah God and He sent Moses to lead them up out of slavery. As they fled their captors they were next in danger from the sea. They later recorded that Jehovah took a personal interest in their delivery both from the captors and from the sea. But the end is not yet! They were next in the wilderness, now without food, now without water. They later recorded that their cries to Jehovah brought action. Food and water came by Jehovah's acts. Lastly, as they prepared to cross over Jordan into the "Promised Land," Jehovah provided an able leader in Joshua.

Now comes the part which intrigues us! As they passed through a dry riverbed on their way directly into the "Promised Land," Joshua wisely commanded that one representative from each of the twelve tribes pick up a stone from the riverbed and carry it with him. Then when all the Israelites encamped, they piled these twelve stones together.

Joshua knew how short memories sometimes are, and he knew how quickly important events can fade from the attention of a people, as new and younger generations come on the scene who were not present when those events happened. So he said to the Israelites, "When your children ask their fathers in time to come, 'What do these stones mean?' then you shall let your children know." Know what? Let them know that God has been active and mighty in the everyday problems of their secular lives. He was active in freeing them from slavery, rescuing them from the sea, solving their inadequate food situation, and in getting them a decent place to live.

N: Chaplain, you said this story is a fine example of how the religious questions have secular answers; can you sharpen the focus on this a bit?

W: All right. When the twelve stones were placed in a pile in the "Promised Land," they became, along with the ark, the chief religious symbols because they were there by God's command. So the people began to think of them as the place where God was. Their religion was in those stones, they felt. If someone had asked these Israelites to point to their God, they probably would have pointed toward those stones, or at least would have felt that those stones were a sacred place where God would be more likely found than anywhere else.

But Joshua shattered this idea by his insistence that the only meaning of those sacred stones was that God was basically not in those stones but was out in the secular world, hard at work, freeing slaves, delivering people from danger, solving the hunger problem, and seeking to find a decent home for the homeless.

N: Chaplain, is it valid to draw any comparisons between those stones and the stones of the Chapel?

W: In my opinion, C.G., it not only is valid to draw a comparison between them, but it is theologically accurate to say that "the stones" of this Chapel were intended to serve almost precisely the same religious function as those twelve stones, namely to remind the old generations and to inform each new generation that God is mighty in action to relieve the distress of the poor, the hungry, the ill-housed, and those in slavery. The function of these stones is to say, "God is out there, not chiefly here."

Last Sunday, Stafford Wing sang here Handel's great prayer, "Thanks Be to Thee," and it was rooted in this mighty drama from Joshua.

Thanks be to thee, Lord, our God
Thy people hast Thou led with Thee Israel,
safe through the sea.

To summarize, we can put it this way: the function of coming together within the stones of these walls is to learn to detect the signs of God's work in the secular world, and to join Him in it.

What is religion all about? These stones? This Chapel? This service of worship? This Bible? Not as ENDS IN THEMSELVES. Indeed, they become hindrances rather than help if we substitute them for walking with God through the slums, and ghettos, and the war-torn refugees of the secular world. They can, however, be helpful if they teach us what religion is really all about.

N: It comes down, then, to this: That we can't always build a house and put a sign on it, saying "God's House," and then expect thereby to capture God in that house. If we try that sort of trick, we may find that God is far away, trying to stop a war in Vietnam, or He is actively seeking to get a "Promised Land" for people trapped in a ghetto. We can't always pour God out of just any bottle that we've decided to stick a "God" label on.

W: The stones of this Chapel, or of your church at home, are not any more sacred than the stones of a gambling casino, unless they come to mean for us that our God is leading us into service for those in trouble. Do you remember the reply which our Lord Jesus Christ gave to the disciples of John the Baptist when John was in prison? They approached Jesus and asked, "Are you he who is to come, or shall we look for another?" What was the reply of Jesus? Did He point to a building He had erected, or recite an orthodox creed, and then say, "Because I built this and because I'm orthodox, this proves I am the Christ"? Did He spin webs of learned theological rhetoric? No, His reply was simply this, "Go and tell John what you hear and see": the blind are receiving their sight, lame people are walking, lepers are cleansed, the deaf are hearing, the dead are being raised to life, and the poor are hearing good news! (Matthew 11:2–5). Perhaps as each of us seeks to answer for himself the great question, "What is religion all about anyway?," he will find it profitable to search in that direction.

Myron Augsburger, then president of Eastern Mennonite College, is the only member of that church to have preached in Duke Chapel, so far as I can tell. He was a great peacemaker and scholar of Christian pacifist principles, true to his church's tradition. At Duke Chapel, Augsburger preached this strong Anabaptist sermon, contrasting an allegiance to Pilate with faith in Christ in a fully Christocentric presentation of the faith.

The Christian in a Revolutionary Age

September 26, 1971

MYRON S. AUGSBURGER

Luke 4:16–21 A few years ago in the magazine *Fortune*, there was an editorial in which this statement appeared: "In days like these what we of the world need is a Word from the Lord. We look to the church for that Word and all we hear is the echo of our own voice." In that statement there is a description of the way society has looked at the church and the way the church has too often disappointed society. As I share today on the subject, being a Christian in a revolutionary world, I do this from the existential involvement that I have found with the risen Christ. Being a part of the life of the church I am in no way simply supporting the institutional form of the church. The modern world must see fleshed out in life what it means to take Jesus Christ with absolute seriousness. As Risen Lord, He becomes in my life the guide for a kind of discipleship that is radically different from the normal life in society.

The Gospel offers a clear note of assurance not as note of pessimism. In our kind of world the Christian cannot afford to be a pessimist. (A pessimist is a person who is seasick on the whole voyage of life.) We ought to be optimists because we know who we belong to, what it's all about, and where we are going. A few years ago an American tourist was in Russia. He met a communist who asked him, "Have you read Karl Marx?" He said, "Yes, I've read Marx." "Well then," the communist said, "you know how it's all going to come out." The American tourist should have come right back and said, "Have you read the Bible? Then you know how it's going to come out." This is our faith, that God has interpreted history from its middle in Jesus Christ, and we know the end from the middle because God has known the end from the beginning. In affirming this kind of optimism the Christian should never imply that he has all the answers. Rather we must be aware that God is not static in terms of His dealing with man. In the dynamic of God's work through the Holy Spirit, He can help us discover in every period of history the meaning and the implications of living under the Lordship of Christ in that particular period.

With many being confused, I am reminded of the delightful little story about the man who ran into a bookstore and said, "Have you got that book, *A Piece of My Mind*, by Rabbi Norman Vincent Sheen?" Many people are about that confused when it comes to trying to find their way through life.

The Apostle Paul gives us a clear word in Colossians 2, verses 6 through 10: "As ye have therefore received Christ Jesus the Lord, so walk ye in him: rooted and built up in him, and established in the faith, as ye have been taught, abounding therein with thanksgiving. Beware lest any man spoil you through philosophy and vain deceit, after the tradition of men, after the rudiments of the world, and not after Christ. For in him dwelleth all the fullness of the Godhead bodily. And ye are complete in him."

Alvin Toffler, in his book *Future Shock*, exposes the problems facing us in society, and interprets ours as a psychological illness of existential uncertainty with respect to the future. A few years ago it would have been more the fundamentalist who would have been talking about the end of the world, but not so today. In fact one of the interesting phenomena today is that you find young people on campuses across the land who are talking about the end of the age.

Some of the best ecologists we have say that by 1979 the seas will be dead; by 1984 it will all be over. I am not at all sure about that. I am glad the whole matter rests in God's hand but these men are speaking to a judgment the Bible makes clear, that man creates his own judgment. It is in the processes of judgment that God works with man.

Our time has been described as revolutionary. That is a trite statement now. I do not mean to elaborate this, except to say that there are factors that cause men to say this is a revolutionary age. I do not refer simply to the much change that we have had, nor to the rapidity of change that has affected us, but rather to the fact it has involved the total of man's experience. One analysis of this suggests four reasons for revolution: change with respect to authority since the 19th century; second, change regarding culture—there is no one culture anymore in a given area of the world; third, the meaninglessness of affluence, in which the middle-class American has suddenly discovered that what he was trying to gain, out of his fear that he might go back to another depression, has left him empty; and fourth, the depersonalization of modern technology. I would like to add a fifth cause, and that is the existential immediacy that characterizes modern life, in that we want everything at the moment. We want instant satisfaction in every level, not only instant coffee, but now it is instant pleasure, instant success, instant sex, instant everything. Dimensions of life we knew in the past are gone.

Francis Schaeffer speaks of this in his writings, describing the modern world as having moved under the line of despair. But there is no reason the Christian should parrot the emptiness of society. We have something to offer modern man that is even more revolutionary because of the radical depth and nature of the change the gospel brings. If revolution comes because of total change, I know of nothing so completely revolutionary as an absolute commitment to be a disciple of Jesus Christ.

About three years ago I flew to Miami, Florida, to share in a citywide preaching mission. Judge Bill Meadows, Methodist layman, was chairman of the committee for that citywide crusade and he took me to television and radio stations for interviews. As we walked into one of these he told me what happened a few weeks earlier. He had gone in for an interview, and as he stepped into the room there was a young man sitting across the table waiting to be interviewed as well. He said that young man stuck out his hand and said, "I am Joe Smith, a disciple of Bhave." Meadows said, "I slapped my hand in his, and said, 'I am Bill Meadows, a disciple of Jesus Christ.'" Vioba Bhave is the successor of Mahatma Gandhi in India, the man who collected from the "haves" to give to the "have nots." He carried through a major program of reform in India. The thing that Bill Meadows said was that he longs to see more young people who will say, "I am a disciple of Jesus Christ." That is my conviction, and I get the feeling that the Spirit of God is creating this all across the land.

I have been in the ministry for twenty-one years, and have enjoyed many varied experiences. It was my privilege to share in the one citywide preaching mission among Protestants that Salt Lake City has ever seen. On the first Sunday afternoon we got rained out on the capitol steps, where the meeting was being held by the kindness of Governor Clyde, and over three thousand people packed the rotunda of the capitol building at Salt Lake City. I had the privilege of preaching the Gospel inside the capitol to that audience.

I could give you other illustrations but I say this for only one reason: having moved across the country, and in other parts of the world, in these twenty-one years I have not seen heretofore what is happening right now. Especially among young people on college and university campuses there is a new awareness that the things they have tried in the last few years have left them empty and disillusioned, and they are turning to Jesus of Nazareth. To me this is one of the most heartening things in our day. I am excited about it, and I don't want to miss out on what God is doing in our time. What we need today is more Christian Christians, people who will flesh out in life what it means to walk with Jesus Christ. We need men and women who will be genuine disciples and not persons who simply have an intellectual or philosophical approach to Christianity. We need persons who are not afraid to say "Jesus Christ is my Lord" instead of talking about Jesus who lived in yesteryear, like Abraham Lincoln. Beware of making a philosophical premise of Christ, or a Christ-kind of ideal. We need persons who actually believe that Jesus Christ our Lord is a living person open for encounter at any moment.

To be Christian in our kind of world is demanding a new thing. Dr. Glover of England said a few years ago, "The early church grew because it outthought, out-lived, and out-died everybody around." The challenge you and I face is the challenge of out-thinking our age regarding Christianity, as well as out-living our age as a disciple, and then being willing to out-die it, if you please!

I suggest three things for out-thinking to elucidate what I have introduced: (1) what people experience determines to a large degree what they believe, (2) what people believe determines how they behave, and (3) how people behave determines the character of brotherhood.

First, what people experience determines what they believe. If all you have experienced is a kind of cold, philosophical, institutionalistic Christianity, then that is what you believe Christianity is all about. If what you have experienced on the other hand is a kind of religion that is altogether other than Christianity, then that's what you tend to believe. Or if what you have experienced is a kind of honest authentic commitment to Jesus Christ in your home with your parents or in your congregation, then you will believe that this is a possibility. In America, where we boast of being a Christian society, many people have never experienced fellowship with persons who know what it means to participate with Jesus Christ. A few years ago I was on the way to Stratford, Ontario, for a citywide preaching mission under the Council of Churches to be held in the Shakespearean Art Theater. I flew on Piedmont from Harrisonburg, Virginia, over to Washington, D.C., and transferred to a jet for New York and Toronto. There had been a peace march in Washington that day and there were some peaceniks getting on the plane. I moved over and took the center seat and a young lady sat down beside me. We were off, and I opened conversation with her. I said, "I presume you were here in the march today." She said, "Yes, I was." I said, "Tell me what brought you here for this march." "Well," she said, "I am against killing." I said, "So am I and many of us are; but why are *you* against it, what brought *you*?" She said, "I am against what is happening in Vietnam." "Well," I said, "So am I and

130

there are a lot of us who are, but why are *you* against it?" And she looked at me and said, "Who in the world are you?" I said, "Well, I happen to be a Mennonite, an evangelist on the way to Canada for a preaching mission." She said, "You are a Mennonite, well you are a pacifist too." I said, "It depends on what you mean by that term; I am committed to Jesus Christ, to be His disciple, and I believe that the way of peace is part of His teaching." She looked at me and these were her words, "Don't talk about God to me; I don't even believe there is a God." I said, "You have no association with the church?" "Oh yes," she said, "I belong to a church but that is just for identification, it doesn't mean anything." For the next forty minutes until we scooted in on the runway at LaGuardia in New York City we talked. I asked her to tell me how she saw the church and how she understood Christianity, and she did. When she got through, I said, "Young lady, if that was what Christianity is I wouldn't want to have anything to do with it either." She said, "You must think of it as something different or you wouldn't be involved in it." And so I told her what I understand Christianity to be. And then as a last hook, because you can't talk truth and remain neutral, I said, "You know it's a strange thing, one of these days it is all going to be over, the world will blow up and it will all be over and there will be not an intelligent mind in the universe that remembers we ever happened." The plane landed and she got up and started up the aisle with her friend, but stopped and turned around and called back over two or three people standing in the aisle between us and said, "You know, Preacher, my position doesn't make much sense does it?"

Now as far as I was concerned I had done my job of evangelizing.

For evangelism is not pressure, not manipulation, not coercion, for Christian faith will stand on its own feet. I don't have to defend it. Evangelism is making faith in Christ a clear option. We must realize that there are many people around who have never experienced a confrontation of Christian faith in a meaningful way. Consequently people tend to believe that Christianity is not a real option.

Many of you are students at the university, and I would like to remind you of one of the things that is a most common mistake. Too many students will go to school; take their "Sunday School level" knowledge of Jesus and put it in a pigeonhole while they advance in psychology, philosophy, sociology, and the arts. Four years later when they graduate, instead of being honest about the fact that they did not put into their theology the same intellectual diligence that they put in the other areas, they will smirk at their "Sunday School level" religion and pose with an academic sophistication that regards the religion they had when they came to college as naïve. They never admit that they are naïve or dishonest in that they haven't given the intelligent, honest study to religion that they have put into the other areas.

What you experience determines in a large degree what you believe. You can experience if you will open your life to see what God is doing around you.

I was out in the Midwest and a university professor came to the meeting and after the service he said to me, "I am an honest intellectual agnostic." I complimented him for honesty, and said, "You are a thinking man and you have a right to your position." He then asked what I would tell him to do. I said, "Try one little experiment—every day for thirty days pray honestly this little prayer: 'God, if You are around help me to recognize the evidence for You today.'" I asked him to do that for thirty days and if nothing happened to forget the whole thing. You know what that man said to me? He said, "Preacher, I am afraid to do that: something might happen!" There aren't many intellectual atheists. There are a lot of moral atheists, people who don't want God in their lives.

I turn now to a second premise: what you believe determines how you behave. I have told you a few things I believe by way of illustration. I believe in Jesus Christ as Lord. I believe in the reality of a changed life because I am committed to Him. I know the joy of experiencing His grace and being born from above. I believe in the reality of the presence of the Holy Spirit. I believe in being a disciple. Now what you believe determines how you behave. If you believe something very deeply then you behave in that way. If you believe that God is known in Jesus Christ more clearly than any other way it will affect your behavior because you will seek to know and understand Jesus Christ—you will go to the Word to do this. You will go to people who have experienced Christ and ask them to tell you how they experienced Christ. If you believe that human personality is the most valuable thing in the world then you will behave that way. There is nothing I know that does more to change the inequities in the areas of political, economic, and social problems than just this basic principle. But it is costly—costly to live by this. With respect to the issues of violence, poverty, race, and war, it is a costly thing to live by this principle; that personality is the most valuable thing in the universe. And if you also believe in reaching men for their good you do not touch them at one level only but at the totality of their being. As in the passage from Luke 4, Jesus announcing His ministry did not simply say that He came to preach, but He came to heal the brokenhearted, to give sight to the blind, to give healing to those who were suffering and the like. If you believe that the Gospel touches the whole life, you will never stop with merely giving a cup of water. You will always give the cup of cold water in the name of Christ, so that men may be brought to God. What you believe determines to a large degree how you behave.

It seems that many have the idea that religion is something you turn on at the eleven o'clock hour on Sunday morning, and the way they behave from Monday to Saturday night or three o'clock Sunday morning has no part in it. That is not Judaic-Christian thought, that is purely Greek thought. You see the old Greeks believed you could separate the real you down inside from what happened to your body. The prostitute operates on the philosophy that she can give her body if she keeps the real self detached from what is happening. Christianity talks about something altogether different. It says, "I" am a personality. The whole being relates to God. When a man is saved, you are saving a person, not just the soul as some little entity down inside. When you are dealing with Christian faith you are dealing with the whole person. If you understand this you are not being honest with your fellow man if you know Christ and do not share Him in an evangelistic witness.

The final thing I affirm is that how people behave determines the character of brotherhood. Dietrich Bonhoeffer, in his book *Life Together*, points out that Christian community is quite different from a mere sociological community. In Christian community we always relate to one another in and through Jesus Christ. Sociological community is a commonality of taste, where we come together because we like the same things, have the same symbols, and dress the same way whether it is one pattern or another.

The Christian community is not that. Bonhoeffer says that Christian community means that I relate to my brother in and through Christ so that he is free and I am free. If you relate directly you may tend to manipulate, to dominate, to intimidate, to coerce. But when you relate in and through Christ you are both free. The kind of community I am talking about is a community of disciplined people — a disciplined people who aren't afraid to say they are committed to Christ and mean to obey Him. People who have made this basic commitment to Christ come to the Bible with their minds already made up to obey it. To really sell out to the Lordship of Christ and say I will come to that Scripture with my mind made up to obey it, that's quite radical! This is the kind of brotherhood in which we give and receive and rebuke of one another honestly. We share to exhort one another in the things of Christ. We will step out like John Wesley and put our hand in our brother's by saying, "if your heart is as my heart, give me your hand." The kind of brotherhood in which we share depends on our commitment. What we believe is expressed in our behavior and how we behave determines the character of our brotherhood.

One group of people in our country today who aren't afraid to talk about obedience are the "Jesus People." I have been amazed by some of the insights some of these persons have in the Word of God, and they haven't studied theology. They can sit in a group and tell you in a few minutes what it means to take Jesus Christ seriously and put to shame many within our churches who have grown up around the Christian faith.

Christianity is not mere mysticism, nor is it legalism or a religion of a code of morality. Christianity is relational; I relate to Jesus Christ at the level of the spirit, of mind, and volition in the same way I relate to my wife or to other persons at that level. Because knowing Jesus Christ is not a mere mysticism, the movement today in which many persons are enamored with Far Eastern religions is not a total surprise. For one reason, American high education is shot through with Greek thought and Greek philosophy and has missed out on the unique dynamic of the Judaic-Christian tradition. Far Eastern religions, Hinduism and Buddhism, are not really religions, they are philosophies. I have spent hours discussing with professors of Hinduism in India their philosophy to find it varies little from Greek philosophy. The Greeks believed that the rational part of man is immortal, and that part will live on and eventually merge back into the universal reason. The Buddhist believes that somehow if one can lose his identity as a person and like a drop of water in the ocean merge back into that universal life, if one can lose his identity and merge into the universal, he will be at peace. In our society people are reaching for some answer and this is the path many are taking.

Another reason for this approach is that the general assumptions about Christianity in America have been moralistic. I do not simply say legalistic, but moralistic; so that we cannot understand the relational aspect of knowing Jesus Christ. In reaction to this moralism we are now trying to find something that translates into the inner psychological awareness we have today. In doing this we are missing out on the uniqueness of what Jesus Christ brought. Moralism reminds me of Dr. E. Stanley Jones's story of the Indian holy man he found sitting on his ash heap, and the holy man said, "I gave up sex forty years ago," but E. Stanley Jones said that for the next forty minutes all he could talk about was sex.

Christianity is not simply moralism, it is a relationship with an actual personality, present in the world to work in one's life — the personality of God as He is known in Christ. Jesus makes clear a personal God who is radically different from that of the mystical religions that many people are accepting today. The story of the Bible is the story of creation, incarnation, discipleship and resurrection. God created a good world; humanness and sinfulness are not synonymous. Humanness in itself is affirmed by Jesus Christ in the incarnation. The fact that God could come in Christ is the greatest compliment to humanity, the greatest affirmation of humanism you can find in history. God affirms man, and when He calls us to be disciples, He does not call us to a popularized Christianity that is an escape hatch from real life. He calls us to put into practice what it means to live for Jesus Christ in a world where this is not popular.

Personally, I am committed to a discipleship that makes me a pacifist; however, the word pacifism is too weak, for really I believe in a New Testament nonresistant redemptive love that seeks to win our enemy to become our brother in Christ. I believe also in working for a relationship between the races that makes me my brother's brother. I believe there is an answer to the problems of "the economic gap." Somehow we must reach across this gap between the "haves" and "have nots," we must help persons understand that values are not measured by money — by what a man carries in his pocket or his bank account. I believe in grappling with the social problems in our world; but I also believe in being concerned about the whole man — his spirit as well as his physical being.

Dr. Elton Trueblood, in his book *New Men for These Times*, says the church is suffering from a polarization between social action on one side and evangelical action on the other. I say this as an evangelist. I may be to a small degree an educator, a president of a college, a writer, but I am first of all an evangelist. Basically this is because of my theology, for I believe "that if a man is in Christ, he is a new creature," II Corinthians 5:17. Knowing this, we can introduce a man anytime, anywhere, and in any culture to Jesus Christ, and He will not Americanize him, He will Christianize him!

While we talk about the importance of freeing Christianity from its cultural trappings, we in America have been guilty of domesticating the Gospel. We have Americanized Christianity so that in many parts of the world people can't really meet Jesus Christ because they don't see Him. I remind you of what happened when Mahatma Gandhi was in Africa. He was turned down by a church by being told, "this church is not for the likes of you; it is for white Europeans." It has been said that what Gandhi rejected was not Christ as much as the perverted picture of Christ he was given. He went back to India, borrowing the teachings of Jesus, but he never became a Christian because he thought that to become a Christian meant he had to accept western culture, and Gandhi was first of all an Indian, not a westerner.

We have so equated Christianity with Americanism that many persons in other parts of the world, hungering for God, miss what it means to meet

God. Often those who profess to be the most liberal are the most difficult to get to understand what it means to lift Jesus Christ above the cultural trappings of their verbalism. Some who want to take the Gospel and put it in modern forms overlook the fact that in other parts of the world these are Americanistic forms, or verbal cultural symbols. To communicate the Gospel in Africa, India, or Indonesia means that we make clear the Gospel of Jesus Christ, the One who reveals God, who calls a man to come and walk with Him. To identify with Jesus Christ in another culture is so revolutionary that the average American liberal doesn't adjust any better than the average American fundamentalist.

The age in which we live is no time for the weak, timid, timorous, uncommitted souls. It is the age for a kind of person who has enough intellectual integrity to make commitments, but at the same time enough humility to always review those commitments. I can only surrender as much of myself to God today as I understand today.

I would like to close with an illustration from Paul Tillich in one of his addresses to Union Seminary students in which he says: "Don't give in too quickly to those who want to alleviate your anxiety about truth. Don't be seduced into a truth which is not really truth even if the seducer is your church, your pastor, or your parental tradition. Go with Pilate if you can't go with Jesus, but go in seriousness with him."

Why do I quote a statement like that to conclude this message? For these reasons: (1) Because the choice that I am putting before you this morning must be that clear—no halfway ground—it's either going with Jesus or going with Pilate. It is that clear. So I say with Tillich, if you can't go with Jesus, go with Pilate, but go in seriousness with Pilate, know what you are doing. Don't just water down Jesus and still claim to be a Christian. Either be a genuine, honest, radical disciple or else admit you are going with Pilate who says, "What is truth, I can't commit myself because I can't be sure." (2) I share this because many people today are choosing to go with Pilate rather than to go with Jesus because it is more palatable in our society. It is more palatable in our academic community because there are some people still believing the myth that the skeptic or the cynic is more honest than the committed person—and that is pure myth. I quote this statement because many people are going with Pilate instead of Jesus who are implying that Jesus is a little less than real sophistication. (3) I share this because of the kind of radical discipleship I have sought to call you to follow. That is a discipleship which says if I take Jesus Christ seriously, and I mean the Jesus Christ of the New Testament and not some watered-down Jesus that people have handed me, that has been domesticated and acculturated, then I will have to fully commit myself to him. I trust that my words have been less comforting than probing and less analytical than they have been affirmative. I share this with you not as a professional preacher, but as one genuinely involved with Jesus Christ. He has not only changed my life but keeps changing it as I discover day by day new things that He has for me, changing my life into His image.

D. Moody Smith Jr. is a renowned interpreter of the New Testament, particularly the Gospel of John. He served for many years as beloved professor at the Divinity School. In this sermon, Smith explicates a strange Johannine event, Jesus' turning of water to wine at the wedding in Cana. He interprets this story as a challenge to modern modes of thought and an epiphany of Jesus Christ.

A Necessary Tension

February 6, 1972

D. MOODY SMITH JR.

John 2:1–22 Just a week ago Miss Carol Feraci astounded a White House gathering in honor of the founders of *Reader's Digest* by addressing the president of the United States and denouncing the war in Vietnam. The guests, who included Bob Hope, Billy Graham, and Mrs. Martha Mitchell, were doubtless as shocked as the nationwide television audience, who witnessed the event on the evening news, when the Ray Conniff singers suddenly produced a prophet. Most of the audience was apparently satisfied by Miss Feraci's subsequent departure, although Mrs. Mitchell was reported to have said that "she ought to be torn limb from limb." Only slightly less astounding than Miss Feraci's audacity were her references to Mr. Nixon's church attendance, her invoking the name of Jesus Christ against the war, and her blessing of the Berrigan brothers and Daniel Ellsberg. One recalled Eartha Kitt's denunciation of the war before Mrs. Lyndon Johnson, if not Micaiah ben Imlah's prophecy before King Ahab's court. Whatever might be said about the effectiveness or the appropriateness of the act, you had to admit it was a very gutty performance. And what of the invoking of the name of Christ? Doubtless for Mrs. Mitchell and the millions who agree with her, it capped effrontery with blasphemy. For many others it seemed entirely apposite. Miss Feraci later conceded she was not particularly religious, but her linking of the president's church attendance, the name of Jesus, and the heroes of the Roman Catholic peace movement cast up in a graphic way the issues that now confront and divide the church.

What does it mean to be a Christian? What is the truth or the essence of Christianity? Who is Jesus? Where is He? What does He have to do with the war, the Berrigan brothers, the draft, and Mr. Nixon's church attendance? Our text for the morning is the second chapter of the Gospel of John, which recounts the wine miracle of Cana and Jesus' cleansing of the temple. It is now the season of Epiphany, which celebrates the manifestation of Christ to the nations. The narratives of both incidents recounted in John 2 are traditionally read during the season of Epiphany, and the association of the miracle at Cana with Epiphany is particularly strong. Here Jesus first manifests his glory and his disciples believe in him. The miracle itself is a rather odd one among the miracle stories of the Gospels. Most of them are healings or demon exorcisms. A few portray Jesus rescuing people from physical danger or death. Here he responds to a situation that is at worst an embarrassment. When you're out of Schlitz, you're out of beer! Not to worry. Jesus makes it all right in a moment by converting six large jugs full of water into well over a hundred gallons of wine. You don't believe that? Quite frankly, there is room for skepticism. But John's point is not that Jesus produces the highest-quality vintage wine, but rather that he fulfills and restores disappointed human expectation. The water of purification does not suffice; the original wine is exhausted; the most one could expect is second-rate stuff. But contrary to all expectation Jesus provides the finest fruit of the vine after the other wine is exhausted. He affirms natural human hopes. Quite possibly we should understand that the wine itself is symbolic. It is the divine affirmation of life that bestows life on despairing and dying men.

This epiphany story embodies a view of Christ. At a certain level he is a wonder worker, a divine figure, possessing uncanny powers. This Christ has always been popular, and he still is today. We sophisticated Christians, who scarcely believe that Christ worked miracles and certainly do not believe he will work one for us, might well remember that among his followers we are still a minority. Yet the story wants to say more than that Jesus can do more than we ask or think in a worldly sense. It means to say that he affirms man's deepest desire and intentionality. He has come that we may have life and have it more abundantly, and he bestows this life without restraint. He bestows it lavishly upon us all, upon Mr. Nixon, the Ray Conniff singers, Carol Feraci, the radical priests, and Mrs. Mitchell as well. In Christ we see God's graciousness to men, His goodness. This goodness is free, prevenient. That is, God is good to us before we are good to Him.

But wait! That God and that Christ are splendid, glorious. Too glorious. The world is not such a place as to encourage belief in them. If Christ has affirmed us so lavishly and lovingly, why do we still hurt? Or, more important, why do we not hurt, when by rights we should? Why do we continue to enjoy affluence and ease when in this rich country children go hungry and in Vietnam and East Pakistan people die like flies? The epiphany of a Christ who simply blesses things the way they are is and always has been a pleasant prospect, so that people are deeply shocked and offended at the suggestion that he may also be among the dissidents—stirring up trouble, so to speak.

Yet John is not satisfied that Christ should appear only at a wedding feast to enhance the enjoyment of the guests. He does that, says John. He affirms life and the poignant human desire that it should have meaning and purpose. Yet at the same time he stands over against our own ways of affirming, hoarding, and ultimately squandering our lives. John is not satisfied to present Jesus at a wedding in Cana. Alongside this epiphany story he places another one, the story of Jesus' cleansing of the temple. All the other gospels report that this event occurred on Jesus' final visit to Jerusalem, and they are probably right. So John deliberately places the story here at the beginning rather than the end. But in doing so he does not falsify the history of Jesus. Rather he exposes its deepest truth. Jesus affirms life, but at the same time he challenges what we make of it. Thus he becomes a judge as well as a Savior. John shows how Jesus challenges the corruption of the house of God, and in doing so he suggests that he challenges our corruption of religion, whether on television or in Duke Chapel. He challenges us most acutely when we deem ourselves most religious. In this challenge he risks himself. "Destroy this temple . . ." This word of Jesus points forward to his own death, from which no supernatural powers are invoked to save Him. His protest exposes him to the wrath of the gods who preside over the status quo, and he succumbs. He gives his life for his friends, and suggests that those who are his friends will prove themselves through similar self-giving.

Near the beginning of his Gospel John describes in a skillful way, in dramatic scenes, the tension that stands at the heart of Christian faith. Moreover, he traces this tension back to Jesus himself. And as much as John paints over the historical Jesus with the colors of Christian faith, in this he is essentially correct, not only theologically but also historically. The Jesus whom we know from the other Gospels also embodies this tension. On the one hand, unlike John the Baptist he is not ascetic. He comes eating and drinking, much to the displeasure of some pious people. On the other, he challenges and judges the status quo and those who are satisfied with it, and they kill him. Finally, after he is done to death by them, his disciples proclaim their faith that he has risen from the dead and offers forgiveness to those who have killed him. The final word is yes to mankind and to life, not no. In this sense Christ himself is relieved of the tension between affirmation and judgment. But in this world he was to the end involved in this tension. In fact, his ministry was defined by it.

Now the temptation of Christians is, and has always been, to relieve ourselves of this tension prematurely. It is easier either to affirm the world or to reject it than to live in critical tension with it. In the New Testament there is already evidence of this. Some Christians go on living easily and happily in the world, accepting its ambiguities and evils as though Christ had not judged it. Others reject the world completely and withdraw from marriage, gainful employment, and civil responsibility. Later on one sees the church affirming, adopting and adapting the institutions and power structures of the world to the extent that its own identity becomes questionable. It is perhaps easier to see this in the age of Constantine and of the medieval church than in the age of prayer breakfasts and White House worship services. Yet it is as real now as it was then. Conversely, the impulse that led some people in the apostle Paul's churches to give up their wives and jobs in the belief that they had already entered into glory, or soon would, has never ceased.

The rejection of this world in favor of the next, or simply in revulsion from it, has doubtless played a role in the rise of the Gnostic heresy and of monasticism within the Christian church. Various present-day sects mirror a similar outlook. It is arguable also that certain forms of Christian social protest contain within them the seeds of such an attitude.

Christians frequently seem to go overboard in one direction or the other. That is entirely understandable, for it is not easy to live with tension. When men hope for the world to come, for heaven, or for eternal life, perhaps also for Nirvana, they express a natural and valid longing for an ultimate resolution of the tension in an affirmation of all that is valid in this life or this world. But to expect such a resolution within this life or within this world is to cherish a vain and delusive hope. If we are to live in this world, as we must — we have no other world to live in — how may we deal with this tension?

Now I am tempted to say to you that we should strike a balance between affirming the world and judging or rejecting it. There would be, I suppose, a certain truth in this. If we were to agree on some such resolution of the situation, we might leave the chapel consoled in the thought that we must neither affirm the world uncritically nor reject it uncompromisingly. But possibly there are times when we should reject it or even affirm it! Moreover, to live with such a comfortable abstraction could be actually to surrender to the gods of whatever is or whoever is stronger.

People in a university setting feel comfortable with abstractions, and rightly so, for abstractions are our business, and they have a certain value, and even utility. Yet life itself has to be lived at the level of the concrete and the specific, and that is disquieting. For example, it was easier for all of us in this intellectual community to accept the abstract idea of school integration than to accept the fact of our white children going to predominantly black schools. When we are realistic we know that life places hard choices before us which cannot finally be dealt with at an abstract level. If I could only show you how to strike some balance between affirming what is and standing in judgment over against it, those of us who have opposed the war in Vietnam might reassure ourselves that our form of action — or inaction — has been wiser than the civil disobedience of the Berrigan brothers, not to mention the impertinence of Miss Feraci. Maybe it has been. I can't answer that question for you, but only for myself. Yet I would not want any of us too easily to assume that our way of living with the tension to which Jesus calls us is better than theirs. For when we act and speak in judgment upon this world in the conviction that it is not what it ought to be, or can be, we do not reject the world, but affirm it. But when we withdraw, when we withhold, when we rise above the tumult when others perforce must live in it, when we retreat into the abstract when others are bleeding in the concrete, and on the concrete, what do we do? We do not then affirm the world that God has given us. We really reject it. Is this right for us as Christians? Is it right on any accounting? Is it in the long run even possible?

Jesus helped celebrate a wedding feast and assaulted some people in the temple. What kind of Christ was that? Probably the only kind for a world like that. And the only kind for a world like ours.

> O God, give us the strength to change the things we can change,
> the patience to accept the things we cannot change,
> and the wisdom to know the difference.
> But if we find ourselves complacent in our wisdom,
> May we have courage to question whether it is from You.
> Amen.

John W. Carlton, who served as professor of preaching at the Southeastern Bap-
tist Theological Seminary until its takeover by the fundamentalists in the 1980s,
was a gentlemanly, learned, eloquent proponent of the gospel. In this sermon, he
employs the insights of prominent contemporary plays as a way of illuminating
Jesus' phrase "the generous eye." Carlton's own generosity of spirit is evident in
this gracious sermon that appeals for that "generous eye" in times of both pros-
perity and adversity.

The Generous Eye

June 11, 1972

JOHN W. CARLTON

Matthew 6:19–25 Thirty years ago there came to the American stage a remarkable play by Thornton Wilder, *Our Town*, which reached into the past
of America and portrays a New England village between the years 1901 and
1913. Wilder brings to us the wind-blown hills, the plowed fields, the sound
of the early train and the school bells—the quiet serenity of Grover's Corners, a little village in New Hampshire. We glimpse the town's untarnished
life as in the first act we arrive at breakfast time and are carried through an
entire day in the lives of such people as the milkman, the paper boy, the general practitioner, and the local editor. Act II, appropriately called "Love and
Marriage," celebrates the wedding of George Gibbs and Emily Webb.

The last act is laid in the village cemetery on a windy hilltop where the
people rest from the cares of life on earth. But there is a new grave, for Emily
had died in childbirth. In a strange retake of human existence Emily is told
that she can relive a day in her life, and with childish ecstasy she chooses her
twelfth birthday. At first it was exciting to be young again, but soon the day
held no joy, for now with the knowledge of the future it was unbearable to
realize how unaware she had been of the meaning and wonder of life when
she was alive. Emily says:

> Live people don't understand, do they?
> We don't have time to look at one another.

As Emily leaves the world of Grover's Corners to return to the company
of the dead, she bids farewell by saying: "So all that was going on and we

never noticed. O earth, you're too wonderful for anyone to realize you. Do human beings ever realize life while they live it?"

The passing years have underscored the relevance of this play. Today we have become habituated to a kind of cinematic, restless vision that leaps about on the surface of things, with neither the time nor the disposition to penetrate beneath the circumstantial levels of reality. Indeed, we are reminded of Captain McWhirr in Joseph Conrad's *Typhoon*: "Captain McWhirr had sailed over the surface of the oceans as some men go skimming over the years of existence, to sink gently into a placid grave, ignorant of life to the last, without ever having been made to see all it may contain of perfidy, of violence, of terror."

We need not marvel, therefore, that we must depend upon our highly paid professionals to guide us backward through half-lived events to recover their content and meaning.

Today we attach ourselves to whatever passes by, so that we are "distracted from distraction by distraction." We hope that reality can be affirmed outside. Yet how often the things we miss seeing are the things we miss being. Being is conscious existence; it is the capacity to respond to reality. Life is what we are alive to. No wonder St. Theresa said, "I require of you only to look."

My mind is drawn to a remarkable saying of Jesus: If your eye be generous, your whole body will be full of light. To be sure, the original context of this saying is not known. Matthew and Luke place and understand it differently. Some versions speak of the eye being single and of the eye being evil. In Jewish metaphor the evil eye was a grudging or jealous spirit. The word in this context translated "generous" can also suggest sound, healthy, single, sincere. It would seem to me that here Jesus is saying, at least in part, "If your eye be generous—wide open, undistracted—you will have a clear and undistorted view of life." By the same token, the grudging and ungenerous spirit will distort and blur your vision of reality.

How much of real life is a matter of attentiveness and hospitality. Even on that elementary level of nature itself there is an aristocracy of the attentive. Within the animal world the ultimate aristocrats are those who pay enough attention to their environment to survive and leave some descendants. Consider the newborn infant. He is literally in a state of suspension—born and yet not born—a creature in the physical world but yet to be born into the successive worlds of meaning and value and relationships.

Surely the generous eye is essential in the realm of intellect. We often speak of the "play" of the mind, by which we mean its animal spirits and its restlessness and activity. This gives range and momentum to the mind, for it lures us beyond pedestrian trails. One does not need to be indiscriminately open to the clutter and clatter of life, but we do need a wide hospitality to ideas and an explorative thrust to the mind. I am persuaded that too many men become too certain about too many things too soon in their lives, and they lack both the wisdom and the knowledge to expose their hastily adopted ideas to further doubts and reflections. In these immature absolutists lies the seed of tragedy.

We live and work within a network of mutuality, perceived by John Donne when he wrote: "No man is an island entire of itself, for every man is a piece of the continent, a part of the mainland. Any man's death diminishes me, for I am a part of all mankind." One of the real tragedies of our era is that we have tried to strike at the primordial oneness of man and have sought to split on the circumference of life that which cannot be split at the center. In the valiant struggles of minorities for recognition and dignity are they not saying to us: open your eyes. Look at us from God's point of view. Our human dignity is a divine bestowal; it is not the grudging concession of sinful men. Surely justice is a vision of the mind and heart long before it is a law on the statute books.

Love by its very nature is a way of seeing: it is the capacity and willingness to penetrate objectively and feelingly the individual self-awareness of another person so that we see the world through his eyes, even when they are petty, mean, or dull. Love sees something of the might-have-been in every life. This love is more than a diffused essence of amiability—it is an invincible goodwill, an unconquerable benevolence, an inward openness to the needs of others, a constructive set of mind and a hardheaded intention to do for another what can be done to achieve his total good, as nearly as we can discern it. Love in any meaningful sense is a communion of being, the sense of the human burden and the burden of being human.

A recent Broadway musical, *Lost in the Stars*, based upon Alan Paton's great classic of South Africa, *Cry, the Beloved Country*, has a stirring song about the power of love to bridge distance and silence and years. Stephen Kumalo has left his little valley church in Natal to search for his wayward son Absalom in the Babylon of Johannesburg. This humble man—always God's servant, though often his bewildered servant—sings:

How many miles to the heart of a son?
Thousands, thousands of miles
Each lives alone
In a world of dark
Crossing the skies

In a lonely arc
Save when love leaps out like a leaping spark
Over thousands, thousands of miles.
Not miles or walls or length of days
Nor the cold doubt of midnight can hold us apart,
For swifter than wings of the morning
Are the pathways of the heart.

Now consider one further dimension of experience that requires the generous eye. It is suggested by our Lord's conflict with the Pharisees and the Sadducees in Matthew's gospel. No doubt Jesus lived among people who could neither read nor write, but the illiteracy he deplored was an inability to read the signs of the times, an essential blindness to what is happening around one. He said to the Pharisees: You can discern the clouds and the fact of the sky, but you cannot discern the signs of the times. Certainly it is not easy to read the signs of the times in today's cosmic hallowe'en of dark witchery and fear. Neither is it easy to discern God's glory, for his glory never looks the way we think it ought to look. There are many epiphanies through which he reveals himself, but often there is no sign on the door, no notice in the paper, no spire on the roof. When our Lord came to this earth there was no Hollywood stage setting for this biblical extravaganza. God's attack of grace upon the human scene took place on a tiny human stage—on a little postage stamp of earth. Perhaps today he comes again into human life, not in the noisy and the boisterous and the bizarre but in the quiet and unobtrusive events of daily life. If only we could read his coming!

We are all easily preoccupied today with what Wordsworth called "the burden and the mystery, the weary weight of this unintelligible world." In the crisis of hope we are experiencing, I see a continuing peril—the possible defaulting of individual man. Sir Kenneth Clark, in his monumental study of civilization from the fall of the Roman Empire to the present day, concludes his great work by saying that while we might not be entering into a new period of barbarism in the human pilgrimage, there is a crisis of confidence and that we can destroy ourselves by cynicism and disillusion as effectively as by bombs. And I do firmly believe that the tragedy of life is not in the fact of death itself but in that which dies inside a man while he lives—the death of faith and hope and human response. Death comes when we no longer care—when the forces that make for righteousness and truth and beauty die in the hearts of men. In this day of such widespread lassitude and failure of nerve, our faith calls us to the enlargement of life in God and to the discovery of our representative capacity.

We make no plea for superficial optimism but neither do we have to settle for a dispirited "waiting for Godot." When our Lord walked upon this earth He read the cosmic weather map and knew that there was turbulence ahead. Did He not say, "The rains will fall, the floods will come, and the winds will blow"? But He also said, "Be of good cheer; I have overcome the world." He leaned more toward the celebration of life than toward the sad endurance of it. St. Paul had something of the same spirit when, after surveying his own "slings and arrows of outrageous fortune," he exclaimed: "We may be knocked down, but we are never knocked out."

Negro spirituals are for witness, and one affirms that history can be incredibly harsh: "Nobody knows de trouble I see." But it ends with as brave a line as literature could invent: "Glory, hallelujah." And only generous eyes can see both the trouble and the hallelujah.

Eternal Father, grant us the gift of the generous eye and the courage of the open road, that we might come to true understanding before thee, for in thy light do we see light. Amen.

In his lifetime of citywide crusades and evangelistic meetings, Billy Graham has probably preached to more people than any preacher in history. On four occasions, he preached in Duke Chapel. In this sermon Graham preaches from Psalm 23, focusing upon the problem of death. He ends with his usual evangelistic appeal, reassuring the congregation that "every person can be a new creation through a personal relationship with Jesus Christ."

Finding Answers

September 23, 1973

BILLY GRAHAM

Psalm 23 It was my privilege to be in this pulpit twenty-one years ago. I have been invited back on other occasions but because of scheduling in various parts of the world I have not been able to come, so I am delighted to have this opportunity to speak to another generation of the Duke family. I have always wanted to come back to Duke University Chapel because of the warm hospitality here.

In the passage of Scripture that was read by the Chancellor a moment ago, David is describing his feelings as a young shepherd under the stars in the Middle East. So much of the world's history revolves around the Middle East today. If you picked up the Raleigh newspaper this morning you noticed that the number one headline had to do with the oil crisis in the Middle East. The whole world is concerned about the conflicts and violence that may come out of the oil crisis that is surrounding the Middle East at this moment.

David was a young man in that part of the world. Writing hundreds of years before Christ was born, he touched upon the three greatest problems that we face in 1973. These are three problems that science has not been able to solve. In all of these centuries and with all of our scientific developments — and knowledge is doubling every fifteen years in the scientific world — we have not been able to solve these three problems; at this very moment they are your problems, they are mine, they are America's, they are the world's. David said, I have found the answer to those three problems.

David touched upon the first problem when he said, "He restoreth my soul." "He restoreth my soul" is the answer to the problem of human iniquity. What causes lust, greed, hate, jealousy, war, social injustice? What is the root cause of it? The Bible says, "For all have sinned and come short of the glory of God." David said, "He restoreth my soul."

Jesus asked a very searching question, "What shall it profit a man if he gain the whole world and lose his soul?" When the Berlin students were rioting some time ago, the press asked, What is the purpose of this trouble? What are your objectives? A student said, "We want to restore the 'soul' of Germany."

When I first heard of "soul music" and "soul food," I asked a black friend of mine in Watts, What do you mean by "soul music" and "soul food"? He said, "Everything, man! Everything that's good in a man is soul." The Bible teaches that you have a body but inside your body is a soul — a spirit. That is the part of you that will live on forever after the death of your body. That's the real you! The part of you that can remember. It is the part of you that feels and thinks, it is the *real* you. That's the soul.

A nation also has a soul. The past few months, America has been going through a soul crisis as we have seen the unraveling of a part of our government on television. The television has been a classroom. We have been taught something about our government — its strengths and its weaknesses. We have asked ourselves, Can the system survive? Can it bring social justice to a nation that desperately wants it and needs it and can it bring peace to the world?

He restoreth my soul. How can the soul of a nation or an individual be restored? That is what Good Friday is all about. That is why every Catholic Church and every Protestant Church has a cross. Jesus Christ came to die on that cross for a purpose — to restore our souls. When He died on that cross something mysterious happened. Something thrilling and wonderful happened. God took your sins and my sins and the sins of the whole world and laid them upon Jesus Christ. He became the world's great sin bearer. Because of that cross, God can say to you and to me, you are forgiven — I forgive you!

I visited a mental institution some time ago. The head of that institution said, "I could release half of my patients if they could only be assured that they are forgiven." You see, one of the greatest psychological problems that we face today is guilt! We don't know what to do with our guilt. That is why Christ died — to take away our guilt. God is saying through the cross, "I love you!" "I love you!" "I love you!" "I forgive you!" "I restore your soul." Your soul was separated from God by sin but he forgives the sin. Reconciliation between man and God takes place at the Cross. But there is another part of that story. They buried Jesus, but as our confession states, "He arose from the dead."

Once I visited a man approaching ninety years of age who was the head of his country. He gave me a cup of coffee, then looked at me and asked, "Young man, do you believe in the resurrection of Jesus Christ?" I said, "I do." He replied, "When I leave office, I am going to spend the rest of my life studying the resurrection of Jesus Christ; because if Jesus Christ is not risen from the dead, I see no ultimate hope for the human race." Christ is risen! He is alive! The message we proclaim today is not about a dead Christ still hanging on a cross, but a risen Savior who is willing to come into our hearts, forgive our sins, and restore our souls.

How can a nation have its soul restored? America needs to repent! Not just the Republicans, but my own party—the Democratic Party as well. We all have something to repent for because there's a little bit of Watergate in all of us. The Lord said to Solomon, "If my people which are called by my name shall humble themselves and pray, and seek my face and turn from their wicked ways, then will I hear from heaven, and will forgive their sin, and heal their land." We as a nation need to corporately repent and confess and turn to God. He will restore the soul of a nation, a soul that we are in danger of losing.

David touched upon another great problem. He said, "I shall not want." The problems of our world are tremendous—poverty, race, pollution, the population explosion, war, crime, drugs, kidnapping, bombing, assassinations. The papers and the television are filled with stories about these problems. What is the answer? David said, "I have found that even though I am poor, 'I shall not want.'" I have found a resource.

Some of my colleagues have just returned from central West Africa. We have set up an emergency relief fund to help the people there. It is estimated that 5–6 million people will die of starvation before Christmas unless the nations of the world come to their aid and rescue. When I was in northeast India, I flew over Bangladesh. I looked down and felt anguish over the statistics and stories I had read about the hunger and suffering.

But there are other kinds of suffering, too. There is suffering even in affluent America or affluent Sweden or affluent Britain. There is personal suffering that comes to students and faculty alike at Duke—boredom, guilt, loneliness, a marriage that went wrong, poor health, getting old, dreams unfulfilled, a friend that betrays you, the pressure of life that seems too great to bear, a child that disappoints you, a broken love affair. Job said, "Man is born into trouble as the sparks fly upward." What are you going to do when the crisis comes? What are you going to do when trouble comes? What are you going to do when the betrayal and disappointment and loneliness and emptiness comes?

We talk about cosmic loneliness today. You can be in a crowd, a party having a good time when all of a sudden for a fleeting second there is a moment of loneliness. That's man's great loneliness for God. We are made for fellowship with God. We try to bring in substitutes, but nothing will work until we come into a relationship with God through Jesus Christ.

I was in New Delhi a few months ago. At the airport I saw hundreds of American university students. They had been there for two weeks sitting at the feet of a guru. Three jumbo jets were there ready to bring them back to America. So I decided to move among them and ask them questions. I asked, Did you find what you came to India to find? They sadly shook their heads and said, "No!"

They could find what they are looking for in their own backyard. Acres of diamonds are there, available to every one of us in a personal relationship with God. We can say with the apostle Paul, "I have learned that in whatsoever state I am, therewith to be content."

There is of course a Christian discontentment. We are discontented with the world in which we live. We want to do something about it, and rightly so. We ought to tackle the energy problem. We ought to tackle the pollution problem. We ought to tackle the war problems and try to eliminate them from the human scene. But what about those millions who are caught up in other kinds of problems? Where are they going to turn? There is a resource that David found. He said, "I shall not want."

The third problem that science has not solved is the problem of death. We have not solved the problem of human iniquity. We still have it. We have not eliminated the problems of poverty and war from the world, we still have them after thousands of years. But the greatest crisis you will ever have to face is the crisis of facing death. David said, "I have found an answer there too, 'Yea, though I walk through the valley of the shadow of death, I will fear no evil: for thou art with me; thy rod and thy staff they comfort me.'"

When C. S. Lewis was a professor at Cambridge he made a statement one day that shook me. He said, "War does not increase death." He added, "You think about it a moment, every generation dies." Death comes to the whole human race. Because of war, some may die earlier, but all die. Every generation passes away. You will die. The Bible says, "It is appointed unto man once to die." Now, how are you going to face that great crisis of death? If you are prepared to die, I believe you are prepared to live.

Death today is a suppressed subject. I spoke to the presidents and deans of eight universities on the West Coast some time ago. The Big Ten schools were represented there as well. I spoke on "The Missing Link in Modern Education." One of the points that I made was that I did not know a university at that time that offered a class on death. There were no classes on how to die, or exploring the possibilities of a future life. When I got through, one of the university presidents came to me and said we are going to look into that. I am glad to say that his university has put into its curriculum a class on death. Do you know, it is crowded out.

Listen to the songs and lyrics of the modern music of young people and you will notice that a great deal of it has to do with suffering and death. When the University of Kentucky took a survey to find out what students were thinking about, they found that university students most often think about, of course, sex. But second, and a close second, was death. We don't admit it. We would be embarrassed even to talk about it just as we were embarrassed to talk about sex forty years ago. We are embarrassed to talk about it but there it is, our greatest crisis. But how much time and energy are we giving to solving it? Modern science has not increased the longevity of life. More people are reaching the age of seventy, but after seventy that is about it except for a small handful, and most of those are in primitive societies.

David said, "When I face death God will be with me." It is a wonderful thing to know that you are prepared to die. It is a wonderful thing to know that your sins are forgiven. It is a wonderful thing to know that when a crisis or trouble or difficulty comes, "I shall not want." It is a wonderful thing to know that when I face the greatest of all crises God is there with me.

Do you know God? You can know God for yourself. You don't have to go through a clergyman or a priest. This was the message of John Wesley and George Whitfield two hundred years ago. They said you can know God for yourself. They went into the fields of England and preached it. That's how the Methodist Church was born. You can know Christ. George Whitfield, one of the founders of Methodism, preached every night on the subject "You Must Be Born Again." Some of the leaders of the church came to him and said, "Why don't you change your text?" He said, "I will when you become born again."

Every person can be a new creation through a personal relationship with Jesus Christ.

Our Father, we thank Thee that these three great problems that seem to be insoluble find their solution in the person of Jesus Christ. And we pray that today, as individuals and collectively, we may commit ourselves totally and unreservedly to Him. For we ask it in His Name. Amen.

The feminist theologian Letty Russell was a new professor of religious studies at Manhattan College when she delivered this sermon in Duke Chapel. Here we find themes that characterized much of her later theology at Yale Divinity School — service to others as a Christian imperative, the need for ministry to be mutual, and partnership as the guiding paradigm for the practice of the faith.

The Impossible Possibility

March 31, 1974

LETTY RUSSELL

Mark 10:35–45 In my undergraduate days at Wellesley College, I used to process with the choir at daily and Sunday chapel, up the aisle, toward a chancel where the words *non ministrari, sed ministrare* were written in huge letters across the upper wall. Each time I looked at those words, no matter how bleary-eyed or distractedly, I believed—believed that this lifestyle of Jesus (not to be ministered unto, but to minister) had something to do with my own lifestyle and with why I was at college.

Today the words, although in modern English, are still with us. Our text, Mark 10:45, reads: not to be served, but to serve. But for all of us, I think, they have become more of a problem than a possibility.

They are a problem for Christians because the very word "service" has become so debased in our culture that most people think of it, at best, as a sort of "band-aid" approach to helping others and, at worst, a "cop-out" from working for a just society.

They are a problem for women, blacks, and other third world groups because service is identified with subordination, powerlessness, and oppression.

They are a problem for ministers and laity because we have created a class of professional "ministers" who serve in structures which deprive the whole People of God of their own responsible servanthood or ministry.

Yet here are the words (Mark 10:42–45): "And Jesus called them to him and said to them, 'You know that those who are supposed to rule over the Gentiles lord it over them, and their great men exercise authority over them. But it shall not be so among you; but whoever would be great among you must be your servant, and whoever would be first among you must be slave of all. For the Son of Man also came not to be served but to serve, and to give his life as a ransom for many."

And here is the lifestyle of Jesus of Nazareth who came to serve and give his life as a ransom for the world. This impossible idea of service is in fact the only possibility for those who would follow Jesus.

I. This seemingly impossible role of service is possible for us all because it is not just a command. It is a gift of God.

Service is God's gift because it is God who serves us.

Think of it. This God of the Hebrew-Christian tradition is like no other god! God is the one who chooses to serve, not just to be worshipped or adored. Other gods have been revealed so that women and men could serve them. This God (the God of the Suffering Servant: the God of Jesus Christ) begins from the other end. God comes to the people, to liberate them so that they may celebrate their freedom by sharing it with others!

In God's service we see what Karl Barth calls the humanity of God. God is first of all not a king, sitting on a pyramid of the world — creating pyramids of domination and subjugation in the hierarchies of church and society. Rather the humanity of God is seen in that God chooses to be related to human beings through service (Barth, *The Humanity of God*).

No wonder our passage from Isaiah 52 says that the servant of Yahweh will startle the nations: "His appearance was so marred, beyond human semblance, and his form beyond that of the sons of men — so shall he startle many nations; kings shall shut their mouths because of him" (52:14–15).

The servant cannot even be recognized because suffering service is not even expected of a messianic figure by those in high places!

Service is also God's gift because Jesus not only calls his disciple to serve but also provides the power and possibility of carrying this out.

In Jesus Christ, we have the representation of a new humanity — the beginning of a new type of human being whose life is lived for others. Jesus came as Immanuel (God with us): to be with all people — the women as well as the men; the ignorant as well as the learned; the outcasts as well as the religiously acceptable; the oppressed as well as the oppressors.

Jesus helps us to see the Humanity of God so that we too can become representatives of new humanity. Here we see what it means to be truly and newly human. This is the image of God — freedom to serve others. This is the image into which humanity is created and redeemed.

The whole story of the New Testament revolves around this one theme: *diakonia* (service). At last someone has come, not to be served, but to serve! Everything that was done by this Son of Man, including humiliation, self-emptying, cross, death, is summarized in one final communiqué: service

(Hoekendijk, *Horizons of Hope*). This communiqué is offered as gift and promise. The disciples of Jesus are called to be servants; to be liberated for others.

II. God's intention for us now is just such an impossible-possibility: through service (God's and ours) we are liberated to be full human beings.

First, we are liberated for ministry (*diakonia*). We are set free from hierarchical structures which place ministry in the hands of a few, to begin carrying out the work of the people.

Traditionally, diakonia has taken three forms: curative, preventive, and proscriptive (Hoekendijk, *Horizons of Hope*):

    a. Curative diakonia is the healing and helping of victims in society.

    b. Preventive diakonia is attempting to curtail the development of social ills which victimize human life.

    c. Prospective diakonia is attempting to open the situation for a free realization and actualization of human life.

Although in the past the church has specialized in individual curative or "band-aid" tasks, recently people have become aware that it is necessary to work together on preventive health and social programs. It has also become slowly involved in prospective programs in which society is so changed that people can take part in shaping their own destiny and that the evils such as war, poverty, racism, and sexism are attacked.

The kind of diakonia that we want in our own life is the latter. We do not want to be helped after we are crushed, but would rather have justice that leads to elimination of destructive social structures.

In being liberated for ministry, we are drawn into the struggle for liberation of all peoples. Men and women, black and white, rich and poor seek to move together toward new ways of life in which those who have been oppressed are free to form their own agenda—to participate in shaping their own future and in deciding whom and how they will serve.

Second, we are liberated for others because we are called to be God's helpers or co-servants.

This is the image of woman in Genesis 2. She is created by God as *'ezer*—a divine helper for man who needs to live and work in community. Just like the image of the *'ebed* Yahweh (the Servant of God) in Isaiah 52, woman, and also man, is seen as a human being who has been given the privilege of living for others as God's representative.

This service in no way implies subordination. Nor does it imply domination of any human being over another. The alternative to subordination is not domination but service. There is no true ministry which is not freely given, in the same way that God's ministry is freely given. Social and church structures in which domination is used to make others serve are a denial of freedom. Just as subordination is a denial of true human dignity.

In this respect, the work of the women's liberation movement and third world liberation movements for new structures of justice, partnership, and sharing sometimes may be disruptive in family, church, and society. But they are not the real troublemakers—the structures of domination and subordination which destroy the possibility of true humanity and service.

Third, we are liberated for God because we can experience the love and service of God in our own lives.

When confronted by the authorities, the apostle Peter boldly proclaimed, "We must obey God rather than men" (Acts 5:29). For the gospel claims our allegiance to the One who serves, beyond any human ideology, beyond any church or social structure.

Such a demand is not easy. It often makes us unreliable in a cause; unable to assert that in fact, any particular program or organization is of ultimate significance. Because Christians seek to live according to a new way of being human, they often find themselves as marginal or misfit people in the games of dominance and exploitation that people play. If we are not misfits, then we need to have another look at how and where we serve.

In the last few years many women have been discovering that they really are misfits and marginal to the male-dominated society in which they live. Some are seeking new ways to go on being misfits for the sake of society. They are working in community with others on the boundaries of institutions where they can try to create new structures for human life (Daly, *Beyond God the Father*). My own experience is that I have always been a misfit, and I am glad to find other women and men who feel as I do—those who are seeking not just to be part of things as they are, but to serve the process of change toward God's intended future.

Not to be served, but to serve. These words—so impossibly-possible as a gift of God—are an instant communiqué of who we are and where we are going as followers of Christ and representatives of an emerging new humanity in which "There is neither Jew nor Greek, there is neither slave nor free, there is neither male nor female" (Galatians 3:28).

Long ago, as I glibly read those words circling that chapel chancel—*non ministrari, sed ministrare*—I didn't know how tough service would be! I didn't know just how much that promise of Jesus meant. I tried to share his baptism and temptations and I often ended up with wrong answers and worse defeats.

I still don't know how much that promise means. But I do know that in spite of all the devaluation and misuse and betrayal of the word "service" in churches and society, these words of Jesus continue to lead us toward a life of freedom. They are words about *a revolution in which everyone wins*— in which everyone finds a way of ministry and partnership on the road to human freedom! (Eric Mount, *The Feminine Factor*).

He was an attorney and author in New York City. He was not a clergyman; in fact, he delighted in castigating clergy for their appalling compromising of Christianity. He was a radical Christian who put his faith into practice ministering in Harlem. He did not mind being a "fool for Christ," nor did he ever shrink from an attack upon the world's "wisdom." William Stringfellow's very first sentence is a bemoaning of the sad "decadence of the American university," an unrelenting assault that typifies the whole sermon. Stringfellow accuses the modern university of being compromised by its mercantile context, a slave to those "principalities and powers" announced in the biblical texts as enemies of God. If any of the decision makers of the university were at church this Sunday, they heard a Sunday sermon that was a call for the university to repent of its sin and regain its true vocation.

The Wisdom of Being Foolish

May 10, 1975

WILLIAM STRINGFELLOW

I Corinthians 1:18–31 In these last years the profound organic decadence of the American university has become visible. My remark is not quantitative: I do not consider that the condition of death in institutions in this society has suddenly or lately increased by so much as an iota; the university is no more fallen today than yesterday, but human perception of demonic reality varies significantly, from time to time, and it may be said to be currently more lucid, or at least less deluded, than it seems to have been a generation or two ago. It is in this connection that the curious presence of Christians in the university has been relevant. The thought and word and action occasioned by them have been important in exposing the wretched situation of the American university and in nurturing some human beings—faculty and students, trustees and administrators, chaplains and campus ministers—to cope with the demonic, incarnate and militant, in the authority, tradition, ideology, and institution of the university. Now we reach a moment when daily events of our common history refute vain and romantic and fraudulent ideas about the university and when political naïveté can no longer conceal and academic sophistication can no longer rationalize the rudimentary status for the university as a principality, a fallen domain, similar to any of the other great institutional powers in which death thrives—like the Central

Intelligence Agency or the conglomerates or the Pentagon or the political technocracy. And the aggressive purpose against human life of the university, as with the other principalities, is no longer reserved or disguised but has become blunt and notorious.

Analytically, there are various rubrics by which to attempt comprehension of the present estate of the American university. I name some, not to thereby exhaust the matter and not to thus treat them as alternatives. These views are not distinct; they overlap; they are congested. Moreover, the discernment of any of us is partial and tentative; we suffer our own frailty; we glimpse but fragments of awesome reality. If any of these rubrics convenience our understanding of demonic existence in this world, we must nevertheless heed a caution that they oversimplify the activity of the principalities and powers. Yet for all of that, I try not to speak about the power of death manifest in the university truthfully, which is to say confessionally. Theologically, the elementary subject is the saga of the Fall. Analytically, it is the actuality of chaos in the present age.

Ideology and the American University

It is increasingly acknowledged today that the university in its identity as a principality has an ideological aspect. This is a tardy and begrudged recognition. The inherited and prevailing view has maintained that the university was ideologically neuter, and further, that this attribute rendered the university an open forum in which assorted and disparate claims of ideology — or of philosophy or of morality or, sometimes, of religion — could contend while human beings, variously persuaded, were left to exercise choices and make commitments. Though the university sponsored this dynamic encounter, the institution itself was conceived to be beyond ideology: aloof, nonpartisan, objective, devoted, purely, to search and research.

The quaint ideal of the university has been, in fact, often contradicted in practice by the exclusion from the pluralistic marketplace which the university was supposed to be of those religions contemporaneously prevalent in American society. There could be courses on Marxism or Platonism or positivism, or archaic religion, but none on Christianity or Judaism, at least in their modern expressions. Paradoxically, this cloture was rationalized as a pragmatic accommodation to American pluralism. Withal there was such a plethora of churches, denominations, and sects, each with its doctrines and versions, that it would overtax the facility of the university to cope with all of them, while to deal with some would imply bias or preference, or even risk proselytizing. No wonder that a premise of some Christians a quarter-century ago regarded the university as alien and hostile: a mission field, as they sometimes referred to it. Bishop Pike, of comforting memory to me and to many, suffered his earliest notoriety because he complained about the prohibitions against the teaching of Christianity in the colleges, a discrimination he thought betrayed their propagation of "an alternative faith" in scientism. Others thought, grandly, of the idea of a "Christian university." Meanwhile, let it be admitted, church-related colleges were proliferating which were frequently narrow-minded both religiously and educationally.

Gradually, as some of our predecessors in the faith foreknew, this feigned objective ethos of the university has been exposed as a de facto ideological stance. If, as an ideology, it be not as elaborated and self-conscious as classical ideologies, it has been no more subtle and no less self-serving.

The American academic ideology emerged from the imperious status accorded to science coincident with the industrialization of this society and from the efficacy imputed to scientific methodology in the technological mutation of society, especially as that has affected human behavior. The exaltation of scientism, and the imposition of the regime of science upon the whole university enterprise, were accompanied in the American experience with the popularization of an inflated — virtually superstitious — belief in education as the veritable secret of salvation. When the mentality of scientism began, more and more, to determine and restrict the conception of education, that fatal optimism concerning education became attached to the methodology of science. Within these past several years, we have beheld a degeneration of this grandiose schema of salvation into most pernicious doctrines. So heavy has been the concentration upon the specific as if that were unrelated to anything else, upon the substitution of technical capability for moral discretion, upon treatment of human beings as data, upon determinism, upon quantification, upon specialization, upon fabrication, upon mechanization, upon compartmentalization, upon prediction, upon manipulation, upon automation, upon technics, that questions of ethics — of belief and conduct, of commitment and decision, of correlation and consequences, of relationship and impingement, of integrity and wholeness — have seemed abolished. The only ethical issues remaining have been radically privatized, disconnected from everything else, narrowed to a matter of proficiency and competence within one's own niche and of loyalty and uncritical obedience at each respective echelon of organization.

Far from being innocuous or neutral, this ideology, in the university and throughout American society, has had, from a human point of view, appalling significance:

Thus, the usurpation of human accountability and the displacement of constitutional government by technical capability occasioned radically genocidal warfare in Southeast Asia;

Thus, a similar moral priority surrendered to technics gluts the market with redundant products which literally waste creation, jeopardize life, deceive intelligence, and program people as compulsive consumers;

Thus, the ethical rejoinder, in Watergate, to the most calculated and insidious threat to the rule of law in American history was reduced to the plea of dutiful obedience to political superiors;

Thus, too, the American abhorrence of such myopic ethics, summoned at Nuremberg, has proven insufficient to forbid or prevent My Lai while the Nazi war criminals found vindication in American ideology when Lt. Calley was rendered the scapegoat for higher authority and corporate criminality;

And, thus, in the American university, a fragmentation and isolation has occurred which is both anti-social and anti-societal in principle, which implies an elemental incoherence of knowledge, and which, incidentally, spreads a pervasive illiteracy among members of the university organized and confined in their respective segments and factions.

But I find no need to multiply this news, though it is necessary to notice that the predatory character of the ideology fostered in scientism, within the university, is quite definite, that is to say, what is involved is a relentless assault upon the mind, what is threatened by demonic aggression is the retention of sanity and the use of conscience, what is at stake is the preemption of those very faculties which distinguish human life as such. It is a fearful — and authentically apocalyptic — happening that the university furnishes such hospitality to the purpose of death in this world.

The Commercialization of the Disciplines

All that has been suggested here about the bestial reality of the ideology incubated in the university is subject to the note that as America moves into an ultimate technocracy, change is accelerating geometrically, the chaotic impact of such change proliferates fantastically, and human beings become demoralized and bewildered, and, sometimes, dissipated in their efforts to comprehend the chaos. Technocracy signifies a most sophisticated totalitarianism and people are delivered into its bondage as much by their own pathetic private attempts to shield themselves or to, somewhere, somehow, escape as by either captivation or surrender.

The matter of ubiquitous, omniscient surveillance aside, the futility of these poignant illusory human retreats is demonstrated in the terms of mere survival dictated in an advanced technocratic society activated by the necessities of redundant warfare and indefinite consumption. Survival in the American technocratic state means indoctrination in operations and skills integral to the technical process. The totalitarianism is so pervasive that there is no way to exist unimplicated in technocracy. Even those discarded by and cast out of this society, those classified as recalcitrant or useless or unemployable — the blacks or the Indians or elder citizens or emancipated women or prisoners or the ill and disabled or unconformed youth — remain basically dependent upon gratuitous official dispensations: food stamps, welfare, rent subsidies, Medicare, social security, and the like. When it comes to college students, the possibility of survival becomes translated into obsessive anxiety about admissions, examinations, grades, the acquisition of marketable "know-how," placement. And these, in turn, are quickly converted into sullen conformity to the status quo.

Paradoxically, and even more pathetically, technocracy now brinks a crisis in America in which, should either or both of this society's basic policies — warfare and consumption — be further implemented, the predictable outcome is national suicide. Hiroshima taught that gruesomely, about thermonuclear war; Vietnam has, ruefully, shown the same to be the fact about any other warfare. Meanwhile, Americans have already pursued the consumption ethic far enough and fast enough to foresee that it can only end in the consumption of everything, beyond any capability of replenishment, in self-consumption. If this be truth, conformity in this society is insanity.

This points to how, under the aegis of scientism, within the ideology prevalent in the university, abetted by the extraordinary momentum of technologically induced change, the disciplines and the arts indigenous to the university have been demeaned and subverted by commercialization. They become commodities. And those who are trained to practice the professions and the arts are consigned a correspondingly humiliated status.

Nowhere is this more sufficiently documented than in the law, the field I know at first hand. When scientism is formulated as jurisprudence it is known as positivism, and it is no happenstance that there is an historical association between totalitarianism and legal positivism. In it, the role of the lawyer is not as protagonist for justice nor as champion of equity nor even as advocate of the rule of law, but the public responsibility and function of the lawyer is abolished in favor of the lawyer as hired technician obliged only to serve the vested interests of a client or the cause of the regime. In America that has come, practically, to mean the nigh exclusive commitment to the advantage of the great corporate powers and principalities to an extent to which the rights, causes, and complaints of ordinary human beings are virtually obviated. And thus, the realities of human need, where not utterly disallowed, are deemed parasitical, while any meeting of those needs becomes super-erogatory.

I have on occasion said that my only comfort, morally, in being a lawyer is that I am not a doctor. It is not a facetious remark, for though I can here only speak as victim and not as practitioner, I observe a corruption in the medical profession parallel to that in law where matters of research priorities, costs, distribution of services, and response to human need are concerned.

And there are grounds to assay similarly the other professions and arts. The language is debased and perverted into jargon, propaganda, code, and other babble; literature is regarded as obsolete and threatened with extinc-tion; the performing arts become stereotyped and facsimilated; any cre-ativity is controversial and is opposed by the powers that be. The situation is quite explicable: technocracy cannot tolerate human creativity because that cannot be quantified, programmed, and forecast; so it must be suppressed, destroyed, or displaced. As often as not, it is substitution which happens, and then, the nomenclature of the art is misappropriated and applied to the anti-art so as, after a generation or two, to even deprive human memory of the art. Meanwhile, it barely requires a footnote, a ridiculous parody of this whole process is technocratic totalitarianism by which the disciplines are corrupted and dehumanized as rendered in the realm of sports, both in the university and in society generally, especially in the political use assigned to commercialized sports to supply distraction or vicarious involvement to habituate persons as spectators to fill up the time, or otherwise to nurture public passivity and enforce ignorance.

Lest anyone mishear my remarks as a diatribe against science, let me make plain that I behold the sciences in the same way that I have cited the profes-sions and the arts and I denounce only the abuse of science, the exaggeration of scientific methodology, the idolatry which is scientism, the overwhelming commercial orientation of the sciences, and the abdication or other absence of human dominion over science.

Respecting all the disciplines of the university, and their potential for human life in society, human originality or creativity, like conscience, which is its next of kin, means resistance to the regime of technocracy. The use of the mind — the exercise of the definitively human faculties — signals that resistance and risks violent reprisal.

An Inherent Violence

What I am saying, analytically, is that violence is inherent in the techno-cratic state in America, and that inasmuch as the American university has been captivated by the ideology of scientism and has been determined by a technocratic model it is governed by violence. Theologically, of course, the straightforward meaning of the Fall is that violence takes the place of relationship throughout the whole of creation and, in that sense, violence reigns in the particular fallen domain of the university. Yet that does not spare us from trying to understand and cope with the immediacy of violence in the contemporary university scene. I am not now recollecting the turbulence of student protests in the sixties so much as reminding that as soon as those protests exceeded the outbursts of late adolescence and indicated a more mature rebellion, the "student movement" was routed, ruthlessly, and devastated by the official violence of political and university authorities. The defeat and repression of the student unrest was, at the time, the most predictable outcome, given the precedent, but a few years earlier, of how the American black revolt had been stopped by a similar deployment of paramilitary police and the federal army. Violence is diverse and, often, subtle, and verbal, psychological, economic, and political sanctions had been enforced prior to the military resort against the students. This serves mainly to disclose that the forms of violence, which are not literally secret, the threat of physical coercion, and, ultimately, the prospect of death are latent in the technocratic DNA of scientism.

All this, as you know already, was enacted in the infanticide at Kent State. It was then and there that message was notarized, that if the offspring of the white bourgeoisie would not conform to the function consigned to them in technocratic society they would die. Quickly, after the massacre, economic reprisals — the cutbacks in scholarships, student loans, subsidies for student jobs, research grants — reiterated the same news. And so, defeated, intimidated by the threat of death, immobilized, scared, the students conformed. They remain so. Quietism is the pervasive political mood on American campuses to this day. Resistance is now nonexistent or is reduced mainly to mock protest like the indulgence of neo-Marxist talk. Appropriately for technocracy, the university more and more has the façade of a fortress, and the ambiance of a factory, and the internal surveillance of a medium-security prison. It is said that the students study more, but that comfort is small if what there is to learn is radically diminished and dehumanized. What, in fact, we behold in the university is a principality bereft of autonomy and integrity, and, instead, consigned to a vassal status, subservient to other powers — the political and commercial and military and intelligence institutions prominent among them.

What can be said of the witness task of the Christian in the university in America?

For that I commend you the word *foolish*.

In the midst of demonic reality, while the power of death is most awesome, in the present age, the Christian is called to be foolish: to be an agitating, patient, resistant presence in the university, confessing the power of the Word of God to renew the mind: to replenish our university.

Almost all of the pastors who served Riverside Church in New York have preached at Duke Chapel, testimony to the connection felt between these two unusual congregations that were born during similar periods of American religious life. Ernest Campbell came from Riverside to preach this sermon on the theme of faith. Campbell was a great storyteller, a preacher who sought to link the historic Christian faith to the contemporary world. In this sermon, Campbell's description of "faith" rarely links itself to the traditional story of biblical faith, the story of Jesus. Instead "faith" becomes part of our story as we move through the present world, or in his words, "all of the reality that rides in upon us."

What's the Story?

May 11, 1975

ERNEST T. CAMPBELL

Genesis 12:1–19 and Hebrews 11:32–40 We hear much these days about four-letter words — some good, some bad. Today I should like to attempt a few improvisations around a five-letter word that is heavily used and frequently misunderstood. The word is faith!

At the risk of being either heretical or simplistic or both, I want to de-theologize this term, take some of the starch out of it, and describe faith as "an act of commitment by which one inserts himself into a new story."

Every life needs a story line. Our years are sequential. Yesterday carries over into today, and today into tomorrow. Some organizing theme must be discerned or ascribed. We cannot live as if life were a patternless mass of unconnected fragments.

For some the story is the self. The perpendicular pronoun becomes the Maypole around which the steps of life are danced. These potent egos trade in society's marketplace under the firm name, "Me, Myself, and I, Inc." Ethical decisions are made on the basis of self-interest: What's good for me is right, what's bad for me is wrong. For all such, the world turns on the narrow axis of the self!

This perception of life can even find support in prayer. Abraham Heschel, in one of his earlier books, talked about a view of prayer that could only be described as "religious solipsism." He described this perversion thus: "The individual self of the one who prays is the whole sphere of prayer life. The assumption is that God is an idea, a process, a source, a fountain, a spring, a power. But one cannot worship an idea; one cannot address his prayers to a fountain of values; one cannot pray 'to whom it may concern.' To whom then do we direct our prayers? Yes, there is an answer. We address prayers to the good within ourselves."

For some the story is the family. The needed meaning is found in family history. It is enough to be a Jones, a Johnson, or a Jenkins. Pride of blood is a centering force for many in our society. There are mail-order houses that apparently do a brisk business tracing family trees and selling coats of arms. The wag rises up and says that the best thing to do with a family tree is spray it! But these people will not be put off by such whimsical advice.

After all, there are three and a half billion of us in this world. We can be forgiven for seeking solace or even enclosure in the family.

But can any family supply all the required meaning? "All in the Family" may be a striking television series, but "all in the family" is not an adequate base for life. Witness the forces at work in our culture pushing in the direction of the "extended family."

Daniel Day Williams has spoken to the point with force and clarity: "Family love does not exempt us from the claims of the Kingdom of God. No person is ever fulfilled in the family alone and no romanticism about love should obscure that fact. The person is fulfilled in the world where God's work is being done. We have to find a union of love in its obligation to those with whom our lives are immediately bound; and love which calls upon each to become a creative member of the full society."

For some the story is the nation. Before and above all else, some know themselves as Germans or Italians, Puerto Ricans or Americans. Surely it is not wrong for one to love her country, but it is dangerous when one begins to love her country uncritically. Hyper-patriotism has contributed more than its share to the national grief that we call Watergate. I fear that we are overly stocked in the country with Americans who happen to be Christians rather than Christians who happen to be Americans!

I was visiting a few weeks ago with an old friend who taught for many years on the faculty of the University of Michigan. He is now teaching at McMaster University in Canada. I asked him what his status is as a citizen. He said, "I am now classified as a resident immigrant. I can go one of two directions, but I am in no hurry to make up my mind. I do not need a national identity to know who I am."

For some the story is the job. They define their lives by their livelihood. Who are you? I'm a plumber. I'm a merchant. I'm a policeman. Back in the Middle Ages there were guilds that served as organizing foci for people's lives — the carpenters' guild, the writers' guild, the actors' guild, and others. Today part of the slack has been taken up by unions and professional associations. I have known people in the academic world whose joy was boundless when they discovered themselves quoted in a footnote of some noted publication in their field.

It is not discounting the worth of work to suggest that there is something questionable about allowing ourselves to be defined by function alone. What we do and who we are should not be completely interchangeable.

A minister friend was trying to get next to a doctor who had a problem in his family that he would not admit to. Finally one day they played some golf together. Long about the sixth or seventh hole their drives fell reasonably close and they walked the fairway side by side. My friend took a deep breath and decided to make one last attempt. "John," he said, "tell me what you are when you're not a doctor." The man bristled, raised his voice, and said, "By God, I'm always an M.D.!" There is both judgment and warning in that well-known epitaph: "Born a man, he died a grocer."

Every life needs a story line. What is the story? What is it all about? Is it self? Or family? Or Nation? Or job? Or are these in fact subplots that stand in constant danger of being falsely magnified?

The good news of the Bible is of another story to which any may belong! "Once upon a time God created the heavens and earth . . . And God said, 'Let us make man in our own image' . . . And the eyes of them both were open and they knew that they were naked." The story goes on and touches down in places like Babylon and Egypt, Sinai, Palestine and Assyria, Judea and Samaria, and the uttermost parts of the earth—including New York City. It runs through names like Abraham and Moses, Saul and David, Isaiah and Amos, Jesus of Nazareth, Saul of Tarsus, Augustine of Hippo, Calvin of Geneva, Francis of Assisi, King of Atlanta, Chavez of Delano, and many, many more.

The beat goes on and the story continues. Of those who have preceded us in this still-developing drama it may be said that "they all having obtained a good report through faith, received not the promise, God having provided some better thing for us, that they without us should not be made perfect" (Hebrews 11:39–40).

Faith is something more and other than mental assent to fixed propositions about a static God! God is not a problem to be solved. He is a worker to be joined. Jesus said, "If any man will do his will, he shall know of the doctrine, whether it be of God" (John 7:17). God is at work in our world. This is what the story is all about. He is at work in the world not simply to "evacuate" souls out of it but to redeem, reconstitute, and recapitulate his vast creation.

There is extant in the church today a damaging "hovercraft" theology. In days to come we will see more hovercraft in the various harbors of our cities. Those contraptions skim over land and sea without touching either. Hovercraft theology touts a God that rides in majesty above the uneven surfaces of life immune to all that we experience. Too many, even in the church, regard God as a timeless essence that floats dispassionately above a mix of pain and pleasure that we call life.

The truth, I believe, is quite other than that. God is at work within our history. By loving lures and beckonings he keeps pulling us forward, working and willing the restoration of the world. Abraham is prototype — going out, not knowing where, breaking with the familiar to venture into the fundamentally unknown.

Nikos Kazantzakis has caught the forward motion of our years as well as anyone I know. Open your tired hearts to his testimony of hope:

> Blowing through heaven and earth, and in our hearts and the heart of every living thing, is a gigantic breath — a great Cry — which we call God. Plant life wished to continue its motionless sleep next to stagnant waters, but the Cry leaped up within it and violently shook its roots: "Away, let go of the earth, walk!" Had the tree been able to think and judge, it would have cried, "I don't want to. What are you urging me to do! You are demanding the impossible!" But the Cry, without pity, kept shaking its roots and shouting "Away, let go of the earth, walk!" It shouted in this way for thousands of eons; and lo! as a result of desire and struggle, life escaped the motionless tree and was liberated.
>
> Animals appeared — worms — making themselves at home in water and mud. "We're just fine here," they said. "We have peace and security; we're not budging!" But the terrible Cry hammered itself pitilessly into their loins. "Leave the mud, stand up, give birth to your betters!" "We don't want to! We can't!" "You can't, but I can. Stand up!" And lo! after thousands of eons, man emerged, trembling on his still unsolid legs.
>
> The human being is a centaur; his equine hoofs are planted in the ground, but his body from breast to head is worked on and tormented by the merciless Cry. He has been fighting, again for thousands of eons, to draw himself, like a sword, out of his animalistic scabbard. He is also fighting — this is his new struggle — to draw himself out of his human scabbard. Man calls in despair. "Where can I go? I have reached the pinnacle, beyond is the abyss." And the Cry answers, "I am beyond. Stand up!"

THAT'S THE STORY.

Faith then does not deal with a fragment of life marked off and labeled "sacred." It has to do with our attitude toward all of life. Commonly when we are asked, "Do you have faith?" we interpret the question to mean, "Do you believe in miracles?" "Do you believe in an after-life?" "Do you believe in the veracity of the Bible?" "Do you believe in the inherent worth of prayer?" "Do you believe in going to church?" "Do you believe in taking theology seriously?" How specialized faith has become! The "two-story" view of the universe is out—the idea that there is an ideal world above, where eternal essences abide, while down below in the flickering shadows of history men put in their time until death releases them to realms above. But what is "in" and has always been "in" is the "two-story" universe. For in, with, and under the events that comprise your life and mine, personal and corporate, the eternal God is at work—hopefully through us.

Our sin against the secular order as a church is grievous and large. William Dixon Gray, the sage of Nashville, wrote recently, "I would like to find funding for what I call an Institute for Secular Studies. My idea is that churches cannot talk with the secular world, the world itself, because they do not bother to study and understand the secular. *The churches even take from their own people who are in the secular world a confidence that the secular is God's interest and love.* Churches want their people to stay unsophisticated, in bondage to an irrelevant idiom."

Here I want to do something that I very seldom do. I want to quote again a paragraph that I quoted previously in this pulpit. I cannot hide my belief that in this statement Bishop Robinson has put an able finger on a common Christian failing:

Much theological language has a way of defining Christ out of universal common experience. If I am asked, "Do you believe in the Atonement?" or "the Resurrection" or "the Parousia," the questioner expects to elicit my attitude to something Jesus is supposed to have done on the cross, something that is alleged to have happened on "the third day" or something that may happen at the end of the world.

Contrast the effect when you leave out the definite article: "Do you believe in atonement?" "Do you believe in resurrection?" "Do you believe in parousia (that is, presence or coming)?" The "the" of the traditional Christian myth removes the reality of Christ from the kind of present where every eye might in fact see Him to the distant past or to the remote future or to "the divine super-world" where Christ lives in a timeless realm, as unrelated to the continuing course of events.

What I am insisting on today is that faith is not the special quality that we have made it. Faith deals with all of the reality that rides in upon us. The aim of faith is to *refine* life where it is coarse, to *soften* it where it is hard, to *reconcile* it where it is lost, to *value* it where it is debased, to *celebrate* it where it is doubted, to *free* it where it is hung up, and to *illumine* it where it is in darkness.

What then of self or family? What then of nation or job? None of these is denied. Each can be fulfilled in the vision of the two-story universe. At best they are vital subplots of the main story line. Viewed thus, they are freed from the strain of trying as *parts* to function as the *whole*.

Faith is an act of commitment by which one inserts herself into a new story. Jesus came to invite us into a new dimension of life. "The time is fulfilled, the kingdom is at hand, repent and believe in the gospel" (Mark 1:15). In Jesus of Nazareth the scope and substance of the story are prefigured. He is its embodiment and the source of our empowerment.

Years ago Josiah Royce described man's life as "a search for loyalty to an adequate cause." What many of us need is deliverance from the subplots into which we have thrown ourselves unconditionally, so that we might connect up with the big story that is pregnant with meaning and excitingly open to the future that God is seeking to bring.

It has been said that the two most important days in a person's life are the day on which she was born, and the day on which she discovers why she was born.

Gracious God, forgive what we have been,
Correct what we are,
And order what we yet shall be,
For *Thy* sake and *ours*—
Through Jesus Christ our Lord. Amen.

W. D. Davies, George Washington Ivey Professor of New Testament at the Divinity School, capped off a brilliant career at Duke, bringing the university international renown through his publications. But despite his erudition, Davies was also a wonderful preacher. Delivering his insights in his Welsh-accented voice, he demonstrated that the finest of faithful biblical scholarship could also be vibrantly proclaimed. When not in the pulpit or on the lecture circuit, Davies was always in his place in the second pew on the right in the north transept of Duke Chapel.

The Bible Today

October 24, 1976

W. D. DAVIES

Psalm 8:6—Thou makest him master over all thy creatures; thou hast put everything under his feet.
Luke 12:15—Beware! Be on your guard against greed of every kind, for even when a man has more than enough, his wealth does not give him life.

In 1964 at the end of one of my classes, when I had been lecturing on the New Testament, one of my students asked, "Why do you get so excited about the Bible? After all, what importance has it for this modern, secular world?" That was the first time that I had ever been asked by anyone to justify my discipline: to defend the importance of the Bible not on cultural or historical grounds, which would have been easy, but on religious ones. I knew then that I was moving into a new world which questioned familiar assumptions. Today I want to share with you the answers I have tried to give to that question: what is the role of the Sacred Book in a Secular Society?

First, what does the phrase the "Secular Society" mean? Fifty years ago it would have been easy to define it. The word "secular" comes from the Latin "saeculum," meaning "the time," or "the age," or "the spirit of the age." A secular society is one bound in by the spirit of its age, confined in itself and content with this world. This meaning still remains, but in our generation the phrase "secular society" has gained a wider sense. Perhaps the chief mark of our age has been the fantastic development of applied science, that is, the growth of technology, the ability of man to control the forces of nature by his intelligence and mechanical skill. I need not labor the obvious.

The term "secular society" is a description of our scientifically conditioned society.

This modern secular society has certain characteristics. It can be technically efficient. It is international: it is evident in Japan as in America, in Vietnam as in Brazil. Its spread seems uncontrollable. It provides us with untold wealth and benefits. It is not surprising, therefore, that the secular society has been highly confident. The achievements of Science have been so spectacular that nothing seems beyond its reach: it seems to be the "Open Sesame" to the good life. The great successes of technology produced in some the conviction that we have now come of age and can stand on our own feet. The primordial notion that we need the help of a divine being or beings or need appeal to another world to adjust the balance of this is superfluous. Our problems will ultimately be soluble, if at all, not primarily at least through the aid of ancient religious traditions. Even the so-called higher religions, Buddhism, Islam, Judaism, Christianity, belong to a stage of human evolution which is past: they can largely be discarded. And much in the history of religions is primitive and reactionary. In many of its forms religion has been callously on the side of privilege and truth. A French philosopher has urged that "God has been a restrictive force in human history." The view has grown that our immemorial problems are to be best solved by scientific research and technology.

In short, there has come about a profound revolution which we call "secularization" on a worldwide scale. In Nietzsche's words this "secularization" assumes "that all the gods are dead and that we must be mature enough to go on from there," leaving all the dead gods behind. The attitudes and institutions of our society are more and more determined not by religious beliefs and movements but by the pressures and demands of the techniques of mechanization and production.

And yet, there has recently been a change. The term "the Secular Society" has come to suggest to many something not altogether desirable. Many find it even frightening. Even in its heyday some of the most intelligent and earnest spirits among the young in the universities and elsewhere rejected it and dropped out. But even more there is now emerging a general recognition that the Secular Society generates its own peculiar problems: extremes of poverty persist despite its benefits, congestion jams its speed, and pollution its abundance. In a world of plenty the rich are getting richer and the poor, poorer. To manipulate nature is to invite unforeseen, perhaps unforeseeable problems. There is a growing disenchantment. To use an overworked cliché, we are experiencing a failure of nerve, intensified also by the cosmological, biological, and psychological knowledge of our time.

One result of this has been a new openness to what the older religious traditions have to say. Recently we have seen an emerging interest in eastern as well as western religions. The search for the sacred is inching its way back, sometimes in unfamiliar and even bizarre ways. In this recent period of the return of the sacred we must dig into the rock whence we are hewn and inquire: What has the Sacred Book of our Faith to do with the Secular Society?

But first we must ask what we mean by the Sacred Book. The word "sacred" is synonymous with the word "holy." And we normally speak of the Holy Bible or the Holy Book. In its root meaning the term "holy" suggests something that is apart from everyday life; something appropriated for strictly "religious" use; the holy is the nonsecular, the separated. A holy place is that space which is set aside from ordinary commerce and used only for the approach to the divine.

In this sense, the Bible is not a "holy" or "sacred" book; it is *not* apart from the secular. We have much to learn from the Jews. They hardly ever use the term "Holy Bible." When they refer to what we call the Old Testament, they speak of the Law, the Prophets, and the Writings, which have very much to do with our everyday life. The Bible deals with the most ordinary, worldly secular things. It describes war, the conquests and defeats of nations; it deals with human love and lust; it speaks of poverty and riches, justice and injustice. It is a disturbingly, at times coarsely, secular book. It is we Christians who have called it "holy" and set it apart from life—perched on a pulpit. It is much healthier to speak not of the "Sacred Book" or the "Holy Bible" but of "The Book"—the Book we use and thumb, because it is in the very midst of our daily life.

In what ways then does this Book confront our secular age? I can only mention two: one positive, and the other negative.

First, then, the positive. The Bible says "yes" to the secular age. This secularization in certain aspects is to be welcomed. Our mastery over Nature can be beneficial; it is under the blessing of God: it is the fruit of God's grace to us. In Psalm 8 we read:

> *What is man that thou art mindful of him*
> And the son of man that thou visitest him? . . .
> Thou hast given him dominion over the works of thy hands;
> Thou hast put all things under his feet.

The benefits of technology are to be enjoyed. The prophets of the Old Testament did not bleat for a simple past in the desert before the complexities of civilized life in Canaan had come. They accepted cultural and technological change as a challenge to their moral integrity. And it is not for us Christians to yearn for what we imagine to have been a simpler world—to long to go back to the Early Church, or the Middle Age, or to the Reformation or the nineteenth century—but to recognize the gifts of God in the marvelous achievements of the human mind in this secular age.

In fact, the Bible is not only *not* a "Holy Book," but it proclaims a faith which is highly materialistic. Christianity is probably the most materialistic of all the higher religions: it is not for nothing that Communistic materialism has been called a Christian aberration. The essence of the Christian Faith is expressed in the first verses of John's Gospel:

> In the beginning was the Word
> And the Word was with God
> And the Word was God
> . . . And the Word became flesh
> And dwelt among us
> Full of grace and truth.

The word became "flesh." One aspect of this might be rendered: "The Divine has become secularized." The Word—the Reason or Thought or Principle behind and in the Universe—has become "incarnate" in Jesus Christ: it has taken his "flesh." This means that all human flesh can become the vehicle of the Divine, so that everything that helps human flesh is to be welcomed, and everything that hinders that flesh is to be opposed. In this sense, we celebrate secular achievement when we celebrate Christ. For example, the notion that it is possible to save souls, as if they could be isolated from their environment and did not exist in the flesh, is again an aberration from Christianity.

But what of the negative aspect of the Bible's encounter with the secular age? The Bible asserts that technology may be and is a good servant but a bad master: it declares that the secular, good as it may be, is not enough. On one way especially—there are others with which I cannot deal today—the Bible puts a question to the "Secular Society."

We saw that for the secularist there often seems to be no need to refer to anything beyond or outside this world for explanation, authority, or salvation. But the Bible confronts us with a strange people, the Jews. Ben Gurion thought that they created God. Most of them believe that they encountered a mysterious living God, who claims ultimate allegiance. This living God of Israel cannot be contained within the confines of our control but rather controls us and our destiny. The Bible compels us to face the Mystery of the People of God both in its Jewish form and in its Christian form, the Church. The Bible speaks of a Traveler unknown, as John Wesley calls Him, Someone beyond and outside even though He is in this world, who has called into being a People *in* the world not explicable simply in terms of this world. I said that the Bible is *not* a holy book in the sense that it is separated from our secular life. Let me now say, equally emphatically, that by confronting us with the mystery of the people of Israel, it points to the Holy.

What do we mean? The most probable origin of all our religious life seems clear. As we walk this earth we become aware of a mystery which terrifies us and fascinates us at the same time. To this mystery we have given the name "the Holy." It is our awareness of and response to this "holiness" that alone makes us truly religious. How shall we know this Mystery which we experience in ourselves, in others, and in the world around us? How shall we approach it? It is to *this* question that the Bible largely applies itself.

All the great prophets and priests of Israel agreed that the Holy One, the Mystery, is not to be understood other than on moral terms. The way to approach the Holy is to do justice. But there is more than justice. And later the New Testament was to assert that in the fullness of time the Mystery appeared, condensed, or concentrated in the face of a man, that is, in the person of Jesus Christ, that in Him the unknown Mystery is made knowable; he himself becomes the mysterious Israel pointing to the Holy.

The secularist too certainly finds life mysterious. There are secular poets, artists, and thinkers who are profoundly aware of the mysterious dimensions of life. Very often they put us to shame by their sensitivity and concerns: we stand in need of them. But the vision is mysterious on its own terms and within its own limits, and man *will* himself be sufficient for it. Here the Bible issues its challenge. Through this Book, and through the Mystery of Israel and of the Christ to which it points, we are confronted in our pilgrimage with One beyond and outside us who claims to be our creator and redeemer. We are challenged to discover ourselves as truly human in an encounter with and response to this Jesus, the personal mystery of God in the flesh.

And this means that the Bible challenges us with the question: "What is the true nature of our human existence? Can we be satisfied within the confines of this world? We need more — a personal relationship and conscious dependence upon the ultimate Mystery who is the God and Father of our Lord Jesus Christ. Human achievements, technical and otherwise, are to be welcomed. But will they ever, even in their most enhanced forms, satisfy? Let us use a simple analogy. A man and a maid get married and set out on their life together. They buy a house: they supply it with all the modern utilities: it is the height of comfort. But in itself, it is not and cannot be a home until there be established within its walls a personal relation of trust. So is it with the universe. We may, indeed, find ourselves able to provide for all our material needs. But without the dimension of personal trust in the ultimate Mystery and commitment to that Mystery who gives meaning to our existence, we can never convert the house of this world, full of wondrous things as it is, into a home. In short, can we be at home without the experience of and resting in God? As an English poet has expressed it:

> We have hands that fashion and heads that know,
> But our hearts we lost, how long ago —
> In a place no chart nor ship can show
> Under the sky's dome . . .
> For men are homesick in their homes
> And strangers under the sun,
> And they lay their heads in a foreign land
> Whenever the day is done.
> In the end, all things betray us who betray God.

This, then, is the challenge of the Bible to a Secular Society: it proclaims the reality and necessity of the Living God, holy, righteous, and loving, and of the practice of this Presence, as an ultimate succor in a world which proclaims the death of God, as an outmoded, primitive overhang.

And secondly, I have time to note one further challenge only. The Bible confronts the "Secular Society" with the demand of the Law of that God of whom we have spoken. One of the effects of the secularization has been to challenge the age-old moral teaching not only of other religions but of Judaism and Christianity. The traditional norms of the Judeo-Christian past have given place in many quarters to moral relativism in which, within the limits imposed by society, everything becomes permissible. In other quarters, the norm seems to have become "doing our own thing." The old guideposts are eroded, forgotten or ignored now in the secular society, and we are adrift on change.

Let us be realistic. There are questions now facing mankind on which the biblical documents can give us no direct guidance: these questions had not arisen when the biblical writings were composed. On such questions all the resources available to us from contemporary knowledge should be exploited. We must frankly recognize the radical newness of many ethical problems that now confront society and be ready to experiment with new forms in the community, in the family, in life and in death. We must espe-cially beware of using the Bible to bolster our own established interests and prejudices rather than as a challenge to necessary change: the Bible is not a sanction for the security of the status quo but a spur to a new and more liberated order.

But this does not mean that the moral teaching enshrined for us in the Old and New Testaments, the fruit of the experience of centuries, is now out-moded. How this teaching is formulated — through the Law, the Prophets, the words and life of Jesus — all this I cannot here discuss. But as the eminent ethicist who teaches here has rightly noted, it is for us to recognize that in these forms the Divine Imperative under which man is to live is presented. It is God's thing that finally we are called upon to do. Very often — more often that we usually recognize — our thing and God's thing will coincide. But sometimes they will not and at that point the Bible issues its challenge.

I will note only one point at which the demands of the Bible come into essential concentration — at the death of Christ. I have spoken of the Mys-tery of Israel which confronts us in the Bible. But Christ is Israel and He died. And to be in the Church is to die with him — to die to the self. At the heart of the universe, for us, is a cross. There is a sense in which we can sum up the moral demand of the Bible in the words of probably the earliest Christian hymn known to us.

> Let this mind be in you
> Which was also in Christ Jesus
> Who, being in the form of God,
> Thought it not robbery to be equal with God
> But made himself of no reputation
> And took upon him the form of a servant
> And was made in the likeness of men.
> And being found in fashion as a man
> He humbled himself
> And became obedient unto death.

The climax of the Bible's demand is here. Far be it from me to suggest that we can die His death. But we are called upon in our measure to die to ourselves. This is fundamental to our redemption.

To sum up, then, the Bible welcomes the positive aspects of our Secular Society, but it also sets before us the question: do we know the presence of God in our life and do we acknowledge the mystery of his commandment? Do we know the infinite succor and infinite demand of the Living God? The

Bible sets a judgment over our closed sterile, stale world of secular values, and it opens our eyes to a life which does not primarily depend on the abundance of things, but on His presence. Our holy book roots us in a past but does not tie us to it. While it is an anchor, it is not a sanction for the status quo but a spur to a new creation.

From the very first sentence of this sermon, Will Campbell displays his gifts of humor, sarcasm, and outrageous prophetic pronouncement delivered with studied Southern redneck earthiness. Campbell, then director of the Committee for Southern Churchmen, was serving as Duke's "Theologian in Residence," as part of a program concocted by the Chapel to bring a prophetic voice to Duke for a month to mingle with undergraduates. It was the first of Campbell's many visits to the Chapel, where, in every sermon, he always managed to present an uncomfortable, unconventional, deeply faithful gospel. Campbell wrote novels, histories, and works of popular theology but he remained always that which God had first called him to be: a Baptist preacher.

That You Might Have Life

January 23, 1977

WILL CAMPBELL

John 10:10 On one occasion Jesus, who might well have been aborted if he had come along in our day because the circumstances surrounding his conception and birth were highly irregular and a terrible inconvenience, was talking to some friends and came as close as he ever came to proclaiming that he was, for sure, the expected Messiah. After talking of imposters, of thieves and robbers, of sheep and shepherds, he said, "I have come that you might have life, life in abundance." Abundance here has been used to explain quality of life. Jesus saying he had come so that we might all have a good day or, as the airline stewardesses say, "a good *rest* of the day," a meaningful existence on this earth. Maybe so. But *abundance* does not really have to do with quality. It has to do with quantity. It means, "a lot of something." A lot of life—like *forever*.

I would like to talk this morning—for not more than twenty minutes, they have repeatedly told me—about one person, one pilgrim, who needed something to serve, someone to worship, who finally took the declaration that Jesus was the expected Messiah seriously and that He did come to offer life. Despite his belief, his pilgrimage was far from smooth. It's just a story. It isn't biographical and it isn't autobiographical. It's just a story.

He was born into a poor family, rural folk, simple people, rednecks was what they were called. The only book they had was the Bible and his Daddy and his Mama used to read it every night. And then they would pray. It seemed to him that they always prayed for the same things — food, shelter, and fairness to their neighbors. When he prayed he thought of a lot of other things to ask for but they always admonished him not to bother the Lord with trivia, that he was terribly busy day and night. They were a close people, each dependent upon the other for something. He said to his father and mother, "I will worship."

But he was a very bright boy and as he grew he became bored with hearing the same stories read and the same things prayed for. In his rebellious adolescence he would sometimes not listen when they read or would sit in a corner reading books of his own collection and selection. He especially tired of one of their favorite readings, of how Mary Magdalene and the other Mary had come running to tell some scared people that Jesus wasn't where they had put him, that he had got up and run off. He resented it when they talked about that meaning that they would live forever, feeling sometimes that they had both lived too long already.

They were forever talking about "Good News." The gospel, they said, meant "Good News." But he could see no good news in the rigid rules their faith seemed to dictate — don't smoke, don't drink, and don't mess around on a Saturday night in town. That, to him, was bad news, and he didn't intend to pay them any mind. And soon he didn't. There was a way out and he took it. It was 1942 and the patriotic fever of global war was in the air. There was a drama and romance about it. He did not hate his father and mother, actually loved them, as much as it is ever possible for an eighteen-year-old to love his elders, but he knew there was more to life than this dull and humdrum existence on a south Alabama cotton farm, and he suspected that there was more to Christianity than their moralistic code. But that would have to wait. He was in no hurry to find what it was. He saw the marching soldiers, watched the banners of Caesar unfurled upon every occasion, even in church, listened to rhetoric designed to gain his ultimate allegiance. So he went away, joined up, or was drafted. And he liked the parades, the formations, even reveille. He even liked the commands, the "Platoon halt, left face, right face, parade rest, attention, at ease, ready, aim, fire." One man said all those things to a thousand men at once. And they were obedient. The cause was just. He needed something to serve, someone to worship, so he said, "I have found that for which I searched in the days of my youth. I will serve my country. I will worship my king."

There were months of it. And then years. Months and finally years of sitting in hot, wet jungles of the South Pacific, waiting for the battle for which by now he was so well trained, an encounter he had long desired.

And then so quickly it came. He found himself splashing through the salty water, running with hundreds of others from the boat called an LST and looking like the hippopotamus he had seen in the San Francisco zoo, rifles held high, listening now for the commands, but now seldom hearing them, storming the beach of a little island called Vella LaVella, looking for the enemy. At first it all went right. Everyone shooting as one, shouting, moving further and further inland, until the army, the unit, the battalion was split into individual pieces and everyone was on his own.

Then it came. Days without food, drinking water from stagnant lagoons, still, though, searching for the enemy. And then he finds him, a slant-eyed soldier, sitting also alone, sitting in days of his own waste from dysentery, making no motion of opposition. Each looked at the other. The pilgrim, the noble warrior, lover of Caesar, knowing the enemy sitting before him could not walk and that he was too weak to carry him as prisoner to the command post on the beach miles behind them. Then the enemy, the slant-eyed little man he knew only as Jap, each unable to speak the tongue of the other, pointed to a spot between his tired little eyes, pointing then to the pilgrim's rifle, never fired before in anger, and then, pulling his pup tent half up over his face so that he could not see, stood facing him.

Now the battle was over and the pilgrim was back on the ship, going, they said to a rest area, then to another training area, and then to another search for the enemy.

He had some time to think. And it was of his earliest beginnings that he thought. "I am come that you might have life." Just those words over and over. I am come that you might have life. And he thought of his simple people at home, and wished that he was there, and he thought of the little Jap lying rotting in the jungle.

Now the war was over and he waited some more, this time to be mustered out, discharged, sent back. He read a little book the chaplain gave him. It was a book about some things that had happened to his people, his flesh and blood. It was the story of an illiterate black man who joined forces with some ignorant and illiterate white people, formed a constitutional convention in South Carolina, got elected to state office and finally national office. And then of Rutherford B. Hayes, who called the troops out of his native South, and the mass slaughter against those simple people who had overcome their fears and prejudice of one another, of black and white together. He read of the death of the black hero, read these last words and thought: "Gideon Jackson's last memory as the shell struck, as the shell burst and caused his memory to cease being, was of the strength of those people in his land, the black and the white, the strength that had taken them through a long war, that had enabled them to build, out of ruin, a promise for the future, a promise that was, in a sense, more wonderful than any the world had ever known of that strength, the strange yet simple ingredients were the people—there were so many of them, so many shades and colors, some strong, some weak, some wise, some foolish; yet together they made the whole of the thing that was the last memory of Gideon Jackson, the thing indefinable and unconquerable."

Now, disillusioned with country and king, as well as his own hollow victory, the shooting of one soldier dying already of beri-beri, he knew that his life would never be the same, that the rest of it would be given to improving his native soil, the South, and improving too the relationships between the races. He would serve this cause, he would worship the people.

But first he must be trained again. This time with books, laboratories, halls of ivy. He had long since deserted his fundamentalist rearing, partly because they taught him that sin was smoking, drinking whiskey, and messing around. He read new books, modern books, that set him on fire, heard learned words from learned people. They taught him that what God cares about is the suffering of his people. And he believed. God cares about human suffering, not little social things like smoking. (Then his reading included a report that said according to the scientist, according to the learned doctors cigarette smoking was going to create more widows and orphans than slavery or war had caused. But he was a two-pack-a-day man, so he didn't dwell on that. But he did wonder a bit about his new theology. If he had not simply substituted one moralistic code for another. One set of do's and don'ts for another set of do's and don'ts. But he went on. His cause was just. His new god noble.)

Now there was a movement raging, something called the Civil Rights Movement. He knew that it was for him, would bring him into the struggle for justice as Gideon Jackson and the others had been. He joined the movement, went to the meetings, marched, sang and protested, learned to say "Cracker, redneck, and peckerwood" in the same venomous tomes he had once said "nigger." But he was against violence. He was nonviolent. But as he watched the soldiers marching on his Christian campus every Thursday afternoon, looking pretty in ROTC parades, learning of war, and as he observed that it was academe that trained not only the warriors but the owners, managers, the rulers, he wondered if the academy might not be responsible for more violence than the Ku Klux Klan that had burned a cross in front of the chapel on Saturday night. But there was so much to do. The movement was just, and the learned doctors so persuasive.

Now there was another war—far off in Southeast Asia. This too he would protest, march against, sometimes to the point when there was a gnawing in his bones that he was betraying his people, his heritage. But he was learning to read the Bible again, in a new light, he thought, and he read the words of Jesus when his family had come to put him in the asylum, "Who is my people? Who is my mother and my brother? They whose cause is just!"

And another movement. Women were everywhere oppressed. In some ways more than black people. Again he would join, and march, and chant supportive songs. Sometimes his movements seemed almost to oppose one another. He had wanted to go and personally kill Bryant and Milam when they murdered a young black man named Emmett Till for insulting a woman. Now he found himself at times wanting to go and kill Emmett Till again for being abusive to a female person. He became confused and confounded. The wheels of progress made strange and now sometimes unconvincing turns.

Through ten years of war not one native American had been killed at the hands of the state. Now we were talking of killing our own criminals instead of political and ideological criminals abroad. Capital punishment was back in the news, strangely missing during those years of war. "It's like we just *have* to be killing someone," he thought, as he made an appointment with his own state's governor, a redneck like himself—or like he once was, a governor who had already opposed death as a means of punishment, saying that is a judgment for God alone to make.

He would go in and commend him, pat him on the back. But he wasn't ready for the words of his governor. "Ah, Pilgrim, I agree. I agree. But now I am having second thoughts. For yesterday you carried, outside these chambers, a sign which said everyone had a right to rid their body of that which it might be carrying unwantingly. If everyone has the right to rid their body of that which it might be carrying unwantingly, unwillingly, and unlovingly, then why doesn't the body politic, which I control, have the right to rid its body of what it is carrying unwillingly, unwantingly, and unlovingly? Ah, Pilgrim, I just don't know."

And the pilgrim went away sorrowfully, for behold, he was very *good*. "What's it all about?," he wondered. "Am I hoping when and where and in what there is no hope? Am I despairing when I should be in hope? Am I perplexed in the presence of certainty?"

Feeling it all so deeply, he went again to his mother's house, the hut of his beginning, and found a feast of a fatted calf. The feast was the reading of his father, now weak and stooped with age:

Why do you seek the living among the dead? He is not here,
he is risen. And then again.

I am come that you might have life . . . abundant life . . .
forever life . . .

And after the world has done all that it can do to you, after all the laws, whether laws of state or laws of the academy, after all the learning, the enslavement of technology, progress, and sophistication, after the firing squad and electric chair, after the madness of the rapist, and the murderer's crimes of passion on the street, after the marching and chanting, after the movement has failed or succeeded, and movements succeeding or failing for life or for what the world calls death, after the surgeon's scalpels have ended a life hardly begun, or the crack of bullets has ended one in its thirty-sixth year, the last word still belongs to God — He is risen, He is not here. Hallelujah!

Is it, the pilgrim wondered, as complicated as the learned doctors of academe had made it sound, or is it just as simple and clear as the words at his father's fireside?

Jesus came that we might *have* life, not that we might deceive ourselves into thinking that we can take it away. Amen.

*He thundered forth from the pulpit of Duke Chapel on a number of memorable
occasions, his deep, Southern-inflected bass voice penetrating the darkness and
the hearts of the congregation too. Carlyle Marney was a Baptist pastor and,
toward the end of his life, a visiting professor of preaching at the Divinity School.
He loved preaching at Duke Chapel. His sermons were visceral, eloquent, often
ambiguous and difficult to grasp. "Not to Condemn Us," which Marney preached
on a number of occasions around the country, is one of his most coherent and direct.*

Not to Condemn Us

April 17, 1977

CARLYLE MARNEY

Jeremiah 3:12–18 and John 3:16–17 There's a text for what I am about to
try to do to you. And I confess to some pleasure always in setting it out to do
for, to, or with you, here. But how did I ever think to do it from here or *there*,
for that matter. Years ago I sat on the last row in my old place to hear my
successor and suddenly I realized I had never seen the back of their necks —
in Church. They seemed somehow to stiffen — in Church. How did I think
to do anything to them in just ten years? It's sheer presumption there — or
here, for that matter. We all have ways of defending ourselves against the
Gospel — preached. But I do bring a text to my presumption.

I have never used it before — not in these decades of "doing" sermons. Nor
have I found or heard or read a sermon on it. Everyone jumps over my phrase
to get to the clincher: "but that the world might be saved through him."

It is really so that we have never believed this text of mine. Neither we
Protestants nor us Catholics have believed it. Only flower children really
believe it, for we were not reared to believe in Grace. Because we cannot
believe in Grace we really forgo believing that:

> God did not send his Son into the world to condemn the world . . .

And how shall I clear it of its obvious masculinity? Why not with an in-
serted "Hail Mary!"? "Blessed art thou among women, and blessed is the
fruit of thy womb, Jesus." And so it can read:

> God sent not the fruit of Mary's womb into the world to condemn
> the world.

Jesus or no, fruit of Mary's womb not withstanding, there is plenty of condemnation around. It oozes up through the floor cracks in all our hovels. We float on a sea of condemnation — not from Jesus. My mail this month, not to speak of the decades of mail; the newscasters from 5:30 a.m. to 11:30 at night who speak of little else but crime, judgment, condemnation. From Utah to the Virginia Board of Fisheries to the U.S. Bureau of Health, columnists, scenario writers, poets, pop artists, singers of domestic infidelities, all accuse us. I accuse! While Business, Government, Medicine, Law, Politics, Domestic Relations Courts, Religionists, Educators accuse and counter-accuse and confess. The very air we breathe is laden with condemnation.

But back to the mail, and the telephone, and the casual shopping center encounters:

Lovely letter, lovely girl years ago at school, now well-placed indeed, and happy except for that between the lines, nearly every line, "I am not worthy!"

Three terribly mistyped pages from an overwrought pastor: "If only I could be born again . . . I am my wife's make-shift son, only she does not know this yet . . . the mice are running me over . . . guts I guess I lack . . . I lack . . . I am . . ."

And at the other extreme, a dear and effective veteran pastor, terminally ill and still working, accuses himself of not dying well.

A psychiatrist in Michigan, "Can you give me information about Mr. _____'s experience there for our appraisal of the basis of his self-accusation and hyper-activism?"

Another psychiatrist in Maine: "Please give me your evaluation of so and so." (In effect, why does this front-line varsity man so despise himself?)

A young woman in State Hospital (I've never seen her) writes how she has hated me for what she thought I had done to her father, until she read in an old book of mine what I had done for Judas, and how she loves me!

Her father, a beautiful, suffering man, who had written, "God is the worst thing that ever came into my life!"

My special, very special, six year-old correspondent, reared in all but perfect permissiveness, already intensely aware of his spelling imperfections . . .

Add on all your stuff, dragged into and out of some sanctuary as this for years — then repeat after me:

God sent not the fruit of Mary's womb into the world to condemn the world . . .

Believe it if you can, and then you must ask, " *Who laid all this guilt on me, then?*" There is plenty of condemnation around, but not from the Christ. Who laid all this condemning in our laps? If not Christ, then who . . . ?

If God sent not the fruit of Mary's womb into the world to condemn us; if St. Paul's "There is therefore now no condemnation to them that are 'en Christo' " is believable at all—who laid it on us?

Answer: a version of Christianity laid it on us all over western Christendom. A bad version. By the sixth century C.E. nearly all the great conciliar gropings into the meaning of the personhood of God and us had been blunted by the understanding of Man as sinner. It came rapidly, by the early fourth century—if in mid-sermon Augustine said "Confiteor" in any context of joy, or grief, or need, the rumble of the congregation beating its breast would interrupt the sermon.

As James McCord put it in an address at Princeton this summer, and to make quite another point, the Greeks had addressed "What is Nature?" The genius of Socrates turned internal, and some call him the founder of modern psychology, except that the *person* in his individuality never really appeared, only the universal, and we are always particular men or women or both. This particularity is really our particularity. This Jesus knew, and introduced *singularity*, and set out to capture the "unique flavor of individuality." At climax, this Jesus, fruit of Mary's womb, demonstrated.

But in the West, Christianity reduced the question "What is Man, that thou art mindful . . ." to "What is man as sinner?" So for at least fourteen of the twenty centuries in which we have been de-Judaizing ourselves, so-called Christian anthropology has focused on Man as Sinner. Our greatest impoverishment is our limited notion of the Human: and its corollary, our limited idea of Redemption. So, in short, we get our condemnation not from the Christ, but from a culture shaped by limited Christianity. To sum it, we got our self-condemnation stance, in part, from the blessed Saints:

Not even Augustine escaped. He was unable to repeat the dying words of his great mentor Ambrose:

> My life has not been such that I would need to be ashamed to go on living amongst you. Nevertheless, I do not fear to die. We have a good Father.

Indeed, as van der Meer recaptures it, Augustine did not belong to those who go hence, like little children, content and confident. Ten days he lay alone, his eyes fixed on the parchment with the penitential psalms, which he had nailed to the walls and he wept continuously as he repeated the words . . . then he died . . . and there was no will . . . the poor Man of God had nothing . . .

We learned our condemnation from, too, the blessed Anselm, whose eleventh-century *Meditations* were still being printed in English six hundred years later, for little Christian girls to spend their Sabbath afternoons reading. Indeed, in an English version from 1704, given us by Lib Dowd for Christmas, inscribed "Elizabeth Ray, 1709, her book," I find her markings at:

> I cannot look upon my past life without horrour. For, when nicely examined, it shows me nothing but Sin or Barrenness, and all my days hitherto seem to have been consumed in living viciously, or living to no purpose. Or if in the midst of this general corruption there be scattered some Few instances of profitable actions yet even These give me confusion too. . . . I can easily discover so much laboured hypocrisie, so great an allay of imperfection, and so many other blemishes of several kinds, as will not suffer me to think they can please and deserve to be approved, but incline me rather to dread their displeasing and being rejected by a Holy and All Seeing God.
>
> And this is the best account that sinful Man can give of himself, that all his actions have been either vicious and damnable, or at least fruitless and vain . . .

He continues:

> (I am) the Scorn and Scandal of my *Species*; more vile than the beasts that perish; more filthy and noisome, than a Carcass already putrified. . . . Jesus, the blessed Jesus. This, This is He, The Judge at whom I tremble. . . .

And, in the same old leathern volume from Bernard, *Jesus The Very Thought of Thee*, we read,

> . . . the Gastliness and Deformity that I discover there, make me a perfect Monster, and a Terrour to my self . . . since every Corner of my Heart is a cage of unclean birds . . . and so, page upon page.

If God sent *not* the fruit of Mary's womb to condemn us, where did we learn to be so guilty?

From the Saints, and the Theologians and Pastors, and the opportunistic, manipulative Evangelists, from our first teachers, and our neighbors, and our playmates, and all our companions of the long, drawn-out confusion. From our Culture of Expectations, and the poverty of our Anglo-Saxon and Mediterranean forebears, from Madison Avenue, and the Media, and Courts and Law and Mores — and just this winter I was made to feel both guilty and stupid because I had already had my swine flu shots!

Now, if the Christ does not condemn us, but *we* keep laying it on us, what do we get out of being so guilty? Just what is this colossal indulgence?

The net profit for us in this culture-wide acceptance of our condemnation for mere sinning is the Great Evasion. First and blatantly, sin really is so much less than the *Evil*; we escape responsibility for the Evil by admitting concupiscence, envy, and greed. Consequently, all our legal, penal, educational, religious, governmental, and commercial systems are geared to deal with our sinfulness but none really is set up to deal with Evil.

Hence War, Famine, Pestilence, and premature Death ride all but unimpeded. But what could happen if we became *responsibly* guilty—guilty of Earth's *real* crimes: War, Famine, Pestilence, Death—mass crimes, mass guilt; *structural, institutional, systematic* guilt. What could happen if we quit using our childhood garden sins to escape our participation in Colossal Evil?

Swiftly now, might it not thrust upon us the broader notion of Humankind and Maturity, mobility toward possibility of a fairer Earth that we fled centuries ago when we learned to give total allegiance to property?

In spite of that nineteenth-century explosion which brought all our newer sciences and newest knowledge of our universe and of human beings onto piles of undecoded IBM drums, principally since 1950; in the twentieth century, humankind still acts in Time and History, as well as in that Nature which we now know we are not above. But like a fast spurt across a wide stage we ran through Empiricist, Determinist, Positivist ideological notions of humanity. Our own young have upended it all. They have caught and taught us that we have come past the end of salvation by ideology. They force us back on our origins; we are pushed back to the primal resources we abandoned for petty condemnation and pettier "salvation by ideologies" and "theories of education."

What if we should now be forced to face the real enemies; what if we discovered within us a new capacity for wishing—willing—deciding? What if we took seriously those nineteenth-century thinkers who began to try to show us a new locus for Evil—as McCord put it—"Evil in our structures of society, not just in the human heart?" Could we not with élan and encouragement let those foolish structures all go before a new recognition of *humanity* as our goal? A humanity beyond War—Famine—Pestilence—Death!

This is *Liberation Theology!* This *is* wholeness—this *is* Imago Christi, we *are* victors, being made able to stand against the real enemies. It rests on the reality of Grace, Community, Relation, Responsible Guilt, Expectation, and what a Pentecost it would be! If we realized and accepted the implications of the "God sent not the fruit of Mary's womb to condemn the world . . ."

This would mean that we should quit saying that our petty misdemeanors crucified Jesus. We would rather see, and say, with William Stringfellow and some others of us, that in Crucifixion we see the triumph of the structures of society that have found War — Famine — Pestilence — Death useful; we would see in Resurrection the triumph of the Species in standing above War — Famine — Pestilence — Death; and we would feel in Pentecost, our being empowered to participate in that Full Humanity that has as its proper place in Creation the calling to stand over against the true Evil and Triumph. We would recover our place in Creation! In Kazantzakis's notion — we would be "resurrecting Christ."

Once, years ago, two dear thirteen-year-old women, now grown, asked me why the Christ did not come again. I tried to answer in a sermon, "because we have not yet caught on to his first coming." I now add, "but he did not come to condemn us." Sometimes I have to turn to some great pagan to help me understand and realize what such a triumph over petty guilt would mean.

Last September, last visit to my great friend Kuykendall — pagan, rancher, eight-goal polo handicap in his youth, hunter of everything he could use from the coon who killed his quail to the twelve-foot cat which dragged off his calves in Mexico; pagan, I say, master sinner, Mexican cook, 150 years, he said, on the same spread, dying now, cancer-ridden spleen, liver, and stomach, great hulk shrunken, nothing in his stomach for three weeks, refusing artificial life support, calls to Maria, eighty-four years old and barefooted still, cook, friend, and conscience — "Bring me Chili!" — he believed he could hold it down . . . and did.

Alice, striking wife of forty-six years sitting on the bed-foot — and dying, he talks — of what? His sins, many, and some say, gross, although, as he said, "never indicted"?

Why no. He talks with Alice and me of his Mother. "What a person," he said of her. Widowed in his infancy, how she taught him everything a woman knows to do in a home and all anyone knows to do on a horse or ranch — how he adored her and had therefore turned a South Texas wilderness into an English park because he loved his Mother and Creation and knew himself part of Mother, and Creation, and Nature too — and it was time.

To salute this ego and species maturity I had to recall what Armand Nicholl at Harvard had used before to describe inner peace. He had said that if a person can love across a long span; if a person has a clear concept of genuine right and wrong with the ability to bear being wrong; if one has a growing sense of identity with responsibility for participation in Creation; and if one accepts the reality-terms of his own death — then is that one approaching true Humanhood.

What a model we have for this. Don't let the innocence of Mary's Baby put you off on this. Nothing incites us more than the refusal of such innocence to condemn us. This is perhaps why so many of the innocent, babies and aged, are *battered*. We can just hardly bear the innocence that lays no guilt on us. What a lead, toward mature guilt that sees the real issue, we have in Jesus. Let us even now go to Golgotha and see.

Carter Heyward, professor of theology at the Episcopal Divinity School, Cambridge, Massachusetts, preached this sermon early in her career, about a year after the publication of A Priest Forever, *her moving account of her ordination as one of the first women priests in the Episcopal church. Throughout her ministry, she has continued her fight for justice, particularly justice for women and lesbians. This sermon contains a central testimony of her work— "I believe we are compelled and empowered to risk whatever we must risk to create, with God, a climate in which* all *people can be who they are."*

The Enigmatic God

November 20, 1977

CARTER HEYWARD

Exodus 3:1–14 and John 8:21–43

May the words of my mouth and the meditation of our hearts be acceptable to you, O God, our strength and our hope. Amen.

We are told that upon completion of "The Hallelujah Chorus," Handel fell to his knees, beside himself, overwhelmed because he had seen God—and the *beauty*, the *power*, the *majesty* of God was extraordinary.

One of your preachers this year will be Elie Wiesel, a man who was incarcerated in a concentration camp during World War II and who lived to witness. In one of his books, Wiesel tells of having watched a young boy—his own age, about ten—being hanged by the Nazi soldiers. As the boy writhed in agony, refusing to give in to the rope, one of the witnesses asked another, "Where is God?" The response was silence. The boy continued to struggle, and the man asked again, "Where is God?" Still the response was silence. Finally, as the boy succumbed, hanging still, the man asked again, "Where is God?" And his fellow prisoner replied, "God is there—hanging on the gallows." Wiesel writes of the *utterly helpless* God.

What of this God—this terrible good, this holy terror—this Father, Son, and Holy Spirit Trinity? This Mother Goddess giving us birth and taking us back again into her womb the earth? This God of many faces? To whom has been ascribed many names? *Who is our God?* I ask these questions, believing as I do — to quote one of my students — that "God does not mechanically answer our questions, but rather moves us to *ask* them." And believing, furthermore, that unless we encounter God honestly — with questions, probing, seeking, risking offense — we do not encounter God at all. And so, I would offer this sermon as a prayer — opening myself, opening ourselves, to the presence of God filling this place.

In the beginning, long before there was any idea of "God," something stirred. In that cosmic moment, pulsating in possibility, God breathed into space, and groaning in passion and pain and hope, gave birth to creation. We cannot remember this easily — for we cannot easily bear to remember the pain and hope of our own beginning. But it was *good*. It was far better than we can imagine. For coming forth from God — in God, with God, by God — (as were all created things) we were shaped by God, in God's own image, formed in the being of God. Daughters and Sons of God. Living reflections of — witnesses to — God's own possibility. It was very, very good. For being human meant being with God, in God, for God — *never without* God. (To be without God would be not to be at all.)

It may be, as James Weldon Johnson suggests, that God created us because God was *lonely*. It may be, as various "process" theologians suggest, that God created us because God *needed* us to help God continue to become; it may be that God created us simply because it is the *nature of God* to create. Or it may be that God created us because God — having begun to "come to life" Godself — realized that the only way to *experience* life, the only way to live into the power, authority, and be-ing of God, would be to *share* it.

And so, we were created in God's own be-ing, to move *with* God, *in* God, *by* God, into the *passion*, and the *pain*, and the *wonder* of creation. What does it *mean* — to move with God, in God, and by God?

Long after the dawn of creation, a small group of people in the Middle East began to speak to one another of God. These people of Israel were the first people in recorded history to perceive that there is only *one* God. Other people — earlier, and at the same time, and still today — believed that there were *many* Gods: gods of rain, of sun, of war, of fertility, vying for supremacy. The people of Israel believed, however, that there is in fact *one* God who is the creator of all and who has created us in God's own image.

Furthermore, the people of Israel, discussing God, heard God say to them, promise them, that God was with them on the earth, moving among them, empowering them to do what it is in the be-ing of God to do: to *love*, that is, to reach out to one another and to creation itself, aware of the worth and value of every created person and thing. God showed the people of Israel that God was and is not a far-distant God, spinning holy wheels off high in the sky, but rather is a God passionately involved in creation, history, and human activity.

Long before Jesus, God made Godself known as One immersed in the affairs of being human. Long before Jesus, *human* history was, in fact, *sacred* history, the story of God's own be-ing moving in creation itself. So it was, in the beginning—the divine and the human, the creator and the creation, the infinite and the finite, *together*—in one process of Be-ing.

The people of Israel, aware of this, wanted to know more about this God in whose be-ing they were bound up. And so, as we heard this morning, one of Israel's leaders, Moses, spoke to God and asked God what he, Moses, was to tell the people God's name was. (For the Israelites, there was much in a *name*—a *name* was a revelation of a person's true character.) So, Moses was asking God to reveal God's identity to the people, to tell the people what they might expect from God. To *clarify* God for the people.

And God responded. God did not give out a long list of credentials. God did not give a speech about the power, authority, and might of God. God did not "spell things out." God responded simply, "I AM WHO I AM" (or, in other translations, "I AM WHAT I AM," or "I WILL BE WHAT I WILL BE.")

God could hardly have given a more enigmatic, elusive reply. The sort of reply that would be totally unacceptable to most of us, or to admissions committees, teachers, psychiatrists, were we to ask someone, "Who *are* you?" and the person to reply, "I am who I am." We would likely hear this as outrageous, impudent, defiant, disturbed. Certainly evasive. God *was* evasive. Elusive. Moses could not "pin God down." Approaching God in fear and tremor, seeking clarification, we are met with a riddle. *I am who I am.*

What about God is God saying?

Could it be that God is *not* being evasive about who God is, but rather that God is being *honest* and *clear*, *straightforward* and to the point about who God is? And that the point is that God *is*, in fact, evasive, elusive, not One to be pinned down, boxed into categories and expectations! God will be what God will be.

God will hang on the gallows.

God will inspire, fill, overwhelm Handel with power and splendor.

God will be battered as a wife, a child, a nigger, a faggot.

God will judge with righteousness, justice, mercy, those who batter, burn, sneer, discriminate, harbor prejudice.

God will have a mastectomy.

God will experience the wonder of giving birth.

God will be handicapped.

God will run the Marathon.

God will win.

God will lose.

God will be down and out, suffering, dying.

God will be bursting free, coming to life, for

God will be who God will be.

If this is so, then God is suggesting to the people of Israel—and to us here in this place—that the very minute we think we "have" God, God will surprise us. As we search in the fire and earthquaking, God will be in the still small voice. As we listen in silent meditation, God will be shouting protests on the street. God is warning us that we had best not try to find our security in any well-defined concept or category of what is "Godly"—for the minute we believe we're into God, God is off again and calling us forth into some unknown place.

God is saying something about the ultimacy of our customs, categories, doctrines, and moral laws. God is telling us that God cannot be "contained" —and that we will be missing God if we try to "hold onto" God, finding instead that we have made unto ourselves *graven images* of God according to what is most comfortable to us. God is saying something prickly to any of us who believe that *our* way is *God's* way—hence the *only* way, and an *unchanging* way. God is alerting us to the fact that God's own growth—God's own movement—will not be stunted by *our* low tolerance for ambiguity and change. God will not be confined to *our* expectations of who God *"ought"* to be.

And God surely knows that most of us cannot bear much God. We cannot easily accept an enigmatic God. When God says, "I AM WHO I AM," our most characteristic response is one of *utter denial*. We do not easily hear what God is saying. Instead, we opt for the creation of our own idol, one in which we *can* believe; a god-idol who, as Sr. Corita Kent said, is "like a Big Bayer aspirin": "Take a little God, and you'll feel better."

But, what if—in seeking to feel better—we are avoiding God's moving us toward growth?

In seeking God always as light, we are missing God as darkness?

In avoiding change, we are missing God's plea for us to move into the wonder of some unknown possibility?

In perceiving God as our Father, we are refusing to be nurtured at the breast of God our Mother?

In seeing God only in our *own* colors, shapes, styles, and ways of life, we are blinded to God's presence in others' colors, forms, and ways of being?

In looking for God in the magnanimous, that which is great, we are overlooking God in the most unremarkable places of our own lives?

In running from death, in trying to hold onto life, we are utterly missing the presence and power of God in *aging*, in *letting go*, in *dying itself*, in moving graciously along with God?

In perceiving God always in that which is *sacred*, holy *otherworldly*, religious, we are failing to see God in the *secular*, *this* world, the *office*, the *home*, the *classroom*, our day-to-day relationships, work and play?

What if, in seeking God always in the Bible, we are missing God in the *newspaper*!

What if simply to be with God, live with God, know God, love God is *enough!!*—in living and in dying.

Might it be that being human—*truly* human—is simply *being with God*, and seeking, and finding, God's presence in *all* reality?

That being alive *is* both a *terror* and a *wonder*, an adventure in living *and* dying—all with God, in God, in which terror and death do *not* "lose their sting"—but are experienced graciously, that is, with God.

The people of Israel had to struggle with this enigma. Trying so hard to *see* God, *love* God, *know* God as *all-powerful*, *almighty*, *victorious*, they did not know quite what to make of God's strange elusiveness. (The Book of Job and a number of Psalms suggest their difficulties with a God who will be who God will be.) Israel's expectations of a "*Messiah*" who was to save the nation, beat down the enemies, rout the wicked, suggests also to me Israel's "need," and *ours*, for a "God" we can count on to bring us: light, life, and victory. I AM WHO I AM is hard to bear.

And Jesus Christ did not come to make God any less hard to bear. Jesus did not come to "clarify" the enigmatic God; to help us put God into an Incarnate box that we can carry around with us and show off as "God." Jesus did not come to reveal God's *power*, God's *might*, God's *victory*, *but rather* Jesus came as one created in God, by God, empowered to move with God, into the pain, the passion, and the wonder of creation itself. *Jesus accepted the vocation of being truly human, in the image of an enigmatic God.*

In Jesus, we are able to discern—if we look carefully—a person in whose *human Being* God was made manifest; and a *God*, in whose holy Be-ing human life was lived fully. *"Christ" is that way of being in which God and humanity, the Creator and the created, the infinite and the finite, are experienced and manifest as One way of being. This we see—in Jesus.*

Jesus Christ: who lived and died to show us who *we* are meant to be; what being human is all about. In Jesus, we see what it means to be a namesake of One who says I AM WHO I AM. In Jesus, we see what it means to be a daughter or a son of God; to bear God's name; in Jesus, we perceive that being human, in the image of I AM WHO I AM, means simply that *we are who we are*!

As God's namesake, *Jesus was who he was*, free of all expectations and categories as to who he "ought" to be. Defiant of any expectation that would stunt his growth as a person of God. Jesus lived and died a life of grace — living into what he believed God to be about. *Going, simply, with God*; allowing himself — by God's grace — the freedom *to be himself*, irregardless of customs, laws, and expectations that he be some other.

The people who wished him to be a political zealot found him to be a person of prayerful spirituality; those who wanted him to be a pious, sweet man discovered they had on their hands an offensive activist. To those who wanted him to be Messiah, he retorted, "Get thee behind me, Satan." And in the presence of those who wanted him to explain himself, he stood silently. A *brilliant* reflection of I AM WHO I AM: The enigmatic God reflected in enigmatic personhood.

When *I* probe the depths of Jesus Christ, I realize that as *Jesus* was who *he* was, so too am *I* put here by God to be who *I* am. *Jesus* could not be who *I* am. *I* cannot be who *Jesus* was. My vocation as a person of God is not to try to "imitate" Jesus — not to try to recreate the being of a person who lived in a very different world, in a very different time, with very different life experiences and possibilities. Rather, my vocation as a person of God is to live with God, in God, for God, here, now — in my own time, as graciously as I can.

Our business, our birthrights, our beings are *in God here now*. As such, individually gifted, with individual interests and persuasions, we are *together* in One Christ: a way of being in which God's being and human being are experienced as *one*.

There are four qualities which, I believe, are ways of God, ways of being I AM WHO I AM, ways of being who we are meant to, ways of being in Christ. No *one* of the four can stand alone — in God. The four are overlapping pieces of a whole cloth, the tapestry of creation itself: *Wisdom. Passion. Justice.* And *Prayer*.

1. *Wisdom*. Wisdom is a virtue close to the heart of God, we are told in scripture. Wisdom is, in fact, an aspect of God, a way of being godly. Wisdom is the perception of the wholeness — the relatedness — of all that is. The wise person, like God, knows that there is more to life than her or his own little world; the wise person knows that there is more to living than pursuing "happiness." The wise person can see well that this world, God's world, is simultaneously a *beautiful* place for those of us who inhabit it — not only in the country and mountains, but in the city, the ghetto — and a place of *terror*, not only for the people in South Africa, but for *all* people, all who suffer bondage when anyone, anywhere is a slave. The wise person

will face reality—ambiguity, tension. She or he is able to live into, not flee from, matters of life—and death. Moreover, she will do everything she can to deal creatively, realistically, empathetically, with conviction, in her everyday comings and going. She is no fool. She is, in the words of St. Matthew, "as wise as a serpent, as innocent as a dove," aware that she is, God with her, put in this world, here, now, to participate fully in the affairs of this world—loving this world as God does—and using everything at her disposal to work cleverly, carefully, wisely for the good of the whole. For the sake of the world. For the sake of herself. For the sake of God. God's creativity, and our own, is a matter of wisely perceiving the *whole* of reality, not simply our own small pieces.

2. *Passion*. Passion is a matter of depth. As wisdom allows us to perceive the *breadth* of God, and of God's creation, the wholeness of it all, so passion allows us to discern the *depth*. I am fond of describing passionate people as those who will dive in, rather than float or tread water or even swim across the surface of the water. To be passionately committed, passionately involved, passionately immersed in God, in life itself, is to be involved and immersed in the *enigma* of it all. To know, to feel, to experience one's own dying as the boy hangs on the gallows. To realize one's own shortcomings and capacities for wrongdoings when Nixon resigns. To realize the extent to which living involves dying, *really* living, *really* dying, and to know that to the extent that we are afraid to *die*, we are afraid to live! In passion, we find our resources, our energy, our courage, our motivation, a Spirited way of being human, as Jesus was human. In passion, we are aware that we are infused by the Spirit of God—this is what birth is all about, what creation is, and what baptism signifies. We are created as Spirited people—holy spirited people. Immersed in passion, we are aware that the BCP (even the new one!) misses the point when it says, "Christ has died, Christ is risen, Christ will come again"—for, in fact, *Christ is dying, Christ is rising, Christ is here again!!* And the wise passionate person will know that Christ has as much to do with the "secular" arenas of our lives as the "sacred"; as much to do with "this" world as with some "other" world; as much to do with the "profane" as with the "holy"; as much to do with the "sexual," the political, the social, as with the "spiritual." For the passionate person who is wise will realize that these dichotomies, these lines of demarcation, are ultimately fundamentally *false*, and that God is, for example, every much as present in the kitchen, the classroom, the hospital, the prison, the bed, as in church. The passionate person is one who can cut through to the heart of the matter—whatever the occasion—and discover God.

3. *Justice*. Suppose Jesus' friends had advised him to speak only of "God"

—and to stay out of religious and secular politics. Suppose they had warned him not to offend people. What do you suppose he'd have said? The Bible as a whole speaks of justice as "right-relationship" between and among people. Justice presupposes *community* as fundamental to human life with God. In justice, there is no such thing as a person living simply for him or herself. I must tell you that I am suspect of anyone who tells me that she or he has "found the Lord," or been "converted to Christ," or is "committed to Jesus" if that person is not passionately committed to justice for *all* people . . . black, yellow, red, white; poor, rich; straight, gay; sophisticated, simple; well educated, poorly educated; sick, healthy; male and female. Some years ago, yearning for justice, I was saddened and angered by white governors blocking the doors to schools and universities to prevent black people—God's people with black skin—from entering. Today, although the racial crisis in this country is far from resolved, other issues too cry out for justice. And I am saddened, angered, fired up by—and compelled to call to account—state legislators who willingly put their own re-electionality, their own economic interests, and their own insecurities above clearly and simply affirming that "equality of rights under law shall not be denied or abridged by the United States or by any state on account of sex." (That is—word for word—the equal rights amendment. Simple. Clear. To the point. *Just.* Right-relationship between women and men.) I do not believe that a person who is truly aware of her or his birthright and responsibility to be with God in ongoing creation can sit back silently in this world. I believe we are compelled and empowered to risk whatever we must risk to create, with God, a climate in which *all* people can be who they are. A matter of doing justice, of standing up to be counted, a stand infused by the passion of the Holy Spirit; informed by wise perception of the wholeness, the breadth, the interdependence of the issues at hand; and empowered by prayer.

4. *Prayer*. It's interesting to me that the gospel that speaks most explicitly about *social activism*—Luke—is also the gospel in which Jesus is most often portrayed to be at prayer. Prayer is the opening up of oneself to the presence and power of God; a matter of listening; a matter of perceiving what is invisible to the eye and hearing what is inaudible to the ear. Without prayer, *passion* may become restless, manic activity—doing for the sake of doing, rather than for the sake of God and humankind; without prayer, *wisdom* is empty and becomes a business of "intellectualizing," counting angels on the head of a pin, spinning conceptual wheels to no particular end. (Without prayer, for example, theology may talk *about* God, but cannot draw us further *into* God.) Without prayer, *justice* is doomed to disillusionment, because without prayer, we are unable to see beyond what the eye can see, and all

we see is injustice — war, strife, discrimination, hate; this terror may lead us eventually to rage, to futile outcry, to apathy; to feelings of helplessness; to violence; to suicide. Whereas *with* prayer, we *know* because we *hear* and we *see* that *something is going on* — something is being born — something is happening, stirring, moving, coming forth out of the awful pains and groans of labor and travail. Something is being born again and again and again wherever there is *any* injustice, *any* wisdom, *any* passion. And in prayer, we know well that this something is God — in us, with us, for us, carrying us along. The enigmatic God, who we meet in prayer.

In the beginning of all that is coming into being, something is stirring. Somewhere in some silent space — within us, between us, around us — something pulsating with possibility. The Spirit of God is breathing forth. And groaning in painful hope, God is giving us new birth — again and again — bringing us into new ways of being who we are, empowering us to live our lives, drawing us more and more into the *terror* and the *wonder* of being human, into the terror and wonder of finding God in ourselves, of finding God in the world, and — in the words of the poet Ntozake Shange, of "loving God fiercely"; a way of being in which our laughter is at the heart of God, and our tears are streams of living water — All.

In the name of God, I AM WHO I AM, Amen.

Clarence G. Newsome, known by his friends at Duke as "C. G.," was a product of Duke, having earned undergraduate and graduate degrees here and having begun his career as a theological educator by serving as a professor of American Christianity at the Divinity School. He has the distinction of being the only preacher to have two sermons included in this collection: he was the student interlocutor in the earlier "What's Religion All About" dialogue sermon. He is currently the president of Shaw University. When he preached this sermon he was a young instructor at the Divinity School at Duke, having just finished his doctoral work there. As one of the very first African American doctoral students at Duke, Newsome undoubtedly had occasion for some righteous indignation of his own. Yet in this sermon he focuses upon the anger of Jesus as a model, not so much of the need to be angry but of the call to righteous acknowledgement of "God as the standard."

Righteous Anger

August 27, 1978

CLARENCE G. NEWSOME

Matthew 21:12–16 The topic of my sermon this morning has to do with the subject of "Righteous Anger." I have come to my topic by way of meditating on a portion of the 21st chapter of St. Matthew, and that portion beginning with the 12th verse and ending with the 16th verse. You heard this familiar passage read this morning as the scripture lesson. I wish now to reread it for the purpose of drawing your attention to its meaning. And if you have a Bible with you, I would like for you to read silently along with me. It reads:

> And Jesus entered the temple of God and drove out all who sold and bought in the temple, and he overturned the tables of the moneychangers and the seats of those who sold doves. He said to them, "It is written, 'My house shall be called a house of prayer'; but you make it a den of robbers."
>
> And the blind and the lame came to him in the temple, and he healed them. But when the chief priests and the scribes saw the wonderful things that he did, and the children crying out in the temple, "Hosanna to the Son of David!" they were indignant; and they said to him, "Do you hear what these are saying?" And Jesus said to them, "Yes; have you never read, 'Out of the mouth of babes and sucklings thou hast brought perfect praise'?"

Now, this passage holds for me memories of my boyhood. For some reason, I was always fascinated by the story of Jesus cleansing the temple. I cannot remember the first time that I heard it. But I can recall that each time I occasioned to hear it from my mother, my father, my grandmother, the pastor of my local church, my Sunday School teacher—each time I was as enraptured as the preceding time. The very vivid image of Jesus overturning tables, knocking over chairs and running people out into the street no doubt intrigued me. As a matter of fact, I can recall that the effect on me was so lasting that I would sometimes, even before I knew how to read well, go to the family Bible or the Bible storybook in our house and hunt for the picture of Jesus cleansing the temple. You know how they have in a number of editions of the Bible paintings and drawings illustrating different Biblical stories. Well, the illustration of Jesus cleansing the temple along with that of Joshua "fightin' the battle of Jericho," in the words of an old Negro spiritual, was my favorite.

As I think back on what fascinated me about the story, I suppose it was the image of Jesus and the feeling of Jesus moving with such evident force and forthrightness. It was, even more, the image, the feeling, and the thought of an angry Jesus. And I suppose what intrigued me the most about the thought of an angry Jesus was the contrast it presented to the image of Jesus which was dominant in my heart and mind. This was the image of a meek, mild Jesus, a Jesus so tender of heart and loving as to be almost passive. Although it was not intelligible to me then, I realize now that this contrast was for me, even at a young age, the focal point of my attempt to reconcile an all-loving Jesus with a Jesus of righteousness, and in as much as Jesus was the Son of God, an all-loving God with a righteous God, yea, even a wrathful God.

Some years after the passing of my childhood, I learned that I had not been and was not alone in my attempt to reconcile a loving God with a righteous, wrathful God. I learned, for example, that though religionists have long agreed that love is indispensable to the Christian view of God's nature—for God is love—there has been much, much disagreement on how God's righteousness, expressed in the form of God's wrath, is reconciled with God's love.

The issue, as I understand it, is in no way new. Years and years ago during the early days of the Church, the theologian Marcion, for example, was among the first to face the problem head-on. According to him, reconciling the Old Testament idea of the righteousness of God with the New Testament idea of the love of God is impossible. The concept of law, as he saw it, is a complete denial of love. His solution, therefore, was to insist that the gospel of Christ is completely new and thus has nothing to do with the concept of righteousness as presented in the Old Testament. As a result, Marcion posited the reality of two Gods: the Creator God of the Old Testament who required obedience to the law of righteousness, and the Redeemer God of the New Testament who is the "good," benevolent, self-giving God, the God of love.

As might be expected, the Church rejected Marcion's view, since the early Christian community did not understand its existence as being completely new in the sense of negating the God of the Old Testament. They believed that they were the authentic continuation of the Old Israel and not its denial. Christ, therefore, did not destroy the Old Testament; he fulfilled it.

But while the early Church rejected Marcion's division and dichotomy between the Old Testament view of God's righteousness and the New Testament view of God's love in Jesus Christ, many questions, and much confusion about the precise relationship between the two aspects, modalities, dimensions — call them what you will — of God's reality have persisted even until the present day.

In the main, we Christians have a tendency to regard God's love as the dominant motif of Christianity while attempting to comprehend God's righteousness in the light of it. But this understanding fails to take seriously the importance of God's righteousness and in this connection the importance of God's wrath, and tends to make, as Professor James Cone of Union Theological Seminary in New York says, "God's love *mere* sentimentality." Most of us fail to regard properly the significance of God's righteousness, God's wrath. This suggests that we tend to see God's love as completely self-giving without any demand for obedience. You see, most of us believe in "cheap grace" as Dietrick Bonhoeffer once referred to this frame of mind and heart. And what's more, we think, behave, and interact as if grace were indeed cheap. For some reason, perhaps a selfish reason with a logic all its own, we seem to think and act as if God is basically not against anybody or anything. And we all know according to the reasons of the heart that that is not the case. How then, do we reconcile God's righteousness, yea God's wrath, with God's love?

In a word, and at the risk of sounding a bit like Marcion, we don't. Play any mental games you want; it is really beyond our ability to fathom it, at least with the powers of the mind. Humble yourself enough to admit it. But given the powers of the heart, we can at least, on the basis of faith in the reality of God — and I am not talking about sheer acceptance of the *idea* of God's reality, but belief in the reality of God — come to a point of view which reveals to us, and reveals to us not as the eclipse of a once illuminated scene as the theologian H. Richard Niebuhr once so succinctly expressed, but which makes transparent to us for all time that God's love and God's righteousness are two ways of talking about the same reality. God's righteousness is, whatever else we may say about it, at least God's constant activity of helping *each* of us to become aware, making *each* of us to realize, requiring *each* of us to see, demanding *each* of our hearts to accept that not all we do is right while God's love is at least God's self-giving to this task in the interest of *all* of us.

It was as the embodiment of love and righteousness, then, that God in Jesus Christ moved through the temple in Jerusalem on a particular day some two thousand-odd years ago. As we consider the account of this event as it is found not only in the book of Matthew, but also in the books of Mark, Luke, and John, there is some question about the precise day. Whether it was at the onset of Jesus' arrival in Jerusalem as suggested in Matthew, Luke, and John, or on a subsequent day as suggested in Mark, is not important, at least right now. What is important is that the scripture makes plain to us that Jesus' temperament on this occasion was one of righteous anger. For as we are told, he "went into the temple of God and cast out all of them that sold and bought in the temple, and overthrew the tables of the moneychangers and the seats of them that sold doves." Why?? This is a question well worth considering.

When I first pondered this question during the early days of my youth, I concluded that Jesus acted so forcefully and so forthrightly because he was merely offended by the actions of the moneychangers, the actions of "those that sold doves," and by the negligence of the high priests in charge of the temple. Well, I am sure that this constituted much of the reason for Jesus' reaction upon entering the temple. But now I can see that his protest, his wrath, was directed at a problem much deeper than their actions. For when I consider what they were doing, I am inclined to sense that Jesus was most likely not *that* upset with the form of their actions. As a result of looking closely at the text, we learn, for example, that the moneychangers and those who sold animals were providing a needed service. In a modern-day society such as ours, where we have grown so accustomed to and become so dependent on 7-11 stores and the like, we can well identify with the kind of business they operated, for theirs was an operation of convenience.

Each day people from outlying areas, Jews and gentiles alike, would arrive in Jerusalem to worship at the temple, the sacred and ritualistic center of Judaism. Once in the city they had need of exchanging their coins for the standard Hebrew or Tyrian money which was required. In addition, they also had need of animals to sacrifice at the temple, animals which had been ritually cleaned, making it too impractical to bring them long distances to Jerusalem. So the moneychangers and those who sold sacrificial animals provided a needed service. This did not, in and of itself, offend Jesus. And curiously enough, although I am sure Jesus was disturbed by their actions, I really do not think that he was ultimately bothered, or primarily bothered, by the extortion and graft that took place in the temple, or the misguided intentions of those who, according to the Markan account, used the temple as a thoroughfare, a shortcut from one street to another, or the sanction, tacit or otherwise, which the high priests must have given these fraudulent and irreverent practices in order for them to have taken place. Rather, my heart tells me that Jesus was most disturbed by the root of these actions, the root of this behavior. My heart tells me that he was most bothered by the fact that they acted and carried on as if there was no wrongdoing, as if what they were doing was in some way permissible in the eyes of God. He was offended by the fact that they did not see that not all we do is right. The chief priests, for example, the leaders of the faith, the custodians of God's temple, had become blind to the errors of their ways, so much so that they did not even recognize the Son of God when he appeared before them. Rather than join the chorus of children who, as we see in verses peculiar to the Matthew text, proclaimed Jesus the Messiah at the sight of seeing him heal and do wonderful things in the temple, the chief priests became sorely displeased. They did not see that not all we do is right. For this reason Jesus saw the need to react with righteous anger, with the wrath of God, so that eyes might be opened. Perhaps he did not move through the temple with a whip in hand as the Gospel of John portrays him, but by overturning tables and knocking over seats Jesus acted with righteous anger so that hearts might be opened, even during the time of his earthly ministry, to the fact that not all we do is right.

When I consider the nature of *our* age, an age of test-tube babies and test-tube faith, an age in which the individual is the measure, an age in which whatever is willed and whatever feels good is right, I wonder if we do not need to be reminded that *God is real* and that there is a dimension of his reality which can so forcefully and forthrightly overturn the ways of each of us so that all of us can see enough for our hearts to make plain to us that in this age of "everything goes," all that goes does not go well with God.

God is a loving God, but God is also a righteous God and He will not be compromised.

Here, I need only remind you that the God who created the heavens and mothered the earth is the same God who called forth the flood. I need only remind you that the God of Abraham, Isaac, and Moses, the God who delivered the Israelites from Egyptian bondage, is the same God who made them wander in the wilderness for forty years. I need only remind you that the

God who out of love sent forth Christ to save the world is the same God who, in Jesus, knocked over tables and overturned seats in the temple in Jerusalem some seventy years before it fell to the earth. I need only remind you that in a society where permissiveness is the rule, God is still the standard.

God is still the standard — and for this reason we had better be disturbed about high divorce rates.

God is still the standard — and for this reason we had better be disturbed about the cavalier attitude parents take in raising their children.

God is still the standard — and for this reason we had better rethink and question a matter so impactful as the recent Bakke decision.

God is a loving God, but God is also a righteous God, and this God of love and righteousness is still the standard.

Amen.

Dr. Howard Thurman was a great Christian mystic, an expressive preacher, someone who fused the African American church's love of the spoken word with the movements of thought that were prominent on university campuses in the latter half of the twentieth century. As a young campus pastor and dean of Rankin Chapel at Howard, Thurman led a group of students to India, where he met Gandhi. It was one of the most important moments in his life. Conversations with Gandhi led Thurman to a rediscovery of the teachings of Jesus and to eloquent engagement with the problem of racial segregation in the American South. In 1953 he became dean of the Chapel at Marsh Chapel, Boston University. Thurman's sermons were more thematic than textual, as he followed some high thought through the twists and turns of his fertile mind, delighting in the language, reveling in image and metaphor in a poetic, stream-of-consciousness sort of style. "The Gothic Principle" is one of his most representative sermons. Here Thurman uses the building itself and Duke Chapel's soaring gothic arches to meditate upon the tension and the congruence of the human and the divine. He preached this sermon just two years before his death.

The Gothic Principle

January 21, 1979

HOWARD THURMAN

There's not a word in my tongue, but Lord, O Lord, thou knowest it all together. Thou hast beset me behind and before and laid thy hand upon me. Such knowledge is too wonderful for me. It is high. I cannot ascend unto it. Whither shall I go from thy Spirit? Or whither shall I flee from thy presence? If I ascend up into heaven thou art there. If I make my bed in hell, hell. Behold thou art there. If I take the wings of the morning and fly to the uttermost parts of the sea, even there shall thy hand lead me. And thy right hand shall steady me. Search me oh, God, God, God. And know my heart. Try me and know my thoughts. And see if there be any wicked way in me and lead me in the way everlasting. Amen.

Jesus Christ and the gothic principle — as a background for our meditation will you listen to these words? It is the judgment scene; the climax of man's life has come at last. The oriental despot sits enthroned. Before him come the peoples of the Earth. Here are no men, no women, boys or girls — struggling for rank, wealth, class, or power. No race or tribe has standing here. All walls that separate, divide by the moving drama are pushed aside. Each life is freed of all pretense. Each shadowy seeming swept away by the might spread of ceaseless light. I was sick — comfortless. I was hungry and desperate. I was lonely, wretched. I was imprisoned, forsaken. Strange awful words from him — words more searching followed after. I know your tasks were manifold, unyielding claims consumed your thoughts. There was no time to be at ease with deeds, to give yourself beyond your creeds. Oh, I know about your temperament and your health. Somehow you could not manage all your chores. Excuses came to reinforce the empty feeling of your heart. I know how hard it was for you. You do not want to be an easy touch. Beyond all else, your tears of blood, charity do begin at home. And besides, you didn't know. But are you sure. Do you recall the fleshes of concern that held you in your place that day. Oh yes, I see, you do remember well. Again they came and then again until at last they came no more — only the hollow darkness of the self cut off from all the pain and pathos of the world. No word of mine now can alter what your deeds have done. The story of your life is what the judge reveals from the relentless judgment; is there no appeal?

One of the great creative visitations of the mind of God to invade the mind of man seems to me to be expressed in the grand concept of the gothic arch, the gothic principle. The pillars rooted in the Earth, grounded, substantial, reinforced by flying buttresses and holding their place, the great sweeping vaulting arches of infinity grounded in the Earth. Holding. Sustained by creature-hood and the sweep of the arches. The timeless and the time bound. The universal and the particular. The body. The Spirit. And yet, these holes in order to make fast in experience the boundless reaches of the infinite, man the time binder, man the space binder. There is some aspect of my life that cannot quite be contained in my creatureliness. I share my creatureliness with all creatures. The face of a man. The body of a creature and something deep at the center that always wants to fly — this is man.

Always caught in the agonizing grapple of the contradictions of life, but never quite able to be certain within the contradictions. Life, death, this is the involvement. But always, whatever may be the nature of the quality of my experiences at any given moment, at any time, they never quite contain all that I am, all that I see. If I were to ask you to select one thing in your life that represented you, that was the "for instance," or what you mean by "you," before the sound of your voice died you would reach for it again because it did not include this or that. Man the time binder. Man the space binder. There is something about the moment that cannot contain you since you've been sitting here looking up in this general direction. You've looked past me into next week, into tonight, into tomorrow, and you remain where you are. Man the time binder, the space binder, so that for this reason man is not ever quite able to say that death is the end of life. For always he thinks of life as contrasted with death. And he thinks of life as containing both life and death so that I may be aware of the fact and the experience of my dying as I die. I, the observer, watching, always watching the actions, the deeds.

After forty days and forty nights, Jesus was hungry and the tempter said turn the stones into bread and be satisfied. For bread, the thisness and thatness of experience, bread is the most crucial thing. But man, man does not live by bread, but he does live by bread. He does not live by bread. He does live by bread. Over and over through the long night watches, bread, how important, how crucial. What would I give for it? Does that exhaust the deep hungers of my spirit? Over and over the conflict, the dualism. Man lives by bread. Man does not live by bread. There is something wrong with the answer and how long I don't know. But finally there came shouting from the hills, from the valleys, from the trees, from the rocks, one word — alone. Man does not live by bread . . . alone, but by every word that issues from the mouth of God. Shall I make them the emphasis of my life? Those things that will guarantee myself against the impersonal operations of the world of nature and society to be sure that the ground of my security is established and solid.

But is there another kind of hunger I have, a hunger of the mind and spirit that these things cannot quite satisfy. Man does not live by bread alone, but by every word that issues from the mouth of God. I shall recognize that life is practical, that I must have bread. I must live by bread. But there are needs of another kind that I have and I must provide for them the bias, the accent, the emphasis of my life must take in its creative sweep the fact that I am creature locked in the Earth as the pillars of the arch. Something deep at my center that reaches into infinity like the sweep of the gothic arch. And I love Jesus for this shaft of light that he throws across my pathway at that point in my darkness. I saw a man pursuing the horizon, round and round he sped. I was disturbed at this so I cussed at the man. I said it is futile, you can never. You lie, he cried, and ran on. I must have bread, but the bias of my life will be on the side of those things that long for more. The timeless dimension of my mind and my spirit.

How precious also are thy thoughts and to me oh God, how great is the sum of them if I should count them, they are more in number than the sands. When I awake I am still with thee. Amen.

*Dean of Yale Divinity School, masterful interpreter of the New Testament, Lean-
der Keck demonstrates great expository skill in this sermon that weaves a number
of biblical texts into a seamless garment of homiletical art. Along the way, he
manages to get in a couple of punches at the contemporary university, the super-
ficiality of some contemporary presentations of the gospel, and today's church.
This sermon was preached the year after Keck had published* The Bible in the
Pulpit, *a book that sounded a clarion call for renewal of truly biblical preaching.
The thesis of that book is beautifully proven in this engaging biblical sermon.*

Seeing and Not Seeing

October 21, 1979

LEANDER KECK

*Genesis 12:1–9, Exodus 2:1–4, 11–15, Joshua 2:1, 8–10, 15,
and Hebrews 11:8–10, 23–27, 31*

The Christian winner is in a precarious position. You know the type. He or
she appears on the tube to tell for the hundredth time the story of a marvelous conversion, after which all doubts are dispelled—and all bills paid.
The scrubbed and beaming Christians want us to believe that now there are
no more hang-ups, no more ambiguities, no more conflicts with spouses,
roommates, or parents, because Jesus has come into the heart. Life has become enchanted, and faith moves mountains every day. The so-called Christian talk shows never present the biography of a person coping with poverty
and hunger. It is the Christian winner that we see, the one who with Jesus in
the heart has overcome everything with a smile and a song. Such a person is
in a precarious position because he or she is being used in today's great betrayal of the gospel and of the life of faith. Whatever may be our own story,
whether we are unhesitant Christians or cliffhangers, we have enough common sense to know that such a portrait of Christian faith does not square
with reality.

To be sure, drastic turnarounds do occur. Life does fall into place, and
people do get their acts together when they center their lives on Christ. None
of this can be denied. Still, the gospel is betrayed and we are put off when
the enchanted success story is projected as the way it is for *real* Christians.

But what about the rest of us, whose lives are not enchanted, but dogged by ambiguity and pain? What about those of us who struggle to believe the truth of the Christian thing? What about those of us who begin to wonder whether life is worth the hassle because there seems to be no clear goal in view, no unambiguous purpose to pattern it all into meaning with joy? Is the story of real faith the biography of never-ending success? Where Christian faith is real, is the cost-benefit ratio always manifest? If it is, then the writer of the Letter to the Hebrews has missed the point — and badly. For this writer understands faith as "the assurance of things *hoped for*, the conviction of things *not seen*." He has no word for Christian winners. But he does have a word for those of us whose bright summer of religious experience may be fading, who sense that the fizz has gone out of life, and who need a sense of direction grounded in reality. Our text has a word for everyone who is threatened by despair because life is falling short of the glamorized success portrayed in the ads.

If our author were to host a Christian talk show, he would not emphasize the glamour of faith but the struggles of faith. And the program would not feature only Christian winners but would include those who seem not to win at all. And if his guests would include a few who did make it big, it would not be their triumphs that he would highlight but the struggles of their soul to be authentic. It is not faith as the key to success that interests him, but faith as the key to life when it has no clear success. This is why he defines faith as "the assurance of what is hoped for, the conviction of things not seen." And to drive his point home, he takes a fresh look at old stories of well-known heroes in the Old Testament. We will be even more selective than he was. We shall consider three mini-biographies.

1. The paradigm of faith is Abraham. When Hebrews was written, every Jew knew that. But now see what our author shows us about Abraham. Everybody knows that Abraham left Mesopotamia to find the Land of Promise. Even today the Abrahamic migration is one of the grounds of conflict between Arab and Jew for the right to possess this land as Abraham's children. But that is not what interests our author. He says that Abraham lived in tents with his son Isaac and his grandson Jacob, and that he did so while he was looking for a city. What are we to make of such a statement?

With Canaanite civilization all around, this man lived in tents. Was Abraham, like the Spaniard Coronado, bivouacking in tents while seeking the seven golden cities of El Dorado? Is that what faith is all about — a tenacious prospecting for gold that does not exist? No. Our text says he sought the city built by God. What Augustine would call the *Civitas Dei*, the City of God.

But how can this author say that Abraham sought a God-built city when literally he kept looking for pasture? Our author sees that this restless Abraham was constantly on the move from Mesopotamia to Syria to the Holy Land to Egypt and back to Palestine, and he wonders what it was that kept him from settling down. And then he sees that what Abraham was looking for is what you and I are looking for as well — the God-built city where love and justice are perfectly matched, the eternal city which is the alternative to all the jerry-built civilizations which are strewn along the trails of human pilgrimage. Brigham Young crested a hill where he saw the great Salt Lake and said, "This is the place," and settled in, but Abraham kept moving on. So our author saw in him the prototype of Christian existence in history. With his eye on the God-built city of the future, Abraham cannot settle for any present city. Indeed, our author insists that Abraham lived in his own land as in a foreign land. The difference between Egypt and Canaan is not as important as their sameness, for both are foreign soil to him or her, whose eye is on the city where human pilgrimage will cease for good.

What makes all this so strange to us is the fact that we have settled down in our air-conditioned Egypts. The punch-card security of the modern welfare state has induced us to call this the promised land. It has taken the triple crisis of energy, ecology, and economy to shock even Christians out of the stupor which has come over us. But the Letter to the Hebrews reminds us that be it ever so comfortable here, we have no abiding city. All our achievements of technology and social engineering are only tents and pilgrim huts along the way. Here faith — sinewy faith — manifests itself in keeping alive the awareness that no human city is the city of God.

Let those who are man enough or woman enough for such a faith pitch their tents with Abraham and Sarah, let them build a dam of justice against the tides of chaos and corruption so that human community can grow, but let them also remember that be it ever so just and ever so prosperous, God's city it is not. Faith, you see, measures what is seen, what is experienced and achieved, by what is not seen, by that eternal destiny, by that transcendent criterion which is the city of God. Faith emancipates us from bondage to what we can plan, attain, and see. To use the idiom of the day, faith raises our consciousness of the plight of the present: it alienates us from the structures and perceptions into which we have been socialized and conditioned from childhood on. Abrahamic faith keeps us unwilling to be satisfied with what we are and what we have done because it always pulls us forward to the city not seen. That is the first.

II. The second thing concerns faith's capacity to keep alive that distance, that sense of otherness. Faith is not simply a moment of distancing: it is also a process of pilgrimage. And so our author bids us look at Moses. What interests the writer of Hebrews is Moses the pilgrim. The writer observes that it was by faith that Moses preferred "to share the ill-treatment with the people of God" rather than enjoy the court of Pharaoh. Abuse for the promised future (what our text calls "The Christ") is worth more to him than the treasures of Egypt. What a scale of values! But how can our author go on to say that Moses left Egypt, not fearing the King? After all, he was a fugitive. But our interpreter's eye is on those years of sheep tending in the desert of Midian, because he adds, "For he endured as seeing him who is invisible." From the vantage point of the burning bush our writer looks back across the desert years to say that what kept Moses going was a sense that God was present in spite of appearances. He saw the God who could not be seen, who could not be inferred from the evidence at hand. Only that God could make good. Had Moses trusted the God that could be seen, inferred from the evidence around him, he would have given up. But what sustained him in the desert, away from family and folk, away from the centers of power which were regarded as the signs of divine presence, was this seeing the unseen God. With no daily religious peak experiences, no sequence of mountaintop epiphanies but only the dusty flats of sheep tending, what kept him going was this relentless trusting of the real God to come through. He did not trust the visible God who is the ground of what is, but the invisible God who is the ground of what must finally be. Only those who live by the vision of the unseen God can maintain the life of pilgrimage, wherever their own desert may lie.

A good deal of life, especially in a university, seems to be sheep tending in Midian, somewhere between a past to which we cannot return and a future we cannot see. When the bleak present appears to lack meaning, when it has no effervescent religious experience, what keeps us going, guards us against despair and nihilism? It is this Mosaic feature of faith, this capacity to see the unseen in the midst of the difference between what is and what is to be. What Moses learned he teaches us — that the desert of life discloses that faith is persistence in the vision despite the appearances. Let him or her who lives in Midian remember Moses and learn from him what faith is all about.

Such a faith may not only strike us as rather strange, but as positively dangerous. We have grown accustomed to thinking that any Christian faith which fixes its gaze on the city of God is otherworldly in the bad sense, that such a faith will end up making us irrelevant in the cities on earth because we become preoccupied with life after death, or pie in the sky. Our author seems to sense this too. So he points us to those who acted in the world because this kind of faith put steel in their spines.

III. He begins with Rahab, the happy hooker, whose house was the place to visit in Jericho. It was faith that prompted her to befriend the scouts from Joshua's invaders. Is our author succumbing to that modern game in which everyone is declared to have faith? Not at all. Rather, he says that "She did not perish with those who were disobedient because she had given friendly welcome to the spies." That is, she saw the spies as a sign of Jericho's impending doom, and risked her life by helping them. Our author does not think that deep down she had a heart of gold and was kind to dogs, children, and strangers. Nor does he think that she had a streak of piety which made her want to "do something for the Lord" in order to make up for what she had done for Jericho. No, our author includes her in this roster of the faithful because faith is not to be confused with such sentiments at all, but is the courage to act in light of the future which is not yet here. Faith is an event expressing the conviction that the things not yet seen are more real than those that can be seen.

This is clear in the next paragraph. Here it is perfectly evident that faith which has its eye on the God-built city of the future, which is not yet visible, really leads to bold action. Listen: "And what more shall I say? For time would fail me to tell of Gideon, Barak, Samson, Jephthah, of David and Samuel and the prophets—who through faith conquered kingdoms, enforced justice, received promises, stopped the mouths of lions, quenched raging fire, escaped the edge of the sword, found strength out of weakness, became mighty in war, put foreign armies to flight."

The forward-looking stance, the conviction that the city of God is the really real despite appearances now, enabled them to persist.

Indeed, they persisted even though they did not succeed. As our author puts it, "All these . . . did *not* receive what was promised." They are heroes of faith because they did *not* see the validation of their commitments come to pass during their lifetimes. They lived and died in the name of a future which they never saw come to pass, but which they bequeathed to those who followed.

Is it so hard for us to see what such a faith is like? Shall we remember Dag Hammarskjöld's passion for peace, or Martin Luther King's passion for justice? You can extend this list to include all those whose eyes were fixed on the God-built city and who therefore lived and struggled to help bring it to pass but died without seeing it happen, yet were confident that in God's own time at least an approximation of it would come to pass. In this list you can include everyone whose life does not add up and so leans into the future for justification. It includes the exploited and the tortured who, like Bonhoeffer whose poem the choir just sang, do not give up because they are sustained by an indestructible confidence that sometime, somehow, it will all come out right and that in the meantime no act of fidelity is for nothing.

And here is the key: their not seeing it happen in history is not their personal tragedy. Rather, their not seeing their dreams fulfilled is a sign that their vision embraced what is noble, enduring, and transcendent. In pursuing it, they were themselves made noble, strong as oaks, and effective in ways they could not see. Because they achieved less than they sought, they actually achieved more. As our author says, "They did not receive what is promised, since God had foreseen something better for us, that apart from us they should not be made perfect." How can he say such a thing? Because on this side of the event of Jesus Christ we know for sure that history is non-fulfillment and that the city of God stands over against all of history. On this side of Jesus Christ, we also know that non-fulfillment is not the last word, for Jesus was resurrected and so became the model, the paradigm and pledge that fulfillment occurs at the edge of history. Jesus is not our model because his was the archetypal success story but because he was faithful to his vision and left fulfillment up to the God he trusted.

If Jesus reveals the way things are, then somehow the author is right when he says of the heroes of the past, "Apart from us, they should not be made perfect." That is, every generation validates the previous ones when it is as faithful as they were. The last runner in the relay makes worthwhile the exertion of those who ran before. When does a martyr die in vain except when his successors deem the cause not worth the trouble for themselves? You see, when the author says that "Apart from us they will not be made perfect," what he has in mind is not a static people settled down in the promised land, not the grinning Christian saved by a slick salvation, but a pilgrim people in history on the move because it is not at home. The motley band of believers whom the author bids us view is made perfect by us—not because we are more successful than they, but because we have received their legacy. Our author calls them a "cloud of witnesses," that band of faithful ones who ran their own races in their time. He says that these women and men are watching us, a generation in danger of losing its sense of purpose because the fulfillment is not in hand, because Vietnam and Cambodia, Watergate and Three-Mile Island, have made it chic to be cynical. There is a sense, you see, in which all our predecessors will have lived and struggled in vain if you and I cop out and hang it up unless we can make it pay off in spades right now.

Beyond facts to be mastered there is truth to be grasped, beyond grades to be gained there is a self to be educated toward humanity, beyond a job to be found there is a vocation to be claimed, beyond a cancer cure there is health to be won for our people, beyond judicial reform there is justice to be gained, beyond a low-cal diet for ourselves there are the hungry to be fed, beyond the antics of politics there is peace to be secured.

A university should be the place where we discern the legacy of human striving for freedom in dignity under God, and where we make that legacy our own with no illusions. And the chapel is the place where we renew our vision of the City of God.

All this leads up to the author's exhortation to "Run with perseverance the race that is set before us, looking to Jesus the forerunner and consummator of our faith." What can I add to this but a single word, "Keep on keeping on." Abraham and Moses and Rahab and King are watching.

C. Eric Lincoln was one of the great interpreters of the African American religious experience. As one of Duke's most prominent intellectuals, he brought the university great notoriety through his research and publications as a sociologist of religion. He was also a poet (two of his hymns are in the Chapel hymnal) and a novelist. Here, in 1983, Lincoln expounds on a great Christian story—the conversion of St. Paul—stressing the need for transformation. Perhaps because he spent his life working for the miraculous transformation of a racist culture, Lincoln had a special word to offer the congregation. In the sermon, Lincoln refers to Paul's temporary blindness. This reference is somewhat foreboding since Lincoln spent the last years of his life without sight. Yet to those who studied with him, he was a man of unusually acute vision.

Have You Been to Damascus?

March 20, 1983

C. ERIC LINCOLN

Acts 7:58–8:3, 9:1–9 We thank Thee, O God, for this day. We thank Thee for the beauties of nature which have burst forth in full bloom. We thank Thee for the hundreds of people who have come here to share in Thy holy worship. We thank Thee for the ministry in which we are permitted to participate. We thank Thee for all of the good things with which Thou hast blessed us, and we bow to Thee in gratitude and in prayer. Amen.

I have chosen for my sermon topic today what might seem to you a strange question. Have you been to Damascus? We could say that since this is the season for going and talking about going, if it were not for the particular place, perhaps it would not seem so strange after all. For within the coming weeks we shall say to each other, "Have you been here; have you been there; will you be going elsewhere?" We will say to our friends, "Have you been to London; have you been to Madrid; have you been to Paris, Johannesburg, Aberdeen, Tahiti, Mexico City?" And as the names tumble from our lips, we will conjure up memories of what our visits to these particular places may have been. Those who have been to London will remember the fog. They might remember the double-decker buses or the bobbies on bicycles, two by two, or Big Ben, and perhaps they might remember—as I do—steak-and-kidney pie. Those who have been to Paris will remember, no doubt, the Eiffel Tower, the Seine, the Sorbonne, the Arc de Triomphe, the French people.

Those who have been to Moscow will remember Red Square, the Kremlin, the tomb of Lenin, the harsh winters. Those who have been to Johannesburg, as I have, will remember the city that looks like any hometown, U.S.A., the Kentucky Fried Chicken places, the Holiday Inns, the Coca-Cola signs, the IBMS, the Apple Computers, the Chevrolets. And they may also remember sadly, as I do, that Johannesburg is not hometown, U.S.A. For there one senses the pervasiveness of hatred, and fear, and unfreedom, and death, and tries to blot out the memory, as I have, of ever having the experience of being there.

But there are other places that we think about, and we revel in the memory of the experiences we have had there. Why Damascus? Who has been to Damascus? Why would anyone want to go to Damascus? Damascus is the oldest city continuously inhabited in the world. There is a great deal of history in Damascus. It is true, perhaps, that they still make the finest sword steel in the world, a commodity for which Damascus was prominent for centuries. Perhaps they even still make the Damas cloth that we in the West have come to treasure so much for our dining linens and other fine tapestries.

But none of these would be sufficient as a reason for making a journey to Damascus. What is in this ancient capital of Syria that would bring one to that city? Not gold. Not silver. Not political aggrandizement. Damascus represents for us a certain rendezvous, a certain meeting, a unique kind of confrontation. The meaning of Damascus is not in the city itself, but in the intentions of those who have traveled there and who, symbolically, have experienced the confrontation which has turned their lives around.

The prototype of the Damascus experience was a man whose name was Saul. We know him primarily by his Roman name, Paul. But he was born a member of the tribe of Benjamin, named for Saul, the first king of Israel. We need to take a look at this man Saul. For in him and in his experiences, perhaps we may find the clue that creates for each of us a sense of compulsion that drives us inevitably toward some Damascus of our own.

Who was this Saul? What is his significance? Why was his trip to Damascus of such great importance to us and to all history? Let us look closely at him that we might better discern what kind of an individual he was. We know first of all that he was a young man proud of his youth, proud of his family, proud of his learning, proud of his city, proud of his Roman citizenship, proud of Jewishness, proud of the fact that he was a Pharisee who had studied with the best teachers of his time. He was a man who stood on the edge of destiny, trying to determine precisely who he was and how his life would be spent.

Saul took up with a certain group, as young men and women often do, in the search for his identity, in an effort to determine precisely where he belonged. So we first see him engaged in an act of rather dubious propriety. Our first vision of Saul is as a well-educated, well-dressed young man who found himself in the midst of a rabble engaged in stoning Stephen to death because of his confession of Christianity. There stood Saul holding the cloaks. He was not yet sufficiently wretched to participate in the actual murder of Stephen, and yet he valued the contacts of those who did participate. He did not want to be completely in, but he wanted to be thought well of by those who were in. So there he stood, holding the cloaks and consenting to the murder of Stephen.

Here I must digress for a moment because of things that have happened in recent weeks that perhaps bring a striking parallel. I am talking about the parallel situation of the ritual murder in the Bedford bar a few nights ago, a situation in which a group of young people found themselves caught up in a situation in which a woman was done to death. I know she was not dead physically, but for all intents and purposes, her life has come to an end. When the psychologists and psychiatrists finish examining the causative factors, perhaps they will find that murder — not sexual gratification — but ritual murder, symbolic murder, was the motivation there.

Somehow the significance of who held the coats and who did the cheering and even who was actually in contact with this hapless victim is all lost in the larger question: *What in the world has happened to civilization?* How is it that here in twentieth-century America we could find anywhere, in any tavern, in any town, fifteen or twenty human beings who could engage in an act like this; who could tolerate an act like this; who could be consenting in act like this? What in the world has happened to America? Is personal gratification — sexual or otherwise — so compelling? Is self-respect so degraded? Is respect for the community, the community of others among whom we live, so eroded that there are no factors of inhibition left? Will we do *anything?* Is there nothing we will not do?

How about the law? Have we lost all respect for the law? One is appalled by the fact that after the attack, nobody ran away. The fun continued by reminiscing and recalling what had gone on the previous two hours. If this is the kind of civilization we have to offer the rest of the world, what kind of hope is there? If the murder in the Bedford bar represents the cryptic consensus of feelings we harbor about society and the individuals who comprise it, then the Holocaust in Germany a mere forty years ago was nothing but a prelude of the fire that is still to come.

There are other signs for us to see that keep telling us that this vaunted civilization of ours has somewhere gone wrong. But our preference seems to be to ignore the signs and to get on with the last big party. I'm sorry for my personal need to digress from Saul and to talk about Bedford. But perhaps in the final analysis, they are one and the same.

In any case, Saul in his day was among those who gave consent—those who gave consent to the structures of evil that characterized his time. He liked the headiness of the company he kept. These were the "in" people. These were the swinging people. These were the avant-garde. These were the bright young folk, the next generation of leaders, and he was prominent among them. In keeping with his expectations for the future, Saul became more and more avid, more and more forthright in his search for approval, at the expense of others.

We see that Saul has moved from being merely a consenter to the death of Stephen; now we find that he is organizing vigilante groups of his own. He has gone to the high priest for papers so that he might search the country-side and drag out all the Christians he can find and bring them bound to Jerusalem, where they might be prosecuted.

We can see his counterpart in contemporary times: let's go, guys, load up your pickup trucks and vans and let's go get the Christians. Let's bring them back; see that they are discomfited as much as possible.

On one such expedition that Saul had organized, to go to Damascus to do evil, something happened to him. Perhaps it was a day like today: the sun beating down, the beauty of nature being expressed all along the way. We can see Saul on the Damascus road with his colleagues, hurrying, hurrying, that they might get to the city by nightfall, in order that they might search out the fugitives, and chain them, and bring them to Jerusalem.

As they journeyed along, suddenly there was a blinding light, and our young protagonist found himself lying prostrate along the ground, sense-less. Something had shaken the hell out of Paul. And when he came to him-self, he knew not where he was, nor what had happened. All he knew was that something had taken hold of him, and whatever it was left him sub-dued and submissive, ready to listen. When he listened, he heard a voice that said to him: "Why do you persecute me? Why do you persecute me? Why couldn't you have gone about your business, weaving cloths, or tent-making, or studying in the temple, or whatever it is you want to do, preparing to be a rabbi? Why do you persecute me?" And at that time, Paul noted that he couldn't see. He couldn't see.

If ever you are without your sight after having had it, you know some-thing of the terrible phenomena in which Saul found himself. How could he chase Christians when he couldn't see? How could he do any of the things that brought him so much pleasure? What was going to happen to his professional life as he prepared for the rabbinate? He couldn't see. Not only was he blind, but for the first time in his life, he was helpless. Somebody—somebody had to take him by the arm and lead him into the city. Somebody had to take care of the reservations for his living quarters. Somebody had to feed him. Somebody had to do everything that he had always done for himself. He was blind. He was out of favor with God. And he was scared.

The long and the short story is that they found a Christian named Ananias to see Paul. Ananias healed his sight and protected him. And Paul became in time the greatest promoter of the Christian cause that history has yet produced. Before this could happen, he had to make his trip to Damascus. He had to have his confrontation with reality. He had to come to terms with himself, with his God, and with his destiny.

The significant journeys we make in this life may have little to do with geography, but they are the journeys from darkness to light, from implacability to reasonableness, from toleration to acceptance, from destruction to support, from hatred to love, from bitterness to appreciation. The road to Damascus is long and uncertain. It is filled with possibilities for evil (Paul's original intent) and possibilities for good.

Pray that on your way to do evil you may be blinded by the light of your own insufficiency; that you, like Paul, may hear a voice that calls you back to the responsibility of being what you are and what you can become. Those people in the Bedford bar (here I go again), and all of the people who have encouraged and who share the responsibility for Bedford by distancing themselves from responsibility at home, are people who have refused to be responsible, refused to accept responsibility, refused to see the relationship between nonfeasance and what is happening to the society at large.

There is a world out there, but it is still to be won. It is a world of men and women, in the mass, but it is also a world of human individuals. Human individuals, locked in an intimate struggle against the bars. And even though we preen and we prance and we prate, with the doubtful confidence of jesters and fools, in our hearts we know all too well that unless we learn to live for each other (and that right early), we may not live at all.

That is the lesson of Damascus. If you have never been there, God grant that you may be going soon.

Marty, as he prefers to be called, was a longtime professor of church history at the University of Chicago Divinity School. He is a prolific author and a widely known commentator on and spokesperson for American religious life. In this sermon Marty preaches with the Bible in one hand and Psychology Today *in the other as he mounts a spirited defense of biblical apocalyptic. In apocalyptic— that strange, "useless" vision of a "new heaven and a new earth"—Marty finds the chief source of any possible human hopefulness in an often hopeless age.*

The Usefulness of a Useless Vision

November 6, 1983

MARTIN E. MARTY

Revelation 21:1-2 From the Apocalypse, Revelation, this vision: "Then I saw a new heaven and a new earth, for the first heaven and the first earth had passed away, and the sea was no more. And I saw the holy city, new Jerusalem, coming down out of heaven." What follows is then the text that you heard today.

This Thursday, November 10th, is the five hundredth birthday of Martin Luther. This is a festival that comes around only every five hundred years. And thus I consider myself pridefully sinful in my self-restraint in that I'm not going to talk about him today. He has his chances this week (I get four with him in this city). He's a media hero—last week's *Time*, tomorrow's *Newsweek* and *U.S. News*. I read in the morning paper that Pope John Paul II will honor him with a sermon next month. Who am I in that great cloud of witnesses? And what is more, a good Lutheran should stick to the lectionary—the appointed festivals and texts of the year. Your bulletin today reminds you that this Sunday follows All Saints Day, and it is also known as All Saints Sunday. Why should we be so economical as to honor just one saint (and he barely one!) when we can have all saints before us?

On the terms of the Christian message, you and I are also and equally to be seen as incorporated in this good news, this message that makes us saints. So we have the business before us of unfolding, or unveiling (that's what Apocalypse means) this text from Revelation, which I'm calling, in a sense, a useless vision, because it seems so remote from our world.

Most people look at the language of vision in the Bible—Daniel, Revelation, Ezekiel—very much the way we in the modern world look at dream.

For a moment in the beginning of our attempt to crack this one open, let's think of "dream" as an analogy, or metaphor, or comparison for "vision." There are numbers of theories about the function of vision, dream, the best known in our time being that of Sigmund Freud, who saw vision and dream simply as wish fulfillment. You could read this text about a new heaven and a new earth as a language of wish fulfillment, on the part of believers, who through the ages have had to live far from heavens in an old earth that is stubborn and intractable and warring and foolish.

But that theory doesn't stand up well. This week's *Times Literary Supplement*, in a review of *The Oxford Book of Dreams*, says (I'm happy to say) that Freud's view is officially on its way out. In the entire *Book of Dreams*, only one can be described as wish fulfillment. The feminist Mary Wollstonecraft says, "Dream, that my little baby came to life again. That it had only been cold, and we rubbed it in front of the fire and it lived. Awake, and find no baby. Not in good spirits." On Sundays we have the dream of new heaven and new earth, but on Monday we awake and find no new heaven and no new earth. And with Wollstonecraft, not in good spirits.

A little closer are the theories about vision and dream that come from Carl Jung, because he says the dream is that which connects the language of the conscious and the unconscious. That's a little closer to what goes on here. For in the unconscious of the believing community are those great stories — memories of saints, heroines, heroes, martyrs, mentors. We recall those improbable stories that now and then, through the glass of a chapel like this, or through the kind of music we've heard, become part of our conscious life as well.

The approach to dream that is currently most fashionable — I have this on the authority of the *Times Literary Supplement* and *Psychology Today* — is that of Sir Francis Crick and Graeme Mitchinson, who believe that dreams are, in a sense, part of a computer mechanism in the mind for mental housecleaning. They help us get rid of images that are not too useful during the rest of the day. They are called "reverse learning" — a damping-out process that makes us more efficient the rest of the time.

Could it be that the language of a new heaven and a new earth, and of a holy city that comes down in the middle of our world, and the light of God, the sun and shield breaking in it, ought to be damped out — discarded, unlearned — because it gets in the way of the practice? If we just gather for an hour in a setting like this and get it all over with, we can get back to the real, practical world.

And yet, that same canonical text (*Psychology Today*) also says that others believe dreams help consolidate memories. This is the opposite of Sir Francis

Crick's and Graeme Mitchinson's view. The view that dreams help consolidate memories would also work, for that is what believers do when they gather and hear the vision, the unveiling, the revelation, the apocalypse. There is in our collective memory a recall of the promise that ahead of us and coming toward us is always the activity of a God who would create new situations for us.

So much for dream theory—but I hope that at least three of those four theories might help us as we crack open this text. What we have to remember is that very often, this dream and vision language of Daniel, Ezekiel, and Revelation is taken literally by people many centuries later. They have often and again applied it to their own time. From one point of view, every later age can say that they have often and again and always been wrong because they prophesied the end of the world. The fact that we are here this morning is empirical evidence that they were wrong. Martin Luther, in the sixteenth century (pardon the reference), read this text and said that the whole book of Revelation is a prophecy against the Pope, the anti-Christ. (The Pope is now returning the favor by coming to preach Christ in a Lutheran church.) So that can't have been right, though Luther's argument that gave rise to that name calling was, I believe, a valid one.

In our time—in what the magazines would call the fashionable theory of the literal view—there are those who apply this book to our world, which will soon be incinerated, probably beginning in the Middle East, at the place called Armageddon. The president of the United States this week confided to some friends (who blabbed to the press) that as he looked at the signs of the time, he joined the fundamentalist-literalists in sometimes thinking, with Lebanon, Grenada, and Russia on his mind, like the Book of Daniel, Armageddon seemed to be coming. The not-so-nice newspaper reporter reminded readers that Armageddon is not in the Book of Daniel; it is in Revelation. But the president here was giving voice to a widespread sentiment: that now we have to have a literal vision of the new heaven and the new earth and the new Jerusalem that replaces the old Jerusalem.

Everything in this book can be seen literally on those terms. I read a tract recently on Revelation 13:7. The tract said the Universal Product Code on what you buy in the supermarket is a fulfillment of Revelation 13:7, which says that no one can buy or sell unless he has the mark—that is, the name of the beast, and the number of its name. I take great comfort in the fact that the best-selling book of our time, *The Late Great Planet Earth*, which is literal about Revelation, has won its author millions of dollars, which he is investing in long-term real estate at the same time as he is telling us the world will end tomorrow.

What these people do to serve us is to keep the images alive, to remind us of end times and urgencies. Yet we have been led through this all to say again, what did this text originally say to the people to whom it was written? Maybe then we will learn why through the ages, All Saints speaks to us.

For the past century, the most serious biblical scholars have said that we will get our best clues if we understand that the John of Patmos, who had this vision from the spirit of the Lord, wrote it in a letter, and sent it to be read in the churches. The churches had in common not saintliness (one of them was lukewarm), not heroism, but the need for a long-term vision. The message is that Christ the crucified is the victor. In the middle of a world that looks far from any new heaven, and is very much old earth, there is therefore a promise, a future. The Roman Empire, the enemies of these believers, all conspired against them. Yet they are to endure, and have hope, and that is why we celebrate them today—all saints.

But this text is not only historical, not only about people who suffered under the Romans. It discloses to us ways of thinking and being that we might not otherwise have entertained. The symbol of the new heaven and the new earth lives on among very practical people. I looked at books in print this week and noticed at least five books titled "New Heaven" or "New Earth." Novelist Joyce Carol Oates. Anthropologist Kenneth Burridge. Historian Cushing Strout, who has traced the way that Americans have again and again done useful things in the light of that useless image, such as work for the abolition of slavery.

"I saw a new heaven and a new earth." The Bible is coming to its end. Revelation 21: "Behold I make all things new." The quality of the life of all saints was to grasp this sense of newness. Ernst Bloch, a maverick Marxist who stood outside the Bible, admired it for what he called "its infatuation with the possible." The God who raised Jesus from the dead is active in our broken world, in our fallible city.

The usefulness of a useless vision—what does it mean for us? We are not to be literal—and you could tell I wasn't siding with that. And we are not to be only historical. After all, we have our own lives to live. We don't live in the past—we have our deaths to explain, our fears to encounter, our hopes, our fighting off of chaos and meaninglessness. What's in it for us?

A great German Catholic with an Italian name, Romano Guardini, once described worship in a very interesting phrase. It applies to my title. He called worship, "schwechtlos aber doch zinvoll." It means, it's pointless, but significant. It's pointless so far as the eight-hour day is concerned. No new product comes from it. You can't look at something built because of it. And yet, it is significant. It signifies, signs, points to, indicates, inspires modes of being that we would not have otherwise entertained.

So let's close by looking at what this text you heard read today would have us entertain. "I saw no temple in the city, for its temple is the Lord God Almighty and the Lamb." This vision that seems so useless comes to all saints, to you and me, with the recognition that in all circumstances, God is Lord for us. Viktor Frankl, the death camp psychiatrist, observed people who were to die that day, and knew it, sharing their last crust of bread. By word and by gesture they imparted hope. Frankl said that they proved there is one freedom that cannot be taken away from us: the freedom to choose one's attitude in any circumstance.

In this second-to-last chapter of the Bible, this last vision says there is a reason in the Lordship of God. A day comes when the Temple, or places like this sanctuary, will no longer be needed, for God is all in all. Then all will be holy. Now, the world is still broken. In Tillich's phrase, the demonic pervades the structures of existence. But we are not to see the world only as God versus Satan, Christ versus Anti-Christ, us good people versus those bad people—we are to see the potential of God active everywhere.

There is in this useless vision the useful sense that behind the windows of this world, behind all that we see, is this light of God. This world is to become ever more transparent to it. The city has no need of sun or moon to shine upon it. For the glory of God is its light, and its lamp is the Lamb. This is a reminder that sun and moon were to this Creator a creation, and that could pass away, but God's light cannot pass away. The more this creation becomes transparent to that light, the more likely we are to be good care-takers of the earth, responsible and caring about the people and the society around us.

Society—by its light shall the nations walk, and the kings of the earth will bring their glory into it. And its gates shall never be shut. By day—and there shall never be night there. This useless vision tells us that in the middle of this world, when nation wars against nation, God comes with a sign of shalom, of peace, and it becomes useful as we grasp it. Harold Isaac says, "Around the world today there is a massive, convulsive ingathering of peoples into their 'separatenesses' and their 'over-againstnesses' to protect their pride and power and place, against the real or imagined threats of other people who are protecting their pride and power and place." This vision tells us that we are always to respond to a day when all nations will recognize this power.

All saints of all ages live and die in this peace. Nothing unclean shall enter that city, and no person who practices abomination or falsehood. Only those who are written in the Lamb's Book of Life will enter—not the "good guys" and "good women" who achieve so much. Instead, it is those who by grace have a vision like this break into their lives that will enter.

A new heaven; a new earth. Behold, I make all things new! Not a bad way, is it, to end a book called the Bible? Not a bad way to begin the week.

In the name of the Father, and of the Son, and of the Holy Spirit. Amen.

Donald MacLeod influenced a generation of Princeton-educated preachers through his role as the Francis L. Patton Professor of Preaching and Worship at Princeton Theological Seminary. This sermon is typical of MacLeod's elegant, literate style. A string of diverse illustrations is used to illuminate his central theme: there is a point in living. Though this sermon dates from the mid-1980s, it sounds reminiscent of an earlier homiletic that sought to combine the best of human wisdom and art with a rich, thematic presentation of the gospel.

There Is a Point in Living

November 13, 1983

Isaiah 49:4—"I thought I had been laboring in vain, spending my strength for nothing."
I Corinthians 15:58—"Your work is not in vain in the Lord."

In one of his poems John Greenleaf Whittier wrote these words: "Of all sad words of tongue or pen, / The saddest are these: 'It might have been.' "

Today if any of you were to ask me to rewrite Whittier's lines to reflect the mood of many of our people, it might go this way: "Of all sad words that are on the loose, / The saddest of these are: 'What's the use?' "

Last year after the primary elections in one of our cities, a civic leader, looking back on all the chicanery, dishonesty, and double dealing, called the political process "an exercise in futility."

Several years ago a Presbyterian minister in Chicago sent out thousands of questionnaires to people in every walk of life. He received over four thousand replies, all of which he carefully indexed and tabulated. In each questionnaire only one point was raised: what is the outstanding question you face in all your thinking and living. 22 percent indicated their problem lay with their families; 48 percent said their problem was personal living and the seeming loneliness, general failure, and the futility of it all.

On the bulletin board of an Ivy League university last spring this item appeared: "WANTED: a young couple to care for an elderly millionaire who has been taking tranquilizers for twenty years. This couple is needed desperately to give him meaning to life. He has nothing to live for."

An editorial in a college newspaper reflecting student opinion said this:

"Our generation has known only death from the time we were born. We have no reason to believe we shall even be alive twenty years from now, much less hope for a better future. And we cannot count on the adults around us to inspire us with a new vision of a world transformed."

Now all these are contemporary echoes of our first text today, which was a cry of discouragement from one of the greatest prophets of ancient Israel. For more that half a century the people of Israel had been exiles in pagan Babylon. But God had not abandoned them, for a new chapter of their history had begun to emerge: out of the North came Cyrus, the Persian warrior, whose pressures on the Babylonian empire eroded its strongholds and set the captives free. What a tremendous hour this was for the prophet Isaiah! Now his hopes were about to be fulfilled; now his prophecies would be vindicated. God had intervened and had opened a highway for the exiles to return to Jerusalem and to rebuild their temple as a free nation. Well might the prophet sing, "O Jerusalem that bringest good tidings; lift up your voice with strength; lift it up; be not afraid; say unto the cities of Judah, 'Behold your God!' "

But people everywhere are so human and even the best among us can be so disappointing. Some of these exiles refused to return home because they preferred the life of idolatry of the heathen. Others decided to come, but were so slow and reluctant that they tried the patience of the prophet. And some others, though they came readily, brought their pagan gods with them. It is not surprising, then, that Isaiah, who was at the peak of jubilation over his prospect of liberty, should on account of the slow reaction of his people be hurled momentarily into the pit of depression and dejection. Hear his lament: "I thought I had been laboring in vain, spending my strength for nothing." This was the day he had lived for; this was the hour toward which his soul had reached; yet so few shared his enthusiasm. And hence in a moment of sorry reflection he felt his life was pointless and useless; he saw no result for his labor; he perceived no rhyme or reason to his exacting toil.

And this, men and women, is futility. Moreover, this attitude and feeling that assailed the prophet Isaiah for a moment twenty-six centuries ago holds many of our people in its grip today. Despite all the benefits of science, culture, and progress, we are a confused, bewildered, and frustrated generation. The great Jewish philosopher Martin Buber was describing a few years ago the temperament of the people of Europe and he remarked, "They are working hard, but they are working in the dark." Now, whatever excuse might be given for this state of mind in Europe, it stirs our curiosity when we discover the disease of futility to be rampant today among vast numbers of Americans who have everything they want. Every day we meet people who seem to go through the motions of living as if they were waiting for a sudden and ominous catastrophe. Walk the streets of any of our cities and how one misses the uplifted face, the flashing eye, and shoulders braced and squared with courage. Men and women seem to believe, like old Sorrell in Warwick Deeping's novel, "Man is fighting a lone fight against a vast indifference." Or, as an Englishman cried out recently, "What is the point of trying when the devil holds all the trump cards?" Something has seemingly gone out of our lives and into the vacuum has come the deadening mood of futility.

One evening Prime Minister David Lloyd George was called to the telephone from a political caucus in a smoke-filled room and a doctor's voice at the other end of the line said, "I regret, Sir, but your daughter is dead." Then and there he was staggered as never before; no political manipulation could do any good in the face of this devastating fact; and turning from the telephone he cried out of sheer futility, "Why doesn't life work?" This problem was not political or economic or national; it was basically moral and spiritual. For if people could believe greatly in something, if they could see the outline of a purpose that would give reason and reality to daily living, then life would wear the radiant image of victory.

By now you are asking: what has Isaiah to do with all this? If he was the victim of futility among the simplicities of his life, what has he to say to the complex situation of the twentieth century? Simply this: although Isaiah was assailed by futility in its bitterest form, yet he met it head-on and defeated it because he was equipped with certain inner fundamentals that came from the mind and heart of the living God. And these were not merely ten little rules for confident living, but were deep convictions which came from observing the way God acts with men and women who were obedient to his will. And St. Paul, too, knew that through obedience to the living and exalted Christ when he said, "Your labor is not in vain in the Lord." Moreover, these spiritual truths by which God's great servants lived are still vital and valid in this generation in which we find ourselves. Let us take a look at this scripture passage in which Isaiah speaks and discover for ourselves three great convictions to sustain us in our struggle with futility.

Isaiah had the conviction that *he had a place of significance and worth in human society*. Note in verse 1 how he puts it: "From my birth God hath made mention of my name."

Now, is not this one of the lost notes in much of our thinking and living today? Constantly we are told to see and safeguard the worth of other individuals — and rightly so — but the conditions of our age demand that we see also the worth of ourselves. The story is told of a group of men and women who were passing through the security check at the gate of a government plant in Glasgow, Scotland. One woman hadn't her ID card and she shouted to her husband who was some distance down the line, "Hurry, Jock, and bring my nonentity card!" This is part of our problem: too many people today are inclined to treat themselves as nonentities. They forget they are members of God's great family and that the quality of the whole depends upon the quality of every single unit in it. But if you and I believe that this universe is merely an accident or that life is (as one student puts it) "a bad joke that isn't even funny," then it is folly to be concerned about ourselves or anyone else. However, if you and I believe that it was God who called us into being, we shall see life from a new perspective. We shall see ourselves to be endowed with a new perspective and be captivated by a new meaning. Now we shall want to make our lives morally and spiritually great in order to count 100 percent in God's plan for all humankind.

Not long ago on the CBS News we saw a view of the newly refurbished interior of the Ford's Theater in our nation's capital. I thought of that fateful night, April 14, 1865, when John Wilkes Booth approached the unguarded presidential box to assassinate Abraham Lincoln. Who was the president's bodyguard and where was he then? His name was John F. Parker. His job: bodyguard to the president of the United States. Someone described him as a man who lived in a dim fog of mind and will. Always he got along somehow. Never could he be a somebody, so he decided to enjoy himself as a nobody. His orders that night were to be alert to any and every danger and to defend the president at all cost. But from where he was standing he couldn't see the stage, so he forsook his post and grabbed a seat. And for over one hundred years our nation has worn the scar of one man's sense of futility. One man failed to respect his task and to feel that at that moment, in that place, he as an individual was indispensable.

On the other hand, whenever you and I see our work and ourselves to be claimed by a righteousness and justice not our own, the quality of human society is enriched and our contribution to the common good is made more real. "From your birth God hath made mention of your name." When you and I believe this, there is no room for futility and no one of us feels his or her work is in vain.

Isaiah had a second conviction: *he was an instrument in the hands of God.* Note what he says in verse 3 in reporting God's word to his own life: "Thou art my servant in whom I will be glorified."

While Isaiah was concerned about the task of counseling and encouraging his people, he was aware that the truth of God was being expressed through him. For whenever men and women put themselves at God's disposal, he breaks into glory through them. And there is no greater inner enthusiasm you and I can experience than when God breaks into glory in and through our human life. But unfortunately Irwin Edman, in his book *Candle in the Dark*, could describe our usual status very aptly: "In the nineteenth century man was sad because he no longer believed in God; but in the twentieth century he is sadder still because he no longer believes in man." And certainly we cannot restore the conviction that we are instruments of God unless and until these deficiencies in nineteenth- and twentieth-century thinking are made up.

The Shorter Catechism says, "God is Spirit, infinite, eternal, unchangeable in his being, wisdom, power, holiness, justice, goodness, and truth." And just as light requires a surface to reflect it, else it is not seen, also God's ways and will are reflected in human witness and character. Therefore when you and I do what is wise instead of what is indiscreet; when we ally our energy with the holy rather than the profane; when we commit our life to justice in place of what is unfair; when we seek truth rather than falsehood: we are on the side of God, doing his will, and through us others see his inbreaking glory.

But it is just here that we continue to fail him.

One day on a playground in Boston some boys were teasing another lad who was a Sunday school boy and whose shoes were broken through at the toes and heels. And they said to him tauntingly, "If God really loves you, why doesn't he take care of you? Why doesn't he tell someone to buy you a pair of shoes?" And the boy answered, "I suppose he does tell somebody, but they just aren't listening." But when people do listen to that call and claim from beyond themselves, they become God's instruments for the benefit and good of others, for he can only work through men and women for men and women. As the late John A. Mackay of Princeton Seminary once said, "We become related to Christ singly, but we cannot live in Christ solitarily." When you and I are committed to him, our lives are directed ever outward to work his purpose for his people. And when we are so involved, the thrill of our enthusiasm outstrips the encroachments of futility.

One further thought: not only had Isaiah the convictions that he had a place of significance and worth in human society and was an instrument in the hands of God, but more—he felt he could trust in God's handling of tomorrow. Note how he testified in verse 4: "Yet surely my judgment is with the Lord and my work with my God." He gave it all over to God and he conquered his sense of futility. He took Kierkegaard's "leap of faith." And this is always the initial step toward a life filled with meaning, direction, and purpose, where futility has no place.

Oh, but you interrupt: this is what all the preachers say, "Simply have faith and all will be swell." But those who talk this way are not sure of what faith is; for them it is believing in what you know to be untrue. And if that be so, then no scientist, no inventor, no explorer, would ever have budged an inch and the resources of this universe would have been left untapped, its laws untamed, and you and I would still be living in caves.

But the men and women of faith, whose lives have cheered and uplifted humanity, have had one watchword, LET GO and LET GOD! As William Barclay of Glasgow wrote, "It is the persons who are in a right personal relationship with God as a result of their faith who really live." And the enemy of this kind of life is our graceless, grasping inner selves which always want our own way, our own comforts, our own ends, and we continue to be miserable and to feel futile with them and without them. Henry Drummond, the great Scottish scientist and Christian, said, "The end of life is not simply to do good or to get good. It is just doing what God wills, whether that be winning or losing, suffering or recovering, living or dying."

At one time in Africa, David Livingstone felt for a while that his work was hopeless, futile, and in vain, but he fell back on Christ's promise, "Lo, I am with you always, even to the end of the world." And later Livingstone wrote in his diary, "These are the words of a man of the most sacred and strictest honor!"

"I thought I had been laboring in vain, spending my strength for nothing." "Your work is not in vain in the Lord." There is a point in living! How happy will be those who find it!

Louis Patrick came up to Durham one September, toward the first of the school year, to preach this eloquent sermon, a poetic appeal for the cultivation of a sense of wonder in a world that is too often demystified. Patrick was pastor at the Trinity Presbyterian Church in Charlotte, North Carolina.

The "Ah" of Wonder

September 30, 1984

LOUIS PATRICK

Genesis 28:10–17 For all of us, this is the day the Lord hath made. But for some of us, the day is a bit more awesome than for others, and not until I stood up here did I appreciate why your ever-gracious dean put on the back of the chair where I am sitting a piece of paper with the word "preacher." It helps to be reassured in this awesome setting that one has come to preach—especially when the text seems so out of place for this context. Genesis 28:17: "Where a man awakens out of doors in the midst of everyday life and says, 'Surely the Lord is in *this* place, and I knew it not.'" And he is caught up with great awe and trembling.

It is about that kind of wonder that I want to speak with you this morning. We are running into it every day, and yet somehow it escapes us. We see the silver rain peppering the pond. And we smell the incense of honeysuckle at the end of a hot and bothered summer day. And at night we listen while the waves lull the shore to sleep, or while some whippoorwill makes its call out of a deep, dark wood. And we think, ah, of such things is the stuff of life. And we do, in this, catch the wonder that lies deep down in things—where life consists not in the number of breaths we take, but in those times when our breath is taken away from us and all we can do is say, "Ah . . . Ah!" That's why no day is lost in which we marvel.

Well, whosoever wonders reigns, and whoever reigns will find rest. Stay yourselves, and wonder: Who makes the streams run and puts the valley's grass on the mountains, shows his goodness to the forgotten, sets at liberty those who are in chains, proclaims the acceptable year of the Lord—but always in terms of the common, everyday events. To see this is to indeed be saved.

But so often this "ah" of wonder escapes us. We look at everyday life, our own life or the life of the world, but instead of the "ah" of wonder, it's the "blah" of what we know and what we somehow think we understand. We see through everything we want to see. Every question has an answer. You come to the "blah" of class after class after class, all questions with answers. The "blah" of a world where we are moved around by virtue of digits assigned to us by computers, known by numerals instead of names. The "blah" of plastic replacing wood, powdered stuff replacing Bess's milk, soap operas instead of real life. Eventually we do indeed see what is in everything until there is nothing left to see, and we look through the slits of our eyes knowingly like some downstairs maid. Until all the prophet can say to the likes of us is, "See, you blind! Listen, you deaf! To that wonder that is deep down in the everyday things."

Annie Dillard tells how as a six- or seven-year-old in Pittsburgh (and goodness knows, Pittsburgh is no wonder city—not even with the Steelers and the Pirates), she would go out when this curious compulsion would come upon her to hide a penny somewhere in that smoky city, along a certain stretch of sidewalk, under a sycamore root or a crack in the sidewalk. And then beginning at one end of the block, she would draw arrows on the ground and write things like "Surprise ahead!" or "Money, this way!" And she then would go hide—she had no desire to see it, just to think about the wonder of someone in the universe receiving a free gift from the universe without regard of merit or desserts or anything. Now, she says, the compulsion no longer seizes her. But since we live in a world that is strewn with pennies, if we would cultivate that kind of healthy poverty, where finding a penny would make our day, we would thereby inherit a lifetime of days.

But in a world where facts are facts and facts are all that matters, who has time to stoop for pennies? What's one more penny? So Dillard says: "The cold frost of fact gives correctly stated death to all that lives, and pennies do not make our days." She means that we have demystified life. Forests are no longer enchanted; sidewalks are no longer full of surprises—just ways of getting places.

You would know this had to come from another generation, wouldn't you?

> Flower in the granite wall, I pluck you out of the crannies
> And I hold you here in my hand, little flower,
> And if I could but know what you are, root and all, and all in all,
> If I could but know what you are, then I would know what God and
> man is.

What do you mean, "if?" Anybody with a botany badge—girl or boy scout—knows what a flower is. Not even the heavens are beyond our knowledge anymore:

Twinkle, twinkle, little star,
I do not need to wonder what you are.
You're just so much combusting mass
Of C and N and hydrogen gas!

Here's how one person put it:

One day I went walking and I found a magic glass—a magic looking glass.
A stagnant pond, said Cass.
One day I went walking and I found a dress—a princess fairy's dress.
A fallen leaf, said Tess.
One day I went walking and I found a brownie's shoe—a brownie's button shoe.
A dried pea pod, said Sue.
The next time I go walking, I'm going by myself, unless—
Unless I meet an elf, a funny, friendly elf.

That's why John Oman said that as long as he was a Methodist—he became a Roman Catholic—if he had seen Jesus walking on water, he would have had to say, "Sir, could you do it again? I didn't get the trick." That's how important it is for us to demystify—to understand so much that it does not so much lead to wonder, but take away our wonder.

What turns God on? With all the mystery and wonder removed from life, we are tempted to say it is goodness that turns God on. And God deals with this very quickly, saying, "Goodness? You think that I get off on goodness? You who went through the long slap of history, the long suffering of the innocent? All this history's excrement of evil being rewarded with good, and good with evil, you think *goodness* is my thing? No. I called it off, because my one thing is *astonishment*. And I never found my audience. I got a few 'hillels' from the Jews, a few 'lacheims.' A few 'Hallelujahs' from the Protestants, a few 'te deum laudamuses' from the Catholics, but I really never found my audience. For astonishment is that in which I delight. Those who can stand before an everyday event and say, 'this is the Lord's doing,' that is marvelous in my eyes!"

Alice Walker says, in her *Color Purple*, "God loves the very things we love, that used to turn us on, only they keep turning Him on. It isn't that He's vain. It's just that He wants to share these things with us, and nothing turns Him off so much as a person who can walk a field of purple, and not stand and stare. So full of care they can walk by a field of purple and not just stand and stare."

Look at the wonder deep down in things — every land a Land of "ah's," every place a place where the Lord is — especially in the everyday places.

And I have taken this long to just somehow get us into the story of Jacob, which will not now take long. Here is a man who has just fleeced his father, flim-flammed his brother, is taking it on the lam until the tempers cool. And the first night out he makes his bed out under the stars with nothing around to remind him of anything but the world as it is — the plain, hard facts. And he lies down, and you'd think he would have a troubled conscience. But he goes to sleep like a baby cradled in his mother's arms. You would think at least God would get at him with some troubled dreams, and instead Jacob gets a dream that would be worthy of a saint. He sees a ladder coming down from heaven to earth and then back up to heaven, and on it angels with feet of burnished brass, wings like monarch butterflies, and they are all bringing blessings to him — Jacob, the flim-flam artist, the con man! And above the ladder is God himself saying, "I will give you the land you sleep on; I will make you a blessing to all the nations of the earth. In you they will find their birthright." And then this codicil to the blessing: "I will bring you back to the land from which you came, and always I will be there with you to bless you."

My soul! You would think at least God would have thrown the book at this crook. No wonder when he awoke from the dream it was with fear and trembling. "*The Lord is in this place! This place!* The last place I would have ever expected to find him!" You could not cheat and put Him there. He was there, simply to give what was on the house — what had been on the house all the time. Everything Jacob had wanted and cheated in order to obtain, it could not be had that way, because it can't be had that way. It has to be had as a gift! That's why he was saying: "This is the gate of heaven. This is the great discovery. The Lord is precisely where I least expected him." And so Jacob became father of the faith. So the stable, so the star, so the man whose name is called Wonderful.

All this "ah" in the midst of the everyday things. In a world full of con artists, of helms and hunts, of family feuds, of attempted getaways, dirty tricks — you name it — ah! Holy, holy, holy, art God almighty! The earth is the place of thy glory. That's why this chapel — to remind us of nothing more than that. Not that He's in chapel, but all the glory that is *here* comes from *There*. Or we would not be here ourselves.

How else can you say it? Lick a finger and feel the now? Listen, Jesus says to the wind, listen, listen. It's out there. The wind, that's the now. That's the gracious coming of our God, who always comes in ways where He's least expected, where we least expect to find Him as in a roomful of Jews smelling of fish in the Upper Room, as on the road to Emmaus, where they thought the one thing they now could be saved from was visitation from any more Saviors. He is always coming to make wherever we are a land of "ah's"!

C. S. Lewis tells how he too as a young boy was one day standing by a currant bush when something overtook him more important than anything that had ever happened to him before or ever since. He has this memory that went back not a few years, but centuries, it seemed to him, to that time when as a young boy his older brother came and brought on a biscuit tin a miniature garden made up of nothing but moss and a few plants. And suddenly, he said, "Even as a child, I found myself filled with the enormous bliss of Eden, a longing for that place where I would be at home, had been at home, would yet be at home again. And though longing I no longer had, then it vanished, and I longed for the longing again. The only really important thing that has happened in my life on that biscuit tin, in that moss and those plants, was to see the wonder of God's creation."

Are you going to say "blah" to that? It's in all of us. How else will you understand this poem? Lewis wrote it many years after that longing had welled up inside him and then quickly vanished.

> The sky was low, the sounding rain was falling, dense and dark,
> And Noah's sons were at the window of the ark
> The beasts were in, but Jack had said, "I see one creature more!"
> There, all belated and unmated, standing there, knocking at the door
> "Well, let him knock," said Ham,
> "Or let him drown or swim — we're overcrowded; we've got no room
>   for him."
> "Oh, but how it knocks," said Shem, "How terribly it knocks;
> Its feet are hard as hooves, but, ah, the air that comes from it —
>   how sweet!"
> "Now you hush," said Ham, "You keep talking, you'll wake up Dad,
> And when he comes to see what's at the door,
> All it's going to mean is more work for you and me."
> And sure enough Noah's voice came up from the darkness down below:
> "Boys, some animal is knocking — knocking there at the door!"
> Ham shouted back, savagely nudging the other two,
> "That's only Jack knocking the bread nail in his shoe!"
> "Boys," said Noah, "no, I hear a noise that's like a horse's hoof."
> "No, no," said Ham, "it's just the dreadful rain, Dad, coming down upon
>   the roof."
> But Noah tumbled up on deck, and out he put his head,
> And suddenly his face turned gray, his knees became loose,

He tore at his beard, and said, "Look! Look! It would not wait!
It turns away and takes its flight!
Oh, fine work, my sons, fine work you've made of it tonight.
Even if I could outrun it now, it would not turn again — not now.
How great discourtesy hath earned its high disdain.
I tell you noble, unmated beast, my sons were all unkind,
On such a night as this, what stable, what manger will you find?
And henceforth, what furrows shall be plowed across the hearts of men
Before you come to stable or to manger ever, ever again.
And how dark and how crooked all the ways in which our race shall walk
All their wondering manhood now like flowered, broken stalks!
And all the world, my sons, will curse the hour when you were born
Because of *you* the ark must sail without the unicorn!"

Have you seen a unicorn lately? That which cannot be had can only be given in the come-and-go of everyday life — can only be had in the faith, hope, and love that come to us in our daily walk. Then you can say, "Surely the Lord is in this place. And I knew it not. For holy, holy, holy, Lord God almighty, the Earth is the place of thy glory."

Amid the declining influence of mainline Protestantism during the last years of the last century, the same mainline Protestantism that had produced Duke Chapel, this sermon was preached in defense of that wing of the Church and its vision. Beginning with an acknowledgment that "Jesus Christ broke the heart of the Roman world," John Vannorsdall, a Lutheran who was then university chaplain, Yale University, admits that it is difficult to be in the mainline church, the Church that keeps "one ear to Jesus and one ear to the ground." Vannorsdall uses a gentle, irenic, chastened voice for this encouraging sermon.

Mainline Churches

February 10, 1985

JOHN VANNORSDALL

Mark 1:14–20, 29–39 They were casting their nets into the sea. A graceful sight, I'd guess, a matter of rhythm and strength, the net arcing up, spreading outward until its weighted edge touched the water, more slowly sinking to entrap whatever fish might lie below. Simon Peter and Andrew, James and John. Jesus cast his net and drew them in: "Follow me and I will make you become fishers of men"; which is to say, "I will make you fishers of men, of women, and of children."

And traditional piety celebrates this casting of the net as the invitation which has eventually drawn millions upon millions of people into becoming followers of Jesus, and many of us as well. I'm not the only one here this morning who learned as a child these words of a hymn: "Jesus calls us; o'er the tumult of our life's wild, restless sea, day by day his sweet voice soundeth, saying, 'Christian, follow me.'" And most of us have no regret. We've been freed by the Gospel, guided by Christ, comforted in trouble, and renewed in the hope of good things to come.

But I'd like you to see this calling of the disciples, this first in-gathering, to see it from the viewpoint of Zebedee and all the others over the centuries who have been left behind in the boat. "Jesus saw James the son of Zebedee and John his brother, who were in the boat mending their nets. And immediately he called them; and they left their father Zebedee in the boat with the hired servants, and followed him."

"Jesus came preaching the gospel of the Kingdom of God." James and John followed him. Zebedee was left in the boat. I'm not worried about the economics of it; the fishing no doubt continued, the family fed. But think how you'd feel, your two sons following a stranger. "The Son of God," you say. But Zebedee didn't know that. He only knew that Jesus was religious, and not one of the mainline branches of Judaism, and that, somehow, makes it worse. I think he was heartbroken.

And I think we have to understand that for three centuries Jesus Christ broke the heart of the Roman world. The people of the Roman world had their religion, you see. The teachings were different, the practices, but religion was alive and functional everywhere. There was a kind of unity. You had a people — the Jews, the Egyptians, the Romans — dozens of peoples. Each people had a land, at least a historic point of origin. And each people had a religion. And the people, the land, and the religion were one story. Religion described their origin, provided their feast days, determined the laws under which they lived, sanctioned what was good and what was to be punished. "True doctrine," wrote Cicero, "was ancient doctrine. The preservation of the rites of the family and of our ancestors means preserving the religious rites, which, we can almost say, were handed down to us by the gods themselves, since ancient times were closest to the gods."

And along comes Jesus with his net and his "Follow me." And it wasn't long before his followers were not just Jews, but there were Samaritans too. Before long the followers were from everywhere, from many nations. Now we have something different. Not one story in the old sense where a land, a people, and a religion belong together. We had a new people who were no people in the older sense. We had people who were not born into a religion but made a choice to be followers of Jesus. We had a people with no land because they were no people, with a religion which belonged to neither a people nor a land. And Zebedee was left in the boat, heartbroken.

In A.D. 170 the Greek philosopher Celsus lamented that Christians would not serve as soldiers and protect the state; they would not hold public office. Another commentator said that Christians did not understand their civic duty. Tacitus said that Christians were aloof, disdainful of the ways of others, people who wall themselves off. Celsus considered it a revolt against the institutions, the customs which made society possible. For three centuries, Jesus Christ broke the heart of the Roman world.

Don't misunderstand. I'm glad that James and John followed Jesus. He was preaching the gospel of the Kingdom of God, announcing in his own life, death, and resurrection the coming of a new age which drew Jews and Greeks into a new nation; created a nation beyond land, a religion beyond a particular land and people, reversed the roles of rich and poor, the ancient rulership of men over women, the ancient tyranny of sin and judgment, and ultimately destroyed the terror of death itself. What Jesus came preaching was tremendous, a reconceptualization of what it might mean to be human beings. It was time for it, time for the new way, the way of God, the true way. It was the fullness of time; they were standing at the very edge of it.

They were standing at the edge of the future; why should they look back to the doctrines of the ancients? Why should they serve in Roman legions, why become involved in the traditional civic duties? Why should they, as Paul wrote, why should they worry about marriage? If married, stay married. If not married, stay single. They were baptized into androgyny: the distinctions between slave and free, rich and poor. Let the fishing go, the nets, the boat. A new world was coming to birth, a radically different world, the future's world; Jesus was preaching the gospel of the Kingdom of God. And Zebedee was left behind.

I want you to see Zebedee left behind, and I want you to have some sympathy for him—because, in the fourth century, Christianity became the established religion. Now Christians were in the army, and did their civic duty, and they were not aloof and disdainful. Now Christianity became the bearer of correct doctrine, of what was true, what was good and bad, the old religion against which prophets spoke, and we ourselves become Zebedee sitting in the boat.

Now, as you see, there are two things going on—always two things—and both of them called Christian. The first century dynamism is still there: the casting of nets, the fishing for men, women, and children, saying, "Follow me. The Kingdom of God is at hand. There's a new way of seeing the world in which there is neither rich nor poor, male nor female, where roles are reversed—see the dawn! Have no attachment to this world which keeps you from seeing the dawn."

But the second thing which is going on is Christianity which is the established religion: the Christianity which has to face the fact that the Kingdom is dawning but not yet here, the androgyny into which we're baptized hasn't yet happened, the rich are still rich and the poor still poor, people still more attached to their own kind than to humankind. In a world which is still broken, in which valleys are still valleys, and not every tear has been wiped from our eyes; in such a world there is the task of fashioning, reinforcing, and celebrating what is possible, celebrating compromises, adaptation, and what is obviously second best.

And those who are first-century Christians among us come to us, mending our nets as though there is a tomorrow, and they say, "Follow Jesus." And maybe you are James and John, and it's the time of your calling: called to look at the dark horizon and see the first rays of the Kingdom dawning, see it with the eyes of faith, sell all you have, and follow Jesus wherever he leads you. But some of us will be Zebedee, and we'll go on mending our nets, quietly mulling issues of pro and con, wondering where, in a broken world still dark, the Kingdom can next have a partial expression.

To be a part of what we call mainline churches—Roman Catholic, UCC, Presbyterian, and the like—means that we are people who know that we live within this tension. You are now in a mainline church, listening to a mainline preacher, and the lesson for today is to get out of your boat and follow Jesus to the edge of time where the future breaks like dawn upon the darkness, and to live by that light. Let go of all that holds you back: live unattached to the nation state; don't serve in the armed forces; if married, stay married; if single, let it go at that; break the law, establish sanctuaries for refugees in the church; pray without ceasing, and be ye perfect.

You are in a mainline church; but I also say to you that you live in a broken world where Christians have responsibilities for whatever time is left: responsibilities to children, for education, for preserving the best of the past, for protecting against anarchy, to be conservative. You must see Zebedee, left behind, and understand Celsus, Tacitus, and Cicero.

What do you think the builders of this Chapel expected? Is it a tent which can be struck or abandoned if the Kingdom comes at midnight tomorrow: "Follow me!" And leave all this behind? Restrooms and lounge? Both organs? It's an establishment church built to last for centuries. What do chaplains do?, people ask. They pray, for one thing: for academic convocations, alumni affairs, official banquets, and the dedication of squash courts. Chapel and chaplains are established. Chaplains reach out to both sides in labor disputes, put on their boots and walk through the barnyards of academic politics; they study reports and write reports, try to figure out how prophetic they can afford to be, try to decide on what issues they will cash in whatever chips, whatever moral or political power, they have. In a broken world, in a time when the dawn is not yet, the mainline church is not afraid to survive by patch and compromise because it has a role to fill within the structure; a touch of salt here, a bit of yeast there, and always a prayer for the forgiveness of God.

But within all of this, restrooms, organs, and stone, there is also another sound, people not with boots but with wings on their feet, soaring high above compromise, singing for joy that the Kingdom of God is at hand. Follow me to the edge where wars are ended and peace comes, where the enmity between men and women ends. Follow me to the dawn arising.

Are we large-souled enough to embrace the whole of it? Without the zeal, the vision of some, change is unlikely. But also, in a broken world, the dreamers will destroy us if the doubters are silent.

It's uncomfortable being a mainline Christian: one ear to Jesus and the other to the ground, one foot in heaven and the other at Duke. Actually, it's absurd and wonderful and humorous, as long as James and John never forget that they are the sons of Zebedee, and as long as some part of Zebedee can rejoice that his children have gone to meet the future which, by God's grace, will be his future also.

Walter Brueggemann retired last year from his post at Columbia Theological Seminary in Decatur, Georgia, after a dramatic career as a professor of Old Testament at Columbia and Eden Seminaries. He was the late twentieth century's most prominent interpreter of the Old Testament. This sermon reveals that he is also a great preacher. Other preachers love Brueggemann's visceral, strong, imaginative interpretation of Old Testament texts and have made him one of the most widely read scholars among the clergy. In this sermon Brueggemann links the grief of David over the death of his son, Absalom, to Jesus' encounter with the young man, tying all of it in to the season of Lent. In Lent, in our losses, God can make us new, but the cost is great.

Slogans — And Hurts Underneath

February 16, 1985

WALTER BRUEGGEMANN

II Samuel 18:31–19:8 and Mark 10:17–31 Grace to you and peace from the God we have come to know decisively in Jesus of Nazareth. I do not know what time it is in the university — so I shall not talk about that. I shall talk about what time it is in the Church. It is the moment when we make the move from Epiphany to Lent. When we end this season about talking about the kingship of Christ and Jesus' sovereignty and we move to talk about Jesus' suffering and crucifixion. This Sunday is called the Sunday of Transfiguration, when Jesus does a metamorphosis from sovereignty to suffering.

About a year ago, I did a series of lectures at a local church near here. It was endowed by a family in honor of their son, who was dead. At dinner, in a room full of people, I said to the father — which was a mistake to ask it in a room full of people — "How did your son die?" And he stood tall and stiff and he said, "He died in Vietnam." And a little later, we were alone in his den together and I said to him, "How do you go on living after you lose your son?" And he got tears in his eyes and he said, "You don't ever get over it."

He had said, with pride, in public, "He died in Vietnam." He said, tearfully, in private, "You don't ever get over it." Both statements were true and the first statement was kind of like Epiphany and the second one was kind of like Lent. And he had moved from this public statement of pride to this private statement of tears. And in that moment he had been transfigured.

So it occurred to me that life is made up of slogans and hurts that live under the slogans. Very much of our life is made up of slogans: "Christ died for our sins"; "Win one for the Gipper"; "Support your local police"; "Make love not war"; "America—Love it or leave it"; "The Bible is the Infallible Word of God." And you can add to that. There are slogans of the right and slogans of the left and slogans of religion and of economics and of politics. And the value of slogans is that they carry a general truth for us that we don't always have to think about. But the problem is that slogans tend to cover things over. So the father said, "He died for his country." Which he did. But underneath that there was something painful and concrete and lingering. And that lingering pain reminds us that the slogans are not quite true and we ought to be suspicious of the slogans.

So my gift to you is this story about King David. David had a lot of power but it didn't work very well and his beloved son Absalom started a coup to get the throne away from his father. So he sent his army to get Absalom, the traitor, and they hunted him down and they killed him. And they were so proud and they came and they told David, "We have caught the traitor and he is dead and your throne is safe." And David should have been as glad as his men. But in that poignant moment this David does not respond according to the slogans—he responds like a father and he is filled with grief and pathos and all kinds of memories that are so specific. And he says, " 'Oh my son, Absalom. My son, my son Absalom! Would that I had died in place of you! O Absalom! My son, my son!' And then the King covered his face and cried with a loud voice, 'O Absalom! Absalom! My son, my son!' "

David got underneath his public role and, like every parent, he could touch the cost and the caring. And what makes David such a powerful figure in our faith is that he treasures the pain and he never quite believed his own slogans. But of course, that's not the whole story. There is this Joab. Joab is kind of the Caspar Weinberger of David's administration, who always looks out for the public interest—or what he perceives to be the public interest. And he comes to the king and he scolds him! And he said, "You've made it clear today that you don't care about any of us even if we risk our life for you! And if your son were alive and we were all dead you'd be happy! And you'd better go speak to your soldiers who've risked their life for you be- cause if you don't they're all going to desert you by sundown." And so the king took his seat at the gate and acted like a king. Joab comes to David and he says, "Stop crying and get out on the balcony and make an appearance with all your campaign posters." (You see, paying attention to the media is not a new thing for a leader.) "Cover over your pain and get on with the business of the public."

Now, I find that story so powerful because I find it is the story of my life and, I hazard, it is the story of your life. Because we are strange mixtures. And we do cry at night and then next morning you've got to get up and go through your paces *again*.

Lent is a time for the Church to be suspicious about the slogans—like "Peace through strength," and "Western technology will save the world," and "Jesus is the only way to well-being." All those contain germs of truth but they are only germs. That is what makes them so maddening, because the slogans bracket out the pain and the hurt. And when the slogans cover over everything that we value, our humanity will be that much diminished.

The wonderful thing about David is that he did not succumb to the slogans. And this other one in whose name we are gathered who is a son of David did not believe the slogans either. Jesus could've succumbed to the slogans. There were all kinds of messianic proposals waiting for Him to pick up and they sang all kinds of hosannas. And now we are finishing with Epiphany, when the wise men bring their gold and frankincense and all that stuff. But Jesus makes a turn in Lent. It is no longer Jesus moving from triumph to triumph. But now He is transfigured and He becomes a man of sorrows who is burdened down by our scars. And His story becomes one of betrayal and arrest and suffering and death and being alone without the Father.

And so when this rich young man comes to Him and asks what to do with his life, first Jesus gives him the rules that everybody knows. And then He cuts underneath that to where people *live*! And He says, "I'll tell you about the cost of being human and the cost is not to believe all that stuff but to give it away and become obedient." And the man turned away because he had too much stuff to get underneath the slogans.

So, through this journey of Lent, I invite you to think through the slogans by which you organize your life. And then to ask what they cover over. I invite you to think about this great King David, who wasn't impressed with his throne but who grieved the death of his son. To think about this Jesus who is transformed before our very eyes from the powerful one to the sufferer who moves toward death. I invite you to think about the public life of this American community, with our surge toward power and our greed for markets and our juggling act of arms and diplomacy and our penchant to arrange people in terms of friends and enemies—all of which is a great temptation for a powerful community like ours. And we are learning, learning, learning so slowly that all of that way of being present in the world does not fully take into account the mothers and the sons and the babies and the old people who live and die and hope and despair and laugh and cry.

And surely it is not different in this great university with the slogans of the academy and the truths we covet in our various disciplines on our way to security and power and competence. And all of these academic slogans contain truth or we would not speak them to each other. But right down in the middle of that, there is this story about this father and this son and this pain and this hurt. And that is what makes this community of faith so crucial in the university. And that is what makes the Church so important and so dangerous in our society: we are the ones who are called to notice and to treasure and to pay attention to the hurt underneath and to see that in that hurt is precisely where comes hope. It is this community of faith that is pledged to pay attention to the tears and the joys and the hurt and the amazements and the gifts. It is *this* community that is resolved to pray over our hurts and to pray for our enemies, because we know that our enemies have deep hurts that are not covered over by their slogans, even as our hurts are not covered over by our slogans.

Now, you know, this is not a sermon to invite you to grovel in our hurts. You know that we are committed to the proposition that our attention to hurts must influence public policy, so that we know that peace and justice are not made by slogans. So in this Lenten season we have the hard work to be asking, "How does the suffering history of Jesus and the suffering history of all of us play upon the great questions of peace and justice?" Well, what we know is that peace will not come from soldiers and arms and missiles. But peace will come when there are enough mothers who say, "It is enough and we will give no more of our sons!" And we do know that justice will not come through more harsh laws — either here or in Poland or in South Africa. But that justice will only come when there are enough people who let their hurt touch the hurt of other people and generate hope.

So my charge to you in this Lenten season, as you walk away from Epiphany, is that you pay attention to the juggling act in which we are all caught. And that you pay attention to the juggling act in which *you* are caught. It is a juggling act between sovereignty and suffering, between controlling and yielding, between selling everything and going away with great possessions. Watch this David who is a great king who becomes a pitiful father. And watch this Jesus who is a miracle worker who becomes a sheep available for the slaughter. And as you watch that hinge point, ask what your life is about and where you think newness comes from. Because you see, David knew more than Joab. David knew that newness does not come from kings standing on balconies. But newness comes from fathers who have enough grief and hurt over their dead sons to do things differently. That's what happened on Friday and on Sunday. Think about this father who said proudly, "He died in Vietnam." And then who tortured his way to the truth of saying, "You don't ever get over it."

You know, you who meet here every week, we are a strange body of hurt assembled here in the presence of the lamb who is slain. And we are assembled here because we dare affirm that in the grief and the hurt and the loss—just there comes God's newness and God's power for life. And the wonder of the Gospel is that the new life that is given there is not a life of fear or resentment or bitterness but it is a life of justice and caring and gentleness.

The move into Lent is the awareness of how precious and how delicate and how fragile life is—*all* of life. We do not believe the slogans so fully because the slogans diminish life. But this God cuts underneath the slogans to start over in pain. We are the ones who confess that God enters the suffering and that God attends to the hurting and God makes things *new*!

But at great cost.

As one of the pioneering women in theological education, Elizabeth Achtemeier taught courses in preaching and in Old Testament interpretation at the Union Theological Seminary in Richmond, Virginia. She has preached in the Chapel on numerous occasions. This sermon, preached in Advent, is typical of her strong, orthodox interpretation of scripture and her deep appreciation for the particular witness of the Old Testament.

Christmas Party

December 15, 1985

ELIZABETH ACHTEMEIER

Zephaniah 3: 14–17 and Philippians 4: 4–9 Just let me say what a pleasure it is to share in this Advent service with you. I bring you greetings from that portion of the church at Union Theological Seminary in Richmond, Virginia, to this portion of the church on the Duke University campus.

From our Old Testament lesson: "Sing aloud, o daughter of Zion! Shout, o Israel! Rejoice and exalt with all your heart, o daughter of Jerusalem!" The book of the prophet Zephaniah ends in almost unimaginable joy. We are presented here in seventh-century B.C. prophecies a picture of the people of God holding Carnival, singing and dancing in the streets of Jerusalem. Friends, eating and drinking together. Crowds, clapping to the rhythm of timbrels. Children running joyously about. It is one grand celebration of a people whose motto has always been, "Lacheim!" "To life!" It is a joyous jubilation over the fact that abundant life has indeed been given to them.

But that is only a picture of the future in the prophecies of Zephaniah — a promise to the people of God that there will come a day when they can rejoice with exceeding great joy because God has given them life in its fullness. "On that day" is the phrase in our Old Testament lesson — "on that day" in the future. And we have to ask, as we ask of all of the Old Testament, if that day ever came.

Well, it is no accident that this passage from Zephaniah is the stated lesson for the season of Advent. For in a sense, every true Christian's Christmas party is a fulfillment of the prophecy of Zephaniah. And the Church's celebration of the birth at Bethlehem is the realization of the joy that our prophet promised. Do we not celebrate Christmas for the same reasons that the people of God are celebrating here in our text? For they are jubilant first of all, says the prophet, because God has cast out their enemies. And is that not what can finally happen for us through that one child laid in a manger? He can cast out our enemies. No, not those petty foes we construct for ourselves at home, or on the job, or in the world—but our *real* enemies, who can undermine all of the goodness in life. Our sin, which can distort everything we were created to be, and destroy every human relationship. And yes, the final enemy, death, which can end all our years of struggle and care and turn them into the meaninglessness of the void and of the grave.

Sin and death—those are the real enemies of abundant human life. And it is precisely those foes that Jesus Christ overcame. He took our evil, our wrong, our pride, our selfishness, and nailed them to his cross, defeating forever their power to rule our lives. He buried sin—buried it with his lifeless body, leaving it behind in the tomb, its sovereignty gone forever.

But then Jesus Christ was raised on the third day, victor over death. And so we now know that that final enemy cannot capture us either, and that if we trust Christ's power, we too can live with him. The grave need not be the meaningless last chapter to every life and every lovely relationship, and because of Christ, we need never say goodbye. Yes, veiled in the flesh of that babe in the manger is our savior from our real foes: in the words of our Scripture lesson, a mighty warrior to save. God can cast out our enemies, as he promised through Zephaniah. And if we trust that, we will be able with Paul to rejoice, and again to rejoice because the Lord is at hand in this Advent season, our God, mighty to save.

There is another reason the people of God will celebrate, according to our Old Testament lesson, and it too is a reason why we celebrate Christmas. The Lord will take away the judgments against you, says the prophet. Certainly that was good news for the faithful folk of the prophet's time. For the judgments of God are fearful to behold in the book of Zephaniah. "I will utterly sweep away everything from the face of the earth, says the Lord." Thus begins this prophecy. "I will sweep away man and beasts; I will sweep away the birds of the air. I will overthrow the wicked; I will cut off humankind from the face of the earth, says the Lord." Indeed, in the opening of this prophetic book, the mighty God declares war against this earth and all that are on it.

The *Dies irae*, it has long been called in church tradition, the day of wrath. The final day when God comes to judge the Earth. But the glad proclamation of Zephaniah is that the people of God will escape His punishment of them. For His warfare against them is ended, and He will come to them not in wrath, but in peace and in love.

I'm sure that our reaction to that may very well be, "What else is new?"

For to our minds, God will always come in peace and in love. After all, that's his business. And that has always been the proclamation of Christmas, has it not? "Peace on earth, goodwill toward men." You see, we are people who do not believe in the judgment of God. And so the cause for celebration in our scripture lesson awakens no similar joy in our hearts. God does not judge us, we think; he loves us. He helps us when we get into trouble. He bails us out when we are desperate. He forgives our sin and promises us life after death. But does he judge us? Not really. We really do not think that we have done anything evil enough to warrant the judgment of God.

When I was speaking up at Harvard a couple of years ago, I learned that there was objection in that church's congregation to a phrase in the general confession. We are all familiar with that prayer. It says, "We have erred and strayed from Thy ways like lost sheep. We have offended against Thy holy laws. We have left undone those things which we ought to have done, and we have done those things which we ought not to have done, and *there is no health in us*." A number of people on the Harvard campus wanted to eliminate that last phrase: "there is no health in us." Because, you see, they believed the same things that we believe: that we are rather decent people who do a lot of good things and who therefore have a lot of healthy goodness within us. To hear, as the people of God heard in Zephaniah's time, that God has removed his judgment from us does not square either with our notions of God or with our assessments of our own character. Why should we rejoice over the fact that God has stilled his warfare against us? As far as we are concerned, He need not and He has not declared war against us in the first place.

Perhaps we may have second thoughts, however, if we ask just what the sins were of the people of God in Zephaniah's time. What were the wrongs that God was coming to sweep from the face of the earth? The prophet is very specific about the answer. "Woe to her that is rebellious and defiled the oppressing city, Jerusalem." And I wonder: do we oppress anybody in our cities these days? "Her officials within her are roaring lions; her judges are evening wolves that leave nothing till the morning." Perhaps we can begin to see similarities to our own society.

But that is not the worst. No, says Zephaniah, the worst thing about the people of Jerusalem is that they have a distorted view of their Lord. They say in their hearts the Lord will not do good, nor will He do ill. In short, these people believe that God does nothing at all. They believe that He no longer governs the world. They no longer even attribute good actions to God, because they do not think that He acts in any way whatsoever. His influence and His effective working out of his purpose are absent from the earth, in their view.

And is that not also what we believe, good Christian friends? That God does nothing at all? Tell me, who is in charge of international relations these days? And who has the last say about the rise and fall of nations? We certainly do not think that God is in charge. No, our lives and fortunes, we believe, are in the hands of the politicians, the economists, the military, and so we hold our breath in fear that one of them will push the nuclear button.

Or who sustains the world of nature and keeps the stars in their courses? Whose faithfulness causes the seasons to change and the rain to fall upon the earth? Well, certainly to our mind it is not God. No, nature is a closed system that works by natural law, and there is no room in it for the working of God.

For that matter, who guides your children's lives, and has set for them a purpose and a destiny? Who breathed into them the breath of life, and who numbers the hairs of their heads?

Or, indeed, who fashioned you — with your unique and unrepeatable personality? And what influences make you what you are? What determines your view of yourself, and what purpose do you have in living?

We answer very few of those questions with the name of God. No, we talk about genes, and environment, and psychological influences. We talk about the images that others have of us. In many of these discussions we never mention our relationship to God. You see, we are very much like the citizens of Jerusalem in Zephaniah's time, because we have invented for ourselves a secular world — a world from which God is almost totally absent. And so we think we are the masters of our own destiny, left to muddle through life as best we can, or we join the climb to get to the top of the ladder of prosperity by stepping on someone else's fingers. We are like the man I knew at a church in Pennsylvania, who said in a discussion group, "Sure, I believe in God, but I don't think He does anything."

We have constructed a society that believes God is absent from the world. But as Dostoevsky wrote, "If there is no God, everything is permissible." There is no one to see what we do, we imagine, and there are no consequences to be paid. We have become the ultimate idolaters who have usurped the place of our creator.

It was because the people of God in Zephaniah's time held very much the same views that God said through His prophet that He would judge them and destroy them and wipe them from the face of the earth. That is very much the judgment of God that we too deserve in this Advent season. The general confession still holds, dear friends: there is no health in us. Advent comes to us first of all as the season when we need repentance.

And yet, the promise is still there. God will keep His word through His prophet. He will take away His judgments against us. But only if we celebrate this Christmas for a third reason given us by our prophet. We are jubilant over the fact that God has come into our midst as our king. Rejoice and exalt with all your heart, proclaims the prophet, the King of Israel, the Lord is in your midst! You shall not fear evil again.

Is that not finally the reason why any people or any one of us has true cause for jubilation? Because the Lord, this mighty one to save, now rules in our midst as sovereign? We are not abandoned in the world to the follies of fortune and the whims of government bureaucracies. We are not left to our own flawed and selfish devices. We do not have to rely on our own cleverness, our own wisdom, our own strength to live whole and good and righteous lives in the world. No, God offers to forgive us — to take away His judgments against us and to come to us to order and to sanctify and daily to guide our lives.

It is only the people who accept that who are celebrating in Zephaniah's picture. The others have fallen victim to their own evil and to God's very real judgment upon them — just as any one of us will fall equal victim if we try to usurp God's throne. He is King over our lives. The Lord of the universe — until we accept His rule in our midst, we can never have His abundant life. He alone has the power to triumph over sin and death; He alone is mighty enough to give us life in its fullness. Because He loves us so much, He will settle for nothing less than that.

He will settle for nothing less for us than a merry, merry Christmas party.

We can participate in that party, if in faith we will welcome the one born in Bethlehem as our Lord and King. For Jesus Christ is the incarnation of that mighty warrior to save that Zephaniah talks about. He is the one who brings forth every generation, who created you for His purpose, who rules every empire, and who commands the stars. If we will accept Him for who He is and give up our petty claims to His throne, if we will trust His guidance through His word and obey His will given us in the Scriptures, if we will seek His purpose for our living by daily prayer and Christian discipline, then we can indeed have a joyful Christmas party. And we can in truth rejoice and rejoice again, because our Lord is at hand in this Advent season. He has promised us that He will never leave us, even to the end of the age.

There is one more thing. In Zephaniah's picture of the exuberant party of the saved, it is not only the faithful who rejoice. The prophet says that God himself is in the midst of that laughing and dancing throng, celebrating with them. He literally shouts over his repentant and forgiven people, "Enjoy in exultation!" The Father, holding a homecoming party for the son who was lost and is found; the shepherd, exuberantly calling out to friends and neighbors that the sheep lost from the flock has been recovered. It is God the Father, you see, rejoicing because we have all come home for Christmas.

Wouldn't that be a Christmas party to top all Christmas parties? Joy in heaven over all of us repentant sinners? The morning stars singing again at God's redeemed creation? The saints of all the years joining in the Hallelujah Chorus? The laughter and good fellowship of the good Father's table? And *joy*, friends! Joy in our hearts — because we have been forgiven and welcomed home and given the imperishable gift of God's good, abundant life. Yes, that would be quite a festival, for God, our mighty one to save, really knows how to celebrate Christmas.

What shall we say to His invitation? Shall we join the party?

Amen.

William Muehl came to Duke Chapel while he was Steven Merrill Clement Professor of Homiletics, Yale Divinity School. Though Muehl began his life as an attorney, he became a lifelong professor of homiletics at Yale. Noted for his creative slant on the gospel, Muehl delighted in twisting the Christian faith in a bit different direction than more conventional interpreters. In this sermon Muehl tackles the historic Protestant affirmation of justification by faith. We are saved, orthodox Protestant theology has always argued, not by our good works, but by our faith in the work of Christ. Muehl offers a good word for good works.

It Matters Greatly

February 23, 1986

WILLIAM MUEHL

Genesis 15:6 and Romans 4 When I hear music of the quality of that that we have heard this morning, I find new and somewhat depressing meaning in Paul's words "the foolishness of preaching." But we do the best with what we have. Will you join me in a word of prayer:

May the words of our mouths and the meditations of our hearts be always acceptable in Thy sight, O Lord our strength and our Redeemer. Amen.

"And Abram believed the Lord and the Lord reckoned it to him as righteousness."

A few years ago, I spoke at a corporate communion breakfast sponsored by a council of churches in central Pennsylvania. The ecumenical spirit was strong in that community. And there were representatives of many denominations taking part in the occasion. As I chatted with my host, who was the chairman of the breakfast, he pointed to a middle-aged man who was obviously at the center of all the action that morning. He was carrying trays, directing other waiters, exhorting the cooks and so on.

"That's Amos Schmidt," my friend said. "He's one of the leading Lutheran laymen in this town. A real fireball in municipal affairs. He's on the Board of Education, he's a guiding spirit in our program of downtown renewal. He singlehandedly sold the city council on setting up a soup kitchen and a house of hospitality for street people. And in his spare time, he coaches a racially integrated Little League team. Now he's my idea of a *real Christian.*"

Well, for reasons which will become clear, I sought out Amos Schmidt and cornered him when the breakfast had ended, and made a point of chatting with him for a few minutes. "I'm told," I said, "that you are a splendid example of Christian responsibility in the community. That you sacrifice most of your leisure time in doing good works and that the people of the town feel beholden to you on many accounts. Why? As a staunch Lutheran, you must believe that you are saved by faith and not by works. Why bother doing so much? Is it simply to show your gratitude to God for the unearned gift of grace?" Well, Mr. Schmidt made all the disclaimers required of any reasonably modest person in such a situation. But when he saw that I meant the question to be taken seriously, he thought for a moment and then said, reflectively: "I suppose that I believe in justification by faith and not works, that's certainly what my church teaches. I guess I believe in it. But," (and here he made a great show of looking around to see whether his pastor was within earshot, and then he concluded), "but I figure, why take a chance?"

Now this conversation dramatizes, for me, one of the more serious problems of Christian faith in our time. Most of our churches teach that we are justified by faith and not by works. Paul proclaimed the doctrine so emphatically that one contemporary theologian has called it the "heart-beat of Paul's gospel." And Paul makes our text this morning the central pillar of his conviction in this matter.

"As Abram was justified by his belief in God's promises, so is every believer made an heir of grace by faith and not by works." And while many theologians insist upon defining the terms in the equation in their own special ways, very few of them fail to affirm that doctrine in one form or another. We are justified by faith and not by works. But it's been my experience that in spite of the enthusiasm of theologians for the formula, few lay men and women really understand and accept its thesis. Oh, in Bible classes and in confirmation ceremonies they will give formal assent to the idea that they are saved by their faith. In their roles as members of Christian congregations, or when the minister in his or her official capacity calls upon them in their homes, they probably nod a vague assent if the "full efficacy of faith" is mentioned.

But because of my professional interest in problems of Christian communication, I have, over the past thirty-five years, raised the question that I put to Amos Schmidt—raised that question with a great many people in contexts free from atmospheric pressure of one kind or another. And I have encountered a disturbing confusion about that central teaching of the faith. Indeed, it has become a commonplace for scholars in both religion and psychology that even people whose denominational theology puts special emphasis upon justification by faith—even such people tend to be caught up in a work ethic of one kind or another. As much so as their non-Christian neighbors. So widespread and obvious has this phenomenon proven to be that a thoughtful commentator has christened it "a central paradox of Christian life."

When this kind of confusion occurs about some significant doctrine of the faith, the tendency of theologians and ecclesiastical leaders is generally to put the blame upon the laity — to attribute its misunderstanding to simple ignorance or an infirmity of commitment. And surely, there is enough of these things to account for most of the problems of the Church in this, or in any, age. But it is, I have become persuaded, not only inaccurate but irresponsible to ignore the complexity of this particular lay ambivalence.

People like Amos Schmidt who are doctrinally pledged to justification by faith but uneasy about depending on it, unwilling to "take a chance," as he put it — such people represent the problem not only for the integrity of Christian theology but for the health of all human community. For while a straightforward rejection of the doctrine — such as one might find in Unitarians or Quakers — while such an honest denial of the doctrine can lead to lives deeply committed to responsible living, the half-and-half stance of the more orthodox can have deeply disturbing consequences for all aspects of human behavior, both religious and secular.

Let me illustrate what I mean and then comment on it a bit. About a year ago, while laid low by an attack of the flu, I passed the dragging hours watching some daytime television drama. And in one of these shows, a group of people was seen discussing a woman known to all of them, and known to be a woman of "easy virtue." One of the characters said, with considerable vehemence, "Why, she's a prostitute!" To which one of the other people present responded, with a kind of righteous indignation, "Prostitute is what she *does*, not what she *is*." And one could tell from the approving smiles and nods of the other people in the scene that this was the message that the writer of the script intended to get over that day. "Prostitute is what she *does*, not what she *is*."

Here we see, injected into the drama, the notion that one who does the works of prostitution is not necessarily a prostitute. And the people who agreed with the speaker's comment to that effect drew a heavy line between being and doing. And in the process, they distilled what I have come to regard as the critical malaise of our time. Now, this dialogue that I have quoted is simply one manifestation of a trend that began long ago. Back in the '30s, to my personal knowledge, and perhaps before that.

The drama critic George G. Nathan once complained that he was getting sick of plays in which the leading character is a philosophical bartender, a bank robber who loves canaries, or a prostitute with a heart of gold. This last was called by Nathan "the cosmic tart." Now, anyone reasonably familiar with the theater in recent times will understand the phenomenon about which the critic was speaking. Here was a play in which the protagonist is a man who spends his life selling rotgut. But every time he serves a child under the age of ten, he leans across the bar and says, "Sonny, they's better things in life than booze, ya know." Or here's the one who makes a living cracking other people's safes, but rushes into the flames of his burning hotel room, at the risk of his life, to save the life of his canary. Or the woman of the streets who sells herself over and over again in rituals of commercial sex, but over her bed she keeps a picture of Mahatma Gandhi and reads Santayana in her spare time.

Now, one can see this same process working itself out in contemporary fashion in the films. You're familiar with this theme, I'm sure. Some person or town is in trouble and when help is requested from the law-abiding, church-going, child-raising, tax-paying members of the community, they all straightway begin to make excuse, as the New Testament might put it. So-called decent people crumble in the face of whatever danger impends. And then, just as all seems lost, there emerges from the tavern or saloon some hard-drinking, womanizing, profane, and irresponsible local derelict. For one reason or another, the interest of this degenerate is piqued by the menace in the air. And while the honest citizens shrink in fear from the challenge, he or she goes out to meet it and saves the day. Sometimes this strange hero is a gun-slinging cowboy of the Clint Eastwood genre. Sometimes it is the marginally honest private eye like Mike Hammer. Often it is the dancehall hostess who moonlights in the rooms above the saloon. But each of them delivers the same message: being and doing are dramatically separable. What one *is* as a person is no dependable indicator of what one will *do* in particular circumstances — and what one *does* as an agent bears little relationship to what one *is*, in whole. Patently honest men and women usually let their side down in a crisis. Patently dishonest men and women are capable of splendid courage and selfless sacrifice in the pinch.

"But she's a prostitute," said one of the characters in the soap opera. "Prostitute is what she *does*, not what she *is*," replied another indignantly.

Now I mean to suggest here that at the root of this kind fairy tale, there lies a vulgarized version of the doctrine of justification by faith alone. You see, when Paul stated this doctrine and tied it into the line from Genesis that is our text this morning, he was working from what might be called a "unified concept of human being." He saw the flow of action in history as moving from believing to being to doing. What people *believed* determined what they *were*. What they *were* determined what they *did*. For him, the behavior of any man or woman *could* be traced back first to character and then beliefs—but the dynamic of the relationship among them moved dependably from believing to acting. So when the apostle speaks of justification by faith, he is establishing the primacy of the individual's self-understanding as a child and as one who trusts in God. He is arguing that works, which are not organically rooted in being and believing, are meaningless in the pattern of salvation. One is not saved in any significant sense by isolated virtues which commend themselves on purely pragmatic or prudential grounds.

Now, if one thinks of salvation in legalistic terms—that is, if one sees salvation as some sort of legalistic bookkeeping only, if to be justified means simply to be lifted by God from the debit side of some heavenly ledger and put down by God on the credit side of that heavenly ledger with no substantive rearrangement of the component elements of personality—if one believes *that* to be the nature of justification, then the idea that human actions are meaningless without a fundamental commitment and trust in God must surely seem unreasonable, arbitrary, even grossly unfair: Why should noble deeds, if done in sufficient quantities, be so utterly irrelevant to our salvation?

But if, on the other hand, one sees salvation as something which reflects itself in the total quality of a human life—if to be saved is to be changed so substantially that all of life is viewed and understood in a radically different fashion—then it becomes obvious, does it not, that the starting point in the process must be commitment to a divinely ordained origin and purpose for human existence. Then faith becomes something which is commended, not because it pleases the vanity of God or changes entries in the book of heaven, but because it engenders that whole-souled understanding of life which makes for the total transformation of being and doing.

Amos Schmidt, the Lutheran layman in Pennsylvania who wanted to play it safe by confessing faith and storing up good works—Amos is an excellent representation of our age. We have trouble with the doctrine of justification by faith because we cannot seem to interpret it in anything but jurisprudential theology. That is, we have been taught to see it as a kind of contractual relationship with God: If I have faith, God will reward me with salvation in the end. It's as simple as that. And so one does a successful end run around history.

I said a moment ago that this vulgarized version of justification constitutes one of the most serious problems of faith in our time. For the modern world specializes in the separation of believing, being, and doing. Many of its purposes—both good and ill, both majestic and depraved—are facilitated by the compartmentalizing of human personality. Society longs to believe that one can, for example, *act* ruthlessly as an employer and *be* a truly good neighbor. Act deceitfully as a lawyer and be a successful parent. *Act* the no-questions-asked, my-country-right-or-wrong citizen and *be* a devout Christian. Our society seeks in multitudinous ways to fragment personality, to sever acting from being and to sever both acting and being from believing.

This is why the popular culture is so replete with the achievement in fictional forms. This is why we are given regiments of winsome confidence men, lovable degenerates, and noble whores. These and their legions of clones in both fiction and real life are eloquent testimony to the conviction that human personality is divisible into discrete and convenient compartments — each with its own set of rules and its own set of goals. One plays to win in each arena. Action aims at success, corrupting neither being nor belief. Being remains a smug center of self-esteem uninhibited by belief. And belief constitutes an endless flow of redemptive energies to be called upon as needed and convenient. And all the while, the watchword of the age is that line from a television soap opera: "Prostitute is what she *does*, not what she *is*."

Now, it would be easy, and for preachers rewarding, to see this corruption of personality as something inflicted upon the race by its inherent sinfulness. It would be easy to cluck our tongues and allow as how even the most majestic creation of God can be tainted by human depravity. But that would be to confound the confusion, not elucidate the problem. At the center of this contemporary heresy is the determination to cling to our legalistic concept of what salvation means. Men and women cannot bear to see their lives defined as meaningless in the eye of God. Men and women cannot accept the notion that what they *do* is utterly without significance in the process of justification. They are demoralized by the news, so often mistaken for the Gospel, that their works are solely consequences and in no sense causal elements of their ultimate destiny. So they surrender to the fragmentation of personality and permit action to engender its own values and dynamics rather than accept salvation as a gift which demeans all of life.

Nicolai Vergieff spoke of one aspect of it well when he said, "The demonic materialism of the western world is the product of a Protestant theology which has so persuaded people that they cannot, by their lives, lay up treasure in heaven that they proceed to do the next best thing and lay up all the treasure possible here on earth." Amos Schmidt will go on professing his belief in justification by faith; all the while laying up for himself a store of "brownie points" and looking over his shoulder to see that his pastor is not within earshot when he speaks the truth about it all. He, and millions like him, will struggle to serve two or three masters rather than admit that life is without ultimate meaning. And this will go on and on and on as the unending disgrace of faith and a fount of corruption to society so long as we cling to a legalistic concept of salvation which makes it quite independent of the total transformation of human personality.

Some years ago, a group of parents stood in the lobby of a nursery school waiting to pick up their children after the last class before the Christmas recess. As the kids ran from the classrooms, each one held in his or her hands the brightly wrapped package that was the surprise, the gift on which the kids had been working for some weeks leading up to Christmas. One little boy tried to put on his coat, carry the surprise, wave to his parents all at the same time, and the inevitable happened. He slipped and fell, and the surprise broke with an obvious ceramic crash on the tile floor. For a moment he was too stunned to speak or cry, but then he sat up in inconsolable lament. Well, his father, in an effort to comfort his son, but also to try to mitigate the embarrassment of those present, went over to him and patted him on the head and said, "Now, son, it really doesn't matter. It's not important, son. It really doesn't matter." But the child's mother, somewhat wiser in such affairs, went to the child's side, knelt on the floor, took her son in her arms and said, "Oh, but it does matter. It matters a great deal." And she wept with the child.

Our God is not the careless parent, who casually pats us on the head in the middle of our struggle and conflict and pain and says, "Just remember: It doesn't matter. It's not important. You are justified by your faith. What happens to you and what you do, these things are not important at all." Our God is the parent who falls to the ground beside us, takes up our torn and bleeding spirits, and says, "Oh, but it does matter. It matters eternally."

Amen.

Thomas G. Long is one of the great contemporary teachers and theoreticians of preaching. Even more, he is a masterful biblical preacher. He is now a professor of preaching at Emory, but when he preached this sermon in Duke Chapel, he was professor of preaching at Princeton Seminary. Assigned a strange text by the lectionary, Long skillfully relates it to the students in the congregation, challenging the "assumptive world" of his listeners, moving them toward that alternative world being evoked by the imaginative power of the gospel.

Jesus' Final Exam

November 9, 1986

THOMAS G. LONG

Luke 20:27–40   This is the second time that I have had the privilege of standing in this pulpit. The first time I did, as soon as I got up here, I felt a surge of excitement go through my body. Well it doesn't get any easier, or different the second time. I want to thank Will Willimon and the Duke Chapel community for providing not only the honor of the invitation to be here, but the thrill of the moment.

The Gospel lesson which the lectionary appoints for this day comes from the 20th chapter of the Gospel of Luke, beginning to read at the 27th verse. Let us hear the Good News:

> There came to Jesus some Sadducees, those who say there is no resurrection. And they asked Him a question, saying, "Teacher, Moses wrote for us that if a man's brother dies, having a wife but no children, the man must take the wife and raise up children for his brother. Now there were seven brothers. The first took a wife and died without children. And the second, and the third took her and, likewise, all seven left no children and died. Afterward the woman also died. In the resurrection, therefore, whose wife will the woman be for all seven had her as a wife. And Jesus said to them, "The children of this age marry and are given in marriage but those who are accounted worthy to attain to that age and to the resurrection from the dead neither marry nor are given in marriage, for they cannot die, anymore. Because they are equal to angels and are children of God being children of the resurrection. But that the dead are raised, even Moses showed in the passage about the bush where he calls the Lord the God of Abraham and the God of Isaac and the God of Jacob. Now, He is not the God of the dead,

but of the living, for all live to Him." And some of the scribes answered, "Teacher, you have spoken well." For they no longer dared to ask Him any question.

Amen.

Those of you who are here this morning who are students, I am not sure that you are going to agree with me about this one, but I think I'm right. I think I'm right when I say that the most difficult part of any examination, test, or quiz is not the student's part but the teacher's part. Now I'm not referring here to the drudgery of grading examinations, I'm referring to the far more difficult part of asking just the right questions. However hard it may be for students to find the correct answers to the quiz, it is at least as difficult for those of us who teach to choose just the appropriate questions. The questions that we write on tests can be tricky when we intended for them to be straightforward. They can be vague when we wanted them to be models of clarity; they can be trivial and easy as pie when we were really trying to develop challenges for the students. I know that students are openly concerned and terrified that on an exam they're going to give dumb responses. But we teachers are secretly terrified we're going to ask dumb questions.

I heard for an example about a geology professor at another university who was writing a question for his final exam in basic geology. Now, I know that he had in mind that the students would respond to this question by naming certain minerals and geologic rock formations, because the question that he asked was, "Name three things that occur on the earth which do not occur on the moon." One of the students, knowing a silly question when she saw it, responded, "Roller skates, Bruce Springsteen, and the Republican Party."

I rest my case. The most difficult part of an examination is asking the right questions. And there is a sense in which this business about asking the right questions is true in a broader and deeper and more serious sense. Because to ask a question is to reveal, to disclose something important about ourselves. No question is morally or intellectually neutral. Because the one who asks the question discloses already in the question an agenda about the answer. Any important question—teacher to student, spouse to spouse, roommate to roommate, police to suspect, attorney to witness, friend to friend—any question already contains in the question a notion about what is important and what is not, what is true what is false, the biases, the angles of vision, the assumptions of the questioner. *In* the question is the assumptive world of the questioner.

You may remember, several years ago, a book called *Between Parent and Child*, written by a man named Haim Ginott. Ginott opens that book by telling us about a conversation that a father has with his son in their New York apartment. The son, suddenly, out of the blue, asks his father, "How many abandoned children are there in Harlem?" The father is surprised, but pleased at his son's sociological curiosity and so he gives him a dissertation—all he knows about abandoned children in Harlem. When he is finished, his son looks up at him and says, "How many abandoned children are there in New York?" The father adds a little bit more data and then the son says, "And how many abandoned children are there in the United States?" Finally, the light comes on in the father's mind and he knows the question which is really being asked. And he sits close to his son and assures him that he is loved. That he is not a child who will be abandoned.

In every question, there is contained the assumptive world of the questioner. That's true about the text that we just read in the Gospel of Luke. In this story, some religious leaders—Sadducees, as a matter of fact, who by the way, doctrinally, do not believe in the Resurrection—ask Jesus a question. As a matter of fact, this question is the third in a series of questions which are asked to Jesus, and one of the ways to view the 20th chapter of Luke is to consider it as Jesus' final rabbinical exam. Each question is more difficult than the previous one.

This question goes like this: Suppose there was a woman who married a man who had six brothers. But unfortunately, the man died before the couple were able to have any children. Now the Bible, the law of Moses, is clear about this kind of circumstance. What is supposed to happen is that one of the brothers is supposed to step forward and take the widow as *his* wife and have children so that his brother's lineage can be continued. So brother number one steps forward, but alas, he dies too. So brother number two steps forward, but he dies. And three and four and five and six—all die. Then the woman herself dies—seven weddings, eight funerals, and no children. Now here comes the question (and you can almost see their lips moistening with excitement as they begin to ask it): "In the so-called 'Age of the Resurrection,' whose wife will she be? (since she was married to all seven)?"

Now you can probably sniff out that this is a trick question, and it is. But it is also a multiple-choice question: Jesus has two choices, A or B. Choice A is to specify one of the brothers. "Why, in the Age of the Resurrection, she will be the wife of the first man that she married" or "She will be the wife of the last man that she married" or "She will be the wife of one of the brothers in-between"—it doesn't make any difference which one he chooses: this is an indefensible choice. That leaves B. And this is the one toward which the questioners are attempting to seduce Jesus. "Well," goes choice B, "I guess you've got me there. She can't be the wife of one of the brothers in the Age of the Resurrection and she can't be the wife of *all* the brothers in the Age of the Resurrection, and, reductio ad absurdum, I guess there is no resurrection.

A or B? Jesus chooses C. But C isn't on the test: that's right, he doesn't answer the question. He *challenges* it. *In* the question is the assumptive world of the questioner and the world which is being born in Jesus collides with that world. Now, what is this assumptive world in the question? Well, to begin with, the question assumes that in the Age of the Resurrection, if there is one, the woman is going to be somebody's property. Husbands in the first century had something like property rights toward their wives. "She's *owned* by seven men. Now, in the Age of the Resurrection to whom will she belong?" As one commentator put it, this might as well be a question about a cow owned by seven brothers. "And in the resurrection, whose cow will she be?" "In this age," said Jesus, "people marry and are given in marriage. But I tell you, in the age to come she will be equal with the angels. She will be a *daughter* of God."

As Rachel Walberg put it in her book *Jesus According to a Woman*, "If only this woman could have heard Jesus' response, she would have known that in the age to come, she, who had been defined by this man and that man and the other man, would be no longer defined by anybody else, but only by her status as a child of God."

A world overturns an assumption. And that assumption about the woman in the question is part of a larger assumption being made by the questioners. And that assumption is that the future of God, if there is to be a future of God, is merely the present extended infinitely into the future. "She's somebody's wife in this age, she's got to be somebody's wife in the age to come." The age to come is really just more of the same.

"Oh, no," said Jesus. A new world colliding with the old. In this world there is death, in the world to come there is life. In this world people are owned, in the world to come they're children of a Living God. Jesus' future is a radically and revolutionarily new age. And that's important, especially for religious people to remember, because it is easy to assume that God's future only contains the possibilities which we define by our questions in the present: God cannot or will not do anything new.

In the church that I go to in Princeton, New Jersey, several years ago, we established a "hunger committee." At the first meeting of our committee, we were focusing on hunger in Africa. But soon in our discussion, we realized we could not focus on Africa alone because we had hunger in our own backyard—especially in the town of Trenton, just down the road. So we asked ourselves the question, "What can *we* do about the hunger situation in Trenton?" Now, notice that in a question is the moral, assumptive world of the questioner. "What can *we* do about hunger in Trenton?" We had "A" and "B."

A? Nothing.

B? Creative, intelligent, committed, affluent people like us can do *something* about hunger in Trenton.

We chose B. We established a program to combat hunger in Trenton. And the most dramatic and challenging part of that was a once-a-month hunger offering we would take during the worship service on Sunday. While the congregation was singing a hymn, all who wished to make a hunger offering would come up to the front and put their offerings in a basket. We were astounded at the amount of money which came in: thousands upon thousands of dollars, more than we ever imagined. We funneled that money into Trenton, and then some harsh mathematics began to take their toll. As we fed the hungry in Trenton, the lines only got longer. Not only that, but we discovered that some of the money that we had earnestly funneled into Trenton was being wasted and misused, and some discouragement began to settle in. We began to wonder if, maybe instead of B, our only choice was A.

Two weeks ago, something dramatic happened. It was time for the hunger offering and a discouraged but beautiful congregation was bringing its offerings to the basket. There was a woman about the third pew back that none of us recognized—a visitor that day. She was rather shabbily dressed. But as the congregation streamed forward, she too got out of her pew and moved forward. She had no purse, she had nothing in her hand, she had no offering to put in the basket. And some of us wondered if maybe she were going to take something from the basket. But when she got to the front, she gave her gift. She paused before the basket, folded her hands, and prayed. She was a visible reminder to all of us that the answer to our question was not A or B, but C.

We're not going to solve the problem of hunger in Trenton. We do what we can as signs and wonders of the age to come. And when we have done what we can, we pray like mad for it to come.

On the other side of all of our questions—What can we do about hunger? What can we do about peace? Whose wife is she in the resurrection? Why do innocent people suffer? Why do little children die? On the other side of *all* of our questions there are not answers, but the Living God who brings in an age more gracious and wonderful and hopeful than we could ever have imagined.

Charles and Yvonne de Gaulle were the parents—this is not widely known —they were the parents of a Down's Syndrome child. They knew that her days were limited and so no matter what was going on in the affairs of state,

Charles de Gaulle would carve out some time every day for himself and Yvonne to spend some time with this child. When they would put her to bed at night in her crib, Yvonne would turn to Charles often and say, "Why is she not like the others? I have *prayed* that she could be like the others. Charles, I *wish* that she were like the others." When the little girl was still an infant, she died. There was a quiet graveside service. The priest read some Scripture, prayed some prayers, and pronounced the benediction. And when the service was over, everybody moved away from the graveside except Yvonne. She could not leave the grave. Charles went back to her and touched her on her elbow and said, "Come, Yvonne. Did you not hear the words of the priest? She is now like the others."

In this age.... but in the age to come, we are all children of the Living God. In the name of God the Creator, Sustainer, and Spirit, Amen.

Grady H. Hardin was a graduate of Duke, a Methodist, and a professor at Perkins School of Theology at Southern Methodist University. He spent the last years of his ministry back home at Duke's Divinity School. Not long before his death, he preached this sermon that begins with an observation from daily life and ends in a strong, theological affirmation of the sustaining grace of God. Hardin even ties in Girl Scout Sunday and a group of visiting Girl Scouts with the First Sunday of Lent!

God under Pressure

March 8, 1987

GRADY H. HARDIN

Matthew 4:1–11 We live with so many calendars now. There was a time in western civilization when you got to the first Sunday in Lent, the whole culture was moving with you. Now, the nearest thing we come to recognition of the beginning of Lent—certainly in the Cajun country around New Orleans—is that it is the end of Mardi Gras. Rio has finished its Carnival. Duke has started its spring break. The ACC finals will be soon. By the time the forty days of Lent have come to an end, we will be almost at the Final Four. For those of you not familiar with the Final Four or the ACC, read Revelation this afternoon, and you'll begin to catch on to it (eschatological dimensions). Last year I was a citizen of Dallas at this time, and the Final Four happened there. The Final Four and Easter were so intertwined that we did not know what to sing when the morning came!

But I'm especially glad for some of the calendars here. The music we have heard has not been the normal music of the Duke choir (which is on break), but there has been the unusually great music from these our friends from the Raleigh Consort. I also want to say a welcome to the Girl Scouts here for Girl Scout Sunday. I remember at one point in my ministry when the calendars converged, and one Sunday it was the first Sunday of Lent, Brotherhood Sunday, and the Boy Scout Sunday. I wonder what we observed. Well, we all dressed up in our Boy Scout uniforms, and observed the other emphases, too. It's delightful to be able to mix up all the variety of interests that we have.

We begin to see at the start of these forty days of Lent this close relationship to the forty days of fasting that Jesus faced after his baptism, when he went into the wilderness. The forty days are those days when we discipline ourselves afresh and anew to the meaning and reality of the Christian faith, to follow the pattern of the early church and prepare ourselves for the great baptism which Easter means to us all. It is the time in which we examine our character.

I can remember hearing from this very pulpit many, many years ago Henry Hitt Crane say, "Lent is not a time to forego, it is a time to go forth." He then led us in a stirring message about what we were to go forth to during this season. It is a time in which we call ourselves to the reality of a character which, by the grace of God, might sustain us in days such as this. And so we see the temptations of Jesus, but we also see the temptations throughout the biblical record, and we begin to see the tests of character of one kind or another.

Read in the book of Daniel about the tests of character that came to Daniel when he was tested by the king to see if he really could interpret those dreams. And he indeed did. And you recall that he did it so well that despite the fact that he was due, he was made chief of staff. They were having a mess in that leadership under Nebuchadnezzar. And so they reached as far as they could go — they reached until they found someone who had shown that kind of stamina and insight in the interpretation of dreams. Or look at the test of character of Daniel, of his faithfulness until finally he was thrown to the lions, and by some great intervention of God, he was delivered from the lions.

Or, read the story I loved to hear as a child — the story in Daniel of Shadrach, Meshach, and Abednego. I suppose the poetry, the beauty of those three words, and the song that went along with it, made it even more thrilling to think about Shadrach, Meshach, and Abednego being faithful even in a foreign land. When all others were bowing down before foreign gods, they would not bow down. And so they were thrown into the furnace, but they were not burned.

This is the kind of hero story that seems strange in this particular day and age. We know better than that. We are sophisticated; we don't listen to stories like that. But one of the things that made it possible for me to tell you these stories was the presence of the Girl Scouts here. Because when they were younger they spent almost five days a week looking at hero stories of approximately the same sort. Have any of you the type of touch with children that makes it possible in the afternoon to watch He-Man and the Masters of the Universe? Or She-Ra, the Princess of Power? Somebody told me, when I was talking about Daniel one time, that she sees that every afternoon with her children. So I began to look at He-Man and She-Ra, and I could hardly draw myself away from it! These are cosmic contests in which the forces of evil are about to win over the forces of good. But wait. This magic wand rises, and the light of it sends back the evil in such a remarkable way that every afternoon, just as evil is about to take over, finally it is defeated by this intervention from outside.

Those of us who don't watch those programs in the afternoon certainly have seen in *Star Wars* and other such cosmic events a belief in the "force." It isn't calling us to temptation; it's calling us to become good guys, so that when push comes to shove, you can grab the right sword and stand there and be victorious. The force will protect you.

What kind of mythology are we raising our children on? What kind of lies are we telling about the universe in which we live? Because you see, these are not tests of character, these are tests of good guys and bad guys — and everybody knows who the good guys are. And all of us know where the bad guys go.

We're in a remarkable state of confusion over saying to ourselves and to our children what life is really about, what the tests of character really are. When we enter the forty days of fasting and discipline and penitence of Lent, before we see the majesty and greatness and life-giving power of Easter, we must come to grips with the cosmic forces that face us in every decision, in every moment of our day.

But there's something so different in the story of the temptation of Jesus than in the stories of Daniel, or of Shadrach, Meshach, and Abednego, or of these current stories of heroes on our television. See, the thing about being faithful like Daniel is that when Daniel was faithful, the lions were impotent. But in this glorious story of character, the hero story of the faith, when Jesus was taken out into the wilderness and began to face up to the horrifying demands of how one lives in the kingdom of God, lions' mouths were not closed; furnaces were not cooled off. Jesus was crucified.

There is a very real difference between the temptations that faced Jesus and the ones that faced so many of the heroes of the Old Testament or the heroes of the present. They can just grab the right wand and hold it up and win. No, no! In the Christian story, the great wand is the cross, and on it you die. There's a real difference there.

That's why I'd like us to look at the temptation story of Jesus. When he went out into the wilderness he first saw the opportunity to turn stones into bread — can you imagine what it would mean in a hungry world to be able to create bread miraculously? This was no hungry Jesus, stomach growling — no, this was Jesus the Christ, struggling with the ultimate meaning of life in the kingdom of God. And one of the greatest forces and powers available to him was the ability to feed the multitudes that were starving.

They took him to the top of the temple and said, "Jump off of here! You are the Son of God; you are all-powerful; you can do anything you please. The way to rule the world, the way to establish the kingdom is to get the attention of the people. And you get the attention of the people by some spectacular deliverance." Even more spectacular than He-Man or She-Ra. And people will follow blindly into the kingdom of God. No, don't tempt God; don't tempt Jesus that way. It doesn't work that way.

That final temptation, when Jesus looked out on the nations of the world, the devil said, "Just bow down to me a little bit, just use some of Satan's trickery, and you will rule the earth!" What a terrifying temptation — to rule the world. To take over in God's name and for God's sake, only by nodding here and there to the forces and tricks of the devil himself.

This is the reason for the title of the sermon. This doesn't seem to me to be just the story of Jesus of Nazareth, who was born in Bethlehem, who went out after his baptism to face up to the temptations of the establishment of God's kingdom and to live in heroic deliverance as the Savior of the world. No, not that. You see, in every part of the New Testament when we talk about Jesus, we are talking about Jesus the Christ, Jesus of Nazareth, the Chosen One. And here, lo and behold, when we see Jesus struggling with these three temptations, it's not just Jesus the man. You can't separate him that way. It is God Almighty facing the terrifying demand to be the kind of God revealed in Jesus of Nazareth.

I think the Church fell into some of these traps I have alluded to. I'm not sure the Church believes this yet, because when we were writing the story of Jesus, we hedged. Read the story of the temptation of turning stones to bread and read the story of Jesus' feeding the five thousand, and see if you don't get a little inkling of the fact that the Church itself would like very much to have a God that turns stone into bread and does something spectacular to meet the needs of the world.

Or read the story of the second temptation: jump off that temple there, Jesus. It won't hurt you. It will get the people's attention. The people will love you for it — they will know that you are the all-powerful God. You see, God, we feel, is going to be a god on our terms. When you read the story of this temptation of casting off the temple, and when you also read the story of Jesus walking on water or any other wonder works that Jesus might have performed, do you get the feeling (and I may be all off, I may be irreverent; I don't mean to be heretical) that even the Church is not able to see God in God's terms as he is revealed in Jesus Christ? We want some wonder worker who can jump off the tower and draw all of us unto him!

When Jesus was out there in the wilderness facing these agonies, and we were writing about it in the New Testament, these gospels would tend to think that maybe just a little bread from a little stone—maybe just a little attention from a miracle here and there . . . No, when we read the story of these temptations, we begin to see a good bit more than just Jesus of Nazareth who has just come up from the river and walked out into forty days of fasting, penitence, and prayer. It's not just Jesus here who is going through the agonies of temptation; it is *God* under pressure. It is God asking God: what's the kingdom like? Is it going to be controlled by some magic wand held in the air? Is it going to be some trickery that delivered Daniel from the lions? Will it be something that makes it hot in that furnace but these three won't be singed?

Uh-uh.

This is God Almighty in the terrifying struggle of the pressure of how to make His kingdom available to us, His children. And lo and behold, the possibilities of establishing a world of peace, a world of justice, a world in which persons respect other persons, a world in which we are obedient to God— all it would take would be the legions that would enforce this on God's behalf. All it would take is just a nod, and say, "Satan, let me use your forces just a little bit and let me take over this sinful world." God Himself in Jesus Christ faces this temptation and this pressure and this awful use of power, and He says, "No, God is a God of love, of self-giving love, God is a God of dependable love, and God Himself reveals God through Jesus the Christ, the Son, the Incarnation, as One who was willing to walk out into the agonies of His day. Under pressure. With God, His Father."

What are the implications of this? I wish I knew. I look at as so vast a thing that we could talk for days about its implications. Maybe some of you could tell me how wrong I am. But if I am right, let me suggest just a couple things that maybe this afternoon would make a difference.

How do you live with a God like this? How do you live with a God that is not going to do something spectacular just to get everybody's attention? How do you live with a God that is not going to use trickery to take care of humans' needs? How are you going to live with a God whose Love is so great that the Love is willing to give itself and die, instead of holding back just a little bit and win? How do you live with a God like that?

I am not exactly sure, but I would suggest that as soon as we make it to the front doors and head out into this afternoon, we tell ourselves again and afresh, "God is dependable, and He is not going to pull any tricks on us. God is dependable, and He is not going to pull some spectacle that makes us all rush to His way. No, God is dependable in that He is self-giving, loving, suffering. And I can count on it. And I can walk out those doors this afternoon knowing that I can depend on God to such an extent that I know God has shown me that if I give up my vulnerabilities and just risk it, He is there. Even if I lose my life, I find it. Even if I love and it doesn't seem to work, I will have the whole godly universe on my side."

The Girl Scouts here learned to swim more recently than most of us. Do you remember when you learned to swim? The water was something in which to drown. All of us sputtered enough to know full well that if we went down into water far enough, it would kill you. And so we held onto the side and looked like (for your mother and father's benefit) we were swimming. Or we kept our feet on the bottom and said, "Look, I'm swimming." But you weren't. And you weren't kidding anyone but yourself. You were protecting yourself from drowning in the water, since water was for drowning. But then we learned in that strange, remarkable, almost miraculous moment that that in which we would sink and die is buoyant enough to hold us up and live.

I would like for us to walk out of those doors, and for the next Lenten days be ready for the glorious good news of Easter that says, "Don't hold back! Walk out in confidence that God is dependable. Risk it all! It may kill you, just like water. But it will certainly sustain you until you walk into the future knowing that below you are the everlasting arms, and out there in the risks, you live!"

Praise be to God. Amen.

Through Peter Storey, Duke Chapel established ties with the church in South Africa that enabled students at the Chapel to be active in the anti-apartheid movement. As a Methodist pastor and bishop, and as president of the South African Council of Churches, Storey worked closely with Archbishop Desmond Tutu. He was Nelson Mandela's prison chaplain on Robben Island. President Mandela relied on Storey in the formation of the Truth and Reconciliation Commission after apartheid. This sermon on Simon of Cyrene was Storey's second sermon in Duke Chapel. Part of the sermon's power is Storey's courageous embodiment of the cruciform faith that he preached. He ends the sermon with a vivid example of cross bearing in the church in South Africa.

When the Cross Lays Hold on You

September 18, 1988

PETER STOREY

Luke 23:26— "As they led him away to execution they seized upon a man called Simon, from Cyrene, on his way in from the country, put the cross on his back and made him walk behind Jesus, carrying it."

Before I preach to you this morning, I want to thank you. Last year, when I preached here, a group of Duke students committed themselves to collect old text books and send them to the Central Methodist Mission in Johannesburg. Those books are now in Soweto, in a little study-library that the church has provided for black schoolchildren. Their homes are very tiny and lack electricity, so there is no privacy, nor any light, for study. On behalf of Rev. Sizwe Mbabane, who runs that study-library, and the crowds of schoolkids who pack into it each afternoon and evening in search of learning, I say, "Thank you." In the Xhosa language there is a saying, "Don't get tired, even tomorrow." Don't get tired of sending those books, even tomorrow!

This morning I want to talk to you about what happens when *the cross lays hold on you.*

He had probably saved all his life to make this pilgrimage. It was some weeks since he had left home in the city we now call Tripoli. The journey had been long and dangerous, but now he was almost there. Surrounded by a chattering throng of pilgrims, he strode excitedly down the hill toward the city that lay like a glorious jewel below them. The whispered promise *"Next Passover in Jerusalem!"* was about to come true for him. For the young Libyan pilgrim, it would be this Passover!

Then it happened: suddenly the flow of the crowd changed, and the mood of excitement was now mixed with the smell of fear. Instead of sweeping on toward the city, they seemed to be pressed in a new direction, mixed in with a different crowd from out of the city gates, baying for blood. Close by, there were shouts of derision and hate. And then Simon—for that was his name—found himself facing a wedge of steel. Right in front of him was a phalanx of soldiers with three bowed and bloody prisoners, each staggering under the weight of a great cross.

And even as Simon tries to extricate himself to go on his way, one of the three prisoners stumbles and falls, and the full weight of the wooden cross falls on top of his body. Simon stares at him struggling—and failing—to rise. Then he feels a sharp sting across his own shoulders: it is the flat of a Roman spear blade, and anyone living in the Roman Empire knows what that means. The person so laid hold of is in Roman service until released. There is no evading this conscription.

Then comes the sharp command: "You there! Carry this cross!"

Before he knows quite what is happening, the cross of Jesus singles him out. It lays hold on him, and Simon the religious tourist, willy-nilly, *finds himself walking behind Jesus, carrying his cross.*

The cross of Jesus has a power all of its own and will confront us when we least expect or want it. Christ says, "You have not chosen me, but I have chosen you," and it is in those moments, not when we choose the cross, but *when the cross lays hold on us*, that we are hurled into the challenges that transform everything for us—forever.

When the cross lays hold on us, *it moves us from religion to faith*. There's a crucial difference between religion and faith. Everybody's got some religion. We pick it up from our parents, like having blue eyes or black hair. We absorb it from the culture, like the Fourth of July and Thanksgiving. We begin to learn that "life goes better," not only with Coke, but with a little religion as well.

Simon certainly had religion, but religion is not enough; religion alone can be deeply destructive and dangerous. It's religious people who murder each other in Ireland. It's religion, among other things, that is tearing Lebanon apart. It's religious people who invented the obscenity of apartheid in my land, South Africa. Religious people were part of the process that crucified Jesus. Religion often becomes nothing more than a label to distinguish ourselves from others and to deepen the divides between people in this world. Religion often becomes a mask behind which we can live out our prejudices and blame them on God. You can keep religion. I don't want it!

On that day, Simon from Cyrene, looking forward to a religious festival, was challenged to move beyond religion, into faith. Faith is coming face to face with the one who God sent into the world. Faith calls you out of the crowd:

. . . out of the safety of non-involvement into risk;

. . . out of hereditary belief into relationship with the suffering Jesus;

. . . out of the crowd into a confrontation with the cross, and the person carrying it.

That is the powerful pressure of the cross, when it lays hold on you. There are those who call it an offense and there are those who call it foolishness, but when it lays hold on you, your life changes forever.

Back in 1960, in South Africa, that's what happened for a young white Afrikaner minister of the Dutch Reformed Church — the church that gives theological justification to apartheid. His name was Beyers Naude and he was already marked for the heights of religious, and perhaps political, leadership amongst the white racist élite of South Africa. Then he attended his first ecumenical church conference, where the racial policies of the state were under challenge by the Gospel. For the first time he was exposed to the thinking of white Christians opposing apartheid, and the suffering and the courage of black South Africans. For the young Beyers Naude it was a confrontation with the cross, the day he had to decide whether he was going to follow the road of dead religion, or commit himself in faith to the Jesus who came to care for the poor and bring justice to the world. He knew then that he could no longer live with the civil religion that had shaped him and that he needed to walk in a new direction. After preaching a powerful farewell sermon to his congregation, he descended from the pulpit, removed his black *toga* — the symbol of a Dutch Reformed pastor's authority, and quietly left the sanctuary. At the door, most of his congregation walked past him in silence. These white Afrikaners wanted a religion that would not disturb them, but Beyers Naude had chosen faith. That day began a forty-year sojourn in the wilderness of resistance to apartheid, one that would bring upon him all sorts of harassment and persecution. He found himself walking behind Jesus, carrying his cross. His lonely witness continues.

So when the cross lays hold on you, be careful, because it may move you from religion to faith. I pray it does.

When the cross lays hold on you, *you bear some of God's burden for the world*.

In Holy Week, at the Central Methodist Mission in Johannesburg, we erect a great cross in the foyer of the church, which opens out onto a pedestrian mall. The milling crowds move past while this cross stands there, mute witness to the meaning of the death of Christ. On Holy Thursday evening, we share the Service of the Tenebrae around the foot of that cross, and then we have to carry it upstairs to the main sanctuary for the great Good Friday service. I did it once because nobody else seemed to be around to help. It was much heavier than I had imagined, and believe me, there is no comfortable way to carry a cross! Now I do it every year. I deliberately stay behind because it's important to me to feel something of the weight of a real cross before I preach on Good Friday.

Some years back, a Cape Town schoolboy read the story of Simon of Cyrene carrying Jesus' cross, and wrote these words:

> Step up, Simon, for today you meet your maker:
> the Nazarene woodman whose load is yours to bear.
> The blood, the burning tears
> fall to the steeply cobbled walk trod by the heel of God.
> Lift upon your powered shoulder the hated tree of death,
> for he bears today the wrongs of man.
> Why are you here, Simon?
> To mock the perfect born, or to give strength
> to one who hangs against the tree?
> Step up, Simon,
> For this tree is yours to bear.

There is a weight to the cross because God so loved the world — because Jesus was carrying it for the whole world. Simon of Cyrene suddenly found that he was called to share that weight, and so are we. We have to decide whether we will stand back from the burden God carries for God's world, or whether we too will give strength to the one who hangs against the tree. Is it irreverent to suggest that God may need our strength? Of course not. From the beginning of his ministry Jesus made this clear by inviting a circle of followers to share his task.

Perhaps the deepest privilege in the world is that of being able to say to Jesus, "Lord, let me carry just a little corner of your cross. You carry it for so many: You carry it for the poor and for the homeless; you carry it for those who are oppressed and tortured; you carry it for the outcast; you carry it for the sinful and the lost. Lord, let me carry just a little corner of your cross."

The fact is that when you encounter the cross of Jesus, you also encounter all those for whom Jesus carried that cross. There's a sense in which he nails you to them. He nails you to your neighbor, and that can be a costly experience.

In my land there is a community that has perhaps done more than any other to try and care for those who are being broken and beaten and wounded by apartheid. I speak of the South African Council of Churches (SACC). Time and again, when there has been a need—for legal defense, or to visit somebody in detention without trial, or to speak out or march against injustice, that council has been out there on the cutting edge.

Just two weeks ago, a car bomb exploded in the basement of the headquarters of the SACC, Khotso House (*khotso* means peace). It was the most powerful explosion to take place in all the violence of our land—stark evidence of the price paid by those who witness against the injustice of the regime and stand for the truth. Yet just a couple of days later I was together with a group of Christians where an eighteen year-old white lad stood up and said, "I have read my Bible, I am a Christian, I follow Jesus, and therefore I will not serve in the apartheid regime's military. I will not go and shoot my brothers and sisters." That eighteen year-old knows that six years of imprisonment await him; he could be in his mid-twenties when he comes out of prison, but I have hope when an eighteen-year-old white youth in South Africa says, "Jesus, can I carry just a little corner of your cross for those you care about? Help me Jesus, when I have to pay the price."

When the cross lays hold on you, *you find it is a healing burden.* When Simon was told to carry the cross of Jesus, he must have been afraid and perhaps resentful as well. Everything he had planned had gone horribly wrong. Yet it must have dawned upon him at some point that by engaging with Jesus in his suffering he was being given the opportunity to become a different person—a whole person. Simon was being drawn into the center of all of life's meaning, which is self-giving.

It's a mystery as to how the cross heals people, but it does.

At the World Methodist Council Assembly in Nairobi in 1986, there was a great procession of the delegations from all over the world. It was appropriately dignified, except for one element of chaos, right at the back. There, dancing and singing along, were the South African Methodists, white and black, including exiles who had not seen their homeland for twenty years, and an archbishop named Desmond Tutu, who had been baptized a Methodist before joining the Anglican church. We kept this up for a couple of miles through Nairobi, and someone came up to us afterward and asked, "How can this be? After all we've heard and all we know of the agony and discord and violence and hate of South Africa—how can you celebrate together like that? How can such joy emerge from such pain?"

But it does. People who have encountered the cross, people who have carried a small part of it, know something that is the source of incredible joy: that evil is only the second-most powerful force in the universe. Do you know that? That is what the cross tells us — that there's something bigger and wider and deeper than evil, and that is the power of suffering love. Do you believe that? Let me tell you why I do:

That day when Khotso House was blown up in Johannesburg, it was very important not to allow this destructive act to defeat us. We made the Central Methodist Mission, just a couple of blocks away, a temporary headquarters for the SACC, and that very morning, just hours after the blast, we gathered the exiled community of about one hundred people into the chapel there, for staff prayers. Of course there were tears of anger and fear and pain and loss, but as we recited the 23rd Psalm about the Lord who is our shepherd, about wanting for nothing, about having or souls restored, about gathering together at a table in the presence of our enemies, about walking through death and fearing no evil, it became overwhelmingly evident that evil was indeed *only the second-strongest force in the universe.*

What was true for that community of South African Christians is also true for you. Whatever it is in your life that may seem to have such a hold on you that it threatens to break you and force you down, you need to know that in the cross there is wholeness and newness and freedom for you. The cross will break through!

That bomb ripped a lot of the frontage off Khotso House, and as it did so, in all the dust and debris, the great banner that hung in the foyer was exposed for all to see: it portrays Jesus holding out his arms, offering his gift of peace to all the world. As the wrecked building was surrounded by heavily armed security policemen, their message was clear: "Do it my way or I'll beat you up, do it my way or I'll blow you up." But behind them, now exposed for all you see, was another message, the way of the cross.

The cross speaks a word to the world, to each one of us, which can be said in no other way. It is a word that makes us whole again. Look at the cross on this altar as we worship and let the cross lay hold on you. God wants to move you from religion — which is not a good place to be — to faith, which is where it can really happen; and God really longs for you to carry just a little corner of God's burden for the world; and God wants you to discover in that faith and in that burden, the healing, the making whole of who you are.

After the magnificent Chapel Choir finished singing, Fred Craddock rose to speak, acknowledging the difficulty of preaching after so great a shout of praise. But Craddock did not need to be so self-effacing. He is one of the great preachers, and great teachers of preachers, of the twentieth century. Craddock pioneered what he called "inductive preaching," preaching in which a preacher slips up on a congregation, from the side, or from behind, making the gospel grab them when their defenses are down. This was the sort of sermon that Craddock preached on this visit to the pulpit of Duke Chapel.

November 5, 1989

FRED CRADDOCK

Luke 19 How can you go to serious preaching after that kind of response? I've got to tell you. I've got a pretty good choir. And I appreciate hearing you all. But if the rest of you are not occupied, I've got a gig up north that you can do on a Sunday morning. We've got a big wide chancel and it sounds very good. I expect you get tired of hearing what a spectacular group you are. The setting provides something very special with it. But for those of you who have ever lived as Methodists or Protestants in New England, you know that I haven't seen this many Methodists in one place for the last twelve years. And although there may be a few of other flavors, we're happy to welcome all of you. I'm just honored beyond belief to be here and I think Will believed that with a service as vital as this, no one could do it any damage. So I wasn't any great risk.

Thou Lord, open Thou our lips and our mouths will surely show forth Thy praise. Amen.

Zacchaeus is not a common name. Very unusual to most of us. Indeed it seems strange. But then Zacchaeus was a strange person. Most of you may not have heard the name Zacchaeus, unless you played Sunday School games and wanted to put it at the end of the game with "Zaccariah" and "Zepheniah," and all those other late "Z's." Zacchaeus was a strange kind of person and particularly strange for Jesus to spend very much time with. Luke, fourteen chapters earlier, had told of our Lord meeting with another tax collector, a man named Levi, who did very outrageous kinds of things and now he is talking about Zacchaeus doing strange . . . And yet most of you won't remember very much about Levi. I hope you will remember a lot about Zacchaeus.

He was remembered because he was successful. He was the chief tax collector. Now if you followed the lectionary, last week had a "publican," that's the Roman word for a tax collector, who had a very short prayer, "Lord be merciful to me—a sinner and a Pharisee." I was getting ready for that sermon, and my rabbi friend said, "I don't know why you make fun of the Pharisees all the time. They're our heroes." So I said, "Well, let's change the name." I said, "Let's not use Pharisee." I decided to rename him. I was going to rename him, "pious one." And then I thought, I've got some Roman Catholic friends who may take serious offense. So the Pharisees are the ones who are always the very pious, the very religious, the model of self-righteousness. But let's not call them Pharisees, lest we be anti-Semitic about this.

But Zacchaeus was a tax collector and he was like the chief tax collector. I remember some years ago, *Fortune* had an article on the richest crooks in the country. And Zacchaeus was rich and he was crooked. He was very rich, but that was a bit of an accident of geography because he was in Jericho where the two roads, main roads, came together. And the Roman system of taxing was not much different than ours. You know how they worked the system. Tax collectors got as much as they needed for the government and everything they got beyond that, Rome didn't ask too many questions about. This was the origin of the phrase "What the traffic will bear." And he got lots and lots from the traffic on that particular road.

But he was also short. Now I try not to make any reference to that because I'm sort of monster-size. But Zacchaeus couldn't see in parades. When you're 6′ 5″ it makes it great for parades, but Zacchaeus had trouble and so he considered it some sort of disability. Finally he was ingenious. He decided to climb up a tree to see the master. And that leaves us to speculate as to why he would ever have wanted to do anything like that? That's one part of the story that is not altogether self-evident. This is my theory. People saw Zacchaeus with the evidences of wealth and power and position. Things that most of us would like to have. But they never saw the empty places, the dark nights, the question marks, the moral voids that he alone knew. He must have heard something about Jesus—the power of his love, the cleansing of his perfect goodness, the great strength that went with his personality. He would have been too ashamed to ask anyone, "Who is this Jesus?" After all, think of my position, he would have said to himself. But he climbed out of his Jaguar and up the tree he went. What did he expect? It doesn't say, but not much different than folks who come to church now. They just come, maybe some of you, not knowing exactly what to expect.

This is clear. Folk seek Christ. And those who seek Christ, Christ seeks.

Christ helps are those who are conscious of their needs—their spiritual needs, their personal needs, their moral needs. Christ's ability to work with them, even with those who seem successful by outside standards, is the important point that this lesson makes.

Now think of the words. Bible words are so, sort of, biblical. They use things like sinner or unrighteous or sick or lost. Who wants to be in a club for losers? Who will queue up to be one of the lost or one of the unrighteous? Oh, it's all right if I make mistakes, but mistakes are all right now and again, but not being "lost in sin." I get lost when I drive to Cambridge. That's the reason I can't go to Harvard very often. We have a thing about Harvard in our part of the world. You just don't ever get there. But I can admit that I make a mistake in driving, never "lost in sin." Or I can admit a mistake because I'm old enough to not feel overly self-conscious about it. But lots of folks can't. Admitting that you made a mistake makes you too vulnerable. Oh, you can dodge by saying, "That's not my field. I haven't much chance to study politics or human rights or human relations or things like that." But we need an excuse. Nearly anyone that is handy will do. And what's that in our society? Most of our people respect only strength, success, and wealth. Is that true? There are very few in the Rodney Dangerfield Club, "I don't get no respect."

It seems like a very modern problem, but it must have been about the same in our Lord's time. We show religious and moral and personal superiority, but scarcely ever want to admit our weakness. Even the church is guilty of that sometimes. A bunch of years ago, Carl Menninger wrote a book entitled *Whatever Happened to Sin?* And he was scolding preachers for trying to act like junior-level shrinks, trying to pretend as though we don't use words like "sin" anymore. And told us to come clean and talk about who we really are and talk about what we really do.

Oh, there's a big exception. The fastest-growing groups that come to my chapel are the six AA groups, Alcoholics Anonymous. And they've got students and faculty and staff and everybody in it. And to get into that you have to have an affirmation of faith. It starts very simply. Step one: we admitted we were powerless. Our lives had become unmanageable. I wonder how many would have signed that one as they came in today? I admitted my life was lost, powerless, unmanageable. I came to believe in a greater power. I decided to turn my life and will over to God, as I knew God. I made a searching moral inventory. I think the reason they can be effective is they start not with denying what's wrong; they start by confessing honestly and easily.

The Christian faith, at its best, should give you the strength—the strength of Igor, the strength of personality to take the first step in seeing the needs in human life, in my life. Jesus comes with beauty and power and love that we need — not some judgmental condemning attitude that is more typical of some of us when we are parents or sometimes of the church. Or for some it may take to coming to the lowest point of life, coming to that point where you see only degradation and fear. But some think it's not necessary to get into the pits before you can take the searching moral inventory. The folks Christ sees are those who know themselves to be lost, as Scripture says, "sick, sin, unrighteous."

Christ stops the whole procession, looks up, and calls to Zacchaeus by name. He says to him, "Hurry. Come down. I'm having dinner and staying with you tonight." One would have thought Zacchaeus would have been fearfully embarrassed, caught up there with his pride and dignity hanging out, all the people watching. But no such thing. He shinnied down the tree in a hurry and joyfully received the master — no reserve, no reservation in that response. Think of the contradiction — the rich tax collector with every-thing to show and the humble master with nothing, and the tax collector shinnying down the tree to entertain at dinner. You get sort of a picture of the Pope greeting the mafia. And see what that does to your images. It's so outrageous, so outrageous.

The other people's responses were all very predictable. They hadn't seen transformation take place enough to recognize what it would look like. "The religious leaders all murmured." That's a great phrase in Scripture. When the scholars go to study, no one ever studies the word "murmur," but you all know what it means, "brr, rur, rur, rur." They were all saying, "He doesn't know what he's doing. Have you heard it?" It's sort of that low-lying hum that people do. "Look at that, he doesn't know what he's doing. He's eat-ing with a sinner." We have stereotypes in religious life that just won't quit. "Things just aren't done that way," we say. And for the master to find fun, food, and fellowship with this social disaster is quite unbelievable.

Jesus' disciples were probably just as surprised, but they kept quiet. Jesus did that kind of thing all the time. And yet his disciples, even now, are not quite prepared for that kind of outrageous behavior. Christ announces the beginning of the change. "Today, salvation has come to this house." The basic metaphor is in the last line of the text, "The lost has been found." The first step into a Christian life of faith and trust in Christ is to come from the darkness into the light, to acknowledge that I was lost and now am found. It may be as simple as turning around to greet one whom you have been alienated from. Christ seeks those who recognize that they have some con-dition or situation that needs Christ's help to say, "I am morally sick. I am personally unrighteous. Religiously, I'm alienated. I'm a sinner separated from God." You can put them in different contexts. The spirit is the same. The first step in faith is to acknowledge need and look for Christ.

But then one outrageous action, Jesus calling him, eating and sleeping with him, calls forth an equally outrageous response. Note, the response is not to earn Jesus' love. It's not to earn salvation. That's already the gift that has been given. Zacchaeus says, "Half my goods, I give to the poor. And if I have defrauded anyone, I give them four times what I have taken from them." Now in your service, just after the preaching, you're going to have responses and offerings. Think what it would be like if someone were really so moved by their own need and the power of Christ's love that they would respond the way he did.

Oh, there are some scholars that say that that was really added later. They do that to all my favorite texts. But it fits the experiences that I know. When everything that is wonderful happens, there is no limit to the outrageous responses that I will make to them. It is never enough only to recognize my need. Some of us love to grovel in our confession and never go on from there to do anything other than that. But the point is that knowing Christ is a radically transforming event. It is not just an emotional high, "I got saved," and then back to life as it was before. Those who seek, whom Christ seeks, and who respond are in a whole new life. It's never enough only to recognize the need. That is clearly the first and indispensable step, but when faith finds you — better be ready for changes, which are as great as any really new love can produce.

If I had to draw on the best personal analogy between saving faith and another human experience, I think I'd always choose falling in love. For it's the kind of thing you can recognize, when it's genuine. That's an experience that changes the way you talk, the way you meet other people. Friends can tell when love is genuine and love is real. They can also tell when it's faked. And it can strike you any time, whether you are ready to receive it or not.

Zacchaeus wasn't mentioned enough for the Church to know or to make a saint of him. But I have a feeling that for our time, Zacchaeus might serve as the patron saint of yuppies or those essentially going-to-be-rich people. I don't know how your student body is: we have some pre-law, and some pre-med, and some pre-dental, and some pre-business. Most of them behave as though, essentially, they were simply pre-rich. They were simply preparing and for them, Zacchaeus ought to be the model. He was rich. He was mildly irreligious. He was ingenious and he was enterprising. What else could you ask? And all of the passions that made him a successful tax-collecting entrepreneur helped also in his response to the Christ—once he found Christ or was found up that tree.

The saints of God are depicted beautifully in these windows and I love them and look graciously at them. But those aren't the kind of saints that are going to transform me very much. They could never inspire me to be the kind of a person that would be totally different. And that's what we celebrate in saints, not those who have been made into stiff, solid stained glass, but those who have decided to change so that they give me the impression that even I could be that way too. Some of God's most peculiar saints are much more like this sawed-off social misfit, who recognized his moral and spiritual and personal weakness enough to climb a tree to get a look at Jesus. And from that one attempt we have a story of one whom Christ sought, and that may be very important for you.

Zacchaeus is not a common name. Indeed it is a very strange name, for Zacchaeus was a strange person. But he may be one who can remind you that in Christian faith we start by recognizing our need, by doing something in that recognition, and then finding that the love and the power of Christ has transformed that life in genuine and real ways. Amen.

There are times when Duke Chapel must become a college chapel and minister to the campus in a time of crisis. This sermon was preached by Richard Lischer on the second-to-last Sunday of the church year, November 15, 1992. Earlier that week a Duke undergraduate student, a beloved member of the Chapel Choir, had been killed in a freak bus accident on campus. That Sunday a troupe of liturgical dancers and percussionists performed solemnly and triumphantly in Duke Chapel. Lischer, who eventually came to occupy the Cleland Chair of Preaching at the Divinity School, preached a pastoral sermon, using the appointed texts for that Sunday.

I Have Seen the Future

November 15, 1992

RICHARD LISCHER

Malachi 4:1–5 and Revelation 1:7ff, 21:3–4, 23 These are the words of the prophet Malachi, the final verses of the Old Testament: "For behold, the day comes, burning like an oven, when all the arrogant and all evildoers will be stubble; the day that comes shall burn them up, says the Lord of hosts, so that it will leave them neither root nor branch. But for you who fear my name the sun of righteousness shall rise, with healing in its wings. . . . Behold I will send you Elijah the prophet before the great and terrible day of the Lord comes" (Malachi 4:1–5).

And these are the words of John, the apocalyptic seer:

> Behold, he is coming with the clouds, and every eye will see him, every one who pierced him; and all tribes of the earth will wail on account of him. Even so. Amen. . . . I John, your brother, who share with you in Jesus the tribulation . . . will show you things which must be hereafter.
>
> And I heard a great voice from the throne saying, 'Behold, the dwelling of God is with people. God will dwell with them. . . . God will wipe away every tear from their eyes, and death shall be no more, neither shall there be mourning nor crying nor pain any more, for the former things have passed away.' . . . And the city has no need of sun or moon to shine upon it, for the glory of God is its light, and its lamp is the Lamb (Revelation 1:7ff, 21:3–4, 23).

Each in his own way, the prophet and the seer, speaks words that we desperately need to take into our hearts. Each says, "I have seen the future, and it belongs to God."

With Advent exactly two weeks away, the whole Christian church on earth imperceptibly begins to lean forward and to yearn for the coming of God. Our lessons reflect that. The lessons read today are not specially chosen for Duke Chapel but represent the whole church's rhythm of faith. For many here today, that yearning for God and a greater revelation is focused by the death of Amy Elizabeth Geissinger, a member of this choir and a sister in the body of Jesus Christ. It is good that we have these lessons, so the whole church can minister to us. It is good that we have dancers and drums today, because much of what we feel cannot be spoken but only danced and furiously drummed. What words we sing will stick in our throats. What words we speak will be nothing more than a groan of faith in the God who is Alpha and Omega, the beginning *and* the end.

God will come. So say the prophet and the Seer. Not as a baby anymore, but God will come in quite a different way to set all things right. In the meantime, we dance and drum, sing and weep, not only because a precious eighteen-year-old has died, but because after the dying and the crying, comes *God.*

Most people imagine that God occupies more of the past than the future. God seems to fit right in in museums with temple friezes, ancient manuscripts, the Old Masters. That is God's element. When we think of God, our minds drift back to childhood, when those Bible stories and Sunday School lessons created a world in which we had a place. "O God of my youth," the poet prayed. When you think about your time in this university, isn't it more comfortable for you to remember the familiar people and events that brought you *to* this place than it is to contemplate the riddle of what awaits you as you leave? The past has a face. The future — and today we must say, Death — is without form or face.

But precisely *here* where life is hardest and most inscrutable Christianity speaks a word into the void. It proclaims a future that has contours and form, and even a face. The God of the Bible, who in the New Testament is known as the Father of Jesus Christ, turns out to be a God of the future. The past, for all its vastness, isn't nearly big enough a place for all that God promises to be for Amy and for all who have preceded us in death. Only God is capable of caring for the past *and* the future.

When I was a grade schooler, a boy in my class drowned. I remember very little about it except that it had a profound effect on me. I couldn't eat or sleep properly or concentrate in school. A few days ago, doubtless prompted by

Amy's tragic death, my mind went back to that event, and I was shocked to realize that for the life of me I could not remember the boy's name. That's the fear, isn't it? When you, her classmates, are old and gray, who will remember Amy Elizabeth's name and cherish her as a person? Who will remember those who are appointed to remember such things? And when we are all gone, who will remember us?

When it comes to remembering, we are not particularly accomplished, but God is. The human generations seem not to be built for remembering. But God—God gathers the jagged fragments of life, the tragedies and losses, writes down all the names, and none is forgotten, not one. When the Israelites were in exile they feared, understandably, that they would be assimilated into the nations and lost to history and the memory of God. God said to Israel through the prophet Isaiah, "Can a mother forget her nursing child? Even these may forget, but I will not forget you. Behold, I have graven your name in the palms of my hands."

Malachi and the Seer paint two very different scenarios for the future but each with the same lead actor, God. Malachi, the unknown prophet, was ministering to a depressed people now returned from exile. Israel as a nation-state was gone; the temple was nothing. Because they had no future, they were hurting, and hurting one another. The book of Malachi reveals something about the nature of God we either did not know or had repressed. The Old Testament does not end with a beatific vision but with a burst of rage. "For behold the day of the Lord comes burning like an oven, when all the arrogant and all evil doers will be stubble; the day that comes shall burn them up, says the Lord of hosts." As it turns out, the God of the future is not the shadowy, benign presence we had imagined but a God who takes sides and says, "I am fed up with suffering and hunger, two-bit tyrants, and evil doers. I will have my day." In the prophet's own words, this is a God who is capable of uttering the sentence, "I hate. . . ."

William Sloane Coffin is fond of saying, "If you love the good but do not hate evil, you are doomed to sentimentality." But a *God* who hates? When our son was a very little person, one of our family projects was to train him not to say "hate." We had nice little talks about it: "That is an emotion and those are words that are not worthy of you," we said (and by the way, that is an argument that doesn't work particularly well with a four-year-old). "You didn't learn to say 'hate' in Sunday School," we said, "not from Jesus." We never let him read Malachi—"Jacob have I loved; Esau have I hated." Or Amos—"I hate, I despise your feasts." Or Isaiah—"I hate robbery and wrong." Or even the Psalmist—"The Lord loves those who hate evil." We are tempted to say to God, "This is an emotion and these are words that are unworthy of you."

But the prophet insists there are some things that are worthy of God's rage, and ours. If you can visit the concentration camp in Dachau and enter by the same gate through which so many prisoners passed, and if you can run your hand over the terrible lie that is carved in the wrought iron — *Arbeit Macht Frei*, work will make you free — and not feel rage, then listen again to Malachi's God.

If you can open the newspaper and see the aged faces on the bodies of children in Somalia without feeling rage — not only at the governments of the world, who can deliver bombs efficiently but not food — but rage at the sheer senselessness of the suffering of innocents, then listen again to the prophet's God. When an unsuspecting young woman is lost on her way to class for no reason at all, you can almost hear Malachi's God say, "I *hate* that my dear child has died."

The Gospel of Mark tells us that one day Jesus was confronted by a man covered with sores and putrid flesh who cried out, "Jesus, make me clean." What scholars take as the original wording of Jesus' reply is very mysterious. The manuscripts read, "And Jesus, moved with *rage*, touched him." No one knows the meaning of that reaction, but might we understand it as God's own anger at the insult to a good creation?

And what of John the Seer's scenario? From the Apocalypse we learn something more about God. The God of the Apocalypse heals our wounds, dries our tears, and promises to minister to us forever. "I have seen the future," says John, "and death, suffering, and weeping will have no part in it." The God of Malachi cuts through evil like a blowtorch; Malachi's God rages with us in our grief. We turn to Revelation, and the anger seems to dissipate. There we see the saints gathered around the throne, and among them high and lifted up receiving the praises of all who have died in the Lord is not the angry warrior we might have expected, but the Lamb. The Lamb is in the midst of them. What does it mean to us in this terrible moment, that at the apex of reality sits not a symbol of death or retribution — not the Grim Reaper or the Terminator — but something altogether beyond our imagining?

A great philosopher once posed three essential questions: Who made the world? What ought I do? What may I hope? Today, the third question is on our minds. Both Malachi and John the Seer offer us hope in God. The same God who thundered over Palestine in Malachi's day is the One who watched his son go to the cross in solidarity with all who suffer and must die. He is the lamb who was slain. What may we hope? We may hope in the God who raised Jesus from death.

Jesus was like the exiles, lost and without a future. Like our sister in Christ, gone before her time. Jesus was like us on our own worst days of sorrow and despair. God made him alive so that that we might live in hope. The gospel is a terrible problem solver. The resurrection of Jesus, which lies at the core of the gospel, is a promise. It is a God-given signal that the slaughtered, the starving, our sister, and all the people who seem to be slipping away from us are not meant to be discarded or forgotten, and will not be. It is a sign that they — and we — are meant to be more, not less than we are, that even death, as authoritative and final as it seems, is not the last word.

The resurrection is a pillar of fire ahead of the whole human race. It is testimony: not only to the depth of human hoping but to the reality of God in Jesus Christ. If you want to know where God stands on the issues of suffering and death, if you want to know what God thinks when he sees you walking away from a cemetery, if you want to know what God *feels* when he sees your tears — then go to the cross and the tomb of God's son, and listen for testimony.

"I have seen the future," says Jesus, "and it is as cold and hard as a tomb. And it is as glorious as the saints in heaven."

Anyone can say it, dear brothers and sisters. You don't have to be a prophet or a preacher but only a man or woman, a little boy or girl, of faith: "I have seen the future. And its name is Jesus."

The evangelical social activist Tony Campolo has been—at least for the past three decades—the most popular evangelical preacher on the college circuit. He was not only a professor of sociology at Eastern College, St. Davids, Pennsylvania, but also the founder of an innovative inner-city ministry and the author of nearly thirty books. Students hear in his raucous, loud, exuberant voice an exciting call to the adventure of Christian discipleship. On his third visit in the Duke Chapel pulpit, Tony preached a sermon on Jesus' demand that each educated, powerful, resourceful intellectual become as "a little child" in order to be part of his kingdom.

Children of the Kingdom

February 13, 1994

TONY CAMPOLO

Mark 10:13–16

Prayer: May the words of my mouth and the meditations of our hearts be acceptable in Thy sight, O Lord, our strength and our redeemer. Amen.

Jesus told his disciples that unless they became like little children, they would not be able to enter into the kingdom of God. Obviously, he did not mean for them to be childish. We have enough childish behavior in the world and certainly a great deal of childish behavior within the church. What Jesus was telling us was that we had to assume certain childlike qualities, certain childlike traits if we were going to be part of his kingdom, part of his people.

Children—I guess I get turned on by children more than most people; I like them. I like their forthright honesty, their spontaneity. A friend of mine, who is a preacher, Chuck Swindoll, has a children's sermon every Sunday at his church. Now they don't do that at Duke Chapel. You know, where they get all the little kiddies down front and the pastor comes and sits, and kind of talks kiddy talk to them. You know what I'm talking about, don't you, with children's talks? Kind of make you puke. He had all the kids down there one day, and all the kids were surrounding him, and he said, "Boys and girls, what's this big, has a long furry tail, and climbs trees?" There was dead silence. Finally, one kid said, "I know I'm supposed to say Jesus, but it sounds like a squirrel."

The spontaneity of kids. I have a friend who teaches in the upper peninsula of Michigan. He has one of those schools that run from kindergarten all the way up through eighth grade, including special ed. One of his students was intellectually slow, couldn't do very well in classes. And when Christmas Pageant time came he wanted to have a part in the Pageant. What's more, he wanted a speaking part. He wouldn't settle for anything less. So they made him into the innkeeper. They figured he could handle that because all he had to do was say, "No room," twice: once before Mary spoke, once after she spoke. The night of the Pageant, Mary knocks on the door and he opens the door, and he says in brusque fashion, "No room!" Mary says, "But I'm sick, and I'm cold, and I'm going to have a baby, and if you don't give me a place to sleep, my baby will be born in the cold, cold night." He just stood there. The boy behind him nudged him and said, "No room, No room, say 'No room.'" And finally, he turned and he said, "I know what I'm supposed to say, but she can have my room."

Kids, who can help but like kids? I think that the thing that Jesus liked about kids, which I like about kids, is that they are aware of their own importance, their own value, their own significance. Kids are absolutely glorious. We run an inner-city school, we run a school for kids who come from disadvantaged backgrounds, basically from low-cost housing developments. And these are kids who really shouldn't have a high view of themselves, but they do. And I know that one of the teachers in the third grade was asking the boys and girls, "Can you name something fantastically wonderful that didn't exist fifty years ago?" And one kid said, "Me!" Better still is a friend of mine who has a little girl, named Jennifer. Thunder and lightning hit, one of these horrendous storms. And as the lightning was flashing and the thunder was roaring, he ran upstairs to see if she was frightened. She was standing on the windowsill, leaning against the glass, spread-eagle. The lightning was flashing, the thunder was roaring. He said, "Jennifer, what are you doing?" And she said, "I think God is trying to take my picture." Well, there's a kid who has a pretty good concept of who she is. She knows that she is valuable; she knows that she is precious.

I don't know where we lose it. I don't know where it gets beaten out of us, but somewhere along the line we do lose it, don't we? We do have it beaten out of us, don't we? The Bible says that what happens is that we sin, and what we do not only alienates us from God but alienates us from ourselves. And in the end we despise ourselves because of what we have done and what we have been, and what we have brought about in the way of pain in the lives of others. In the end we find ourselves down on ourselves.

Everywhere I go I meet depressed people. Depression is the malady of our time. And behind depression lies self-contempt. People are down on themselves; they don't like themselves; they despise themselves. Oh, they may put on a good front, but down deep inside they know who they are, and what they've done and what they have been and how they've hurt people. And they hope that nobody finds out about them. They have lost their sense of being precious before God.

I know that's happened to me. I went to Eastern College as an under-graduate, where I now teach, and I had an English teacher and I came into class late. I had just settled down when the professor, Dr. Ingles, called on me to pray — it's a church-related college and we do that. He said, "Mr. Cam-polo, would you lead us in prayer?" And so I started praying. And I said, "God, we thank You for this day and all Thy blessings to us. I thank that You love us all. I'm grateful that You love me in spite of the fact that I am so worthless." And he said, "Just a minute, just a minute." You know, and everybody looked up. He said, "Mr. Campolo, you are not worthless. You are so precious that if you were the only person who ever lived, Jesus would have died just for you. That's how precious you are. The word you should have used was unworthy. You may continue the prayer." Somehow it kind of took the edge off of it for me.

People, we may be unworthy, but you are not worthless. Sin in your life, which is a factor that not only alienates you from God but worse than that, gets you down on other people and down on yourself. Those things that you've done, those things that you've been, that you look upon with con-tempt, this is what the cross of Jesus is all about — that on the cross he is willing to take all of that out of you. Like a sponge he will absorb it from you. He will bear it in his own body. He will absorb it into his own flesh. I don't know how to explain it to you: nobody does. But believe me, that on the cross everything that you don't like about yourself, he is willing to become. He literally absorbs that into his own personhood. He personally becomes sin who knew no sin. He lifts us up and he affirms us and makes us feel valuable, makes us believe that we are of worth. If you are here today and you are depressed about yourself, and don't think that you've been what you ought to be, or done what you ought to have done, if you feel in some way that you have failed to be what you have been called to be, the good news of the gospel is that Jesus has atoned for your sin. And because of the cross, because of what happened there, everything about you that you don't like he is ready to absorb into his own personhood and free you from it. So, Jesus loves you. He is here to declare you wonderful. You are precious to him.

There is another thing about kids; kids have this spontaneous joy about them. The joy of kids is wonderful. I remember taking my boy to Disneyland years and years ago, back before they had a general admission, when you had to buy tickets for all the rides. It was 9:30 at night and we were leaving, and as we were leaving my son said, "Dad, I want one more ride on Space Mountain." I said, "I am out of money and I am out of time." He said, "Jesus wants me to go." I said, "That's intriguing, where did you get that?" He said, "Sunday, when you were preaching. You said that whenever we cry, Jesus cries. That whenever we're sad he is sad with us. You said that whatever we feel he feels with us. If that's true, then when I am feeling happy and laughing, he feels happy and laughs. I think that he would enjoy it if I had one more ride on Space Mountain." Now that's not bad theology.

If there is anything that I have to say about Jesus today it's this: Jesus came into the world not just to free us from sin, to save us for heaven, but — this is the good news — he came that his joy might be in us and that our joy might be full. A Jesus that comes to create joy in us — oh, I like that. I like that! Jesus, the joy creator. I always liked the words of Lord Chesterton, who said that "Jesus may be the only child left in the universe." Though all the rest of us have become old and cynical because of sin . . . oh, we are old and we are cynical, especially universities. People have become too mature. They have lost that childlike joyfulness.

How did God function if he was a child? Well, you know children. You take a child, throw him up in the air, bounce him on your knee, set him on the floor, the kid will yell: "Do it again." Throw him in the air, bounce him on your knee, set him on the floor, the kid will yell: "Do it again." You do it again, he yells for it to be done over and over again. Fifty times later the kid is still yelling: "Do it again, do it again."

Now I ask you a theological question: How do you think God created daisies? Do you think he just said, "Daisies, be"? Do you really think he's that high church? Or did Jesus, like a child, create one little daisy and something within the childlike heart of Jesus and God said, "Do it again!" And he created daisy number two, and something within God said, "Do it again!" and he created daisy number three, and four, and fifty billion trillion daisies later, the great God who spun the universe into space, this great God, is jumping up and down yelling, "Do it again, do it again!"

Oh, a God who not only has a quality of childlike joy but comes to us to infuse us with that joy. "I have come," he said, "that my joy might be in you and that your joy might be full."

It is a joyless world out there. I teach at a college campus, and I get to more university campuses than most people, and they are pretty joyless places. People are pretty bored and serious. Walk down the halls of the university. Look into the classrooms. Watch them sitting there. There isn't much joy there.

I was in New York—there's a joyless place. I got on an express elevator; it was full of dead, joyless people. They were just standing there with attaché cases. And when I got on I did my thing. I waited for the door to close—you know how people stand and look at the door and look at the numbers. And as soon as the doors closed I turned. I thought I might bring a little joy. I smiled at everybody and in New York they can't handle that. You see, they kind of backed up away from me. And I said, "Lighten up guys, lighten up. We're going to be traveling together for quite awhile. What do you say we sing?" And these suckers were so intimidated by me, they did. I mean you should have been there. They were holding their attaché cases going, "You are my sunshine, my only . . ." I got off at the seventieth floor and this guy got off with me. I said, "Are you going to the same meeting I am going to?" He said, "No, I just wanted to finish the song."

And you say what in the world has this got to do with being a Christian? Jesus came not only to deliver us from sin so that we can approach ourselves with love and love other people, but he came to infuse us with an incredible joy. And the fruits of the Spirit are these; right under the word love is the word joy. Joy, Joy.

When Blaise Pascal was converted . . . You know about Pascal—one of the guys that helped invent calculus. You wondered who that was. It was Blaise. He was about nine years old when he was sent to his room to be punished. And that afternoon, he invented calculus. It was his way of getting back at everybody. But this brilliant scholar, who Einstein calls "the greatest mind of the last thousand years," writes in his diary: "I met him, not the God of the philosophers, not the God of the mathematicians, not the God of the scientists, but the God of Abraham, Moses and Jacob. Joy, joy, joy! Fire, fire, fire! Joy, fire. Joy, fire. Joy, fire. Unspeakable joy, oh, the ecstasy of the joy of the Lord!"

John Wesley wanders into a chapel in Aldersgate Street in London and he hears them reading from the preface to the Epistle to the Romans and writes in his diary. Out of the depth, out of the depression, out of the dimness of his soul he writes, "Suddenly, suddenly, my heart was strangely warmed and there was an unspeakable joy."

Jesus came to recreate the joy, to re-instill the aliveness. Christianity, the gospel, the good news, the message of Jesus isn't simply about how to get people purified so that they are fit for heaven. It's an invitation to surrender to a presence, to surrender to a resurrected Jesus because the same Jesus who died on the cross is alive and here right now and will invade us, and when he invades us we not only are capable of expressing a new kind of love but we are radiant with an incredible kind of joy, unspeakable joy, a childlike joy. Jesus said, "Unless you become like little children you will in no wise enter the kingdom of heaven."

I ask you a very simple question: Do you know Jesus personally? I mean has he invaded your life? Has he taken possession of you? Has he absorbed from you the dark and negative things about yourself that you know keep you from loving yourself? Has Jesus invaded you and infused with his joy and his aliveness and his ecstasy, so that you've got the joy of a child?

The last thing that Jesus does is this: he recreates dreams and visions. That's of ultimate significance to me because we live in a generation in which people have lost their dreams and visions.

I was speaking at UCLA a while back and it was a give and take from the lecture hall. And finally, I got into a heated dialogue with one student and I said to him, "I'm fifty-eight years old. I'm fifty-eight and you're twenty-three, and I am younger than you are. I am younger than you are, because people are as young as their dreams and visions and as old as their cynicism. What makes people old is not their age, but the losing of the dreams and the visions. Jesus said, the Scripture says, the Hebrew Bible says: when people no longer have their dreams and their visions, then the people perish.

There is a perishing in this land. Just a couple of weeks ago I was at Yale University. I was going to the train station and a young man was driving me and my wife. My wife said, "Where do you see yourself in ten years? What do you hope to have gained in ten years?" And in dead seriousness he said, "Ten million dollars." I said, "That's it?" He said, "Yes." I said, "No, really, I mean what is it that you really want to have?" He said, "Ten million dollars." I said, "That's it?" I don't want to be nasty, but I really can't stand yuppies. It's not that they are immoral; it's just that they are so stinking boring. I mean a Jacuzzi and a Porsche, that's what it's all about? Is that what this precious thing, life, is about?

Are they your dreams? Are they your visions to "do well"? I'm in New York. I'm watching the musical *Man of La Mancha*. The woman next to me starts yelling at her husband, "John, stop it. Stop it. You're exposing yourself. You're exposing yourself." Needless to say I lean forward. Here's this guy in a three-piece suit, crying his eyes out. And I knew why he was crying because the man up front was singing, "To dream the impossible dream, to fight the unbeatable foe, to strive with the last ounce of courage, to go where the brave dare not go, and the world will be richer for this, that one man bruised and covered with scars still strove with his last ounce of courage to reach the unreachable star." And I knew why he was crying. He had a dream once. I don't know where it hit him, at a Baptist revival meeting on the fiftieth verse of "Kumbaya." Oh no, Baptists—that would be "Just as I Am." It's the Methodists who are into "Kumbaya." Somewhere, someplace it hit you. At a campfire, at special meeting, at a youth conference, I don't know where it was, but somewhere it hit you—the possibilities, the possibilities of your life. What you could do and what you could be if you just totally yielded yourself over to Jesus and let Jesus take you and use you and place you where he wants to place you. In the words of that great captain and theologian, Captain Kirk, "To boldly go where no man has gone before." That's good isn't it? "To boldly go where no one has ever gone before."

The dreams, the visions, they beat them out of you. You were going to be a missionary. You were going to go someplace; you were going to touch lives. I've watched them in the inner city, because I work with inner-city kids. I like to walk in the streets of the low-cost housing projects of Philadelphia. I like to talk with the kids that are there. What are you going to do when you grow up, what are you going to be? And they have their dreams. I'm going to be an astronaut, I'm going to be a lawyer, I'm going to be president. I'm going to be this, I'm going to be that. Oh, these kids in the ghetto, they have their dreams. It's no wonder that they become violent and mean. No wonder they are so angry, and they *are* angry. For what is more angry than a kid who loses his dreams, a child that loses his visions? What is angrier than that?

We work in eighteen different neighborhoods in the Philadelphia area, and each neighborhood, during the summer, has its own program. And we get volunteers from colleges and universities to come and work with us and run these programs—children's programs, teenage programs, sports programs, tutoring—you name it, we do it. And each of the neighborhoods has a sports program and has a basketball team. At the end of the summer one year I put together an all-star basketball team from all the neighborhoods. And I scheduled a basketball game at Eastern College, where I teach, between this all-star team and the Philadelphia Eagles football team. Well these kids were higher than kites that day. I brought them out to the campus. I showed them the classrooms. I gave them the feel of the campus. And when I got them in the back room to give them a pep talk just before the game I said, "Guys, I hope you like being on this college campus because I want you to come back here and be students. You know you can be anything you want to be. Dream some dreams, have some visions," I told them. And they sat there and intensely listened. "I hope that someday you are going to be my students right here on this campus." And at that point the coach of the team spoke up and he said, "Don't listen to this man. I grew up where you grow up. And they told me I could get out. And I tried, I really tried, but I never got out and I'm going to die in this place and you're going to die there too. So don't listen to him." I couldn't believe it. I said, "No, don't listen to him. Listen to the mustn'ts, child. Listen to the don'ts. Listen to the never could bes. Listen to the won'ts. Listen to the never have beens. Then, listen close to me. Anything can happen, child, anything can be. God is here."

He not only wants to remove the sin and infuse you with joy, but He wants to rekindle the dream and give back the vision. He wants you once again to believe that you can be done with lesser things, and do something incredible for God and for others in His name. He wants to do that spectacular thing that they beat out of you. He wants to infuse you with the courage to take the risk, to take the dares. And when people . . . You say what do you want me to be, Mother Teresa? Not bad, not bad. That's where the joy is, to live out radical commitment for Christ, to let him take you and do something . . .

We have a lot of older people here too. Don't get the idea that this is a talk for college students. I mean it's for older people too. I mean Abraham was ninety-four years old when he got the call. Woke up one morning— "Sarah"— got the picture? "Sarah, I just had a vision." There's a whole new approach I hadn't thought about before. Poor old lady, she said, "What kind of vision, Abe?" "We're going to create a new age, a new humanity, a new beginning for the human race, a new epoch in human history." Poor old lady, she's ninety-two. "How's this new humanity start, Abe?" "I'm glad you asked, Sarah." Now if you don't think that God has a sense of humor, try this next scene. It says, "Now Abraham, when his life was far spent," which is a King James way of saying: the guy is half dead, "left the Ur of the Chaldeans not knowing where he was going." Do you have this picture, this ninety-four-year-old guy walking down the road in a walker? And his ninety-two-year-old pregnant wife . . . Don't tell me that this is not a funny scene. And people are yelling, "Where are you going, Abe?" "I don't know." "What are you going to do when you get there?" "I don't know." "Well, why are you leaving?" "Because God has given me a vision."

People, God has given you a vision. You know he has. I don't have to tell you what to do with your life; he has already spoken it into your being. He has already gone into the depths of your heart and he gave you a dream and a vision, and somebody told you to be realistic, practical. Dear Lord, take away those practical, realistic people and give back to me the dreamers and the visionaries. I want a generation of Don Quixotes because the world cannot live without them. I ask you very simply and directly the question: What will you do with your life?

Incidentally, there's an invitation to all the young people who are here to come and work with me during the summer and work with these inner-city kids. Give me your name and address at the end of the service. I'll be glad to send you the material. I want to recruit you. I want you to come and work with these inner-city kids. You say, "I need money to come back to Duke." I'll write a guilt letter to your home church. We'll get the money. We'll raise the money. But you need to come and be with those kids and experience their joy, and their spontaneity, and dreams against insurmountable odds. You need to be rekindled in your own vision and your own dreams and made to believe that this is what is important, to minister to people who hurt, to give yourself to people who are suffering, to make a difference to those who are in need. You need this. Give me your name and address on the way out of here; I want you to come. I want you to be there; I want you to make a difference.

Once a year at my church, it's an African American church in west Philadelphia, we have student recognition day. And the young people come and one by one they come to the rostrum and they tell what they are doing. "I'm studying music at Juilliard; I'm studying engineering at MIT; I'm studying law at Harvard." And the old folks, the old folks in my congregation, who lived at a time in American life when brilliant people who were African American couldn't realize their dreams, couldn't fulfill their visions, are there. I've seen these young people. One of them, his name was Stewart, I took him with me to Haiti. I showed him our hospital up in Limbe that had seven hundred people lined up in the morning, one doctor. At the end of the day we turned away more than six hundred people. He said, "I am going to come back here, and I am going to serve these people, I'm going to complete my medical training, come back here and make a difference." I met Stewart just a year ago in New York. He became a doctor, but he didn't go to Haiti. You know what he is doing? He's performing cosmetic surgery, and not the kind that makes any sense at all. A dream gone down the tubes, a vision evaporated.

But I have another student, Bryan Stevenson. Graduated Eastern top of the class. Went to Harvard Law, graduated top of the class there. He's from my home church. He clerked for a federal judge. Do you have any idea what a Harvard grad, African American, who clerks for a federal judge can earn? A quarter of a million dollars a year, I think so. But he is not making a lot of money. Instead, he's living in a one-room apartment in Montgomery, Alabama. And every morning Bryan Stevenson gets up and goes down to the jailhouse and defends the poor people, especially those who are on Death Row. And when I asked him about capital punishment he said, "You miss the point. In this country they don't put criminals to death, they put poor people to death. Because there are two kinds of law: one for the rich and the powerful — they get the lawyers that get them off. There's another kind of law for the poor and the oppressed, and the poor go down the tubes, Tony. Because the poor have no one to speak for them." And then he smiled and he said, "Except in Montgomery, Alabama, because in Montgomery, Alabama, Tony, I speak for the poor. I speak for the poor, Tony." And he said, "Tony, I'm good. I'm really good." And I said to myself, "Bryan, you don't know how good you are. You didn't let them kill the dream. You didn't let them stifle the vision."

And as these young people tell what they are studying and what they are becoming, the old folks in my congregation just sit there and go, "My, my, thank you, Jesus. Oh, yes. Yes. Yes." And there's a groan and there's a moan that makes music that is even more beautiful than the music we heard today, the music of joyful moaning of God's people.

And when they were finished my pastor looked down at these kids and he said, "Children, you are going to die, you are going to die" — that's a good thing to tell college kids, because they don't think they are going to die. He said, "You are going to die. They are going to drop you in a hole. They are going to throw dirt in your face and they are going to go back to the church and eat potato salad." Ain't it the truth. He said, "When you were born you were the only one that cried, everyone else was happy. Not important but what is important is this: When you die will you be the only one that is happy and everyone else will cry? Good question. Depends on what you live for. Did you live selfishly, or did you live out the dreams of Jesus and serve other people? When it's all over what will you leave behind, these titles that you're accumulating? Are you going to leave titles or testimonies?" Oh, that's good, that is really good.

And he did what only my pastor can do; he swept through the Bible in five minutes. He said, "There was Moses, and there was Pharaoh. Pharaoh had a title, a good title: Ruler of Egypt — that's a good title. But when it was over that's all he had. He had the title but Moses had the testimonies." Oh, that's good, that's good. He said, "There was Jezebel and Elijah the prophet that she was going to destroy. Now Jezebel had a title; it was queen, Queen Jezebel. There's a good title, Queen. But when it was over that's all she had. She had the title but Elijah had the . . ." It gets to you, doesn't it? I'll give you one more shot, just one more, so get ready. "There was Nebuchadnezzar, King of Babylon. Good title, King. Good title, King. King Nebuchadnezzar, he was going to throw Daniel to the lions, but when it was over that's all he had. He had the title of King, but Daniel, Daniel had the testimonies."

People of God, one day they are going to drop you in a hole, count on it.

They are going to throw dirt in your face, count on it. They are going to go back to the church and eat potato salad, count on it. Here's the only question: When it's over will you have lived out your dreams in such a way, will your life have counted in such a manner that you'll have more than titles, that you'll have people standing around your grave giving testimonies as to how you've blessed them?

And Jesus said, "Unless you become as little children," unless you rediscover that sense of worth, recover that sense of joy, recover the shattered dreams and visions, and become a follower of his, "you will in no wise enter the kingdom of God."

Carol Marie Noren, professor of preaching at North Park Seminary in Chicago, preached this sermon while she was a professor of preaching at Duke Divinity School. The sermon is typical of her careful craftsmanship, her close reading of the scripture, and even her references to Wesley's life (she is a United Methodist). Here she walks the congregation through a reading of Mark's story of the storm at sea, noting the peculiarities and the distinctive aspects of Mark's rendition. Then asking, "So what do you suppose Mark was trying to show . . . ?," she spins out the relevance of the story for a contemporary congregation.

Storm at Sea

June 19, 1994

CAROL MARIE NOREN

Mark 4:35–41 There are few stories in scripture that have so captivated the interest and the imagination of Christians as this morning's reading from the Gospel of Mark. Three symbols that appear together draw their life from this text: the boat, the sea, and usually a cross symbolizing the presence of Christ. We see these three symbols together in the logo for Duke Divinity School. They're marketed, these three symbols together, on stoles and banners for decorating our churches. Some of you may have seen a contemporary interpretation of this story: a picture of a sturdy, wholesome-looking youth at the wheel of a great ship, the waves are pounding against the side of the ship, and standing behind the young man is the Savior with one hand on the boy's shoulder and the other hand pointing the course that he should take. But the most memorable rendition of this story that I have ever seen was one I encountered two years ago: a church altar painting in a small, Danish fishing village. The first thing you would notice when you walk into this church is a model schooner made of wood hanging from the rafters over the center aisle. Now, I know this isn't common in Durham but you see them in churches all over near the North Sea. And straight ahead, over the altar, is this painting; it features a wide-awake Jesus standing on the hull of a completely capsized boat and gesturing toward lighter clearer skies. And next to Him, in the water up to their necks, are no fewer than four anxious disciples, clutching madly at the hem of Jesus' robe, at the boat, at each other, anything they can get. It is a vivid and unforgettable picture. The problem is, nowhere in the Bible is such a scene presented.

In this morning's text we see Jesus asleep in the stern of the boat, and then a few minutes later calming the sea. In the next chapter, or a few chapters later, we have the story of Jesus walking on the waves. And in Matthew's Gospel there is also an account of Peter trying to walk on water. But nothing quite like this artistic interpretation of the passage. On closer inspection there are still other differences in this altar painting. Ice is beginning to form on the beards of the apostles struggling in the water, and the boat itself looks like those crafts used a hundred years ago by life-saving crews on the North Sea. Like the painter of that church in Denmark, we borrow the symbols and the action of this story to try to make it our own. We claim our identity as those disciples of Jesus fearful in the boat when we sing " 'Tis the Old Ship of Zion" or "My Soul's Been Anchored in the Lord." We liken the storm on the Sea of Galilee to our own personal inner turmoil when we sing "Jesus Savior, Pilot Me," "Master, the Tempest Is Raging," or "Lonely the Boat, Sailing at Sea." We identify with the saving work of Jesus in songs like "Throw Out the Lifeline," "Rescue the Perishing," "Let the Lower Lights Be Burning." The British Methodists even have a song using this imagery which they use to exhort one another, "Will your anchor hold in the storms of life, when the clouds unfold their wings of strife; when the strong ties lift and the cables strain, will your anchor drift or firm remain?"

It is a good thing for theology to be contextual, for it to speak to worshippers where they live. The stories and teachings of the Christian faith ought to intersect with the particular circumstances of peoples' lives. And who could count the ways that these symbols of the boat and the sea and the cross appearing in artistic and musical renditions have strengthened or even awakened faith in people through the centuries? I don't know about you, but I have been blessed by singing such Gospel songs. At the same time, we can't overlook the license that is taken in interpreting the passage. First of all, there is no anchor mentioned in this story from Mark. Far from being the pilot, Jesus is asleep in the stern. There is nothing to suggest that the disciples threw out the lifeline or rescued the perishing from other boats in the Sea of Galilee. And I think, hardest for those of us who are evangelicals, we cannot pull from the text the conclusion that Jesus will calm any storm if we only have enough faith. I wish this weren't the case. I wish this miracle story had the same upbeat conclusion as one that appears a little while later, when Jesus healed the woman with the issue of blood and said to her, "Daughter, your faith has made you well. Go in peace and be healed of your disease." I wish the disciples, during that storm, had spoken to Jesus as Son of the Most High God, the way the demoniac in the next episode did. Then the rest of this sermon I could meditate on the wonderful and miraculous things that are in store for those who believe in Jesus as Lord and Savior. But that's not what the Bible says here. When all is said and done, Christ calming the wind and sea is not about faith, but about the absence of faith. And what is worse, the disciples don't seem to have much more faith after the miracle than they had before it. According to Mark's Gospel, this incident occurred during Jesus' Galilean ministry, just before he went on a preaching tour on the other side of the Sea. From previous chapters we know that the disciples Andrew and Simon, James and John, had heard a man with an unclean spirit address Jesus as the "Holy One of God." They had watched the Messiah heal the sick and cast out demons and forgive sins. They heard some witnesses identify him as the Son of God. The Master appointed these twelve, and sent them out to preach and have the authority to cast out demons. They spent far more time with the Master than most people did. And earlier in this chapter in Mark it says, "To them was given the secret of the kingdom of God." So you would think that if anybody ought to believe in the authority and power of the Son of Man, these twelve should. But no, the immediate followers of Jesus admired him and they worked with him and they learned from him, but they did not recognize him for who he was. We can't even be certain that they were asking him for help. Unlike that incident where Peter was sinking, and he cried, "Lord, save me," in this incident they only accused him: "Teacher, do you not care that we perish?" They may have hoped that Jesus would pray for them, or lend a hand in bailing water, but they clearly did not expect that he could or would calm the tempest. Their surprise after the miracle and their puzzlement over his identity are evidence of that, and Jesus' rebuke "Where is your faith?" is the proof. Mark does not paint a flattering picture of the disciples here. The story presents them in a very bad light. Matthew's version isn't quite so damaging; at least they call him "Lord" as he tells the story. But not Mark. The most that he grants them is awe after the miracle.

So what do you suppose Mark was trying to show the early church through this story? It seems to me that Christians who were facing persecution and uncertainty would see in this story a reminder. A reminder that the very worst fear in life is not caused by storms, whether real or metaphorical. The worst fear is caused by forgetting God's promises and what God has done in the past. It's strange: the men in the boat that night had been brought up as people of God's covenant. They had been taught about the Lord whose purposes were accomplished through the deluge in Noah's time. They learned how the Almighty had guided Moses and the children of Israel through the Red Sea. They knew that God had brought Jonah into and out of the depths in order to proclaim the word of God. But they forgot divine power and purpose, and that's why they asked Jesus, "Don't you care if we perish?" If they had remembered, they wouldn't need to ask. A church in any place or age that loses its memory is a church running scared. It is a church that looks forward only to despair and death.

I know a congregation in Chicago, though I realize there are countless others like it across the country. It started out many years ago as a small struggling group of mostly blue-collar Christians. They met in homes and then managed to finance a modest church building. They were very creative in their evangelism and dedicated in their stewardship; eventually they outgrew the building and built themselves deep into debt just when the Great Depression came. In danger of foreclosure, they agreed that what they needed to do was pray and worship more and engage in more outreach, and eventually the crisis passed. But many of the second and third generation moved away. The neighborhood began to change, and this time the congregation began to rent out more and more of their building to make ends meet. Finally the remnant decided it wasn't worth the struggle and risk to stay in the city, and they relocated in a nearby suburb. Today this congregation is grayin', not growin'. The members dream of keeping the doors open long enough so they can have their funeral from the church. They have forgotten what they once knew about God's providence and purpose. But a church that recalls and retells the mighty acts of God has a future. The first-century followers of Jesus who sang hymns as they were marched into the lions were not in a state of denial. No doubt their hearts were pounding and their palms sweating as they faced a terrible, painful, and mysterious passing from this life to the next. But they sang praise to their redeemer, for they remembered the acts and the promises of Christ, and their faith lives on. Centuries later the same memory and confidence were shown by Christians such as Hugh Latemir, whose last words before his martyrdom, being burned at the stake, were, "We shall this day light up such a candle by God's grace in England as I trust shall never be put out." He remembered the Lord to whom wind and sea and even death are subject. His witness encourages us today. And lately the news media have reported the slaughter of priests and ministers among others in Rwanda, the persecution of Christians in China, the perilous existence of some missionaries in third world countries, and we have to ask ourselves, "Why don't they flee to a safer place?" It is because they recall what God has done in ages past; they claim God's purpose and promises for their own. And where is the church of Jesus Christ growing larger and stronger day by day? In these frightening places where the people of God remember.

Mark shows us something else in this story of fainthearted followers; something that is good news if, like me, you have more in common with their fear than with the courage of modern martyrs. The good news is that even our failures in faith can be used by an all-powerful God to proclaim the Gospel. Peter's mighty confession of faith a few chapters later and Christ's calling him the "rock" on which He would build His church have much more impact because we know what Peter was before, and how far he had come. The shortcomings and bitterness of Jonah's witness make our Lord's mercy to Nineveh stand out in bolder relief. Or somewhat closer to our own time, we cannot truly apprehend the triumphs of God's grace in John Wesley's life without also recalling his despair and shame in 1736 on a ship bound for Georgia caught in a storm. He wrote in his journal, "About eleven, I lay down in the great cabin, and in a short time fell asleep but very uncertain whether I should wake alive, and much ashamed of my unwillingness to die. Oh how pure in heart must he be who would rejoice to appear before God at a moment's warning! Toward the morning He rebuked the wind and the sea and there was a great calm." By contrast, Wesley noted, the Moravians on board sang hymns and remained tranquil throughout the storm, trusting the Lord of wind and wave whether they were to live or to die. Their faith appears more vividly because of Wesley's lack. And in the years that followed, when John Wesley led the Methodist revival that swept across England, he didn't hire spin doctors to expunge or rewrite this episode. He knew, like the apostle Paul, that God's power can be manifested even through human weakness. Mark's version of Jesus calming the storm is a gift to every imperfect disciple. If we read it as a promise that the truth of Christ can be proclaimed even through the likes of us.

And finally, this episode in the boat in a storm shows us something of the nature of Jesus Christ. This Jesus is the Lord of sea and wind and all creation, the sovereign of all time and space whose power is infinite, and who is love. The Savior did not abandon the disciples because of their unbelief. He did not let the waves of death encompass them alone. God's love made visible does not give up on people. His mercy is renewed over and over; it's made new every morning. The signs of God's love and power do not fail, if we only have eyes to see them. Now, as fellow travelers with Christ we may not find that the water is smooth or the wind is calm. Servants of God, as Paul reminds us, may marvel at His love in the midst of afflictions and calamity and tumult, imprisonment, beatings, and all kinds of situations that we would rather give a wide berth. But the good news is that no storm will have the last word. In love Christ has promised to remain with us now and forever, until His kingdom comes in its fullness and we behold Him on the throne in the New Jerusalem. Until that day, as the Word assures us, when there is no more sea. Thanks be to God for His inexpressible gift. Amen.

Few visiting preachers at Duke Chapel draw larger or more appreciative crowds when they visit than Peter J. Gomes, minister and Plummer Professor of Christian Morals at Harvard's Memorial Church since 1970. When Gomes went on sabbatical in the late 1990s, he chose to spend his leave at Duke. When Duke offered its first honorary degree to a clergyman in nearly two decades, it awarded that degree to Peter J. Gomes. The Chapel congregation adores Gomes's eloquence, his wit, and his way with scripture. This sermon shows Gomes at his best, with a lively, rich, elaborate rendition of the story of Joseph and his brothers.

An Impossible Ethic

February 19, 1995

PETER J. GOMES

Genesis 45:8 and Matthew 5:1–14

> Prayer: Help us, Lord, to become masters of ourselves that we may become the servants of others. Take our hands and work through them. Take our minds and think through them. Take our lips and speak through them. And take our hearts and set them on fire for Christ's sake. Amen.

There is a text for this sermon, and it is the 8th verse of the 45th chapter of the book of Genesis, from which the first lesson was taken. "It was not you who sent me here, but God."

The Old Testament is wonderfully explicit in its stage directions, and that's why I think for most of us it is the easier of the two testaments to respond to. It makes it clear, for example, for whom we are supposed to be cheering, who are the heroes, who are the villains in the lessons. And there is no doubt in the long epic that constitutes the story of Joseph, this morning, that it is Joseph who is the hero. Joseph is the fellow to be taken seriously. In case there's any doubt in any of your minds: the story of Joseph is about Joseph. And we are meant to take Joseph seriously.

But at the start of this sermon let's be honest, or at least let me be honest and confess to you at the outset that young Joseph is, for me, one of the more obnoxious figures in all of scripture, in the whole biblical narrative. And I can readily see why his brothers would want to wring his neck. He was self-centered, this Joseph. He knew he was the favorite son of his father's old age.

Favorites always know that, they always know how to play the card with ma or pa. And he knew through his dreams that great things were going to happen to him and he wasted neither time nor effort, this dreamer, in lording it over his brothers.

There's something of the Eddie Haskell in this Joseph — this spoiled brat, the precocious A-student. His hand always up in the seminar, he always has the right answer. His dog never eats his homework. And he doubtless has a long string of perfect attendance pins from his Methodist Sunday School on his bosom. All of us know such people. All of us grew up with such people and if we could, or dared, we would have loved to beat them up just for the sheer fun of it, just because of who they were. Confess it, you know that it is true.

And so, initially at least, this is an exercise in my own perversity. My sympathy is all with the brothers. Now surely they didn't have to be jealous, these brothers. Surely as older and wiser, they should have had better control of their feelings, been more in touch with their emotions. Surely they should not have contemplated murder, nor sold their brother into slavery, lied to their old father. That's wrong, wrong, wrong. But I think I know why they did it. And this is the reason I posit to you why they did it: you and I, contrary to popular rumor and expectations, you and I do not flourish in the presence of pure and undiluted virtue. We love it in abstraction, but to live with it is a real pain where we sit down. The presence of pure and undiluted virtue is like being in too bright a light, like these lights, too bright and blinding. And rather than illuminating, they blind and intimidate us. Too much of a good thing, contra to Mae West, if it is human, is not terrific; it is tedious. It is boring. Can you imagine small talk with Elie Wiesel, or Florence Nightingale, or a long train ride with Mother Teresa? In theory this is great, but in practice most of us would rather not bear it. It is too much to handle.

"Come let us slay this dreamer and then we shall see what will become of his dreams." We know those vengeful words of the brothers and we know them in our own hearts. We associate those words nowadays with not only the contemplated death of Joseph but with Martin Luther King Jr., and we hear them each January when people read this passage from Joseph and say let us slay the dreamer and hope to kill the dream. We think we can stand the moral light, but most of us cannot. The Josephs of this world do not inspire in close proximity; they annoy, they intimidate, and they drive us often to desperate and even despicable measures. And so, the brothers got rid of him, not by murder as was their first plan, but by selling him into slavery, a much more profitable enterprise. They could get some cash for him by getting him out of the way; it was a win-win proposition.

Now, to put it mildly, this family of Joseph is what we might call dysfunctional. Think of his father, dear old Jacob. Here is a conniver from his birth. He is the one who stole his brother's birthright and tricked his father and sort of lied and cheated his way from the womb to the world — that's the father in the case. Then the half-brothers, they quarrel with each other all the time, they are united only in their treachery. If this is an exercise, this story of Joseph and his family, if this is an exercise of the Bible's view of family values, then things are very bad off indeed. Of course, as you know, and this is a footnote, the Bible is full of dysfunctional families. Mary and Martha are at each other's throats hammer and tong. Cain and Abel are a lethal profile in sibling rivalry. Even Jesus tells his mother off at Cana, tells her to leave him alone. And then, of course, there's Joseph and his brothers. The whole thing is an exercise in perversity. Arrogance, jealousy, treachery . . . this is stuff hardly fit for a family newspaper. Are you sure you want your children reading this stuff?

But perhaps it's the point of this story, at least, to remind us that proximity, which is that family unit, proximity often stimulates perversity. That is why the worst fights are family feuds. The worst quarrels are between people who love each other, and the worst of all imaginable wars is a civil war. Satan likes close quarters, and it is in the most intimate of settings that perversity thrives. And in this story, dare we note, things only turn out right when everybody, not just Joseph, picks up, leaves home, and starts up all over again. If you're looking for something to admire here, it is not the family. Perversity is what gets our attention in this story at the start. But the perversity is necessary so that it can be encountered by providence. That's the point of the text. "It was not you who sent me here, but God." Such remorse as the brothers may have had at that moment is irrelevant. Joseph one-ups them by transforming their perversity into God's divine plan for himself. You see he is still obnoxious. What the brothers intended for evil, God intended for good and the form of God's goodness here is not where we might think it is.

For us the sign of God's providence might be relief from the famine, the provision of food and cattle, all of the things that would advance life and protect people against the ravages of natural resources. Famine means death and God, through Joseph, gives life through famine relief, we all know about that. We know about famine relief for the famines of Africa — Save the Children, Sally Struthers, and all of that. We remember our high hopes for famine relief in Somalia. We know what is supposed to happen, but here God's providence, in the story of Joseph, is not the relief of the famine. It is in the place where all the trouble and perversity began in the first place. It is in the family where God's providence is displayed. God's providence is made real in the reconciliation of a broken, dysfunctional, screwed-up family. Joseph, himself, cannot pretend to be any longer what he is not. He cannot hide under his pseudonym in front of his brothers. He cannot keep them in suspense anymore. He breaks down into tears, reveals who he is, and he and they have a reunion. The human desire for a little bit of revenge and justice is overcome by the divine desire for reconciliation and reunion.

It takes a lot of work to maintain anger and estrangement. Those of you who have been involved in maintaining your share of your family's feuds all these years know how hard it is to remember that you are supposed to be thoroughly disgusted with your sister-in-law for something she did forty years ago. It takes a lot of work to maintain that sort of rigor in the face of God's providential design for reconciliation and reunion. And that is what happened here: providence is the agent of reconciliation, reunion, and forgiveness.

Now before we rejoice too fast in the providence of God and this act of reconciliation, we have to know how contrary to human instinct Joseph acts here. And let's confess again that had we been put into slavery by our brothers, had we been deprived of our birthright and now found ourselves with kingly power, with life-or-death power over them, most of us would be sorely tempted to a little rough justice at least for a few minutes. They should be made to suffer just a little bit longer than the text suggests. Indeed, why should they get off so easily? Indeed, why should forgiveness come rushing in like the cavalry at the last moment and rescue the dramatic tension from the justice it all deserves? Forgiveness sometimes is too cheap. Forgiveness sometimes is too easy.

Did you read a couple of weeks ago about the terrifying remarks of Elie Wiesel at the fiftieth anniversary of the commemoration at Auschwitz? He prayed, Wiesel prayed that God would never ever forgive the Nazis, never forgive the crimes they committed against humanity. It was a chilling, agonizing, terrifying moment. I think I understood why he said it. I know I cannot accept that he said it or nor cannot I expect that of the God I worship, to whom he addressed it. But I understand what drives that kind of powerful emotion.

An example of another sort. I was present not many years ago, not long before his death, when Daddy King preached on his son Martin Luther King's birthday in the Memorial Church in Cambridge, and it was an incredible occasion when he mounted our pulpit and began. But the most incredible thing about that preaching in Memorial Church was at the beginning of his sermon where he said, "Let me tell you at the start, I have no bitterness in my heart." And then he described how his son had been murdered, how another son had drowned, how his wife had been shot in church before his very eyes and after each of these recitals, with tears in his eyes, he would say, "But I have no bitterness in my heart, God won't allow it."

Forgiveness may be too easy for us but it is the stuff of the providence of God, as Joseph's brothers discovered. "It was not you who sent me here, but God." Perversity has become an instrument of providence.

Now that all may be true; it is all supposed to be true. It is all assuredly true—you heard it read from Holy Writ, you hear it proclaimed by me—it must be true. But Joseph is both a paragon of virtue and long dead. What has this impossible ethic to do with us? Most of us know more of perversity than of providence. And if you are having a miserable time at Duke this year, or this term, or this week, or even at this very moment, and God sent you here, then God is even more quirky than we think. Are we really meant to take this stuff seriously? What do we do with Jesus, who tells us in these verses from the Sermon on the Mount that we are to love our enemies, we are to use well those who despitefully use us, that we are to do good to those who hate us, we are to turn the other cheek, and—that most frightening of all things for us—you are to lend and expect nothing in return. Are there any bankers in this congregation this morning? Any lending officers, anybody from the financial aid office at Duke University? You are to lend and expect nothing in return.

Wouldn't it be wonderful if some biblical scholar in the Divinity School, through careful research of the Greek text and some new discoveries in some old broken jars, discovered that these verses from the Sermon on the Mount really don't mean what they say? They have been mistranslated, misconstrued, taken out of context—all this stuff about turning cheeks and lending freely—that's really not what Jesus had in mind at all. This was meant for some ascetic, saintly, religious community, not for very real people like you and me and other failed Christians.

You remember that great line of Mark Twain who said, "It's not the things I don't understand in the Bible that worry me; it's the things I understand perfectly clear that worry me." And these are among the things that you understand and are perfectly clear: you are to love your enemies, you are to turn the other cheek, you are to lend without expectation of return. There it is, square in the middle of the gospel, hardly ambiguous at all. I know lots of Christians, lots of them, who want to take the Bible literally, as inspired, infallible, inerrant, the sole sufficient rule of faith and practice. I know them and you know them, and maybe you are among them. They struggle over obscure rules of conduct in the book of Leviticus and the holiness code, they are eager to adapt themselves in every way to the standards of Rome or Ephesus, or any of Paul's cities, but they come to a sputtering halt at these verses in Matthew 6 where the expectations of a rational and macho society of red-blooded capitalists like you and me are turned on their head. Now that is what I call perversity.

But the impossible ethic, and that is what it is, is the only one that counts. Had Joseph not behaved impossibly and been reconciled to his dysfunctional family, all would have perished. God's plan would have been thwarted and frustrated; there would be no future worthy of the Name.

Look at South Africa if you will. Who would have imagined a decade ago, five years ago, even a year ago that a policy of reconciliation would be the order of the day in that much divided country? Who would have imagined that even with all of its troubles today, the nation would be renewed and the families of that nation reunited by one whom the white majority had thrown into prison? Who could imagine that Christian idealism, that impossible ethic, with its ethic of forgiveness and reconciliation and the extra mile, would become an effective instrument of nation building? Who would have thought it possible? But the impossible ethic sputtering along is the thing that is guiding that country from darkness into light.

Now, we wouldn't dare try that in this country. That's not written in any contract of which I am familiar, at least not yet. We want, in this country — you want to be lean and mean. Somebody must pay. We want to straighten out and tighten up. We will stand for nothing and so we will fall for anything. We cannot bear the thought of Abraham Lincoln . . . I think of reconstruction . . . What good it might have been if Abraham Lincoln had practiced the impossible ethic? You and I might have been talking to one another a lot sooner than we did. Or Martin Luther King — what might have happened had we allowed Martin Luther King and his impossible ethic to live? And even Jesus, who we call the Christ, what could have happened if we let him down from his cross to practice as well as preach his impossible ethic?

Do you know what Joseph means in Hebrew? Of course you don't, so I shall tell you. It means: may God give increase. What a wonderful name: may God give increase. And we know that his story, obviously enough, is an epiphany story, a story of disclosure, revelation, light, manifestation, and reconciliation. We know that because this is the seventh Sunday after Epiphany and we are a liturgically correct congregation. The gospel is about light, manifestation, and disclosure. Perversity is the human condition more or less, and providence is the business of God by which we see our way through the darkness and in that light. And by that light, wonder of wonders, even the impossible is both possible and plausible. "It was not you who sent me here, but God. For God sent me before you to preserve life." And so he did, and so he does, for which we thank God.

Eberhard Bethge spent most of his life in the shadow of another preacher, Diet-
rich Bonhoeffer. What we know of the great Bonhoeffer, contemporary theologian
and martyr of the Nazis, we know from Bethge's tireless, courageous preserva-
tion of his lectures and papers, as well as his fine biographical work. Bethge, who
served as a pastor in Germany during the years of the Third Reich (until his im-
prisonment) as well as a professor in Bonn, was an astute theologian in his own
right. This sermon, which Bethge preached in Duke Chapel a few years before his
death, is illustrative of Bethge's unique gifts: a defense of the faith, but not an
uncritical one; a reminiscence of Bonhoeffer that reveals, in a few simple refer-
ences, the way that Bonhoeffer continues to challenge the Church; and an honest
wrestling with the issue of the Church and the Jews.

A Chief Text of the Church

April 23, 1995

EBERHARD BETHGE

Matthew 16:13–23

The grace of our Lord Jesus Christ be with us all.

Now I'm going to preach about one of the chief stories of Christianity, which
had such a mixed history and reception.

It had at least three different phases, this chief text of the Church.

First, the Church triumphant. Remember, if you may have ever been in
Rome the golden mosaic letters in St. Peter's rotunda in Rome, each letter
so huge, "TU ES PETRUS," shining down at the masses without suggesting
any human limitations in St. Peter and the Church.

And second, it became one of the controversial chief texts, Roman Catholics and Protestants fighting about its meaning up to this day, whether this
text is sufficient basis for the office of the Pope. And the consequences of
this fight for six centuries written ineradicably into the geographical maps,
especially of Europe, and some of the consequences still being suffered in
former Yugoslavia.

And third, it has become a cruel chief text. Christians have applied this
text to the Jews, who refused to confess Jesus as the Messiah, and on this
account have taken away their houses and property, have restricted their

careers, deprived them of decent occupations, freedom, and even life itself. Thus, this chief text of the Christians has become a surveyor's rod, a whip in the hands of the absolutists to justify the lines of separation between human beings and to nourish hatred.

And during my own life, I have had my own experiences with these rather differing usages of the chief Christian text, these three interpretations. First, let's begin with the second letter. As students even before 1933, of course, we were excited about the controversy referring to Roman Catholic claims on St. Peter, on St. Peter's see, the Vatican. As German Protestants, we liked when our teachers explained in the New Testament courses that there was nothing written about a successor of Peter in the Vatican on this passage, and of course nothing about his priorities. In the meantime, of course, things have cooled down a bit. Roman Catholic interpreters used to read the text as we do — namely, about this great promise upon the Church and how her foundations do not rest on Peter's character, or Peter's personality, or his strengths. The confession revealed not from flesh and blood but from the Father in heaven.

The second usage of this chief text, the triumphant establishment of the Church on the foundation of the confession of the Messiah, took on a new quality for us, especially for me and for my friends, in the year of 1933 in Germany. Suddenly, my church had to resist new gods, new idols. There were suddenly altars in some of our churches on which you could find the picture of Adolf Hitler.

On the 23rd of July, 1933, there were the famous church elections in Germany all over the country. On the evening before, Hitler visited the Wagner opera at Bayreuth, I think it was the performance of *Parsifal*, conducted by Richard Strauss, and during the break he spoke over the radio to all Germans. He was interested for his German Christians, that Nazified Christian party, and enthusiastic followers of the Church who wanted to force everybody to confess, next to Jesus, not America, not other countries, but Germany and Adolf Hitler. They wanted to remodel the church institutions according to Nazi principles, including the indoctrination of the anti-Semitic, or so-called Aryan, paragraph into the church constitution. And the German Christians, in fact, on the next Sunday won the elections with more than 70 percent.

On this same Sunday, there in July '33, Dietrich Bonhoeffer preached in one of the Berlin churches and he preached this very text: Matthew 16. And everybody in the church understood at once that word of the one, and only one, Messiah whom you should confess to. And excluding a claim that Hitler was in any way a German Messiah, Dietrich preached of a church, I quote, "which cannot properly do anything other than spread the confession of him alone," Jesus Christ. As long as she was doing it, so she has the firm rock under their feet. There is, as he said, "Church, do not look at any other pillar. Church, remain the church; confess, confess, confess this man." And still today, I breathe faster when I remember the effect of this confession text in this kind of context, which then created what we know now as a confessing church. And that remained, for years, the formative experience for me and for my friends in those days.

The passage provided us with even some vision for the persecuted ones, for the Jews, so that we protested the introduction of the Aryan paragraph in those days. We know now, of course, how little we understood and how poor our attempts were then. And let me add, when I saw for the first time in my life the rotunda in St. Peter's Church in Rome, and that was in 1936, together I visited Rome with Dietrich Bonhoeffer, I loved that golden inscription. Was it not only comforting, was it not even true, yes, the persecuted church stands on rocks. We were both still full of the last days in Berlin, which we had just left during the days of the Olympic games there in Berlin, and had seen and read graffiti on the walls, done by the storm troopers, stating in wonderful poetry that after the Olympiad, we will smash the church to marmalade. And here we read now in the Roman Cathedral: No! The doors of hell will not overcome the Church — the confessing Church.

But then later came another stage, and that period is still with us and going on — the period in which that brave and firm appeal and reference to this text did not come any more so easily to our lips. In West Germany, after the war, we were aware that now our church was again in pretty good shape. Respected again, majority again, having back all the privileges. What a difference; to confess Matthew 16 in what they called *en stato confessionis*, in persecution, in the status of the small, of the weak, of the powerless minority. Or, to do it now again in the status of comfort and well-being. When that confession of the underdogs became once again the confession of the one on top, suddenly the creed of this confession became the status symbol in society. The confession to Jesus the Messiah became the surveyor's rod. Thus, what in the text had been an experience of liberation of blessings, opening up gracious truth, justice, love, that exactly turns into a means of pressuring others. Love becomes threatening and manipulative. A bit too crafty.

When, after Auschwitz, we began in Germany very slowly, very late to study this long history of guilt, which helped to make possible an Auschwitz, we became aware how this chief text of Christianity had developed into a cruel story for them, for the Jews. For centuries, their refusal to confess Jesus as the Christ had brought them sanctions, not only in Germany, of course, but in a merciless sequence of nations and centuries in ever new experiences of deprivation and death. The same text, which was such an affirmation for us, for me an edification, for them it was the source of a constant running of the godless in Christian society. Which means, the text written by Jews, telling Jewish experiences, filled totally with Jewish concepts and Jewish hopes, had become the most anti-Jewish passage with shocking consequences, severe consequences.

Now this has become one of our problems in our church and in our German theology and my home church too. Now we are trying to deal with it. But those insights are a warning to Christians of the world, how our Christian possessions, even this creed, might become a weapon against non-Christians. Here an alarm sounds that more is necessary than a verbal confession that Jesus is the Christ. Now exactly at this point, our text says something very precisely. Belonging to the Messiah Christ, to the person, is important, as Peter and his other fellows discovered, but it includes being set on a distinctive way: the way of readiness for suffering.

In the first part of Matthew 16, everything circles around the person of Jesus the Christ, and around being related to that person in confession. But in the last two parts the story circles around His way. Therefore, it says, you cannot have the name of Christ, you cannot be called a Christian, without His way. The following passages in Matthew speak of that way. But what has happened in the story of Christianity? Consent to the person of Christ has mainly been accepted as making you a Christian. Consent to active participation in His way of suffering has mainly been left out. Suffering was generally left to those who declined their consent to the person of the Messiah. Of course, the church praised Christ's passion all along. She made it the center of her sacramental liturgy. It became exclusively a passion of a Christ for me. It provided a medicine to free us from sin and suffering. The church made Christ's passion a pharmacy for healing, but participation in Christ's suffering was shifted to the outsiders who would not confess Jesus' messianic uniqueness.

In these lovely painted prayer books of the Middle Ages, you find the most extraordinary examples of great art and of great mystery presenting the gospel. For instance, a picture from 1421 in Bologna, of the elevated crucified Christ. With His right hand He crowns a proud female figure riding on a proud horse: the *ekklesia*, the church. Out of the body of Christ spills His blood, and the woman catches it in a cup for Holy Communion, and this lady *ekklesia* is the queen and she spends the food of salvation. However, with His left hand Christ pierces deeply the body of another woman with a huge sword, the bold figure of the synagogue riding to death, to hell on a most ugly he-goat. This separation between the person and His way is now condemned even more in our text itself. This is being told to us: that Peter, who just had totally understood, that same Peter in the next moment does not understand at all. The highly praised rock of the church receives the most outspoken reproof: away from me, Satan. And Matthew, who is so much interested in the role of Peter, told that without moderating it at all.

What did Peter mean? We touched on that a moment ago. When Jesus combines the glorious royal role of Peter's confession — "You are the Christ" — with that most unroyal way of his coming sufferings, just then Peter wants to separate the person and his way. And exactly this comes under the total judgment of Jesus. Apparently very soon Peter was not able anymore to know really what he had said with his confession: "You are the Christ and we belong to you."

But if this happened to Peter, how can we know? How can we think that we would understand better than he? Do we realize what field we have entered claiming his name for us? And also, do we realize what we do to this name, which we think is now our name, when we demand of others that they must make this confession?

So Scripture says here, yes, to the person of Christ, which remains isolated from the way of Christ in this world, that is Satanic. That is evil. That is seductive. It cannot be Christian faith.

Now there are the Jews, who doubt our confession and call into question what we say and claim for their ears — that we are already with the Messiah. Considering our ways, our steps, our lack of discipleship, I think they do us a necessary service. In this connection we rather lately discovered that illuminating word of Dietrich Bonhoeffer, in his ethics, when he says, "The Jew keeps open for us the Christ question." Being said by a man who is so much Christ-centered, whom we would expect to say that the Christ question is forever closed, no, here he says it is open for us — or it keeps open for us the Christ question. So he wrote in 1940. And I think that is profound truth. And we need those Jews mistrusting our Messianic claims, to prevent us from making Christ into a sweet, cheap idol, a false god, a pagan god. All as Peter was going to do.

As a theologian of the Reformation, Dietrich Bonhoeffer was always afraid that we would fill our imaginations, our pictures of Christ, maybe with philosophical, with Greek contents, with non-biblical concepts. Church history shows many examples and so do our hymns, our prayer books. In Nazi Germany churches and theologians had promoted Jesus into a pagan heaven of gods and idols. Jesus plus the swastika flag. That was made now a Teutonic, hero god, who even had to protest the racist purity of the Germans. And always too, and in your country maybe an example, for here, Jesus first and here, the American flag too. Vice Bishop Ludwig Mueller, Hitler's man in the church, a Nazi bishop, turned the Sermon on the Mount into a book in 1936: *German Words of God*. Or perhaps there are some other places too, maybe in America too, being created words of God, being invented today. But what has this Teutonic, this Greek, this American god Christ got to do with the representative of the God of Abraham, Isaac, and Jacob, with the God of Moses and of the Prophets, with the God of the Jews and the God of Jesus — of those Jews who have suffered for his justice, for his grace, who have testified for this through the centuries?

Is Bonhoeffer not right? The Jews keep open the Christ question for us. Thus, we see with our decision for the person of Jesus, the Christ, we have entered another field. We have accepted a norm; we have assumed the goal that is defined by the discipleship of the Sermon on the Mount, by the hymn of love in I Corinthians 13. We have entered a field which is under the promise of compassion and thus, under the promise of resurrection.

So simple is the confession to Jesus the Messiah and so complicated at the same time. So God-forlorn and so certain. So threatened and so firmly built upon a rock. So much Good Friday and so much Easter.

Some years ago, I was asked to put down in my own words, who is Jesus of Nazareth for me. I said then I will not succeed with putting away the name after which I am called a Christian, even if I wanted to. This name will remain a measure, which I cannot escape and flee. Even when half the world would permit me to forget, the Jew might stand up and bind me back to this name. And I won't have to agree; I even hope I would do this with my whole heart because Jesus of Nazareth remains the basis and the measure of my life even when the measures do not fit anymore or well enough. And may I add, today, he, Jesus, binds me to the first commandment and still separates me from all the other gods, created again and again in this world: the false gods. Amen.

David G. Buttrick preached this sermon when he was professor of homiletics and liturgics at Vanderbilt Divinity School. For decades Buttrick was a dean of American homileticians. His large book Homiletic, *published in 1987, was a magisterial treatment of the art of preaching. In this sermon Buttrick defended a love for, and adaptation to, the secular world, basing his sermon on Jeremiah's words to the exiles of Israel. The sermon was heard by many as an attack on Dean Willimon's book (with Stanley Hauerwas)* Resident Aliens. *That book took the opposite view from Buttrick's. The secular world is the enemy, not the beloved friend.*

A Sermon at Duke University

October 15, 1995

DAVID G. BUTTRICK

Jeremiah 29:4–9   Here is the text of the letter that Jeremiah the prophet sent from Jerusalem to the leaders of the exiles, to the priests and the prophets, and to all the people whom Nebuchadnezzar had deported from Jerusalem to Babylon. "Thus says the Lord of Hosts, the God of Israel, to all the exiles whom I have exiled from Jerusalem to Babylon: Build houses and settle down; plant gardens and eat the produce; take wives and have sons and daughters; take wives for your sons and give your daughters to husbands, so they too may give birth to sons and daughters; multiply there, do not become few. Seek the welfare of the city where I've exiled you, and pray for it to the Lord, for in its welfare is your welfare. For thus says the Lord of Hosts, the God of Israel: Do not be deluded by the prophets and diviners who are among you. Do not listen to the dreams they get you to dream. In my name they are preaching a lie. I did not send them. Oracle of the Lord!"

Some years ago *Life* magazine published a pathetic picture. The picture showed an Arab prisoner of war standing behind barbed wire in a Middle Eastern prison camp. His clothes: a pair of shorts and battered canvas shoes. Around his neck on a chain was a large key, the key to a house in which he had once lived. He stood with his hands spread helplessly, saying, "How can I live here?" Well, nowadays the question seems to echo in our churches. "How can we live as displaced people in a secular land?" So listen to the prophet Jeremiah writing a letter to exiles. Listen, for perhaps he is writing the letter to us.

Exile: "Exile does seem to be a metaphor for Christians in America these days. We live as exiles in a secular land. Oh, once upon a time America was settled by true believers — Puritans in New England and Catholics down in Spanish Florida. In between there were the Dutch Reformed in New York City, German pietists in eastern Pennsylvania, and aristocratic Anglicans sprawled all over the state of Virginia. But now, to borrow Stephen Carter's phrase, we live in a "culture of disbelief." Church bells used to ring out on Sunday mornings, but now we've got champagne brunch in Durham's fashionable restaurants or stay-at-home, bathrobed breakfasts with the *New York Times* crossword puzzle. Once upon a time atheists had to rally to defend their position, but subtly times have changed and nowadays no one believes that God will come back to America any time soon. Exile: "How can we live in a secular land?" The question troubles us these days.

Well, listen to the voices all around; voices in our churches. "How do we live?" — there's no shortage of advice. Some Christians are still chasing the bright dream of religious revival. Every now and then *Time Magazine* does a feature on baby-boomer faith and our churches swoon! Or there's a rumor of charismatic laughter spreading in suburbs of Toronto, and church people here start listening for giggles. But somehow revival never seems to happen. Other Christians have joined a militant "Christian Coalition," eager to recapture the land from secularists by political power. Although you do wonder how an outfit that supports military spending, favors slashing welfare for the poor, wants an absolute ban on abortion, demands imposed prayer in schoolrooms, is anti-feminist, gay bashing, and eager for the death penalty can claim to speak for Jesus Christ. Of course, most churches are simply trying to hold onto themselves for dear life; survival is the name of the game. Did you see that Doonesbury cartoon some months ago? It showed an almost empty gothic church. Two little old ladies in a front pew with a decrepit old gentleman behind them. And in the pulpit, a young priest with an arm raised up, saying, "Our day will come again!" We laugh but not too loudly, because the promise does seem unlikely. Exiled in our own land. How can we live for the Lord in an alien secular world?

Jeremiah speaks. Jeremiah, the prophet, has a word for us. Listen: Build houses and settle down, plant your gardens and harvest them. Get wives, he writes, and breed children, yes, grandchildren and great-grandchildren. Look, even in exile we are in God's creation — a world filled with good things for human pleasure: Build your house, breed your young, feast on the harvest of earth. Notice you will not get Jeremiah to support Christian ghettos, even stained glass ghettos on Church Street, USA. For everywhere, yes, even in exile, we live in God's good creation, human beings with human beings on the earth together.

A new neighbor moved into our neighborhood. A corporate wife, she'd moved too many times in too few years. But she had a picture book with photos of all the houses she has had. In every picture there was the same table and always a flower garden. "I move in the same old kitchen table," she explained, "and then I plant my garden." Build and breed and feast on the earth. So Jeremiah writes to the exiles. Says Jeremiah to us, "Join the human world!" For everywhere is God's creation.

Now stop and ask a question: What prompts his faith? How can Jeremiah be sure he's handing out the word of God? Look how the letter is addressed: the Word of the Lord "to all the exiles whom I have exiled!" We talk of the secular world as if it rose up separate from God. But no, somehow God has been involved all along in shaping our exile. Was God delivering us from religious triumphalism? Perhaps. Or had God decreed that if we insisted on wandering from God's will we would end up in confusion, the strange confusion of unbelief? Maybe. But the secular world is still God's world, and incidentally a world God loves! So old Dr. Brown, a missionary leader, stood on a platform before the fledgling National Council of Churches and shouted his faith: "I do believe," he exclaimed, "beneath the surface of things moves the mighty current of God's eternal purpose." For heaven's sake, secularism began with the Protestant Reformation. In the mid-nineteenth century, it became an "ism." Secularism has spread, emptying churches all over Europe and now here in America. The secular world has been shaped by science, by industry and labor unions, universities and political parties, and yes, by churches. But God somehow has been involved in all. "To the exiles who I have exiled." The secular world is still very much God's world.

So, guess what, we can serve God in a secular age. "Seek the welfare of the city," sings Jeremiah, "Pray for the welfare of the land where you are." We cannot withdraw into our churches and pull the covers of faith over our heads. No, we are to be active in the worldly world working for the common good. So you will not devote yourself full time to a church school class, but also to the School Board. God knows, we need good schools for everybody's kids. And you do not simply be a Church leader, but work with secular people politically to plot a better world. The danger now is that Christians may clutch their Bibles and retreat into a safe, sweet, sheltered churchiness. No, we must speak the word of God to the world, the secular world in which we live. Speak to Congress — an irony: think of a hundred rich senators trying to legislate morality for the welfare poor. A double irony: think of churches saying nothing about it! A few years ago there was a big book of pictures done by Sunday school kids. In the middle of the book was a centerfold, a big picture of stick-figure people in pairs bending down toward each other like waiters waiting on tables, all over the pages. Underneath in crayon letters was a caption: "Kingdom of God." Every pagan place is still the kingdom and every moment a usefulness to neighbors. Work for the welfare of the city; pray for the welfare of the land.

So how do we live in a secular world, exiles in faith? We settle down, yes, and breed our children and work for the welfare of all. And we feast, yes, feast as the family of God, trusting in the providence that so surrounds our lives.

In the 1960s Duke Chapel began what was to become one of its most distinctive traditions; the annual student preacher. An undergraduate student was selected to preach on a Sunday in the Chapel after a campus-wide sermon competition. Aspiring preachers submitted sermons to a committee, usually on the assigned lectionary text. Patrick Clark, a senior who was active in campus religious life, preached this sermon, in which he interwove personal experience with the biblical text. Soon after preaching this sermon, Patrick became a Catholic, having received instruction at Duke, and then went on to graduate study in theology at Boston University.

Awaiting New Wine

February 27, 2000

PATRICK M. CLARK

Mark 2:13–22 Sometime during the late 1950s, when my mother was twelve or thirteen years old, she was baptized in a small Church of God in southern West Virginia. Here she dedicated her life to Christ, and accepted His call. On the first of September of last year in a hospital room in Seattle, her lungs were too bloody and ravaged by chemotherapy drugs to function any longer. Here she dedicated her death to Christ, and He accepted her home.

These two defining moments of her life Paul might refer to as her burial and resurrection — dying in her baptism and rising again through her faith in God's power to raise. Such a backward way to think of life — beginning with burial and ending with resurrection. It's hard to completely understand. Yet I sense Paul's words hold within them a clue to a puzzling thing my mother told me before she died.

She was in the hospital by this time, and was several days past her bone marrow transplant. One day as I was reading in the corner of the hospital room, she awoke and told me she wanted to talk with me. She wanted to discuss what life might be like if she should be gone. She probably knew that my fear forbade me to consider this topic on my own. I was full of protests and denials, and even swayed on the edge of tears in my resistance to her. Through all those barriers, however, one piece of that conversation still remains with me: she took my hand, looked at me with a motherly-warm firmness and said, "Patrick, I want you to know that even though I may not be cured of this disease, I have already been healed."

She said it like a creed, like a battle cry rising from a soldier already fallen. She held it in her voice like a treasure—a pearl swallowed up to keep away from the thieves. It was the way she said it that still burdens me. I've explained it away a hundred times over, but none of my solutions seems to quite capture the light that was in her eyes. What were those words and those eyes trying to say?

"Even though I may not be cured, I have already been healed." I tell you all of this, because I believe that Jesus says something to us today about healing and curing in the story that was just read. And in the cracks between my words, I pray that God might reveal it to us.

The story is set in the lake town of Capernaum in first-century Palestine. There swirled a rumor that a local lame man was dropped by his friends through a roof of a building in town, and that he walked out its door. Not only that, but they say his sins were forgiven as well. Those who heard about this man wondered which was the greater miracle—that he walked or that he was forgiven. We see already the traces of two sorts of restoration.

One of the men who must have heard of the rumor was Levi, a toll collector on one of the nearby roads. He must have been intrigued by what he heard, and especially by the questionable company Jesus kept—company like himself. Passing along one day, Jesus called him to follow with no justification or explanation—only the words "Follow me." What was it about Christ's eyes, or about His voice or about the way He moved that would jar Levi up from his table to follow Him? He had no diseases or handicaps, so what did Jesus have to offer him?

The Pharisees and doctors of the law—the religious right of that day—they were also perplexed with why Jesus chose Levi. "Why does he eat with tax collectors and sinners?" they said, "What kind of priest or prophet would concern himself with the rogues and the whores, with thieves and charlatans? A man truly of God would gravitate toward his own: the strong, the rich, the devout and the accepted. What was He trying to do with these sinners?"

Jesus told the Pharisees His reasons for keeping the company He kept, but as with so much, it seemed to escape their understanding. Jesus was challenging their conception of God, and was threatening their sense of security. Such a threat gave birth to reactionary condemnation: "Look! The righteous are fasting, even John's disciples are fasting, but you, you are here feeding your belly. Where is your purity that you can make others pure? What makes you worthy? Why don't you fit?"

Christ's justification is simply that He and His band of followers were celebrating. Jesus claimed that He and this shabby bunch of His, crammed into a dusty house eating an ordinary afternoon meal, were celebrating a wedding of which He was the bridegroom. Strange. I'm not sure I would have had the eyes to see the celebration there through the dust. Could it have really been more than just a meal at that table of sinners? Could it have really been the solemn and joyous commemoration of a coming victory and reunion? I'll have to leave that question to your eyes.

Jesus gives a further answer, however: "No one sews a patch of unshrunk cloth on an old garment and no one pours new wine into old wineskins." What does He mean? What do the two even have to do with one another? There's no answer key left behind for these questions. I can't really explain to you what this new wine is, but I also can't help but sense its burning importance. Could this new wine be that elusive thing we seek in the depths of our hearts? The object of that longing for which we can never find full description?

But where can we even start to look for it? Well, we can start with where we are—you most likely will see wine before you leave here today: this is Christ's blood, shed for you. If an unshrunk piece of cloth is sewed onto an old garment, or an old wineskin holds new wine, they both tear. Here we have common ground—in the tearing. Funny how Jesus gives us no notion of how to fix holes in old garments or how to use old wineskins—only how not to. He only speaks of tearing. It seems as if He cares more about describing the problems than the solutions.

All He gives us is a protest directed against the self-assured, whose hearts have been stiffened and narrowed by the rituals, laws, and methodical habits of their mapped-out faith. Jesus directs His protests not at the known sinners, but at the sinners in denial. Everyone in this story has empty places in their souls— both the pious and the thieves. All of us here today as well have useless wineskins lying empty inside us; we all have gaping holes in our heart's garment. Jesus tells us here merely what not to do with these places.

You see, the Pharisees' patch was religion, and the tax collectors covered themselves with wealth. We all have our own patches to cover the emptiness inside us. But those patches aren't good enough—they cannot hold the grace God intends. They lull us into a false security, and lead us away from true freedom, risk, fulfillment, and the keeping or saving of our souls. The world tells us today that if we want spiritual cleansing, we must go to a mountaintop, and stay away from the noise of the city where the homeless lie drunk and dying. Like the Pharisees, we want more to appear healed than to be healed. We would rather be freed from our weakness than by our weakness. Our nature tells us the lie that peace comes with a change of the external—more money, more security, more experiences—but Jesus warns us that filling the heart with things it was not made to contain will only tear it even more. He invites us to live a life without anaesthetic.

Jesus tells us here that problems of this world cannot be solved with solutions of this world. Our ways are not His ways. But our wounds are indeed His wounds, and by those wounds we are healed. Our hope is His presence within us, and the triumph of the cross, which that presence constantly proclaims. If we can gather up our wounds, our holes, our sin, and our pain and have the courage enough to simply wait in the silence, I believe the strength we need to hope for our healing will find us. If we could only trust enough to wait for the new wine, we might find that in our expectation, our empty wineskins may become new as well. This is the substance of our hope. We must cling to that hope. We must cling wildly to that hope.

On Friday, the 13th of August, I realized that my mother was sick beyond cure. Only a few strands of her hair remained, and I stood stroking them back as she looked at me with her eyes, now filled with blood. I sang her the alphabet song—ABCDEFG—like she used to sing it to me when I was in the bathtub, as she washed the shampoo from my hair, stroking it back. Her face lit up with joy in the midst of my tears, and she told me she remembered how she used to sing it to me. At that moment I first began to understand what she meant when she talked about the difference between curing and healing. As I fought through my fear of standing there, I felt healing begin to seep in. At such a painful farewell, there was strange joy, because I saw that she believed that, in her baptism, her sounds were no longer merely hers. They became trophies of her Redeemer's victory, and her goodbye became a celebration of grace. You see, death never really was the enemy. The real enemy is fear, the fear that the new wine will never come. But we are surrounded by a cloud of witnesses that urges us on in our expectation. I know my mother is in that cloud, and I am sure many of you know others there as well. They stand at the end of this hard journey, and they call to us from the feast of sinners at Christ's table.

You are invited to that table today. Come and see if your eyes can catch a passing glance of that celebration for which we wait.

L. Gregory Jones returned to Duke to become the eleventh dean of Duke Divinity School in 1997, having earned his PhD at Duke just a few years earlier. Dean Jones then led the Divinity School through a period of remarkable growth and development, making the school one of the premier theological schools in the nation. He is a renowned scholar, and his writings on theology and ethics, particularly the ethics of forgiveness, are widely acclaimed. As a frequent preacher in Duke Chapel, Dean Jones is a popular communicator of the gospel. This sermon, preached at the Founders Sunday celebration, weaves a biblical theme with a consideration of the university's mission.

We Do See Jesus

October 8, 2000

L. GREGORY JONES

We live in a world of people offering answers to unasked questions. We see it especially during a political campaign season when people—even as we are gathering here for worship—are appearing on the talk shows, where well-intentioned questioners on "Meet the Press" or "This Week" will ask a question to which the candidates or their spokespeople offer whatever they came to say, regardless of the question. Periodically a persistent questioner will repeat the question again, to which the spokesperson repeats what they came to say, regardless of the question.

But it is not only in political worlds where we run into those problems: it's also in the church where all too often people of faith offer answers regardless of the questions. We know what the answers are supposed to be, so we don't bother to listen to what the question is that's being asked.

One Sunday morning the pastor had gathered the children up at the front of the church for a time with the children. The pastor said to the children, "Now what I'm thinking of is brown, has a bushy tail, and gathers acorns around him every fall. What am I thinking of?"

After a period of silence, finally a little boy at the back raised his hand and he said, "I am sure the right answer is Jesus, but it sure sounds like a squirrel to me!" All too often we want to offer answers without attending to what the questions are. And yet we're gathered here this morning, in this Chapel and on this weekend in which we recall with thanksgiving the founding of Duke University. We have gathered because we believe that in some sense, the right answer is Jesus. And we need to try to ponder what the question and questions are to which that is the response. We gather in this Chapel because the founding of Duke University was predicated on, and the founders of Duke University were rooted in, the presumption that learning and faith go together. Eruditio et Religio.

And so it was with foresight and farsightedness that the Duke family wanted this glorious Chapel, which soars to the heights and lifts our imagination to God, to be at the center of the university geographically and also to be the heart of the university. And that the Divinity School would be geographically proximate to the Chapel, and the first professional school established. Because they had a conviction that knowledge and faith, when brought together, respond to the deepest questions. And when either is left separate from the other, it is to the detriment of both. I suspect that it wasn't simply because they lived in North Carolina in a time of a Protestant culture that they recognized the linkage of knowledge and faith. For we see even in this time and culture, when there are so many changes, the resilience of those questions that are coming back to us about how we understand the relationship between faith and knowledge. After all, St. Augustine put it well more than a millennium and a half ago: "Our hearts are restless until they find their rest in thee, O God."

We have tried over the course of the twentieth century in various and complex ways to find ways to avoid the intersection of faith and knowledge. We tried putting our faith in weapons, we tried putting our faith in technology, we tried putting our faith in consumer goods, we tried putting our faith in ourselves — yet each and every time we fall short and greater and greater destruction comes.

And so it is that on this weekend, we celebrate the founding and the founders, and the continuing commitment of the men and women of this university, to sustaining the questions at the heart of the intersection of faith and knowledge, of faith and learning. Eruditio et Religio. In our lesson from Hebrews this morning, we come to perhaps the most important question that could be raised, the question of the Psalmist, from Psalm 8, that the writer to the Hebrews lifts up and now puts into the context of his own letter: "What are human beings, that thou art mindful of them? Mortals that thou dost care for them?" What does it mean to be human? How do we understand human life? It's a basic question. In some ways a very simple and straightforward question, and yet it addresses the greatest complexities that we face. In recent months we have discovered how to map the human genome, and even as we look forward to all the advances in knowledge that this knowledge provides and the hope for therapies and other interventions that could make our life better, that could help us with the environment, we also know the dangers that this knowledge presents. It is dangerous unless we continue to ask the question, "What are human beings, that thou are mindful of them? Mortals that thou dost care for them?"

In the Divinity School's Institute on Care at the End of Life, we grapple with that question as we look at people who are in their dying days, whether in a neonatal ward or at the end of a long life, struggle and face the fear of isolation and the abandonment of others. They wonder whether they are any longer a human being, because they are no longer a productive consumer. They are no longer able to work. Or because the pain seems like it could be overwhelming. We try to bring people together to look at the question of how to care faithfully and effectively for others at the end of life — we do so because we believe that human beings are made for relationship with God and with one another.

Studies have shown that after pain management, after wanting to find a way to control the pain in their dying days, the second thing they want most is peace with God, a sense of spiritual completion and a sense of reconciliation with God and with their families and loved ones.

Universities are great places to sustain the question of what human beings are like. And when we do it in a context that opens up the horizons of who God is, and how God is related to the world and why we were created in the image and likeness of God, we uncover an opportunity to bring together advances in research with humane care that nurtures our lives and sustains us with hope.

"What are human beings, that thou art mindful of them? Mortals that thou dost care for them?" The Psalmist has put the context of what it means to be human in relation to God in a majestic way. But notice how often we turn the question of what it means to be human into a source of cynicism. Somebody's caught with pornography and what's their excuse? "Well, after all, I'm only human." Somebody's caught dumping toxic waste into a river without any regard for the people who live down the river, much less succeeding generations. And what do they say? "Well, after all, I'm only human." People abuse and destroy other people and they say, "Well, after all, we're only human."

Why don't we look at the people whose lives truly are a little lower than the angels — people who live good and holy lives? Why don't we look at them and say, "Well, after all, they're only human?" Why don't we look at a Benjamin Newton Duke, who despite his own physical frailty worked so hard for Duke University, who never turned away a needy Methodist preacher, who supported children's homes and hospitals and even in the

1920s was reaching out and supporting black colleges in a time when that would have been unthinkable to so many? Why don't we look at his life and say, "Well, after all, he's only human"? Why don't we look at the mother working the second or the third shift to try to save up enough money to send her daughter to college, so that she can be the first generation to go to college and have a sense of hope for a better life, of the expansive ways in which learning and faith can go together to create a better world? Why don't we look at that mother and say, "Well, after all, she's only human"?

Too often in universities as well in other settings, we turn the question of what human beings are like into a refuge for cynicism, rather than as an opportunity to sustain communities of hope. Of discovering ways to connect a love of learning and the desire for God that becomes manifested in care for other people both near and far. "What are human beings that thou art mindful of them? Mortals that thou dost care for them?" The writer to the Hebrews does indeed end up answering that question by saying the right answer is Jesus. But he does it in a very rich and complex way. In the context of asking the fundamental question, he then says we don't see everything. The world is so complex. As this university is complex—people are off studying the most minute scientific data at the same time that people are reading Dante's *Paradiso*.

The writer to the Hebrews says we have the confidence that it all holds together in Christ. As the writer puts it, "We do see Jesus." And in seeing Jesus we see a way to live through the questions and to sustain ourselves even in the midst of all that we do not know. We do see Jesus. We need that sense of learning how to see well, even amidst the questions. Simply to understand some of the moves that the writer to the Hebrews makes occupies a lot of our attention over in Divinity School classrooms. Learning the Hebrew of Psalm 8 and the Greek of the opening verses of Hebrews and the ways in which the rhetorical beauty of those passages can't really be translated. But then to look at those opening words. "God spoke to our ancestors in many and various ways by the prophets, and in the last days has spoken to us through the Son." How do you understand what it means to see Jesus in that way? To understand the complex relationship between this passage and other passages in the Old Testament and the New Testament, and how to see Christ as the fulfillment of the hopes of Israel without displacing Israel in the kinds of ways that lead to destruction?

It takes time and study. Then when you are presented with the interrelation of the passages for this morning, we do see Jesus in conjunction with that difficult passage from Job, which President Keohane read a few moments ago. Job points us to all the suffering in the world, indeed what some

333

would describe as deeper than suffering — a sense of affliction. Of the pain of the separation that comes from the most acute isolation. Affliction names Job's isolation, sitting out on the ash heap wondering why he was being cast aside. It names those times in all of our lives when darkness seems to overwhelm us, when we are afflicted and feeling despair and isolated, wondering if there is anyone who cares. Have you ever thought of the miracle that is a hospital where people care for those who are in intense suffering? It is a miracle that we remain present to others — we don't simply abandon people. Nurses and physicians and clergy and families and care givers go and are present and sit and hold hands and sing and pray with people, even when a cure is not possible.

The writer to the Hebrews says we see Jesus perhaps in the midst of suffering. That the glory and honor of Christ is not a glory and an honor of simply discovering that you've won an esteemed academic prize or that you have pride of place in a great university. That glory and honor is found also in solidarity with all those who suffer. And maybe even that very difficult gospel passage this morning about divorce is at least in part an attempt to point out that in a world in which we are so prone to perpetuating brokenness and division and destructiveness, God's intention is for reconciliation — for faithfulness. For finding ways to bring people together in communion. A vision of us connecting with one another that we see Jesus in the miracles of people forgiving and reconciling, of people giving and receiving hospitality. When in the midst of pain we continue to offer presence to one another.

The questions are real. And at their heart they have to do with who human beings are and what it means to be mindful of them. The assurance that we have in this Chapel is that God has created us in God's own image and likeness. And that God in Christ has forgiven us and set us free from all that binds and divides and destroys for the sake of bringing us together to care for one another. To reach out to one another.

And that is at the heart of this university which, over seventy-five years as Duke University and drawing on the previous legacy of Trinity College, has insisted on a convergence of both an outrageous ambition and an extravagant faithfulness that brings learning and faith together for the sake of the pursuit of that truth which heals, which redeems, which liberates.

We do see Jesus whenever we see human beings who are living faithful lives. Who are seeking truth above self-interest. Who are reaching out to others. This weekend even as we remember all that has been accomplished over seventy-five years, we also celebrate a gift that has been given in part to help further Duke's relationship with the community of Durham. To reach out in service to a community nearby even as we also seek to be of service throughout the world. We do see Jesus in the work that goes on in the laboratories, in the seminar rooms, in the ways in which graduates go forth from this place to serve and make this a better world. And it's no accident that the heart of this university should be a Chapel and a Divinity School that emulate the university's motto, Eruditio et Religio.

Seventy-five years ago, when the Duke family established the indenture that created Duke University, they also formally maintained the strong linkage to the Methodist Church. Over the years, Methodists have cared deeply about education. And some of our sister institutions around the world have trained and educated some of the greatest people of the last century. My wife Susan and I were privileged to go to South Africa this summer as part of the Divinity School's efforts to establish a partnership with churches in South Africa. While we were there, we traveled to some of the places where Methodist institutions of higher education had been founded. They were places that educated some of the greatest people who have transformed South Africa. People like Robert Sobukwa, Peter Storey, and Nelson Mandela. The apartheid government saw that these Methodist institutions were a challenge to their unjust ideals because they represented that bringing together of faith and learning and justice that would be a risk. And so they shut down those schools and confiscated their land. And it was with pain that we looked at the police complexes and the commercial institutions that had been thrown up on land that had been previously devoted to Methodist institutions of education. But then we went and we saw some instances of what the Methodists now call the "chain of hope." Over the last several years, the Methodist church of Southern Africa has started more than sixty preschools in and around Johannesburg. They have done so as a way of re-establishing their commitment to education, preschools in the churches that bring together faith and learning for the youngest of children in the conviction that we cannot afford any more cynicism but we need to be establishing communities of hope. We went to see that "chain of hope," preschools in some large churches and also in some of the townships. In one township of Ivory Park, every time they start a new congregation to worship God, they simultaneously start a preschool and they also start a program of economic empowerment. A Chain of Hope. As we visited one of those preschools, the pastor said to me, "I'd like to come to the United States and study because some of the questions we're trying to address about leadership and about the future of the church and the future of education are questions that really need complex study. I hope we will be able to do that." They recognize what's at stake.

We are blessed at Duke to have had visionary founders and men and women of extraordinary leadership over seventy-five years who have been committed to furthering the linkage of faith and learning.

Why do you think Nelson Mandela has been such a powerful leader? Well, after all, he's only human. Why would these people establish these preschools and this chain of hope in the midst of so much suffering? Well, after all, they're only human.

"What are human beings that Thou dost care for them?"

In the midst of our lives, let us ourselves aspire to the true humanity that we see glimpsed in Jesus Christ. In faithfulness to God that our learning and our living might always cultivate a community of hope because . . . we do indeed see Jesus.

This year Ellen Davis, professor of Old Testament and preaching at the Divinity School, gave the prestigious Beecher Lectures at Yale Divinity School. In those lectures Davis stressed the need to combine a close reading of the biblical text with a willingness to be astonished by the text. She embodies that creative interpretation in this Epiphany sermon. Why were these magi, who first worshipped at the manger, filled with such joy? What epiphany led them to such jubilation? Might it be a joy that is contagious to our time and place?

Stargazers

January 5, 2003

ELLEN F. DAVIS

Matthew 2:1–12 "Seeing the star stop, the Magi were wildly happy" — but why? This is what I want to explore with you today: what lay behind the Magi's joy that night? Because, when you stop to think about it, there is no obvious reason those astrologers from the East should have been so wildly excited. They had not seen anything that ordinary eyes would interpret as a revelation of God. They had seen a star rising in the East, a tiny point of bright light. And because they were trained to take the heavenly bodies very, very seriously, they followed it, probably hundreds of miles: from Mesopotamia (the ancestral home of astrologers) across the northern edge of the Syrian desert, down into Roman Palestine, until they got to the little and not-obviously-distinguished city of Bethlehem. Then that star somehow led them through the maze of narrow streets and stopped over one particular house. (The Evangelist Luke envisions a stable, of course, but for Matthew it's just an ordinary house.) And at that point those Magi "rejoiced with a really, really big joy," as the Gospel literally reads. "And coming into the house, they saw the child with Mary his mother; and falling down, they worshipped him." Those highly educated foreigners, distinguished enough to be summoned for a private consultation with King Herod — they were the very first ones to worship our Lord. "And opening their treasures, they presented him" with tribute fit for a king: gold, frankincense, and myrrh. They took that baby for the real article, "the one born king of the Jews," whose birth prophets had foretold — yet remember, they had heard no angel choir (again, that's in Luke's Gospel). All Matthew's Magi saw was an ordinary Jewish mother with her baby. And even if we agree (as I suspect we would) that there is simply no such thing as an ordinary baby; and even if we imagine further that Jesus was maybe an especially beguiling infant (why not?) — even so, this birth would seem, to ordinary eyes, to be a small-scale wonder of God.

So my question is this: How, having seen so little that was identifiably the fulfillment of God's promises — how they could feel so much joy? That may be something more than an idle question, because it seems to me that for many of us (and I include myself), joy in Christ has more the status of a pious wish than a deeply felt reality. And I wonder how those Magi — who knew so much less than any one of us knows about the life, death, and resurrection of this one born king of the Jews — I wonder how they felt something that I, with all my theological education, feel all too little: that really, really big joy in the Christ child. I think the answer must be this: the Magi had mastered the art of hoping in God. It is a saying in the book of Proverbs that leads me to draw that connection between joy and hope. I think it is the boldest teaching on hope in the whole Bible. Listen: "The hope of the righteous is gladness" (Proverbs 10:28). Their hope is gladness — the saying is so bold that one very popular translation changes it into something more cautious and commonsensible. The NRSV renders it, "The hope of the righteous ends in gladness." Now that's a very reasonable idea; it makes sense that the righteous will in the end be rewarded by actually getting what they hope for. But the proverb as it stands says a lot more about people like our Magi. "The hope of the righteous is gladness" — already now, in the present tense. Those who train their sights on the faithfulness of God, "the righteous" — they already experience joy, even before they see their hopes fulfilled, even if they never live to see (in this world, at least) the clear fulfillment of all that God has promised. The righteous are those who trust God so much that they have learned, as the Apostle Paul says, to "rejoice in hope" itself (Romans 12:12). That is the kind of joy that burst forth that night on the streets of Roman-occupied Bethlehem, like flowers springing suddenly out of stone pavement. It was joy that takes root in nothing more (or less) substantial than hope itself.

Epiphany is the great season of the Church's hope. In this season, all the prayers and Scripture readings aim at nurturing our hope — indeed, at helping us learn the art (because it is an art) of hoping in God. And so it makes perfect sense, when you think about it, that the ones to usher in this season should be Magi, stargazers, for they were masters of an art that opened their minds toward a world beyond our own. That is of course the essence of all true hope: stretching our minds and our faith beyond the confines of what we can clearly see and touch and control.

Therefore the message we get today and in the weeks to come is not one that magnifies our sense of control. The message of Epiphany is not "God is born in Christ, and all's well with this old world." Thank God that's not the intended message. Looking at our world, who would believe it? The message is not even "Jesus is born, and all's well with us who believe in him." Thank God that's not the message. Looking into our own hearts, who even among us would believe it? Rather, this is the message of Epiphany: "Jesus the Christ is born into our world, and for us who believe in him, there is a clear focus for our hope." Like the Magi who saw his star rise in the East and followed it, we Christians are stargazers, discerning a bright point of light in the darkness and following it as we travel a long and unfamiliar road, guided by the light of the one born king of the Jews.

I think of the people I know who radiate most powerfully what I see as "the joy of Christ"; all of them are, in a sense, stargazers. They are adept at the art of looking into the darkness, finding the one bright point of light that leads to God, and orienting their lives toward it. Two of the people who have been sharing their joy with me most consistently over the last year or so — one of them has been enduring rigorous treatment for cancer; the other is nursing her husband in an advanced state of Alzheimer's. In both cases their joy has much less to do with present circumstances or doctors' prognoses than it does with their continued ability to experience God as faithful, true to the promise of abundant life given in Jesus Christ. In situations that are uncertain and difficult on a daily basis, they nurture a bright hope that often bursts out as a flame of joy and laughter. Thus they attest to the truth of St. Paul's teaching that in the characters of the faithful, there is a real connection between enduring suffering and hoping in God (Romans 5). Christian hope is something very different from the natural feeling of elation that comes when things are going our way. No, hope is not a feeling that ebbs and flows. Rather, it is a way of living that we choose; and gradually, day by day, we learn to be graceful in it. Hope is a way of living beyond our own limited vision and natural fears, a way of living into God's faithfulness and there finding fullness of joy forevermore.

Within his brief account of the Magi, Matthew gives us a thumbnail sketch of King Herod, and their intertwined stories show how hope opposes and ultimately, by God's grace, faces down evil — and not only natural evil, like cancer or Alzheimer's, but also the worst human evil, exemplified by Herod, who was not, you know, a real king of the Jews. He was a foreigner, a puppet king set up by the Romans, an Idumean pretender to the throne of David. When Herod heard about the one whose star had risen in the East, "the one born king of the Jews," he felt his unstable throne shake beneath him. He could read that sign as well as the Magi; it meant that his own days were numbered. So, consumed with fear, Herod launched a desperate new security program. First he tried a closely targeted operation, a "smart bomb"; he tried to get the Magi to give him the baby's exact whereabouts. But when the Magi evaded him, then Herod settled for a general slaughter, killing every child in and around Bethlehem, two years old and under.

History remembers Herod with special loathing. He was a ruthless despot, who did not scruple at murdering his close associates, and the wife on whom he doted, and three of his own sons, because he feared they were plotting against him. It was said of Herod in his own day that it was better to be his sow than his son (Alan Hugh M'Neile, *The Gospel of Saint Matthew*, 1955); the pig in the royal barnyard had a better hope of survival. Yet even if Herod didn't have a friend in the world, or a trusted ally, nevertheless he had companionship in his fear. Matthew's observation is telling: "Herod was terrified, and all Jerusalem with him." Herod could not have secured the deaths of all those children, if he were the only one who was afraid. Matthew is pointing to the clearly documented fact that fear is contagious, and it readily crosses party lines. When fear reaches epidemic proportions, as it did that year in Jerusalem, then it inevitably unleashes destruction on a massive scale. "Herod was terrified, and all Jerusalem with him." Fear spreads like plague through an unhealthy system, infecting not only those who are powerless to defend themselves — the Jewish families in Bethlehem — but also infecting the relatively powerful, the ruling élite in Jerusalem, who sensed (with that gut-gripping fear that comes in the middle of the night) the fragility of the base on which their power rested.

So Matthew is giving us an artful picture of two opposed entities: on the one hand Herod and all Jerusalem, and on the other the Magi, following the promise of God and one bright point of light as they travel in a country not their own. But the gospel story is artful — and more, it is revelatory — because both halves of the picture tell us something about ourselves. This is not a simple picture of them and us, as we would prefer to believe. Rather, if we read the story deeply and honestly, I think we will identify both with fearful Jerusalem and with hopeful Magi; for they both reveal aspects of our own situation that we have not seen clearly before.

In the fear that grips "all Jerusalem," we see an image of the fear that has grown insidiously to become such a dominant factor in our own public life. Columbine, the Washington sniper, the Twin Towers, global warming, decline in the Dow Jones, Al Qaeda, Saddam Hussein, North Korea — it is a dread litany, highlighting but not exhausting all that we as a people have come to fear, at home and abroad. Like "all Jerusalem," we are afraid even while we are still powerful. We are preparing for war because we are afraid, and because we are powerful. Yet we know that on the other side of that violence, we, like Herod, will have no less to fear than we do now.

So there is judgment for us in that picture of Herod and all Jerusalem. Matthew holds it before us like a mirror, challenging us to acknowledge our fear, to recognize the violence that springs from fear and will doubtless perpetuate it. Yet Matthew does not consign us to despair. For alongside that mirror is a second one — you might call it a glass of vision, for it shows us something a little ahead of where we are now. It shows what we as a church can and will look like if we stand against the tyranny of self-perpetuating fear. We will look like the Magi. For those first worshippers of Christ are, of course, the very first biblical image of the church. Look at them: those three travelers in a country not their own, in a land literally governed by fear. Yet in that country, they constitute a very small but powerful community of resistance. Their hope empowers their refusal to be co-opted by Herod's reign of terror. "The hope of the righteous is gladness"; having experienced the surpassing joy of Bethlehem and knowing it came from God, the Magi listened to the dream that also came from God and warned them not to return to Herod. Instead they "departed by another road for their own country."

Matthew is showing us a way forward in this Epiphany season, this season of hope in which we are gripped by fear. He challenges us to be the community of resistance that the church has been, he tells us, from the beginning. He challenges us as a church to examine and deepen our understanding of the systems that generate fear for ourselves and others. He challenges us as a church to find ways out of those systems — not to despair, though the systems are large and powerful, but to find and commit ourselves to the small steps by which we may depart from the country governed by fear and go by another road to our own country, that place we call the kingdom of God. Matthew's Gospel challenges us to live boldly in the hope of the Magi, so that having rejoiced with them at the first coming of Christ, we may at his second coming know fullness of joy forevermore. Amen.

Fleming Rutledge once published a book of her sermons, Between the Bible and
the New York Times. *The title of that collection typifies much of her preaching.
She begins with the Bible, taking it as the authoritative, challenging word, then
she moves to a sermon that is as contemporary as today's headlines in the* Times.
*She is an Episcopal priest, a strong, evangelical Christian communicator of the
gospel, and a frequent visitor to the pulpit of Duke Chapel. She preached this sermon during the first days of the war with Iraq. Not everyone in the congregation
that morning agreed with her strong word, but everyone knew it was a biblical
word from a preacher who is passionately committed to being biblical.*

The Enemy Lines Are Hard to Find

Third Sunday in Lent 2003
March 16, 2003

FLEMING RUTLEDGE

Psalm 19 — Who can tell how often he offends? Cleanse Thou me from my
secret faults.
Romans 11:32 — God has consigned all men to disobedience, that he may have
mercy upon all.
I Peter 3:18 — For Christ also died for sins once for all, the righteous for the
unrighteous, that he might bring us to God.

A friend of mine who is a child psychologist told me about something one of
her young patients said. It is common practice to give toys to children in the
treatment room so they work out their conflicts through play. This particular little boy was given toy soldiers, which he laid out and began to deploy.
After he had done this for a while, he looked across his little battlefield with
a puzzled expression and said, "The enemy lines are hard to find."

In late 1944, while the allies were rapidly advancing across Europe after
the success of the Normandy invasion, J. R. R. Tolkien, the author of *The
Lord of the Rings,* wrote a letter to his son Christopher, who was serving in
the R.A.F. (the British Royal Air Force). Tolkien himself, the father, had
fought the Germans in World War I; he was in the infamous trenches of the
Battle of the Somme. These were not pacifists, in other words. The father
wrote to the son that he was very disturbed by the way the British press
was relentlessly depicting all Germans as irremediably evil. One of his local

papers was seriously advocating "systematic extermination" of the entire German nation because "they are rattlesnakes and don't know the difference between good and evil." *What of the writer?* "The Germans have just as much right to declare . . . the Jews exterminable vermin, subhuman, as we have to select the Germans: in other words, no right, whatever they've done" (*The Letters of J. R. R. Tolkien*, 93).

In other words, whenever a person takes to himself (or herself) the defining of another person or group as evil, he is in more danger than he knows. It is in the very nature of the human being to judge other people and groups as evil. We can then give ourselves permission to treat those others as less than fully human, to ostracize them or persecute them and eventually to destroy them. And once we have begun that game, it takes on a life of its own and it begins to dominate us without our even noticing.

Who decides who is evil and who is not? Two weeks ago, a *New York Times* article told of some Afghan boys who were displaced by the American bombing. (There will be a TV documentary about this on the Discovery Channel on March 25.) The boys are now living in Karachi, Pakistan — if you can call it living. The children in this particular news story live in the garbage dumps. They are paid pennies to pick through the rotting food, broken glass, and discarded syringes to salvage items to sell. They are indescribably filthy and smelly, and they are hungry much of the time. What is their hope? Their hope is the *madrasas* — the Muslim religious schools. We all know now, if we did not before, that many of these schools in Pakistan are run by hard-line extremists, and they were the breeding ground for the Taliban. (According to the article, about 40 percent of the ten thousand *madrasas* in Pakistan are moderate; 60 percent are run by the hard-line Deobandi sect.) The *Times* reporter interviewed some of these Afghan refugee boys at the garbage dump. They are thrilled at the possibility of being taken as students by one of the *madrasas*. They said, "We'll get free food and clothing. It will make us very happy." The reporter asked them what they thought of Americans. "They are very cruel to us," said Muhammed, one of the boys. "They kill our people." Another boy named Shaheen said, "I want America to be finished. They destroyed Afghanistan. They bombed the whole country" (*New York Times*, March 7, 2003).

It is an easy matter to teach children who is evil and who is not. I have another article in my files from a few years ago, when the Albanians fleeing from Kosovo were in Macedonian camps by the hundreds of thousands. A father was catechizing his young son about the Serbs. "Who are our enemies?," asked the father. The child seemed confused, so the father answered for him. "The Serbs are our enemies! They killed our people!" he trumpeted;

"and what will you do when you grow up?" This time the boy was ready. "I will kill the filthy Serbs!" he answered. The father was very pleased with his son.

One day it's the Germans, the next day it's the Serbs, today it seems to be the French. The enemy lines are hard to find. We should remember that the *madrasas* were financed in part by the U.S. government during the '80s when the Afghans were fighting the Soviets, and then we left Afghanistan to the tender mercies of the Taliban. The axis of evil lies here, there, and everywhere. Václav Havel, recently retired as president of the Czech Republic, wrote that during the rule of Soviet communism in Czechoslovakia, there were so many everyday acts of compromise on the part of so many people that it became impossible to tell who was a collaborator and who was not. These are his words: "The line [between good and evil] did not run clearly between 'them' and 'us,' but through each person. No one was simply a victim; everyone was in some measure co-responsible . . . Many people were on both sides" (Timothy Garton Ash, "The Truth about Dictatorship," *New York Review of Books*, February 19, 1998, 36–37). Alexsandr Solzhenitsyn says almost exactly the same thing in *The Gulag Archipelago*: "Gradually it was disclosed to me that the line separating good and evil passes not through states, nor between classes, nor between political parties either—but right through every human heart. . . . This line shifts. Inside us, it oscillates with the years. And even within hearts overwhelmed by evil, one small bridgehead of good is retained. And even in the best of all hearts there remains . . . an uprooted small corner of evil" (part iv, chapter 1).

The season of Lent reminds the Christian community that the line runs through you and the line runs through me. It reminds us to beware of drawing lines between ourselves on the good side and others on the bad side. Those of you who were fortunate to be in church on Ash Wednesday will know what I mean when I say that reading Psalm 51 together on our knees, as we do on that day, is a very powerful act. We are acknowledging the truth about ourselves. In the words of that Psalm, "I know my transgressions, and my sin is ever before me." In the words of our Psalm for today, "Who can tell how often he offends? Cleanse Thou me from my secret faults."

When we cannot hear such things about ourselves without bristling and becoming defensive, we are in trouble. When we are unable to utter a sincere apology and ask for forgiveness, our primary relationships are in trouble. When a nation treats dissent as unpatriotic, the whole world is in trouble. Repentance, the Lenten theme, is necessary for human well-being. Our leaders in former times seemed to know this. Our two greatest presidents, George Washington and Abraham Lincoln, both called the nation to repentance. It is hard to imagine any president of either political party doing that today.

I recently read an article about repentance by Frederica Mathewes-Green, a well-known writer on Christian themes. She grabbed my attention with a new definition. "Repentance is not blubbering and self-loathing. Repentance is insight" ("Whatever Happened to Repentance?," *Christianity Today*, February 4, 2002).

Repentance is insight. Repentance is not groveling. I'm sure you will recall that many people were turned off when Trent Lott seemed to be groveling. Moreover, repentance is quite a different thing from saying "I'm sorry if anyone was offended" a dozen times. Repentance involves trying to understand *why* people were offended, *why* people were hurt, *why* people would like to hear a true and sincere apology, and why we ourselves have been offenders. "Who can tell how often he offends? Cleanse Thou me from my secret faults."

Repentance means insight. That's what Tolkien meant in his letter to his son when he said, "What of the writer?" He meant that the newspaper editor lacked insight. He was so quick to label others as evil that he did not understand his own inclinations. That's the problem with the headlines that stir up readers to easy identification of Saddam as evil, and his sons as evil. That makes it so easy for us. We relish looking at the evil of *others* because it distracts us from the need to examine *ourselves*, a much more difficult task. I wonder if you have seen the movie *The Pianist*. In my opinion it is the best movie ever made about the Holocaust. Among other things, it raises the question in the most acute way: What would I have done if I had been there? I have never seen a movie that illustrated so vividly the way that the line between good and evil becomes blurred under pressure. This movie offers insight.

Two weeks ago I was preaching in another church and I mentioned the book by former Senator Bob Kerrey in which he tells how when he was in Vietnam he got swept up into a massacre of women and children. Reflecting on this later, he wrote, "I did not recognize the person I had become." A man came up to me afterward and said that he had had the same feeling about himself. He too was a Vietnam veteran. He had been a door gunner in a helicopter, a position which, I am told, is very dangerous. He told me that he was sure he had killed as many women and children as Kerrey had, though from a bit of a distance. More important, he said he had felt a rage and hatred within himself that he had not known was there. His exact words were, "It scared the hell out of me." He meant that he was more afraid of his own impulses than he was of being in the door of the helicopter.

The paradox of this is that when a Christian makes a confession like that in the context of the Christian community, though it is deeply sobering, it is also liberating. We make our confessions in the secure embrace of the gospel. What is the gospel? Listen to this verse from St. Paul's letter to the Romans: "God has consigned all human beings to disobedience, that he may have mercy upon all."

All of us share in the human condition; that is the meaning of Lent. All of us have dark impulses that could have become murderous had we been brought up in a garbage dump or been catechized by a father full of hate and revenge. Who knows if Saddam's sons are evil? Do you know? How do you know? Who told you? And if they are evil, who knows what influences made them evil? Let me be clear: action has to be taken against evil deeds. But the Christian will beware lest more evil deeds begin to erupt *from within* as well as from without.

It is God's plan to have mercy upon us. He *has consigned all human beings to disobedience, that he may have mercy upon all.* The epistle of Peter puts it another way: *Jesus Christ also died for sins once for all, the righteous for the unrighteous, that he might bring us to God.* The righteous died for the unrighteous: that is to say, he, the only truly righteous one, died for the *un*righteous. And again Paul: "While we were still helpless, Christ died for the ungodly" (Romans 5:6).

The one great mistake we could make today is to think of ourselves in the wrong category. The Lord Jesus did not die for the righteous. He did not die for the godly. He did not die for the exceptional so that we, the saved, could delight in our own superiority and gloat over others. The Bible teaches us to see ourselves as God sees us. Suppose you and I were at the mercy of what our enemies think of us. Thanks be to God, the ultimate destiny of human beings is not to be determined by enemies. We live and die at the mercy of God, "to whom all hearts are open, all desires known, and from whom no secrets are hid." "Cleanse Thou me from my secret faults, O God."

God sees you as you really are and He loves you. God sees those parts of you that you hide even from yourself and He loves you. God sees us all dividing up the world into good and evil but He, the only One entitled to divide the evil from the good, the One who could have remained enthroned above our struggles, out of His love came into the world to be "numbered among the transgressors" (Isaiah 53:12). Through His Son Jesus Christ He has entered into our condition, bowing His head under the onslaught of human vengefulness, indifference, cruelty, and hate in order to show mercy to us all, *especially to the perpetrators.*

He died the death of an outcast, He died the death of a condemned man, He died the death of one who was declared an enemy of all the righteous of the state and of the church. With the last breath of His body and the last drop of His blood He has wrought the salvation *of His enemies*, that is to say, the salvation of each and every one of us. Amen.

After this sermon, Barbara Brown Taylor, an Episcopal priest and one of the most popular of Duke Chapel's guest preachers, said to me, "I fear that my sermon was too weird for them." Not too weird at all. It was a wonderfully engaging, vivid exposition of a strange biblical text, a creative linking of one biblical image—Moses' lifting up of the serpent in the wilderness—with another—Jesus' being "lifted up" on the cross. Weaving a sermon out of the assigned lectionary texts for the fourth Sunday in Lent—John 3 and Numbers 21—Brown Taylor gave us quite a sermon on a Savior who saves in ways that we do not always find congenial with our expectations for salvation.

The Snake Savior

March 30, 2003

BARBARA BROWN TAYLOR

John 3

Come Holy Ghost, our souls inspire. Enlighten us with your celestial fire.

It's always a toss-up on a Sunday morning, whether to take one hour off from what's happening in the world or whether to bring the world into this hour, in hopes of finding some holiness in it, calling some holiness down upon it, any sign of God's presence will do in this wilderness of our own making where we humans never seem to run out of the energy or the zeal for digging new graves.

I'm going to split the difference between those two this morning and talk about snakes, which until just a few years ago rated as the thing that Americans feared the very most. It's almost sweet, isn't it? That, that recently, that long ago, the things that Americans were most afraid of were not exploding airplanes or chemical weapons attacks or the collapse of their 401(k) plans but ordinary, old-timey reptiles? In a Harris poll of 1999, 36 percent of all adults in the United States identified snakes as their worst fear. Worse than heights. Worse than spiders. Worse than speaking in public. Making ophidiophobia, remember that for the next time you're on "Jeopardy," the number one fear in America. And yes, there were gender differences: 49 percent of all women polled said that they were scared to death of snakes, while 22 percent of men said the same thing. Whether you write that off to Eve or to

Freud, you have to leave room for women like me who are perfectly happy with snakes as long as we are not surprised by them.

Every year around this time, when the hay in my hay loft is getting really low but the horses are still demanding to be fed, I approach the bales that are left up there with a little more caution than usual. Because I know that sooner or later, I'm going to lift a bale with a very long snakeskin attached to it. Last year it was over a yard long, with a little inside-out snake face at one end of it and a little tail cone at the other. So far the snake has always been gone by the time I got there. But I remain exquisitely aware of its presence. Because I know that it's still around there somewhere.

Last fall I watched it sunning itself on the bottom rail of the paddock fence, a fat, satisfied-looking black snake, with a little barn mouse–sized lump about a third of the way down. My snake is a good snake, in other words, as opposed to the southern copperheads and timber rattlers that I've also seen around my place. Most of my neighbors don't bother with such fine distinctions, however. As far as they are concerned, snakes are snakes, and preemptive strikes aren't even debatable. You see a snake. You reach for a garden hoe. It's that simple. The only good snake is a dead snake.

Some scientists apparently think it has something to do with evolution, that since snakes have been dangerous to humans for as long as both of us have been around, that we humans have developed a kind of snake-hating gene that makes us natural enemies. Now I don't know about that. Especially since many children I know seem to be very curious about snakes, at least until their parents teach them to scream when they see one. But I do know that whatever this thing is, between humans and snakes, has been going on a really long time.

Take this morning's story about the poisonous serpents from the book of Numbers, for instance. Now that's an old story, but it's not as old as Egyptian stories about the hooded cobra on Pharaoh's crown who spit venom on his enemies, or the Samarian legends about Ningizida, the god of healing, who walked around with two snakes on a staff, before anyone ever heard of the American Medical Association. Asclepius, the Greek god of healing, only carried one snake on his staff, but then he could turn into a snake as well. Snakes show up in the ancient iconographies of India, China, Africa, and the Americas, as well as those of the Middle East and Europe. Half the time, they show up as saviors—guardians of some kind. And the other half of the time, they show up as demons, which may have less to do with snakes themselves than with the various ways in which human beings respond to them. We simply don't know what to do with creatures that inspire such a wide range of feelings. I mean, it's hard not to admire a creature who can travel six miles per hour without feet. And who can climb trees without hands. The skin shedding business is also a major fascination, especially for those of us who are carrying around enough dead cells of our own—to long for new life.

At the same time, it's hard not to fear a creature that can bring you down with one bite, even if you did not mean to step on it, even if you apologize every way you know how while you're waiting for the venom to reach your heart. Snakes have teeth. They live underground in the dark and plenty of them only come out at night, which makes them powerful symbols of the human unconscious. Any of you who've spent much time in therapy probably already know this—take a snake dream to a therapist and stand back. You're about to discover way more about your depth than you may want to know.

All in all, I find that most of us prefer soft, safe creatures, like young bunnies. But bunnies don't show up in any depth lexicon that I know about. They're just not complicated enough. They're just not dangerous enough to have captured the human imagination. There are no bunnies in the Bible. I checked. But there are snakes, which show up just as paradoxically as you might expect.

At the same time that Moses was ushering the people who worshipped YHWH through the wilderness of the Negev, other people who worshipped the thunder god Baal were gazing upon statues of Baal or his consort, a *starta*, who was often carved with a serpent wrapped around her lovely body. If you want to get technical about it, this may be why the writers of the Hebrew Bible put a snake staff in Moses' hand, both here in the book of Numbers and in the book of Exodus. Because they wanted to make clear that the snake worked for Moses and not the other way around.

But if you're content to stay inside this story, then there is definitely something funny going on here. What are a bunch of monotheistic Hebrews, with a clear commandment against graven idols, doing gazing upon a brass serpent? And not just gazing at it, but looking at it? Scripture says, "in order to save their lives." Aren't these the same people who have already been through a really awful scrape with a golden calf? And isn't this the same Moses who offered to give up his own life in order to atone for that very great sin of the people? Where did this snake savior come from?

According to the book of Numbers, it came from the mind of God as an antidote to the venom of the poisonous snakes that also came from God to bite the people who had the gall to call heavenly manna, also from God, miserable food. They were tired of being lost and unsure. They were tired of living on desert welfare—eating pot after pot of the only thing that God's food stamps were good for. They wanted to go back home to Egypt, and that would have been bad enough if they had only thought it, but then they said it out loud. And right after that, Scripture says, "God sent poisonous serpents slithering across the sand to kill them for complaining." And some God-fearing parents don't want their children reading *Harry Potter*?

Now even if this sounds to you like someone's supernatural explanation for what happens when a bunch of tired hikers don't look where they are going, please do note that all the snakes in this story belong to God. The live one. The brass one. All of them. For some reason, Christians seem to jump to conclusions whenever there is a story with a snake in it. Sinister music starts playing in our heads. We sniff the air for brimstone as we reach around behind us trying to find the hoe. This is probably because we all believed our Sunday school teachers when they told us that the snake in the Garden of Eden was really Satan in disguise. Or maybe it's just that old snake-hating gene looking for a just war theory? But whatever it is, it won't work in this story. There is no Satan in Torah. All of the snakes belong to God.

If this is not clear in English translation, then it's at least more astonishing in Hebrew, where the serpents are not poisonous but *seraph* serpents, or fiery serpents. Apparently some interpreters believed that fiery was a metaphor for how your ankle feels when a poisonous snake sinks its fangs in. But my two Hebrew commentaries leave that word untranslated, right there on the page. So that it's hard to miss a connection between seraph serpents in this passage, in the book of Numbers, and the seraph that tends God's throne in Isaiah's vision in his book in chapter 6. While one species of seraphim has six wings, and the other crawls on its belly in the dust—they are both fiery ones, sent by God to frighten, burn, rouse, revive and ultimately heal the people of God. They are very scary angels, in other words.

Now this may be biblical, but it won't sell in any Christian bookstore where I live. Where seraphim come decked in pink organdy with satin ribbons in their hair. Have you ever noticed how much our angels tend to look a whole lot like us? If you doubt me, then check out www.seraphimhouse.com the next time you're near a computer. There you will find a porcelain collection of very Caucasian seraphim who are for sale with names like "Abigail, Amanda, Amy, Anna, Ariana, Anabella, or Ashley," and those are just the "A's." You find that you prefer "Meredith," the red-headed guardian of celestial music, who plays a large harp on a snowy cloud that's sprouting with beds of pink roses. Or you may prefer "Flora Ella," guardian angel of nature, who stands surrounded by deer and birds and, yes, bunnies, but no snakes.

You may even select a new patriotic seraph named "Jennifer," who's piecing together a red, white, and blue quilt on her lap. She costs sixty-five dollars, plus tax and shipping.

Now if you collect these figures, please forgive me. But even if you do, I'm counting on you to be the first to admit that if "Seraphim House" had offered you a collection of fiery serpents for your china cabinet, then you would have kept on shopping. I mean, who wants frightening angels that bite? Who wants wilderness, for that matter? Or a steady diet of anxiety? Or a leader who truly believes in the Promised Land, but does not seem to know how to get there? These are not the things we've been led to expect for those who follow YHWH — the way a head is supposed to be lit, the difference between good and evil is supposed to be clear. God is supposed to protect us from biting snakes, and fiery serpents are not supposed to work for God. I don't know where we got our story line, however, since the Scriptures that we call sacred have quite a different one.

In the story at hand, fiery serpents, sent by God, bring the people to their senses. Burying their dead, they remember how much they love being alive. And they furthermore realize what a lot of nerve they had to speak against God and Moses, who happen to be doing everything in their power to keep the people alive. So the people in this story, they apologize to Moses. "We are sorry sinners," they say to him. "Please ask God to call off the snakes." Then Moses prays for the people, but God won't call off the snakes. Instead, God tells Moses to put one on a pole so that even though the people go on suffering snakebite in the wilderness, they won't have to die from it any more. When they are bitten by one of the deadly snakes on the ground below, God says, "then they shall look at the saving snake up on the pole." And looking up, instead of down, their lives shall be saved.

You and I might ask a few more questions about how that's going to work, exactly, but Moses doesn't. Moses chooses brown for the snake, our translation tells us, which is presumably as close as he can come to the color of fire. Then he makes a replica of the very thing the people fear. Without actually reaching into a hole and pulling it out of the ground, he still takes the source of their anxiety out from under their feet and places it high up on a pole, where none of them can miss it. Now they can see that the seraph of death is the seraph of life — not an evil snake and a good one, but one snake. And somehow, in this utterly mysterious parable, the law of kill or be killed is suspended for a time. It's not quite Isaiah's vision of the messianic age, with babies playing over adders' dens, but it's on the way. Snakes don't lead people into sin in this story. Snakes lead the people out of sin, by scaring them so badly that they leap back into the arms of life.

In spite of its many, many difficulties, this story remained a powerful one for the people of God. So powerful that the brazen serpent was preserved for hundreds of years after Moses was dead and the wandering days of the people were over. So powerful that King Hezekiah finally broke it into pieces to stop the people from worshipping it. So powerful that according to John, at least, Jesus used the brass serpent as a figure for himself, one night while He was trying to explain the mysteries of heaven and earth to a seeker named Nicodemus. He did not succeed that night. But that single reference may help explain why the early Church Fathers referred to Jesus not only as the Good Shepherd but also as the good serpent. Who, like the fiery prophets before him, fell to the hoe. The venom his killers feared turned out to be theirs and not His, but it took setting him on a pole in order to see that. Then God lifted Him even higher so that venom turned to anti-venom and even those who had killed Him were saved when they looked upon Him.

I can't tell you how it works. All I can tell you is that it's easy in a world like ours to believe that we know the difference between good serpents and evil ones, and we can be trusted with hoes. That's what we hoped to gain, anyhow, in the Garden of Eden by reaching past that first snake for our fill of forbidden fruit — the knowledge of good and evil. Today, the snake's back to see how things are going. He's no less scary, but he still works for God. And this time, in this story, the knowledge he offers is not the forbidden but the saving kind. Hung on a pole, shinning like the sun, he is God's own fiery reminder that enemies and angels can look a lot alike. And that the only one who truly knows the difference between them is the one to whom all, all the snakes, belong.

Combining thoughtful biblical interpretation with African American Pentecostal fervor, James Forbes is quite a preacher. A native of North Carolina, pastor in the United Holy Church of America, Forbes was called to teach preaching at Union Theological Seminary in New York and from there was called to the pulpit of Riverside Church. On a hot June day, Pentecost, Forbes came down from New York to stir up the Duke Chapel congregation with this lively sermon on (among other things) a text that Forbes calls the "best-kept secret in the Bible."

The Best-Kept Secret in the Bible

Pentecost
June 8, 2003

JAMES A. FORBES JR.

Matthew 13:24–30 Brothers and sisters, I am delighted to have yet another opportunity to worship with you, here in Duke Chapel. I bring greetings from the Riverside Church in New York and I want to express thanks to you on behalf of my congregation for the gift of ministry, which you provide: first, through the writings of Will Willimon; and also, he's a visiting fire person around the country. He came by Riverside Church and preached, I think it was last summer, and left a flame. I think it was in August. It was really hot when he left. Thank you so very much for his ministry to us.

Now, you may think it's strange that I should be here on Pentecost Sunday. I mean, Jim Forbes, North Carolina, Pentecostal Church background, away from Riverside on Pentecost Sunday. Is it because the Spirit is so high there that he needs to go off some other place to try to stir up another congregation? That is not the explanation. The explanation is that this morning at Riverside Church, one of my former, one of the former ministers of the church, Ernest Campbell, is giving the Word. And I am sure he will handle it well and allow me to see if I can stir up these bones of ours here in Duke Chapel. They said the first time I preached here, I was so rambunctious in the Spirit that the Dukes woke up downstairs and walked around. I do not think that is true. But at least I am happy to have this privilege to be with you.

Now the first thing I want to do is to bring you a word from my congregation. You know all over the nation today, because it is Pentecost Sunday, people will close their service with the hymn that was presented by Harry Emerson Fosdick on the occasion of the dedication of the Riverside Church in 1931. People will be singing, it's so appropriate for Pentecost, "God of Grace and God of Glory. On thy people, pour thy power. Crown thine ancient church's story. Bring its bud to glorious flower."

Now there is something I need to tell you about that hymn. It is probably the case that people liked an upbeat tune, so we've got the *Cwm Rhondda* tune, "God of Grace and God of Glory. On thy people, pour thy power."

Except Fosdick's favorite rendering for this particular hymn that he wrote was *Regent's Square*. I think the difference is that we sing this hymn mostly as a triumphal affirmation of the power of the Church. We almost forget that the words of this hymn are words offered in prayer, not in, "Yeah, we have achieved the vision of the glorious church." I asked my congregation a few Sundays ago to try to sing this tune as a prayer. Not that we have won the victory, but a deep longing that the sentiments of Fosdick might be revealed in our time. And I'll tell you why that might be the case. If there ever was a time when Christian churches across this nation should receive God's power and need wisdom and courage to face this hour—it's now. Because lo, the hosts of evil round us scorn thy Christ and assail thy ways. From the fears— and oh, how fearful we have been since 9/11. These fears have bound us and somehow we can't seem to get free from them. It will be the second anniversary in a few months of that awful day. Somehow we need to have our hearts freed up for faith and praise, not cowering in fear and steeped in the spirit of revenge. How can we sing this hymn triumphally? "Cure thy children's warring madness." This is a prayer. Lord, whatever has gotten in us in the wake of that awful day, won't you cure church folks' warring madness? And Lord, can't you bend our pride to thy control? Can't you shame our selfish gladness, rich in things and poor in soul? It's not a triumphal song, "Grant us Wisdom, Grant us Courage, for the living of these days."

No, no, no, no, no . . . we wish somehow on the Pentecost Sunday God could lift us and set our feet on lofty places. And gird our lives that they may be armored with all Christlike graces, pledged to set all captives, not just those of us, but those around the world, pledge to set all captives free. And the tune, even if it is *Rounder*, would be more like Lord, "Grant us Wisdom . . . Grant us Courage . . . that we fail not them nor thee. That we fail, not them, nor thee."

So this Pentecost finds me in a mood, wishing that this prayer would be fulfilled. I wish that I could get a grant to have a kind of teleconferencing church where all Christian churches, making allowance for the time change, would worship at one time. And that we would . . . and I'm not speaking of prophetic progressive churches such as the one I'm supposed to be a part of, but I'm speaking, what it would be like if we could get together, hooked up on-line. On Pentecost Sunday they were on one accord. An old man said, "That means they were all on the same chord." Maybe all in the same channel: conservatives, liberals, hawks, doves, pro-lifers, pro-choicers. Those who believe that we are called to domination and empire building. Those who believe we are called to a humble affirmation of concern for all God's children, rich and poor, all hooked up. And I wish I would be given an opportunity to be on the program. And if I were on the program, I would understand that for Pentecost Sunday the requirement would be whatever you offer has to make sense and be respectful of each of the elements represented in these congregations, all across the land, north and south, east and west. And you've got to give the talk, whatever it is, in such a way that it will actually challenge and speak to the hearts of all of them. And since it's Pentecost, by the end of the day you know that they will have courage. You know they will understand each other because that's what the speaking in tongues part was about. Not that they had this extraordinary linguistic variation in communication. It was that they were able for the first time to hear something of truth from those over there. And something of truth from those over there. That they heard God's name praised. They heard the praises of God, even though the language seemed to be different. Even though the accents, even though there were regional perspectives, even though there were ideological differences. That on Pentecost, for the first time, they were able to be one people, many-tongued, singing one song. And if I were on the program, I would ask to have a chance, not to preach, just to do Bible study. And the text that I would offer, which I believe could gather us all, all who call themselves Christians, the text is one that I have not heard preached on in fifty years. Nowhere—and I've been all over. I travel in conservative circles. I go to liberal churches. But I have not heard this text preached on in fifty years. Maybe you have. You know the parable of the wheat and the weeds. You've heard it lately . . . okay. But for some of the others, let me just read it one more time, just to make sure you get it. I consider this text the bearer of one of the best-kept secrets of the Bible. I know the topic says "*the* best-kept," but I think I better not make such staggering claims since there is at least one person who knows it here—that it is one of the best-kept secrets in the Bible. Here is what it says:

> The dominion of heaven may be compared to someone who sold good seed in the field. But while everybody was asleep an enemy came and sowed weeds among the wheat and then went away. So when the plants came up and bore grain, then the weeds appeared as well. And the servants of the household that came and said, "Did you not sow good seed in your field.

Where then did these weeds come from?" The householder answered, "An enemy has done this." They responded, "Then do you want us to go and gather them, the weeds," but the householder replied, "No, for in gathering the weeds, you would uproot the wheat along with them. Let both of them grow together until the harvest. And at harvest time I will tell the reapers, 'Collect the weeds first and bind them in bundles to be burned. But gather the wheat into my barn.' "

I'm on a national network now. I'm talking to both sides of the church. It would be my best bet to describe what I'm trying to say or what I think the parable is trying to say, though usually parables, you work up slowly, up on people's blind side, but not on this occasion. I may lose somebody unless I tell you right off the bat what I hope this sermon is going to be about. What this lesson is. So I violate my own homiletical rule. The homileticians would say, never tell anybody what the point is in a parable. You got to work it in slowly, to get below the level of their awareness, sneak it in, slide it in. But no, I am not risking. Somebody may click off the station before the sermon is over. I propose to teach that God is more invested in empowering our growth and development than in punishing us for our imperfections. And that God wills us by grace to press on with the best we can do in faithful service, while the negatives about us, around us, beyond us, are being transformed. The outcome of this sermon, if it is effective, would be that those who hear it would become aware of the negative consequences of hyperjudgmentalism projected upon God. That they would believe and receive God's grace. That they would offer up for service all that they are, relying on God to sort out the good and work with the weeds in our lives. That's what I would want to say.

For it has been half the time allotted to me. But you get the point. Let me see if I can elucidate just a little bit on this particular idea. The first thing I want you to notice is that this parable would gather us, all sides of the church, to define our theology of God. One theology would put it this way: God is holy, demanding holiness of us. If we've missed the mark of righteousness an avenging angel will come quickly to punish us. That's one theology that we bring to this table.

It also includes this notion: that the wrath of God can hardly restrain itself from swooping down on us to force us into righteousness quickly. Lest we do more harm than we've already done. This theology would say that God is watching us and will have nothing to do with us until we get certified as worthy of God's grace. Oh, this may be a bit of a caricature, but what this theology would do is to make others, who are different from us—I'm a liberal — this would make me treat conservatives by dissing them and dissociating myself from them. And I would go around as a liberal, as a progressive, and I'd have some stickers like you use at the automobile inspection center. Where I would inspect them and then I'd put a rejection sticker of disgrace on their faces to indicate that they went in for inspection before God, but couldn't pass the test. And furthermore, that God is going to get 'em yet. They may get by for a few days, but you know, you reap what you sow.

This isn't much of a caricature, is it? Do you know folks that think like that? That is their God. And this is a bad theology from my perspective. First of all, it misrepresents God, I think. In fact this parable is Jesus' way of getting at that very spirit. In fact this parable is so unusual that I should submit it to the Jesus Seminar down there in Atlanta. Did Jesus actually tell this parable? This theology that Jesus might have been addressing does bad things to people. When we see our shortcomings, if that's the way God is, it makes us feel the need to cover up and to draw attention away from our flaws by pointing out the flaws of others. It's this theology of the God who is holy demanding righteousness right now — can't wait to swoop down on us and beat us on the head until we get right. If that is the nature of the God we serve as Christians, no wonder we lack the strength we need when we find ourselves to be flawed. In fact, this is why. Now I understand it. This is why some people distance themselves from God. They don't want the rejection sticker. Better to stay out of sight, because if God sees me and discovers that there are things in my heart that are not worthy of the glory of God. Then I'm just staying . . . there are a lot of folks that would be in church today unless they really believed that God is this kind of God. "I'm going to get you. Get you soon and quick."

Well, I think this text is trying to tell us something about God that's different from the caricature of God that I have given. Are you still with me out there in Los Angeles? Are you still riding with me in Utah? What about Oklahoma? Are you still on the line? Let me tell you about a different kind of God and I hope that I will caricature this one just to counterbalance the caricature of the other. That God in this parable sees and knows all about us already. He's not snooping under our beds to see what we are like. God already knows our down-sittings and our uprisings. Not only does God see me and know me, God even knows why I am as I am. The God that Jesus was talking about in this parable; the priority of this God, as I have already told you, now I say it again, is the growth in maturity of the good wheat. God is not looking around and — pardon me, sound man, please, I know you won't pick this up — to see which of these weeds doesn't belong in this crowd? That is not the God Jesus is talking about. God makes arrangements for the weeds. Since you might tear up the design of "is-ness," trying to be so fastidious about "oughtness." God sent not the son into the world to condemn the world. God already knew that. But God in this parable is patient, understands the complications of life, knows that some days we are up and some days we are down. Knows our thoughts from afar off. God compasses our lying down and is acquainted with all our ways. The God of this parable knows and understands, but the God of this parable is patient . . . patient. The God of this parable, I think, knows that the church where there is East Coast, West Coast, north or south, liberal or conservative, that the churches across the nations are fields of wheat and weeds, all of them. The best of them, weeds in them; the worst of them, some wheat there. Now you understand why we don't hear this text very much. People are scared. I preached it fifty years ago myself, but the congregation didn't like it. They said, "Man, if you preach like that, you will be letting people off the hook. Don't you know that it will free them up to do wrong?" Well, they haven't needed my freedom yet. They've been doing wrong all along. They didn't need this sermon to do wrong. Let me tell you we need a God who can deal with folks who are like a Hanes t-shirt. One of the professors at Union had a t-shirt she would wear, and it simply said, "I may not be perfect, but parts of me are excellent." That we need a God who understands that we are not perfect, but there is some good in us. That's the kind of God we need. A God of a gospel who is not interested in disgracing us, but taking us where we are and having patience with us that maybe before too long some of the weeds may experience botanical transmutation and might become wheat in us. I've lived long enough to see the Lord take some of my weaknesses and work with them until they are perhaps the source of some fruitfulness in my ministry.

Well anyway, if it's on the air, they wouldn't give me much time. You gotta share the time with the rest of the people. So why don't I simply sort of say, if you buy this, please help me to tell somebody. This should not be a secret. There are a whole lot of folks out there that need God, that are scared because they see this wrathful, vengeful God. Tell them that it's out now. Jesus has put it out that God loves us in spite of our flaws. That God cares for us even when we are weak, not so much to beat us down but to build us up, to give us vitamin enrichment so that we can be strong. And the churches across the nation need to know that if we can get this message out across the nation, then the nation will not be so fearful. Then the nation will not be so vengeful, because having received grace upon grace we are prepared to give it to others. We can be more patient and even — I hope this is on in Washington: I want it to get to the judiciary, to the executive, and to the legislative branch—I want them to see that it may even impact nations. Nations need not spend all of the resources seeking out those evildoers around the world. Nations may begin to be more patient with each other. We receive grace and offer it to others: that's what I hear.

Well, this is communion service today, so I guess I had better bring the sermon to a close by saying to you, at the end of my Bible discussion I would propose a song. You know the song, but you would almost think it is out of place. At the end of my Bible discussion on this teleconferencing, one church, all listening together, I would ask that for the closing hymn we would sing a hymn which has been usually designed for sinners, for weeds. This hymn is a hymn usually dedicated to weeds that are sinful and that need to be yanked up and put out to pasture unless we can find it through Christ's undergoing this botanical transmutation. It's the hymn we associate with the Billy Graham revivals. You know what that hymn is, right? Well some of you were saved in those revivals—come on. The hymn is a hymn written by Charlotte Elliott, and I offer this one because she understands what it is like to know wheat and weeds. She was for most of her life an invalid. She was on one occasion hoping that somehow she could get strength to help her brother-in-law, who was trying to build a house for children of preachers so that they could get an education. But her physical condition would not allow her to get up and help and she was quite frustrated about it. Here was an invalid wanting to do good. Wanting to offer wheat, but feeling like she was weeds. Nevertheless she remembered her God, and in remembering her God, at home, not able to be there with those who were doing the good deeds, she wrote this hymn, which we used to have George Beverly Shea and the choirs sing at evangelistic services, where we were trying to get the sinners to come to the altar. She wrote this hymn: "Just as I am, without one plea, but that thy blood was shed for me, and that thou bidst me come to thee, O lamb of God, I come."

We used to sing ninety-nine verses of it until some sinner would come forward. On this teleconferencing worship service, don't sing it for sinners, sing it for the saints that are assembled on-line, on one accord. Because if the Holy Spirit comes alive, if God's power manifests itself in the churches, we at long last will understand that we are wheat, yes, but we are weeds and weeds are unprofitable. They look like it, but they are not like it. They will not advance the cause of the kingdom. This may be a mystery, but only when the Holy Spirit descends upon us and seizes upon the core of our being and offers us up to the God of patient grace. Only then will we know this hymn is for us as well. I think it also could be used for communion Sunday.

Just as I am, thou tossed about, with many a conflict, many a doubt. Fighting within and fear without, oh lamb of God, I come, I come.

Communion Sunday, Pentecost Sunday, "Just As I Am." There are things in me, born of my fear, my anxiety that makes me want to shoot the rest of the world. Destroy countries around the world. Build up my military power. Nuke the rest of the world if necessary to protect myself. Yes, Lord, yes. But I know I get vengeful sometimes and I know I hate others that do not see the world as I do it but:

Just as I am thou wilt receive, will welcome, pardon, cleanse, relieve. Because thy promise, I believe. Oh lamb of God, I come, I come.

Let's make it a communion hymn:

Just as I am, thy love unknown has broken every barrier down. Now to be thine and thine alone, O lamb of God, I come.

Help me get this out! Help me preach this sermon! Help me teach this lesson that God is patient and also for those who want hellfire and brimstone! Only the Lord knows where it is and only the Lord knows who ought to be put there. Let's leave it up to the Lord. Let's don't do any prejudging and start the hellfire prematurely. Let's leave it up to the Lord! But for the time being, get this secret out. God loves us just as we are. God's working on us. God lets us grow up. God knows that we got wheat and weeds. Help me get this message out. It will change our nation. It will draw our churches closer together. It will rob us of this anxiety and fear and replace it with joy and hope. Help me get this secret out. Holy Spirit come on Pentecost Sunday and run us out of this church so we can tell our neighbors, "Oh, I want you to know about this God whose love and grace is such that we need not fear, but go forth in hope to proclaim a kingdom is on the way." And for those who are given eyes to see and ears to hear, that's the best news that's been kept in silence far too long.

I can't seem to stop this sermon, so will you complete it somewhere?

Although our usual practice in Duke Chapel, at least for the last two decades, is to use the texts appointed by the Common Lectionary for sermon texts, sometimes we have a sermon series. In the fall of 2003, we had a series of sermons, "Weird, Wonderful Women of the Bible." This sermon was the third in that series. The sermon begins with two undergraduates enacting the dialogue in John 4, Jesus and the woman at the well. I then delivered a sermon for the first Sunday of the school year on the need for open minds, open hearts, and heightened imagination when dealing with the claims of the gospel.

Confused, yet Curious, about Jesus

August 31, 2003

WILLIAM H. WILLIMON

John 4:3–29

"Come see a man who told me everything I have ever done! He can't be the Messiah, can he?"

In a recent critique of American higher education, *Clueless in Academe* (Yale University Press, 2003), Professor Gerald Graff says that the most important work that professors do is to "begin an argument." Students come to college thinking that reality is fixed, self-interpreting, just sitting there needing only affirmation and reiteration. Higher education, worthy of the name, begins an argument about what's real, what's there. It encourages students to do less assertion and more conversation, engagement, and interrogation.

Which brings us to a curious conversation in John's gospel: Jesus and the woman at the well. Jesus is out in Samaria, far from home, far from his own people. And while journeying on the margins he meets someone who lives on the margin, a woman. And there he engages her in conversation.

JESUS: Give me a drink. It's hot out here.
WOMAN: You, a Jew, ask a little old Samaritan girl like me for a drink?
JESUS: If you only knew the grace of God, who it was saying to you, "Give me a drink," he might give you some living water.
WOMAN: Hello? You've got no bucket! The well is deep. Where can one get

hold of this "living water"? Our ancestor Jacob (blessed be his name) dug this deep well. Can you dig wells deeper than Grandfather Jacob?

JESUS: Everybody who drinks this water gets thirsty all over again. After a swig of my living water you'll never thirst. It's eternal life!

WOMAN: Well, give me some of that "living water" so I can quit lugging my bucket to this stupid well twice a day for water.

JESUS: Go get your husband.

WOMAN: What husband? I've got no husband.

JESUS: You got that right. You've been through five husbands and the guy you are living with now is not your husband.

WOMAN: Well, it seems that here we've got us a real prophet! Tell me, prophet, where is the right place to do worship? This mountain, like we Samaritans say, or up at Jerusalem where your people say?

JESUS: Woman, to tell you the truth, it's not about this mountain or Jerusalem, it's about worship in spirit and in truth.

WOMAN: Er, I know that the Messiah is coming. When he gets here, he'll cut through this doubletalk and explain all this religion stuff to us, make it clear.

JESUS: Open your eyes. I am.

WOMAN: Hey! Come see a man who told me everything I've ever done. He can't be the Messiah! Can he?

And now I stand up and explain Jesus to you. Now is the point in the service where I tell you the point. I take this enigmatic, ambiguous Jesus and — with three points and a poem — explain Jesus, make him accessible. User friendly. I take this ancient, enigmatic scripture and boil it down to some sweet, sappy thought that you can take out of here and assuage some of the misery of Calculus 102. Having gotten a grip on Jesus, made him relevant, accessible, and comprehensible, you have been to worship.

Well, forget it. It's the Gospel of John, it's Jesus with the woman at the well, and I can't explain it to you no matter how high you scored on the SAT! I can't explain it to myself, and I deal with this sort of thing for a living!

For some time now, some churches are having what they call "seeker services," at "seeker-sensitive churches." It's church for the unchurched, church where the music can be sung without effort by everybody, sermons able to be comprehended by any fool who stumbles in off the street, worship dumbed down to a cross between "American Idol" and "Sesame Street."

What concoctors of seeker services say that seekers seek are *answers*. Christianity Lite. What seeker services would do with enigmatic John 4, Jesus and the woman at the well, I wonder.

Jesus wanders way out in Samaria at noon. A woman shows up. Rabbis of that day don't waste their wisdom on women, much less Samaritan women, and much less women of uncertain marital estate. Jesus is out on the fringe with a woman on the fringe. Jesus says "living water," she wonders, "Where's your bucket?" She says "thirst," he counters with "eternal life." He says, "husband," she has none now, but five before. Worship? Spirit? Truth? She plays Gracie to Jesus' George Burns. Costello to her Abbott. By the time Jesus gets done with her, it's "Who's on first?"

Odd, but Jesus misses a great opportunity to explain things to this woman, and to us. She flunks the exam, as clueless at the end of the sermon as when it began. OK. Jesus was tired. I'm not at my best, up before a class, when I'm tired. (Can you tell that I went to bed last night at 7:30 so I would be rested and ready for you this morning?)

She's a Samaritan. She doesn't have the scriptural background of her Jewish cousins. Maybe that's the problem. She's a woman. In that day, in that part of the world, women couldn't go to school and study theology. Couldn't Jesus be a bit more "user friendly," put some of his "spirit and truth" talk down on the bottom shelf for the "educationally disadvantaged"?

No. Jesus gives her theology with both barrels, talks to her like she's a Duke Ph.D. Jesus doesn't back off from engaging her; she doesn't back off from being engaged. She risks being confused and Jesus risks the stupefaction of a Seeker.

You know what really gets me about some of you? It's not your behavior at parties on Saturday night, it's that some of you are making judgments about Jesus on Sunday morning on the basis of a puerile, nay, infantile, understanding of Jesus that you had when you were eight. I can't stand for an adult, with an arrested religious development, to dismiss Jesus on the basis of what that adult thought he knew about Jesus at age six.

Taking physics this semester? "No, I took physics at my exclusive, expensive elementary school where I learned that whatever goes up comes down, and it all seemed so obvious and trite to me, so, no, I've had it with physics."

That attitude, applied to Jesus, gets me.

Student comes to the rabbi in our basement and says, "Rabbi, God has appeared to me and asked me to. . . ." (to do something or other, I forget).

Rabbi responds, "What is your major? How are your courses going? Stressed? What's your relationship with your mother like? Are you dating anyone? How is that going? Have you ever been treated for mental illness?" On and on.

In desperation, the student protested, "Why, when I come in here and tell you that God has spoken to me do you seem so intent on disproving that and confusing me?"

The rabbi retorted, "Because, kid, if you can't explain it some other way, then it couldn't be God! God is large!"

Rabbi Jesus met a woman at the well. And far from explaining it all to her, making everything unequivocal, he dives deep, goes ambiguous, mysterious, moves quickly from the anthropological to the theological. Yet she dared to let down her bucket with Jesus. She stuck with him, through each twisting and turning of the strange logic. The conversation ended, not with "I got it!" but rather with yet another question, "He can't be the Messiah? Can he?"

Professor Graff says that the greatest challenge, for a teacher of undergraduates, is to get them into an interrogative conversation. A teacher's got nowhere to go if all students have is certitude, answers. Ask a question, a teacher is off to the races.

I think we preachers are guilty of this. I get confused into thinking that's my job: explaining Jesus to you. I get confused into thinking that my job is to take some perfectly strange, outrageously inaccessible story like Jesus and the woman at the well and explain it to you.

"Here is what the Gospel of John was *trying* (in his ignorant, first-century Jewish way) to tell you about Jesus. Here is what John would have told you about Jesus if he had the benefit of a seminary education like me!"

Jesus for Dummies. That is an insult both to you and to Jesus.

Visiting at a high, Anglo-Catholic sort of parish in Waban, Massachusetts. After the incense service led by the boy choir, I was drinking coffee with a condescending woman in the parish hall. She declared to me, "I drive one hour in each direction to be here on Sunday!"

"I'm in the church business myself," I told her. "What draws you here from such a distance?"

"Father Warren!" she said. "A friend invited me to one of Father Warren's Wednesday lectures. He spoke for over an hour on the Christological controversies of the fourth century. Spellbinding."

"Wow. He must be good to be able to make something like that interesting," I said.

"I didn't understand a word of it," she said, "and I am a Wellesley graduate. So of course I had to come back the next week. Father Warren spoke then about the formation of the Creed. I understood even less. I've been here every week since. Did I tell you I am a Wellesley graduate?"

Here was a persistent woman for whom the world had been explained, flattened, trivialized, and belittled. She had at last found a church that didn't insult her intelligence by making the truth trivial and immediately accessible.

When we send out a questionnaire to the folk who worship here, asking you what you like and don't like, what you find helpful and not helpful about our Sunday service, you always rate music right up there at the top, more highly rated than the sermon. I try not to take it personally.

I think the music here means so much to you because, when compared with many other acts of worship — the reading, the praying, the sermon — music is where you most fully, inexplicably, yet undeniably experience the presence of the risen Christ. Music reminds you of the most important reason for being here. Our serious business is not to give you answers, but to give you Jesus. My job in the sermon is not to explain Jesus but to put you next to the presence of Jesus.

Jesus isn't for dummies. Jesus is for those who are willing to seek, to question, to persist, daring to be confused, dislodged, disoriented intellectually, willing to begin with assertions, "When Messiah comes he'll explain it all to us. . . ." And ending with, "He can't be the Messiah, can he?"

If you asked me, "What is the biggest impediment to evangelism, the making of Christians, at Duke," I think I would answer, "Scripture." The Bible. Stories like this one with Jesus and the woman at the well. Scripture is more difficult than it should be, full of odd twists and turns, irony and subterfuge. We have spent years educating you into the conceit that you have all you need to grasp the world, to understand, to figure it all out, to get the truth, to use it, make money off of your knowledge, grab reality by the tail and twist.

Yet here in the Chapel things are larger than elsewhere. Here is truth, not as abstract ideas but as encounter, as entrance into mystery, truth with a name, a face, a sovereign truth that is beyond our ability to grasp. "I am the way, the truth, and the life," Jesus says later in this same gospel. You don't grasp him; he grasps you.

At the very end of the Gospel of John, when Jesus is raised from the dead, another interrogating woman — Mary Magdalene — in a garden meets the risen Christ. Mary at first thinks He is the gardener. But then Christ speaks to her, calls her by name, "Mary," and she, in her joy, grabs His knees. And the risen Christ tells her, "Don't hold me"

Jesus will not be held — even by those who love Him most. He will only be encountered in all of His living, glorious, majestic, and free otherness. He will have you thus or not at all.

The woman at the well — take her as your hero — is not put off by the intellectual demands of a meeting with Jesus. She sticks with Jesus. She stays with the conversation until the end. She doesn't yet understand all there is to know about this stranger at the well. But a door has been opened. Clueless no more, but not yet fully comprehending, she worships, in spirit and in truth, she worships. "Come, see!" she calls to her friends, and thus becomes the first evangelist.

Will you, like the woman at the well, be willing not to get Jesus, but dare to let Him get you? Will you risk the possibility of stumbling out, rather than striding forth, from this service, questioning the whole world? He can't be the Messiah, or can He?

Index to Scripture

Library of Congress Cataloging-in-Publication Data

Sermons from Duke Chapel : voices from "a great
towering church" / William H. Willimon, ed.

p. cm.

ISBN 0-8223-3483-6 (cloth : alk. paper)

1. Sermons, American—20th century. 2. Universities
and colleges—Sermons. I. Willimon, William H.

BV4310.S46 2005

252—dc22   2004025080